Tudor Networks of Power

Tudor Networks of Power

RUTH AHNERT AND SEBASTIAN E. AHNERT

OXFORD
UNIVERSITY PRESS

Great Clarendon Street, Oxford, OX2 6DP,
United Kingdom

Oxford University Press is a department of the University of Oxford.
It furthers the University's objective of excellence in research, scholarship,
and education by publishing worldwide. Oxford is a registered trade mark of
Oxford University Press in the UK and in certain other countries

Published in the United States of America by Oxford University Press
198 Madison Avenue, New York, NY 10016, United States of America

British Library Cataloguing in Publication Data
Data available

Library of Congress Control Number: 2023935846

ISBN 978–0–19–885897–3

DOI: 10.1093/oso/9780198858973.001.0001

Printed and bound by
CPI Group (UK) Ltd, Croydon, CR0 4YY

For Frank & Judith

Acknowledgements

One might argue that the origins of this book go back to a cocktail hour at New Hall (now Murray Edwards College), Cambridge, in 2003, when the pair of us first met. With Sebastian ensconced in a Physics department and Ruth in the Faculty of English, we were always quite happy that our disciplinary backgrounds precluded any competition with one another; when we married in 2007, never did we suspect that we might one day collaborate. However, in 2008 Sebastian had a visiting fellowship at BarabasiLab, the Center for Complex Network Research at Northeastern University, and Ruth thought she should read up on the field of network science to understand better what he actually did. As a result the chapter of the doctoral thesis she was writing at the time (and the corresponding chapter in her first book, *The Rise of Prison Literature in the Sixteenth Century*, Cambridge University Press, 2013) engaged with network analysis as a framework of thought. The seed was sown in her mind, however, of a collaborative experimental project, to establish whether network science could reveal anything new about the collections of early modern letters she was working on. In 2012 we began a study of a small corpus of 289 letters written by the Marian Martyrs, held in Emmanuel College Library, Cambridge, and the British Library; the results were the basis of our first co-authored article. Buoyed by the success of this experiment we decided to pursue a much larger project using these methods. Thanks to guidance from Evelyn Welch and the late Lisa Jardine, we decided to focus on the Tudor State Papers.

The journey from acquiring the data in 2014 to the publication of this book was much longer than we imagined, and we have accrued many debts of gratitude in the process. For the provision of the data, we thank Gale Cengage and particularly Julia de Mowbray, who also helped us to secure permission to release our datasets openly for reuse. The project would have taken even longer if Ruth had not secured funding to support this work. We therefore thank the Arts and Humanities Research Council for the Early Career Leadership Fellowship, Stanford Humanities Center (SHC) for the year-long external faculty fellowship, and to the Folger Shakespeare Library for the two-month fellowship. Thanks to permission from the Royal Society, which was supporting Sebastian's research, and a well-timed sabbatical, he was able to join Ruth on the two residential fellowships at the Folger and Stanford. These fellowships brought not only protected time to work on the project, but also a wonderful community of support and intellectual exchange. At SHC Ruth would especially like to thank the Director Caroline Winterer, Deputy Director Andrea Rees, and the other fellows Rumee Ahmed, Eli Alshanetsky, Lanier Anderson, Claire Rydell Arcenas, Rebekah Baglini, the late Bernard Bate, Scott Bukatman, Lisa Burnett, Vanessa Chang, Jason Cieply, Willie Costello, Lindsay Der, David Driscoll, Frederico Freitas, Jenna

Gibbs, Niloofar Haeri, Stefan-Ludwig Hoffmann, Jennifer Iverson, Christopher Krebs, Reviel Netz, Katharina Piechocki, John Rick, Gabriella Safran, Kay Kaufman Shelemay, Alexander Statman—and especially to Blaine Greteman, who was also figuring out his own project on early modern networks that year. Sebastian is grateful to the Center for Spatial and Textual Analysis (CESTA) for welcoming him and for providing a space to work and collaborate. At CESTA we both benefited greatly from our exchanges with Mark Algee-Hewitt, Nicole Coleman, Dan Edelstein, Sarah Olgilvie, and Elaine Treharne. Thanks to a workshop that Ruth co-convened with Elaine, and funded by Elaine's endowed Chair, we were able to invite a raft of exciting scholars interested in networks (writ large), including Blaine, Jayne Caroll, Max Schich, Dan Shore, Greg Walker, Scott Weingart, and the wider CESTA community. This exchange formed the basis of the spin-off book, *The Network Turn: Changing Perspectives in the Humanities* (Cambridge University Press, 2020) that we co-wrote with Nicole and Scott. The debates and co-writing sessions that led to that publication shaped our thinking on the use of network analysis for humanistic research in important ways. We would also like to thank SHC and CESTA for funding two undergraduate research assistants, Tani Thomsen and Emily Shah, who undertook data cross-checking for us. CESTA, and specifically Director Zephyr Frank, helped us secure sponsorship to bring over Jose Cree, who had a White Rose College of the Arts and Humanities placement grant to work on our project for a month. We are hugely grateful to Jose for the work she did helping us clean and geo-code the place data. The geo-coding was completed by Lotte Fikkers; thank you to her, and to the Queen Mary University of London Innovation Fund for funding this additional work.

Several further communities need mentioning. We are grateful to the Folger Library, not only for the fellowship, but also their invitation to be involved in two of the Early Modern Digital Agenda Summer schools in 2015 and 2017, the second of which Ruth co-directed with Jonathan Hope. For his masterful organisation of these events, we thank Owen Williams. These events facilitated more exchanges than we can list here, but we would just like to mention those who have become more frequent interlocutors: Anupam Basu, Mel Evans, Michael Gavin, Jon Ladd, Laura Mandell, Rachel Midura, Jessica Otis, Ingeborg Van Vugt, Chris Warren, Mike Witmore, and Heather Wolfe. We would like to thank the Arts Humanities and Complex Networks community, assembled by Max Schich, Isabel Mereilles, and Roger Malina at satellite workshops to NetSci, with whom we have shared work-in-progress and many productive exchanges. Chats with Lizzy Williamson and Neil Johnston helped clarify our thinking when we were undertaking the final edits to Chapter 1. We express our huge gratitude to Howard Hotson for his ongoing collaboration: firstly for inviting us to be involved in the phenomenal COST Action Reassembling the Republic of Letters, which brought together scholars from thirty-one countries whose thinking has been hugely valuable to our thinking and practice. Secondly we thank him as a collaborator on the AHRC-funded project Networking Archives, on which we have continued to think creatively and critically with him and the wider team—Philip Beeley, Arno Bosse, Miranda Lewis, Esther van Raamsdonk, Yann Ryan, and Matt Wilcoxson—about letter networks.

Ruth would like to thank the English department at Queen Mary University of London, and especially Warren Boutcher, Andrea Brady, Jerry Brotton, David Colclough, Markman Ellis, Rachael Gilmour, Joad Raymond, and the late Catherine Silverstone for support and encouragement at key moments. It has been her pleasure to supervise Caitlin Burge over this period as she was the first person apart from us to systematically analyse the data we prepared for this book. Ruth is also very grateful for the wonderful community of collaborators she has had the pleasure to lead on the Living with Machines project at The Alan Turing Institute since 2018. Sebastian would like to thank the Royal Society for its support through a University Research Fellowship during the initial years of this collaboration. The freedom of this position, and explicit encouragement by the Society to make the most of that freedom, facilitated this highly interdisciplinary collaboration. He would also like to thank King's College, Cambridge, which provided an interdisciplinary community of Fellows as well as support of meetings and events organised as part of the Networking Archives project, and financial support towards publication costs associated with this collaboration. Several people need special thanks. We enormously enjoyed and benefited from our collaboration with Kim Albrecht on the interactive visualisation of our data for this book. He brought fresh eyes, brilliant insights, and endless patience to the challenge, and we think the result is truly beautiful. We would like to thank Jo Guldi for reading most of the following chapters and providing such incisive comments; we are, as always, awed by her brilliance. And to our editors Stephanie Ireland and Cathryn Steele, and the two anonymous reviewers, we wish to express our gratitude for their comments and direction. These have all helped us shape the final manuscript; any remaining faults are, of course, our own.

Finally we want to acknowledge the broader context in which the research and writing of this book occurred. The genesis of this book was so long that we have travelled through a number of life stages together. During the project we have lost two very important people: in 2017 Sebastian's father Frank passed away, and in 2020 Ruth lost her mother Judith. We know they would have been the first two people to read this book, and it is for that reason that we dedicate it to them. But we have also welcomed two new people into the world, our wonderful children Jasper (born 2017) and Sidney (2021). They have filled our lives with joy (and chaos) in previously unimaginable ways. Through these events we have been supported by our family Graham, Lewis, Amanda, Freddie, and Jude; Bridget, Thomas, Verena, Leopold, and Clara. And our friends have provided both practical help and happy distraction: thank you especially to Lydia, Axel, Mary, Sarah, Eleanor, Robert, Fiona, Çinar, Eesha, Christina, Naomi, and SJ. But most of all we are thankful for each other, and the fact that we are lucky enough to have each found our perfect collaborator for projects both academic and domestic.

Contents

List of Figures

List of Abbreviations and References

In quotations from manuscript letters and early printed books, we provide semi-diplomatic transcriptions: raised (superscript) letters are lowered; contractions are expanded and supplied letters italicised; and terminal -es graph with '-es'. These have been silently expanded. Deletions in the text are signalled with a strikethrough, and editorial insertions with [xxx]. Titles from early modern printed books have frequently been truncated for brevity. We use the following abbreviations for books and reference works that are cited frequently:

BHO	*British History Online*
BL	British Library
CSP	Calendar of State Papers
LP	*Letters and Papers, Foreign and Domestic, of the Reign of Henry VIII: Preserved in the Public Record Office, the British Museum, and Elsewhere in England*, 21 vols., ed. J. S. Brewer et al. (Longman, Green, Longman, & Roberts, 1862–1910)
ODNB	*Oxford Dictionary of National Biography*
PRO	Public Record Office
TNA	The National Archives
SP	State Papers
SPO	*State Papers Online*

Foreword

This book is a marriage of science and history. It brings together a set of methods developed in the field of network science to the study of government communications. In light of recent history, we have become familiarised with the roles that network analysis plays in the surveillance strategies employed by governments to manage their national security. From the 2013 revelations about the US National Security Agency's surveillance programme Prism—which allowed the agency to reconstruct its citizens' social networks from metadata gathered through nine internet companies—to the more recent exposés concerning the exploitation of the social network platform Facebook to sway voter behaviour through micro-targeting, it has become increasingly apparent that a government's success or failure is determined by its mastery of communication networks. The communication networks under scrutiny in this book, however, are not the digital communications of the modern era, but rather the analogue communications marshalled by a much older government: a large corpus of Tudor letters held in the British government's State Papers.

State Papers are the documents kept by governments to record discussions, options, and decisions by officials, departments, and civil servants. In this particular historical context they are the working papers of the Tudor monarchs' secretaries of state (known as the Principal Secretary), and include 132,747 letters dating from the period between the accession of Henry VIII and the death of Elizabeth. These are the communications between the monarch's Secretary and local government officials, the communications from overseas embassies and military missions, intercepted and seized correspondence, as well as the petitions to government from across Tudor society—from widows seeking legal control of their deceased husband's land to prisoners seeking leniency. They are, therefore, a vital source not only for political historians, but also as contextual information for all manner of early modern scholars. This is one constituency for whom this book is written. It is also addressed to readers interested in how computational approaches can be used to harness the archive's digital turn. As our cultural assets are increasingly being turned into digital resources, we have an opportunity to study this material in a new way, and at an unprecedented scale.

The physical body of the Tudor State Papers is dispersed over a number of locations, although the majority of the papers are now in the ownership of The National Archives, and preserved in an archival store located in salt mines in Cheshire.[1] Until relatively recently the only way of accessing these missives was via the original manuscript copies or, more accurately, via the microfilms of these documents, due to the fragility of the papers. However, in 2008 the State Papers became available as a digital

---

[1] <http://www.deepstore.com/>.

resource, *State Papers Online* (SPO), which brought together the digital surrogates of the manuscripts with the vast collaborative scholarly work of the nineteenth and twentieth centuries, the Calendars of State Papers, a chronologically organised catalogue of the contents of this vast collection of documents. Following the logic of these catalogues, it also united in virtual space the holdings of The National Archives with other key State Papers held at other locations such as the British Library and Hatfield House.

While the interface for *State Papers Online* was designed with a particular kind of use in mind—browsing and searching—the greatest potential of this initiative resides in the encoding of the underlying information with metadata, rendering it machine readable. For each document metadata fields have been created which tell us, for example: the name of the document author, the recipient (if it is a letter), the place and date of writing, where known, the manuscript and Calendars references. These are the fields that the search function queries; but if you can get at the underlying data it can be analysed in even more powerful ways. Just as the NSA used telephone and email metadata to reconstruct the social networks of its citizens and foreign targets, we are now able to reconstruct and computationally analyse the communication patterns of all those within the purview of the Tudor government. With approaches from network science we have reconstructed the communication networks documented in this archive, and analysed it with tools and methods akin to those employed by modern intelligence agencies. For the first time (as the result of a painstaking effort to clean the data, detailed in Chapter 1) we now know that the Tudor epistolary network is composed of 20,560 separate people, covering a geographical span whose peripheries stretch from Manila to Aleppo, Moscow to Havana, Goa to Terceira.

But what exactly is network science, and do we really need it to understand the epistolary culture of the Tudor government? Network science is an interdisciplinary field that emerged from a series of key publications in the 1990s and early 2000s, in which scholars such as Albert-László Barabási, Reka Albert, Duncan J. Watts, and Steven Strogatz showed that a huge variety of real-world networks—neural networks, transport networks, biological regulatory networks, and social networks—share an underlying order and follow simple laws, and therefore could be analysed using the same mathematical tools and models.[2] The application of mathematical and computational techniques developed by scientists working in the field of complex networks to the arts and humanities is growing apace. And there is particular appetite within the early modern community: in the past decade early modern historiography has seen the emergence of several digital network projects. These fall roughly into two camps. On the one hand we have projects like *Circulation of Knowledge and Learned Practices in the 17th-Century Dutch Republic*, and its database *ePistolarium* (Huygens Institute,

---

[2] See Duncan Watts and Steven Strogatz, 'Collective Dynamics of "Small-world" Networks', *Nature* 393 (1998), 440–2; Albert-László Barabási and Reka Albert, 'Emergence of Scaling in Random Networks', *Science* 286 (1999), 509–12; Reka Albert and Albert-László Barabási, 'Statistical Mechanics of Complex Networks', *Rev. Mod. Phys.* 74 (2002), 47–97; and Mark E. J. Newman, *Networks: An Introduction* (Oxford University Press, 2010). For a general overview, see Albert-László Barabási, *Linked: The New Science of Networks* (Perseus, 2002).

Amsterdam),[3] *Cultures of Knowledge,* and its offspring *Early Modern Letters Online* (EMLO, University of Oxford),[4] and *SKILLNET: Sharing Knowledge in Learned and Literary Networks* (Utrecht University),[5] which have amassed large amounts of epistolary data into corpora (or what EMLO calls a union catalogue) for analysis. These databases have become the basis for ongoing enquiries into the circulation of knowledge in the early modern world, focusing mainly on the Republic of Letters. By comparison the projects *Six Degrees of Francis Bacon* (SDFB, Carnegie Mellon University)[6] and *Mapping the Republic of Letters* (MRoL, Stanford University)[7] are more concerned with the development of tools that enable such data to be analysed in order to reconstruct communities from early modern correspondence or other textual witnesses. MRoL gained widespread attention for demonstrating how data visualisation techniques could produce research insights from correspondence databases like EMLO and *ePistolarium.* While this project continues to generate academic outcomes, perhaps its most far-reaching impact has been the release of a suite of data visualisation tools, especially Palladio—a network visualisation tool designed with humanities researchers in mind.[8] SDFB, by comparison, is a visual reconstruction of the early modern social network that scholars and students can collaboratively expand, revise, curate, and critique based on relationships inferred from the entries of the *Oxford Dictionary of National Biography.*

What unites these projects is their service to the broader communities. They are underpinned by substantial and generous acts of labour: the painstaking curation of datasets and the development of general tools. Such work takes a long view of scholarly labour, recognising that these are the necessary foundations for the histories that can be reconstructed once such work is complete. However, because of the large amount of work that goes into such foundational endeavours, the research outcomes that we are more used to encountering have been slow to emerge: so far most interventions from these projects have been articles, rather than monographs, although there are several exciting books forthcoming in the next few years. One of the first book-length studies to occupy this space is Blaine Greteman's *Networking Print in Shakespeare's England,* which uses the tools of network theory and analysis to examine early English print networks and to demonstrate the way changes in the communications system reshaped early modern literature, thought, and politics.[9] It is based in part on *Shakeosphere,* an online tool that Greteman built in collaboration with data and information scientists with the goal of mining and mapping major print and

---

[3] <http://ckcc.huygens.knaw.nl/>.

[4] <http://www.culturesofknowledge.org/> and <http://emlo.bodleian.ox.ac.uk/>.

[5] <https://skillnet.nl/>.   [6] <http://www.sixdegreesoffrancisbacon.com/about>.

[7] <http://republicofletters.stanford.edu/>.

[8] Their tools are listed here: <http://hdlab.stanford.edu/tools/>. For a discussion of the affordances of *Palladio,* see Ruth Ahnert, Sebastian E. Ahnert, Catherine Nicole Coleman and Scott B. Weingart, *The Network Turn: Changing Perspectives in the Humanities* (Cambridge University Press, 2020), chapter 4, DOI: <https://doi.org/10.1017/9781108866804>; and Catherine Nicole Coleman, 'Seeking the Eye of History: The Design of Digital Tools for Enlightenment Studies', in *Digitizing Enlightenment: Digital Humanities and the Transformation of Eighteenth-Century Studies,* ed. Simon Burrows and Glenn Roe (Liverpool University Press, 2020).

[9] Blaine Greteman, *Networking Print in Shakespeare's England: Influence, Agency, and Revolutionary Change* (Stanford University Press, 2021).

manuscript catalogues like the English Short Title Catalogue, OCLC-WorldCat, and Early English Books Online Text Creation Partnership.

The overview of these long-view projects is instructive because our book begins with a similar narrative about the foundational importance of creating data and tools. Chapter 1 is dedicated to the history of the data on which our analysis rests, from the early modern creation of the archive, via its process of being catalogued, to its transformation into metadata as part of an online database (SPO). It concludes with an account of the time-consuming work we undertook to turn it into data suitable for network analysis and (as far as possible) 'cleaned' of errors and inconsistencies that could prevent meaningful analysis. In many ways we believe that the outcome of this data preparation might be our most important contribution: the dataset presents a massive terrain of possibility. The book maps that terrain for the first time, providing a demonstration of what can be done once we have data in that form, with the right tools and approaches.

To that end we have sought to make that data available for others to use through two means. The first is what is known as a data publication: it is a practice consisting in preparing certain data for public use in order to make them available to everyone to use as they wish; these are then sometimes contextualised within short articles that describe the data and its preparation, and make it citable for others.[10] This is an integral part of the open research movement. We are thankful to Gale Cengage (the owners of SPO) for permitting us to share the data in this way. While SPO itself remains unaffordable for the majority of university libraries and is inaccessible to public users,[11] we hope that by releasing this dataset we will enable greater opportunity for academic exchange. However, the release of a dataset is only useful to those who already have the skills to manipulate it. For that reason, the second way that we have made the fruits of our labour available to general users is through an interactive data visualisation, working with knowledge designer Kim Albrecht to produce an intuitive interactive interface called *Tudor Networks*.[12] It provides a new way of accessing, understanding, and deriving insights from this catalogue data, fulfilling Mitchell Whitelaw's definition of a 'generous interface': a visualisation that will offer multiple ways in, support exploration and focused enquiry, and 'enrich interpretation by revealing relationships and structures within a collection' (discussed further in Chapter 1).[13]

This book goes far beyond the insights that can be derived from visualisation, however, harnessing both established network analysis metrics and developing bespoke

---

[10] See Ruth Ahnert, Sebastian E. Ahnert, Jose Cree, and Lotte Fikkers, '*Tudor Networks of Power - Correspondence Network Dataset*', https://doi.org/10.17863/CAM.99562.

[11] On the ways that subscription models for many digital resources such as SPO are 'reinforcing and amplifying old inequalities and hierarchies', see Andrew Prescott, 'What Price Gale Cengage?', blog post available at: <https://medium.com/digital-riffs/what-price-gale-cengage-668d358ce5cd>.

[12] <http://tudornetworks.net/>. For an introductory video, see: <https://www.youtube.com/watch?v=Ze5IBlkIBDA>.

[13] Mitchell Whitelaw, 'Generous Interfaces for Digital Cultural Collections', *Digital Humanities Quarterly* 9:1 (2015), <http://www.digitalhumanities.org/dhq/vol/9/1/000205/000205.html>.

methods to analyse this important digital archive. It is of course in no way the definitive word on the State Papers archive. Libraries full of books have been written using
the sources that it contains, and the extent of the opportunities revealed by this new
dataset means that the book only scratches the surface of the huge potential presented
by the digital manifestation of this archive. But we proffer a set of routes into the data
that allow its potential to be harnessed. The chapters should therefore be viewed as
a set of experiments. We choose the word experiments here pointedly, to evoke the
scientific aspect of our approach, and to differentiate the way in which this kind of
research—which might broadly be described as a manifestation of 'digital humanities'—
proceeds from more traditional research methodologies in the humanities. There are
a whole host of centres and communities in the field of digital humanities that have
labelled themselves as laboratories, from the University of Virginia's Scholar's Lab,
Stanford University's Literary Lab, to Harvard University's MetaLab, to name some
of the more famous examples.[14] This trend makes a similar point about approach.
A laboratory is a facility that provides controlled conditions in which scientific or
technological research, experiments, and measurement may be performed. We follow
the values of Stanford's Literary Lab: 'Experiment is presented here not just as a test of
reliable knowledge but as a style of intellectual growth: "By frustrating our expect-
ations, failed experiments 'estrange' our natural habits of thought, offering a chance to
transcend them"', in the words of Franco Moretti, the Lab's first director.[15]

This description is a useful way of understanding the manoeuvres that we employ
in the research underlying this book. There is a kind of estrangement in the way we
look at and describe our objects of study. In our hands, letters and the information
about them become 'data' and 'metadata'. Although our analysis still engages in close
reading to validate our approaches, we usually begin our analysis by applying algorithms. In mathematics and computer science, an algorithm is a set of formal instructions that can be interpreted by a machine, often with the aim of processing large
amounts of information in a systematic way. In the context of our network of 132,747
letters connecting 20,560 people, an algorithm can run through this large tangled network in a few seconds and tell us whose epistolary habits were most similar to one
another, model women's role in petitioning and mediation processes, or understand
the most important news items in a given period. The chapters therefore contain references to the names of these algorithms, the quantitative results from these computational queries, and more graphs and charts than one might normally expect to find in
a history book. But the estrangement is not wilful or complete. Rather these features
are employed only to reorient us as scholars, so that we can encounter this archive
from a different perspective and gain new insights into a source that is well known to
historians of Tudor government and politics.

---

[14] On the concept of the Lab in humanities disciplines see Darren Wershler, Lori Emerson and Jussi Parikka,
The Lab Book: Situated Practices in Media Studies (University of Minnesota Press, 2022).
[15] Ted Underwood, 'The Stanford Literary Lab's Narrative', (2017) <http://www.publicbooks.org/the-stanford-
literary-labs-narrative/>.

In so doing, we want to show how network analysis in particular, and computational approaches more generally, have the ability to create a bridge between what C. P. Snow famously described as the 'Two Cultures' of science and the humanities.[16] These also happen to be the two cultures in which we, the authors of this book, were originally educated and trained. The benefit of our respective backgrounds has led us to devise a research process predicated on the values of ongoing development and iteration, seeking to move repeatedly back and forth between research approaches traditionally designated as scientific or humanistic. Sometimes in the process of researching our chapters we began with the computational approach, using an existing algorithm or set of algorithms to see what they can tell us about the structure of the communication network: for example, who are the people in the network with the highest 'betweenness centrality' (an approach we took in Chapter 3)? By contrast, sometimes we began with a historical and methodological challenge: can we reconstruct people's itineraries from the various locations from which they wrote (Chapter 7)? The initial results of such a query would then be scrutinised by a process of moving from statistical overview—for example, a ranked lists of people sorted by their betweenness centrality, or a ranked list of people by the total mileage they travelled across all the letters they wrote—to a close analysis of the documents associated with that person, in order to understand how these results were generated. The insights from that close reading invariably raise additional questions, which then require additional layers of analysis to be developed in order to further filter those results based on interesting features, or to push at more nuanced or complex historical questions.

We have sought to illustrate the mechanisms and effect of that constant shifting of 'views' in our book *The Network Turn*, co-authored with Nicole Coleman and Scott Weingart, through the metaphor of the use of aerial photography in modern archaeological research.[17] Aerial archaeology has enabled the discovery of hundreds of previously unknown archaeological sites, but it has also helped to make sense of known, clearly visible prehistoric landscape features, such as the Nazca lines in Peru, which form a large-scale pattern that only makes sense when viewed from a great height.[18] The aerial photo sacrifices resolution for the ability to find large-scale patterns. A particular altitude and a particular type of imaging technology are chosen. Features that are recorded in the aerial photograph can then be investigated on the ground, for example in the form of an archaeological excavation. An iterative cycle might then be entered: findings on the ground can inform further rounds of aerial photography, perhaps in other regions, or with other imaging techniques—perhaps ones that are more sensitive to the features of interest on the ground. The same is true of network analysis. The network view offers a bird's-eye view or 'distant reading' of the entire archive,

[16] See C. P. Snow, *The Two Cultures*, with an introduction by Stefan Collini (Cambridge University Press, 1998).
[17] See Ahnert et al., *The Network Turn*.
[18] For a similar metaphor, but used to a different end, see Bruno Latour, 'Anti-Zoom', <http://www.bruno-latour.fr/sites/default/files/P-170-ELIASSON-GBpdf.pdf>.

but by zooming into the ground level and digging into the text through close reading, we can generate new questions or more sophisticated analytical frameworks through which to analyse the network perspective.

The network approach that we have taken maps onto this shift between views. A network, as described in more detail in the following chapter, is an abstraction of information, a complex system simplified into a set of 'nodes', which refer to a set of objects or entities, such as the individuals in the State Papers archive, and 'edges', which mark the relationships between the nodes. For example, in an ecological network different species would represent the nodes and the edges might represent which species feeds on which other species; in the World Wide Web, the web pages would be nodes and the hyperlinks edges; and in our network the senders and recipients of letters are the nodes, and the letters give rise to the edges. When we identify an important node in this giant network we can focus on their immediate neighbourhood: to see how many neighbours they have and who these neighbours are. But it is still an abstraction. When we study a neighbourhood network we do not see the contents of the letters that passed between them, but merely the existence of those communications. However, by enriching the way we encode this information into our databases, it is possible that the nodes and edges can become portals between two qualitatively different kinds of information: between metadata and data. We can imagine going 'into' an edge to see all the letters that constitute that connection between two nodes, excavating the material evidence.

The archaeological metaphor is perhaps also useful for emphasising that, like aerial photographs in archaeology, quantitative approaches in the humanities do not seek to replace traditional methods, but to provide a complementary approach that can both facilitate the discovery of specific new case studies as well as give rise to a vantage point from which local patterns merge into a more meaningful large-scale view. In this way we hope to show how network analysis can act to bridge the binary oppositions that have, perhaps unhelpfully, characterised 'scientific' method versus the humanities: distant and close reading; quantitative and qualitative approaches; numbers and words; and the nomothetic and idiographic approaches to knowledge. The nomothetic approach is based on what Kant described as a tendency to generalise, and is typical for the natural sciences. It describes the effort to derive laws that explain types or categories of objective phenomena, in general. The idiographic model is based on what Kant described as a tendency to specify, and is more typical for the humanities. It describes the effort to understand the meaning of contingent, unique, and often cultural or subjective phenomena. Our contention is that connecting examples of the contingent and unique to their position within or beyond general trends has huge benefits for research. These benefits are normally expressed in terms of the power offered by new technologies for the study of culture. But the benefits do not (or should not) all flow in one direction; researchers and big tech organisations that are using AI to process text or images desperately need the skills of those trained in the humanities to provide cultural and historical context, and to examine the biases that so often problematise the outcomes of these innovations.

There are, however, not that many established precedents for working in this way, and thus a lack of models for how to write about the resulting processes. The mode of writing that we have developed is determined largely by the audiences we have selected for this work. In choosing to write about this research in a book-length study, we are making some assertions about the readership that we imagine. We know that a key audience for this work is the community already working in digital humanities, because of the innovations in the methods we are using. We are not simply employing the range of existing network analysis algorithms available in coding libraries, but also finding new ways of combining measures, and developing new methodologies to address historical questions. For that audience there will also be interest in the way we use network measures as a heuristic, or tool for sketching out ideas at the beginning of a research process. Running some well-selected algorithms can help a research direction to take form iteratively, informed by patterns to emerge from the sea of data. Taking that further we have sought to experiment in whether it is possible to use a combination of algorithms to select candidates for close analysis: in other words, to assist in the kinds of decision making in which literary historians constantly engage when shaping their narratives. However, the book also has a definite aim to stretch beyond that digital humanities community and speak specifically to the research communities in which these sources are most often studied: those with a background in Tudor political history and in early modern epistolary culture. To these readers we want to demonstrate the power of computational methods that make it possible to ask research questions of an entirely different scale and nature, but that can also facilitate the kinds of work that we love, the discovery of new histories, and the opportunity to pore over individual manuscript letters piecing together clues. This has directed the way we have crafted the book that follows, beginning often with explanations of algorithms or graphs representing statistical results, before moving to an archival deep-dive, telling the stories of individual lives excavated from letters, from local administrators to merchants in foreign ports paid to provide the Tudor government with local intelligence.

In making that choice of audience, however, there are also some things that we could not do, as this may have been too 'estranged' from what we expect to encounter between two covers of a history book. For that reason, we do not tend to provide extensive detail on the code that we employ in ways that are scientifically reproducible. For those readers who have the interest and skills to engage with that side of our work, we have sought to follow best practice by making our code available via an openly accessible repository on GitHub, complete with documentation.

The rationale for making our work available in different formats—as datasets, as documented code, and as a book—is not just about reaching different audiences, but also thinking about the challenges of longevity posed for those working with digital methods and outputs. If we optimistically imagine someone reading this book in twenty years' time, chances are that the web address of the visualisation might no longer work, or at best take the reader to an archived version of that interactive visualisation.[19] The data, by contrast, is likely to still be of use, especially as we have chosen easily readable formats that are not specific to any particular application. Whether Github will still be in existence is a different question. The code's value at that point is less clear: we would hope that technology would have moved on to an extent that these kinds of computation will look quaint. Our decision then to publish in the traditional format of the monograph is motivated by our certainty that this at least will last: paper records have survived in libraries for centuries, as the subject matter of this book can attest.

In our desire to speak to those who might be sceptical of computational approaches, we face a couple of challenges that those working in the field of digital humanities for any length of time will have encountered. The first is the tendency for people to argue that the computationally derived findings are obvious or just confirm what we already knew. But as Matthew Lincoln has persuasively argued, scholars 'are particularly susceptible to confabulating these post-facto rationalizations with the idea that we somehow knew the results of this quantitative work already (and, implicitly, that we didn't need to waste our time doing it)'. Rather he is keen to stress the difference between what 'in retrospect sounds reasonable' from 'what we actually knew before'.[20] Moreover, it is important to understand how such objections cut off discussion in unhelpful ways. Sometimes it is also important to find ways of computing things we knew before because it helps us to identify additional evidence to support such assertions, and because it lends support to findings using those methods that might push *against* received wisdom, or that might identify neglected individuals or groups of people as worthy of further study.

The other challenge is created by the ways that computational approaches often lead researchers outside the disciplinary territories they might have previously occupied. Scholars have observed the power of digital methods both to extend the temporal and geographic parameters that can be tackled in a single study. Jo Guldi and David Armitage have argued in *The History Manifesto* that digital approaches can reverse the retreat of the *longue durée* perspective in history theses and books in the decades since 1968.[21] Similarly, the rise of digital scholarship has been directly linked to the transnational turn. As Lara Putnam has observed: 'Source digitization has transformed historians' practice in ways that facilitate border-crossing research in particular. Web-based full-text search decouples data from place. In doing so, it dissolves the structural constraints that kept history bound to political-territorial units long after the intellectual liabilities of that bond were well known.'[22] However, while

---

[19] A summary of key studies on web-archiving can be found at <https://webarchivehistorians.org/the-web-archive-bibliography/>.

[20] Matthew Lincoln, 'Confabulation in the Humanities', available at: <https://matthewlincoln.net/2015/03/21/confabulation-in-the-humanities.html>.

[21] Jo Guldi and David Armitage, *The History Manifesto* (Cambridge University Press, 2014), p. 39. For a rebuttal to their claims, see Deborah Cohen and Peter Mandler, 'The History Manifesto: A Critique', *American Historical Review* 120:2 (2015), 530–42.

[22] Lara Putnam, 'The Transnational and the Text-Searchable: Digitized Sources and the Shadows They Cast', *American Historical Review* 121 (2016), 377–402.

Guldi and Armitage are raising a rallying cry to historians, Putnum is issuing a warning that our 'ability to read accurately the sources we find, and evaluate their significance, cannot magically accelerate apace. The more far-flung the locales linked through our discoveries, the less consistent our contextual knowledge.' As the following pages show, ours is a study that spans almost 100 years, and traverses Europe, with brief forays into Russia, Iran, and the Azores. It therefore may appear to be an exemplar of the approach Putnam criticises. The counter-argument to this returns to the ideas of scalable reading outlined above. The breadth feared in Putnam's argument is an indiscriminate one of the 'web-based full-text search'. By contrast the breadth of perspective offered by the manoeuvres outlined in this book is algorithmic and, crucially, scalable. It allows close-readings to be connected in new and powerful ways, and historical arguments to be encoded as algorithms and thus explored at scale across large corpora of correspondence, drawing out the relevant primary sources in the process.

There is also a more practical argument for these digitally enabled forays made by the archive itself. The Tudor State Papers constitute the working papers of the monarch's Principal Secretary, comprising heterogeneous materials which include letters, papers, reports, memoranda, treatises, grants, commissions, state trials, treaties, and ambassadors' reports. Although letters are just one among these categories, they contain a plethora of information, including important government correspondence between central government offices, letters sent between the Secretary and local branches of government, petitions to the government, foreign intelligence reports from diplomats and informal networks of agents, as well as correspondence intercepted and seized by agents, postmasters, or the Secretary himself. What unites all this information was that it was regarded as being within the purview of the Secretary: it documents in microscopic detail the requests and tasks submitted to the holders of this office, their network (both in terms of the administrative structures they oversaw and the web of informants they marshalled), and the information that they needed to master in order to execute their job. One of the tasks of working with this archive, and what is enabled by network analysis, is a way of fully grasping the extent of that purview, which brings with it the challenge of recapturing some of the breadth of expertise expected in that post. It is testament to the demands of the role that it takes a twenty-first-century analytical framework to fully capture the complex information system that underpinned the Tudor government.

PART I
FOUNDATIONS

1

Introduction

Tudor Letters in the Digital Age

One cannot—or at least, should not—analyse data without knowing its provenance. In this introductory chapter we begin with the archival history of the letters now grouped within the State Papers. We trace their journey from the Principal Secretary's office, where they were filed, through the nineteenth-century efforts to catalogue them, their twenty-first-century translation into a digital resource, and their final transformation into network data. It is vital to pay attention to what Alan Stewart terms the 'archival afterlife of correspondence' if we are to correctly interpret the information held in this large collection of letters.[1] The reason for this is twofold. Firstly, it reveals the historical contingency of the 'archive'. We place the term archive in inverted commas here—and ask readers to mentally add these when we use the term throughout the book—because the State Papers are not an organic archive that has passed down to us from the time of its creation, but rather the product of a series of administrative decisions, and accidents, that occurred over a period of centuries and up to the present day.

Secondly, it also helps us to change the perspective of how we encounter these papers. Rather than foregrounding the scholarly *users* of this archive, we draw attention instead to those we might think of as its *caretakers*: those who have expended labour on organising these papers, and making them navigable, at different stages in their afterlife. These include the clerks and secretaries working in the office of the Principal Secretary, the early modern keepers of the State Papers, the Victorian archivists and editors that 'calendared' the papers (and those who re-calendared sections in the twentieth century), and the workers who in recent years turned these calendar entries into metadata fields that could be queried for the online resource *State Papers Online* (SPO). The final stage of caretaking that will be described is our own process of transforming the XML data from SPO into network data.[2] As detailed below, this involved a long process of data cleaning, as well as the addition of geo-coordinates, before it could be formatted as nodes and edges. The contention of this chapter is that early modern filing processes, editing, metadata entry, and data cleaning are all acts of

---

[1] See Alan Stewart, 'Familiar Letters and State Papers: The Afterlives of Early Modern Correspondence', in *Cultures of Correspondence in Early Modern Britain*, ed. James Daybell and Andrew Gordon (University of Pennsylvania Press, 2016), chapter 11.

[2] XML stands for extensible markup language. It defines a set of rules for encoding documents in a format that is both human readable and machine readable.

Tudor Networks of Power. Ruth Ahnert and Sebastian E. Ahnert, Oxford University Press. © Ruth Ahnert and Sebastian E. Ahnert 2023. DOI: 10.1093/oso/9780198858973.003.0001

curation which, in Elizabeth Williamson's words, are 'simultaneously transformative and embedded within an existing and continuous history'.[3]

That transformation is in essence structural: each of these acts of curatorial labour imposes a new organisational structure, which builds upon those preceding it but also acts as a radical remix of its contents. That process of remixing not only transforms the way the letters can be found and accessed, but also the very system of knowledge within which they are framed, thus transforming the way that users conceptualise the archive in their minds. Each generation of labour that has been expended on this archive therefore has contributed vital new knowledge: new ways of accessing this archive, each offering different opportunities for historical scholarship. By positioning our own data preparation within this continuous history we wish to stress the vital importance of the labour in its own terms, not just as precondition for analysis but as a system of information that can be harnessed by others to access the archive to study social interaction, individual agency and collectivity, time and space—which we might argue are the basic fields common to all social human understanding. In doing this work we are standing on the shoulders of giants, and their monumental acts of labour. The idea of transformation, however, must also be tempered by an understanding that each act of remixing also entails a trade-off of some kind, the removal of contextual information, which may still be discoverable in the layer below, but in some cases is not easy to retrieve. In describing the opportunities and trade-offs at each stage, we seek to show that a network view of this letter archive allows us to better understand the contours and contents of this dataset, and to unpick its complex entanglement of early modern communication patterns, archival history, and data provenance.

Keepers and Finding Aids

The State Papers began their life as the working papers of the monarch's Principal Secretary, the equivalent of the modern Secretary of State. The Principal Secretary and the various clerks and secretaries working in their office, therefore, were the first caretakers of the letters under examination in this book. We have some information about how the clerks and secretaries would have filed and stored the letters, both based on general early modern practices and specific written accounts. Generic advice on organising, filing, and recording correspondence was available in various secretarial guides from the sixteenth and seventeenth centuries, as discussed by scholars such as James Daybell.[4] After being read, the letter would be re-folded, and the Principal Secretary, or their clerk would write on the top of the outer leaf an endorsement consisting of the date (of composition, not receipt), the name of the sender, and (often)

---

[3] Elizabeth R. Williamson, *Elizabethan Diplomacy and Epistolary Culture* (Routledge, 2021), p. 203.
[4] James Daybell, *The Material Letter in Early Modern England: Manuscript Letters and the Culture and Practices of Letter-Writing, 1512–1635* (Palgrave Macmillan, 2012), pp. 2018–20.

a brief summary of the letter. The letter would then be filed in a bundle with the endorsements visible for easy recovery from closets, cupboards, and chests where they were often stored. The secretaries and clerks would have worked with a set of such inherited practices, but also sought to formalise the process for the Principal Secretary's office, as can be observed from treatises by Robert Beale (who acted as Principal Secretary during periods of Francis Walsingham's absence from this office), and Nicholas Faunt (who was one of Walsingham's secretaries). Faunt's treatise advises that letters should be sorted into three bundles—home letters, council matters, and diverse matters—which would have been employed for daily use, and then subsequently dispatched for storage in a chest, cabinet, or coffer.[5] Beale's treatise also provides various advice, such as that lengthy endorsements should be utilised for items to be discussed by the Privy Council.[6]

Daybell has observed that it is also possible in some instances to glean from material clues—fold lines, areas of discoloration, and the positioning of endorsements—how letters were originally filed before they were stored flat (in other words opened), and bound into volumes by archivists.[7] Amanda Bevan has postulated that perhaps 'filing systems could be reconstructed by printing off the backs of the letters and folding them into the original shape as delivered or filed, to compare endorsements, shape, and so on: it would be interesting to see if different office practices emerge, allowing the rediscovery of original arrangements'.[8] Williamson has also drawn attention to the intriguing clues to the organisation of Walsingham's collection of State Papers provided by a small book found in the British Library, known as 'Walsingham's Table Book'. It contains three indexes: the first 'lists 67 unique items under "A Note of all the written bookes in the Chests or abroad"; the second details the contents of several of these books; and a third section, unlike the other two, lists mainly loose papers touching various countries and subjects'.[9] Williamson shows how the first index informs us how letters and papers were not left simply in bundles and boxes, but formed into 'concrete and identifiable "books"', making the papers both a more portable and permanent collective unit. The second index provides a navigational aid to these resources listed in the first index. Williamson thus concludes that it was 'intended to be perused as a quick reference guide; a finding aid or index to the great number of books connected to the office of the Principal Secretary'.[10] However, understanding this 'key' to the organisation of Walsingham's papers is at once exciting and frustrating, because the system that it unlocks is sadly lost to us.

---

[5] See Charles Hughes, 'Nicholas Faunt's Discourse Touching the Office of Principal Secretary of Estate, & c. 1592', *English Historical Review* 20 (1905), 499–508. Williamson discusses this work in *Elizabethan Diplomacy*, pp. 173–4.

[6] Robert Beale, 'Treatise of the Office of a Counsellor and Principal Secretarie', printed in Conyers Read, *Mr Secretary Walsingham and the Policy of Queen Elizabeth*, 3 volumes (Clarendon Press, 1925), vol. 1, pp. 423–43.

[7] Daybell, *The Material Letter*, p. 218.

[8] Amanda Bevan, 'State Papers of Henry VIII: The Archives and Documents', *State Papers Online 1509–1714* (Cengage Learning EMEA Ltd, 2007), available at: <https://www.gale.com/intl/essays/amanda-bevan-state-papers-henry-viii-archives-documents/>.

[9] See Williamson, *Elizabethan Diplomacy*, p. 176.   [10] Ibid., p. 177.

The loss of the State Papers' original organisational structure is due to a range of factors, but two administrative episodes play significant roles. The first was the emergence of the State Papers Office in 1578, and Thomas Wilson's appointment as the first 'Keeper of the State Papers' (although the formality of this appointment is unclear). As described by historians of this archive such as Daybell and Williamson, Wilson worked tirelessly 'to reduce [the boxes of papers] into the set form of a library' and to locate them 'in very convenient rooms near the old Banquetting House at Whitehall'.[11] He was personally involved in creating several different catalogues and indexes—more keys—to enable consultation of the papers. However, this centralising impetus was compromised by various centrifugal forces. Crucially, many papers of respective principal secretaries stayed in their possession when they departed from office, and were passed down as family papers. The example of William Cecil, Lord Burghley's papers, is instructive: though they were bequeathed to his son Sir Robert Cecil on his death, they were subsequently divided up: Wilson took control of the bulk; Cecil retained a proportion at Hatfield House (known as the Cecil papers); and others, which stayed with Burghley's secretary Michael Hicks, passed down through his family until bought by the Earl of Shelburne, later Marquess of Lansdowne, who gave his name to the British Library's Lansdowne collection. While some State Papers made their way back into institutional repositories, like Burghley's, many were thus lost to the vicissitudes of time. A second complication was that Wilson's project as the 'Keeper of the State Papers' was undermined by others with competing personal projects, most notably that of the antiquary Sir Robert Cotton, who was amassing his own private library of matters pertaining to the state.

While the first attempt to centralise the State Papers was compromised, the second may be regarded as a greater success. The formation of the State Papers Commission in the 1830s was intended to unite the scattered papers and thereafter publish the most significant documents. The first publication emerged as *State Papers published under the authority of His Majesty's Commission, King Henry VIII* (11 volumes, 1825–52). From 1852, the State Paper Office came under the authority of the Public Record Office (PRO, now the National Archives, hereafter TNA), which planned a larger rearrangement of documents and a much grander publication plan which comprised the multi-volume *Letters and Papers, Foreign and Domestic, of the Reign of Henry VIII*, edited by John Sherren Brewer, James Gairdner, and R. H. Brodie (1860–1932), and the Calendars of the State Papers Domestic and Foreign for the reigns of subsequent monarchs, which began with Robert Lemon's publication in 1856 of the *Calendars of State Papers Domestic: Edward VI, Mary and Elizabeth, 1547–80*. Here the editors become the caretakers of the letters. This editorial labour rendered the archive accessible and navigable in two ways. Firstly, these editors laboriously created descriptions of the contents of each and every item collected within these papers—letters, papers, reports, memoranda, treatises, grants, commissions, state trials, treaties, and ambassadors' reports. This was a monumental task, especially for

---

[11] Ibid., p. 167.

Lemon's successor Mary Anne Everett Green (née Wood), who improved on his over-concise habit of 'indicating rather than describing' the document contents, and produced forty-one volumes over a period of forty years of editing.[12]

Secondly, and perhaps more importantly, these editorial caretakers imposed an entirely new organisational structure on the papers, placing them in date order (hence the 'calendar'). This was not just a virtual reordering of the papers, within the pages on the new Calendars, but a physical rearrangement on the shelves of the PRO that was formalised and fixed by rebinding the State Papers chronologically by topic, dividing the domestic from the foreign concerns (sometimes a difficult distinction), and further dividing them into royal letters and Irish and Scottish correspondence, for example. This process, as implied above, necessarily destroyed the previous arrangements of these papers—sadly without leaving a record of what these were. This radical reorganisation has had a profound effect on how this archive is accessed and how it is imagined. The calendaring process therefore not only provided a new key to the archive, but also a new *archive*. Williamson puts it more strongly still: the calendaring is 'not a neutral or natural process of organisation, but an extended socio-political project that destroyed the fabric of archival provenance: the calendars do not just represent the state papers, they refashioned them into a new archive.'[13]

The value of the editors' endeavour, however, was undeniable. The Calendars unlocked the potential for research that was previously impossible. A. F. Pollard was the first historian to make use of *Letters and Papers*, writing his 1905 biography of Henry VIII from the document descriptions. And even though Geoffrey Elton criticised Pollard for the 'avoidable weakness' of relying on these secondary accounts, he too was indebted to the Calendars to help him navigate the vast archive;[14] without their aid it would have been impossible for him to find the mass of correspondence needed to make the argument, for example, at the centre of his ground-breaking monograph *Policy and Police*, published in 1972.

The latest instantiation of these papers as *State Papers Online* theoretically makes the leap from Calendar to document easier to overcome—for those who are able to access this expensive resource, at least.[15] The power of SPO is that, for the period 1509–1714 the resource links over 3 million facsimile images (converted from microfilm reels, and for later modules by scanning the original documents) to their instantiation in the text-searchable Calendars. Perhaps more importantly still, it seeks to overcome the scattering of the papers that frustrated the project of the first Keeper of the State Papers, Wilson, by 're-uniting the Domestic, Foreign, Borders, Scotland, and Ireland State Papers of Britain with the Registers of the Privy Council and other State Papers now housed in the Cotton, Harley and Lansdowne collections in the

---

[12] On Green, see Lisa Jardine, *Temptation in the Archives: Essays in Golden Age Dutch Culture* (UCL Press, 2015), pp. 24–5.

[13] Williamson, *Elizabethan Diplomacy*, p. 214.

[14] G. R. Elton, *Studies in Tudor and Stuart Politics and Government: Papers and Reviews 1946–1972*, vol. 1 (Cambridge University Press, 1974), p. 113.

[15] See Andrew Prescott, 'What Price Gale Cengage?', blog post available at: <https://medium.com/digital-riffs/what-price-gale-cengage-668d358ce5cd>.

British Library'.[16] This digital resource is, then, another act of remixing. It is a remix not just of these catalogues and papers, but also of the *way* that these entries are made accessible to the user. This is where we can observe the next layer of labour. In this case, however, it is not from the highly prestigious roles of editors or 'Keepers' but from workers who scanned the microfilms and manuscript pages, and those who manually rekeyed the Calendars and converted them to XML files—the latter of these tasks was outsourced to India. This work process crucially created metadata fields for every document in order to render them searchable.

The search box offers the possibility of infinitely remixing the archive to suit the user's research questions. SPO can be accessed via a general search box on the front page, or via Advanced Search that allows one to search particular metadata fields, such as 'document title', 'place of writing', 'writer/author', and 'recipient' amongst others; and to filter by dates, Calendar, or archival location. The benefit of this mechanism is that users can amass information quickly that would previously have required hours, days, or even weeks of scholarly effort. However, as Ian Milligan and others have warned, the search box is a 'black box': the use of search means that 'historians can lose an understanding of historical context when keyword-searching directly to sentences or individual documents removed from their broader context'.[17] In this case, while the Calendars are the source of the metadata that makes these contents searchable, the organising principles of the Calendars are rendered invisible in the list of search results. This means that the documents returned by the search query are divorced from their chronological ordering of documents that precede and follow them, as well as from the thematic contexts of the volumes. Theoretically, in the current version of SPO, users can flip to the Calendar from the search result, subsequently re-contextualising these results; however, this facet is removed in the new version that is being trialled as part of the Gale Primary Sources Platform. Moreover, the search box hides from view larger issues around what is and is not included in the resource—due to the long history outlined above—and how documentary absences have an impact on the outcomes of the search. Scholars must bring this contextual knowledge with them to use the outputs wisely.

The brief history of the archive outlined above shows us that these letters passed through the hands of generations of caretakers—the clerks, the keepers, the editors, and the workers rekeying the Calendars and entering the metadata—and accrued value at each stage, via the frameworks in which they were placed. These frameworks include both the physical reordering of the documents (the projects of the State Papers Office and the State Papers Commission) and virtual keys to the archive (indexes, Calendars, and the search function). Our project of recasting the letters from this archive as a network is another act of transformation in this long history. This virtual reordering, or remix, was created by one further act of curatorial labour, which builds

---

[16] 'About State Papers Online', *State Papers Online 1509–1714* (Cengage Learning EMEA Ltd, 2007).

[17] Ian Milligan, *The Transformation of Historical Research in the Digital Age* (Cambridge University Press, 2022), chapter 2. Available at: <https://doi.org/10.1017/9781009026055>.

directly on the metadata created by the workers behind SPO. Its value is that it provides a new kind of framework that allows us to attend to the broader context of the data.

Network analysis is particularly suitable for the study of historical correspondence because, as Gary Schneider has written, early modern letters were 'sociotexts [...] material bearers of social connection, instruments by which social ties were initiated, negotiated, and consolidated'.[18] Letters were the method by which people sought patronage, garnered favour, and engineered their social mobility; they were a means of communicating alliance, fidelity, and homage; and they could be used as evidence of social connectedness. We see examples of all of these kinds of communication within the State Papers. Because of this relational dynamic, it is easy to see how letters fit the framework of a network. Networks are abstract representations of entities (usually referred to as 'nodes'), and the connections between them (typically referred to as 'edges' or 'links'). In this context, senders and recipients become 'nodes' and the letters sent between them are the 'edges'. Network analysis therefore allows us to study the patterns of connectivity formed by the written communications that underpinned government business, the contacts sought, whether they were reciprocated, the way that information moved, and, by implication, how power was distributed via letters. More importantly, it helps us to understand the role of letters in the administration of the office of Principal Secretary, and what the archive can and cannot tell us due to its underlying logic and subsequent history.

The transformation of letters into network data is aided significantly by the previous generation of metadata as part of the creation of SPO, described above. Crucially, UK copyright law gives subscribers to a database the right to access and analyse the underlying data. Cambridge University's institutional subscription to SPO therefore enabled us to gain access to the XML metadata. Gale Cengage helpfully supplied the data on two hard-drives. By systematically extracting the relevant data fields, such as sender and recipient, we had the data necessary to generate an epistolary network. However, before it was suitable for analysis another tranche of labour was required, in the form of data cleaning or data curation.[19] The primary reason for this is the fact that the Calendars are the source of this metadata: as C. S. Knighton cautions, 'Care should be taken in using the older Calendar entries, which contain misdatings and other faults.'[20] As we went through the data, the precise character of these faults became apparent—and not only in older Calendar entries. We encountered inconsistency of naming practices with regards to both people and places, dating inconsistencies, and

---

[18] Gary Schneider, *The Culture of Epistolarity: Vernacular Letters and Letter Writing in Early Modern England, 1500–1700* (Newark, DE: University of Delaware Press, 2005), p. 27.

[19] On the problems of the term 'data cleaning' see Katie Rawson and Trevor Muñoz, 'Against Cleaning', in *Debates in the Digital Humanities 2019*, ed. Matthew K. Gold and Lauren F. Klein (Minneapolis: University of Minnesota Press, 2019), chapter 23. <https://doi.org/10.5749/9781452963365>.

[20] C. S. Knighton, 'The Calendars and their Editors, 1856–2006', SPO, available at: <https://www.gale.com/intl/essays>. These errors have been mitigated to some extent: corrections made to the copies of the Calendars in TNA, The Institute of Historical Research, British Library, Bodleian Library, and University of Cambridge Library have been included in SPO. Researchers are also able to submit further amendments and corrections to the project for the benefit of future scholarship.

varying ways in which uncertainty is expressed (regarding authorship, dates, and places of writing). While these issues are often apparent and can be surmounted on a document-by-document basis, when processing data at the scale of over 130,000 documents, a process of data preparation or cleaning is required. The remainder of the chapter provides an account of how that work was undertaken, in order to bring the history of the caretakers of this data into the present, and show the value it adds by opening up new ways of accessing and understanding the shape of this archive.[21] It explains how the approaches we chose were determined by the particular complexities of this data, as well as for the audience to whom we are presenting them.

Data Cleaning as Curation

A key feature of the current remix of the archive is its focus on just one document type: the letter. We began by extracting all documents in our dataset that have both an author and a recipient field in the metadata. This process also captured a small number of documents with an author and recipient that were not letters (e.g. certain kinds of legal documents), but we were able to exclude these from our dataset as a result of the cleaning process. The main need for cleaning, however, was created by the list of names derived from the author and recipient fields, which required both disambiguation and deduplication before we could create a list of unique nodes in our network, or put more simply we had individual people denoted by multiple name labels, and name labels that denoted multiple people. This is due to the fact that the metadata fields in the SPO data are derived directly from the Calendars, which feature these issues due to editorial policies (and inconsistencies), early modern naming practices and modes of address, changing titles and roles of individuals, and marriages. These are worth rehearsing briefly to explain the complexity of the issue and scale of labour entailed.

There are a number of factors affecting names. The first is that early modern names often occur in variant spellings: while senders would almost always spell their name in a single way, names in the recipient field feature many of the usual early modern variations, as well as some more creative spellings. For example, the auditor Anthony Bourchier's name is spelled in twenty-two variants. Secondly, it was common practice for letters to be addressed to a titular office (e.g. the Archbishop of Canterbury, Mayor of London, Sheriff of Nottinghamshire, etc.), or honourable title (e.g. earl, duke, or marquess; 'Norfolk', 'Somerset', or 'Essex'). These titles were held by several individuals during the ninety-four-year period of this study; and in the case of mayors a new holder was appointed every year. An individual's title could also change as they accrued further honours from the monarch, or held other posts. William Cecil, for example, appears in the dataset by forty-one variant names, including various combinations of his name and titles. A third problem is the unimaginative naming

---

[21] For further suggestions on ways this dataset might be used for future research, see the Afterword.

practices of Tudor families. Both men's and women's first names tended to be drawn from a limited pool of favoured appellations: from a list of over 20,560 unique people, more than 10% our network (post-data cleaning) were called John, and the nine most popular first names account for at least 40% of all individuals.[22] Further confusion is added by the recycling of family names. Eldest boys often bore the father or grandfather's name, inherited the same title, and sometimes even held the same governmental offices, to the great confusion of subsequent scholars. The fourth main complication is introduced by marriage: if a woman married, her surname would change, and, in elevated circles, her title too. An additional issue arises from the Dowager status. A widow would usually keep her title after the death of a husband, but his title would pass to a son or other male heir, and if that male heir had a wife of his own there could be two women with the same title. The problem of identifying women addressed by their surnames or titles only is rendered even more problematic by the historic lack of scholarship on early modern women. A final, more minor confusion is created by the Calendars' habit of referring to a sender or recipient by surname only. The reasons for doing so are clear: usually that person has been referred to recently within the chronological order of documents listed therein. This is acceptable in the context of the Calendars, but when they are turned into searchable metadata, the letter can be pulled out of sequence by a query, and the context no longer tells us to which Smith, for example, the letter refers.

The above factors meant that while the process of data extraction gave us 37,101 names, we knew that these were likely to denote a smaller number of unique historical people. However, at such a scale the process of disambiguation and deduplication required computational aid. It is worth pausing here briefly to reflect that we had a choice about whether to automate the process, and that other projects with different goals might choose a different route. Automation might fairly easily deduplicate and disambiguate something like 70% of cases, but developing the automation process to make accurate matches beyond this could take almost as long as curating the data by hand, and would still require manual checking to validate its accuracy. Given the nature of the problems posed by early modern names listed above, there would likely be various errors in an automated system that could introduce issues into our data. As outlined in our Foreword, our aim was to facilitate a scalable reading of the archive, that allowed us and subsequent users of the dataset to navigate from large-scale patterns in the data down to individual people and documents. While a 90% accuracy rate for an automated system might be good enough for certain applications in other domains, if 10% of the individuals in our network (which amounts to 2,000 people) were wrongly disambiguated or deduplicated this would make this work unpersuasive and even risible to historians. Moreover even such a relatively small proportion of misidentified nodes would significantly affect the results of any network analysis.

---

[22] These statistics are based on an automatic extraction of first names (with some filtering and corrections) and are therefore almost certainly underestimates. The true distribution of Tudor first names is likely to be even more skewed. For a study of early modern naming practices, see Scott-Smith Bannister, *Names and Naming Patterns in England 1538-1700* (Oxford University Press, 1997).

We therefore chose an approach of assisted manual cleaning, using a bespoke interface. The benefit of manually cleaned data is that the result is much more trustworthy (at least when performed by a scholar versed in the field of study), and provides those undertaking the work with a very powerful grasp of the shape of the archive under investigation. The preparation of the name data was undertaken by Ruth working largely full-time on the process for nine months, plus several further months part-time, using a bespoke interface built by Sebastian called the Disambiguation Engine (shown in Figure 1.1).[23] There are existing open tools on the market for undertaking data cleaning of this type, the most obvious being OpenRefine,[24] which would suit the needs of many projects. Our tool fulfils a similar function, but we wanted to supply additional contextual information in the interface for swift decision making, due to the specific challenges presented by names outlined above. The Disambiguation Engine accelerated this process by allowing us to move deftly between: (1) the basic metadata fields extracted from SPO; (2) the supplementary information, such as letter abstracts, added by the editors of the Calendars; and (3) the digital scans of the original manuscript letters themselves (where available). Before loading the data into the Disambiguation Engine, each name label was assigned a unique Uniform

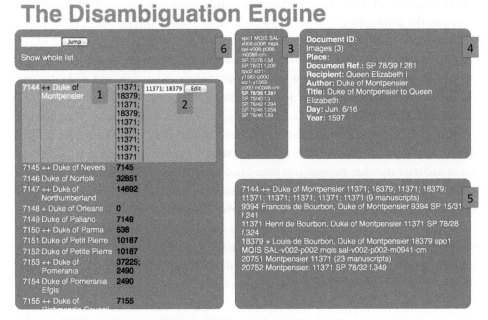

Figure 1.1 The interface of the Disambiguation Engine.

[23] The code for this tool can be found at: <https://github.com/tudor-networks-of-power/code>. An updated version of the tool with additional functionality has also been developed as part of our follow-on project, *Networking Archives* (AH/R014817/1), which will be released in due course. For an account of the tool, see Eero Hyvönen, Ruth Ahnert, Sebastian E. Ahnert, Jouni Tuominen, Eetu Mäkelä, Miranda Lewis, and Gertjan Filarski, 'Reconciling Metadata: Semi-Automated Tools', in *Reassembling the Republic of Letters in the Digital Age: Standards, Systems, Scholarship*, ed. Howard Hotson and Thomas Wallnig (Göttingen University Press, 2019), pp. 223–36.
[24] See <https://openrefine.org/>.

Resource Identifier (URI), in this case a number. The tool then allowed us to record our disambiguation and deduplication decisions by mapping these URIs to other existing URIs, or to new URIs.

In many cases the metadata alone might be enough to provide a positive identification. For example, the highlighted label in Figure 1.1, 'Duke of Montpensier' (item 1 in the figure), can be disambiguated in the editable box (item 2) using the dates of the letters supplied by the metadata (item 4, provided for each letter listed at item 3), cross-referenced with historical lists of title-holders, some of whom appear in the list of search results for Montpensier across the entire list of names (item 5). Indeed, where the holders of an office are well documented it is possible to automate the disambiguation process by constructing a mapping rule that is conditional on the date of writing. However, in cases for which no date is provided (or the date provided is insufficiently precise) it is often necessary to examine the description of the letter provided by the Calendar entry, or even to examine the text of the letter or the signature on the digital scan of the manuscript. This is the most definitive way to make a positive identification in ambiguous situations, but also where the most labour is expended in data cleaning. One example is the case of James Fitzgerald, Earl of Desmond. Over the entire period of the Tudor State Papers, four separate individuals with the first name James held the title of Earl of Desmond, and in addition the title was challenged on the earldom's second creation (when it was held by James Fitzgerald, the 1st Earl of Desmond) by James FitzThomas FitzGerald, the Súgán Earl of Desmond. Confusingly the 1st Earl and the Súgán Earl were both imprisoned in the Tower of London around the same time, and both petitioned the government for mercy, thereby creating some difficulties in telling them apart. In this context their signatures are often the only way to distinguish them. As the case of the Earls of Desmond show, these decisions cannot be made using information intrinsic to the dataset, but must be cross-referenced with biographical resources[25] and handlists of official offices.[26]

Another place where expert *human* decision making was necessary was in the case of aliases. Aliases were employed by correspondents who wished to disguise their identity—used both by agents of the government and conspirators against the throne—and intended to frustrate exactly the kind of identification we are setting out to achieve through deduplication. The previous labour of the Calendar editors means that we have inherited numerous helpful notes identifying aliases, but these are not applied systematically, and where multiple names were used, much additional mapping of

[25] We used online biographies because of the value of adding linked data to our datasets. LOD (linked open data) is added to our list of names where available (around 16% of all people). Due to the relative obscurity of certain figures (especially women) we used a variety of sources for verification. These included but were not limited to the *Oxford Dictionary of National Biography*, *The History of Parliament Online*, *Clergy of the Church of England database*, Wikipedia, *A Who's Who of Tudor Women* (<http://www.tudorwomen.com/>), and *The Virtual International Authority File* (<https://viaf.org/>).

[26] The most valuable ones for the disambiguation process for this project have been Arthur F. Kinney and Jane Lawson, *Titled Elizabethans: A Directory of Elizabethan Court, State, and Church Officers, 1558–1603* (Palgrave Macmillan, 2014); and Gary M. Bell, *A Handlist of British Diplomatic Representatives* (Royal Historical Society, 1990). Bell's book unfortunately only lists English ambassadors abroad, and not foreign ambassadors to the English court. The identities of those figures have been ascertained from a number of additional lists published in journal and online databases, as well as internal evidence within our own dataset.

names is required. In addition there are doubtlessly numerous aliases that have not been identified by past scholarship. For example, in the process of researching Chapter 4 we noticed that the handwriting of the letters from one Thomas Sansellen to the double agent Gilbert Gifford (who acted as a courier in the plot that entrapped Mary Queen of Scots) was the same as that observed in the letters from the Catholic exile and conspirator Thomas Morgan. The content seems to confirm that Sansellan was an alias of Morgan: the letter refers to numerous people within Morgan's network; it uses the same method for referring to Mary Stuart as in Morgan's other letters (as 'A', and using the male pronoun); and on the address leaf it addresses Gifford by the same alias ('Nicholas Cornellys') employed in Morgan's correspondence.[27] We have not been able to find any scholarship which explicitly identifies Sansellan as an alias for Morgan, so the decision to map these name labels to the same URI is an act of argumentation as much as an act of data cleaning. These kinds of decision making explain both our decision not to automate the process of disambiguation and deduplication, and the extent of the labour that this process entailed.

A key principle that guided our decision making during this process of data cleaning was to over-disambiguate. In other words: it is better not to collapse John Smith and J. Smith unless we could find evidence they were the same person: for example the same handwriting, biographical details in a letter, or writing to the same people in the same time window. Similarly if John Smith wrote twenty letters, it is best to create twenty unique URIs unless it could be demonstrated the letters are by the same John Smith. The reason for this is determined in part by the purpose for which we prepared the data. The results of a network analysis of a falsely over-connected network could erroneously exaggerate a person's significance, creating connections between communities that were in fact separate. If in doubt, therefore, under-connection is preferable. For this reason, we took the case of aliases very seriously, and only mapped aliases to the same URI where there was persuasive evidence.

However, names were not the only metadata field that required cleaning. The place of writing presented a similar problem to names, as places can be known by different appellations in different languages (such as Cologne versus Köln); and often the same place name can denote several unique locations, such as the place name 'Sutton' (five different geographic locations across the eleven letters in which it appears). Moreover, misspellings and variants are as common with place names as they are with people. We therefore implemented a similar cleaning process to the person names, again developing our own tool.[28] The cleaning of the 7,981 place names was undertaken by Jose Cree and Lotte Fikkers. Cree made the suggestion to add contextual information to the tool: by situating each letter attached to a given place of writing within the chronological order of the author's letters, it becomes possible to infer a likely itinerary that can help to discount unlikely mappings of place name to a geographical location.

---

[27] 'Thomas Sansellen' to 'Nicholas Cornellys' (Gilbert Gifford), 9 July 1586, SP 53/18 f.80.
[28] See https://github.com/tudor-networks-of-power/code.

In the process of disambiguating and deduplicating the place names Cree and Fikkers also assigned geo-coordinates for the locations.[29]

These geo-coordinates also enabled us to identify errors in our data, which could have been introduced by the Calendar editor, by erroneous decisions in the data-cleaning process, or by the wilful misdirection of the authors of the letters. One example of the way in which geo-coordinates can highlight likely errors is to calculate a 'velocity' for a given individual by dividing the geographical distance between two subsequent places of writing by the time that elapsed between these letters. If an individual writes from two different locations that are hundreds of miles apart on the same day or on subsequent days, this velocity will be impossibly high, and an error in the data very likely. This approach uncovered a whole host of errors introduced at different stages in the letters' long afterlives. For example, Sir Robert Jerningham is listed in the Calendars as writing from Bologna and Boulogne on the same day (Boulogne is the error). In another example it appears that Nicolas Raince, a Parisian clergyman who was a secretary at the French embassy in Rome from approximately 1521 to 1537, was writing from both Rome and Cambridge on 31 May 1531 (918 km apart). But given that all his other letters are written from Italy (the most recent, twenty-one days earlier, also in Rome), it seems that the author has been misidentified. Looking at the original print copy of the *Letters and Papers* we can see why: the letter description is '___ to the bishop of ___'. However, the blanks have been filled in on the SPO version of that Calendar using information from the entry above, carrying over the identical sender and recipient (seemingly based on the fact the recipient of Raince's letter was also a bishop).[30] Here we can see how the data-cleaning process helps to improve on the labour of the previous caretakers of this archive.

To test the quality of our work we followed the assisted manual process of cleaning that we had undertaken using the Disambiguation Engine with systematic computationally run checks. These were implemented by writing an algorithm to extract chains (e.g. instances in which we were mapping person 1 to person 2, and mapping person 2 to person 3) and loops (person 1 mapped to person 2, person 2 mapped to person 1). Such erroneous cases will inevitably arise in a large data-cleaning effort.

We also checked the metadata fields for the date of composition. The date of composition is encoded in two separate fields to allow for uncertainty. Of a total of 132,747 letters, 110,037 have the same date in these two fields, meaning that an exact date of writing is given in 82.9% of cases; 10,281 letters are given a year-long window

---

[29] Wikipedia was used as a source for the geo-coordinates. There is currently no temporally appropriate gazetteers available to scholars working on the early modern period, although there are efforts being made to address this. See, for example, Katherine McDonough, Ludovic Moncla, and Matje van de Camp, 'Named Entity Recognition Goes to Old Regime France: Geographic Text Analysis for Early Modern French Corpora', *International Journal of Geographical Information Science, Special Section: Spatial Computing and Digital Humanities* 33 (2019), 2498–522; and McDonough, 'Putting the Eighteenth Century on the Map: A Proposal for Early Modern French Geospatial Data Development', in *Digitizing Enlightenment*, ed. by Glenn Roe and Simon Burrows (Oxford Studies in the Enlightenment/Liverpool University Press, 2019).

[30] 'Nicolas Raince' to 'the Bishop of Montmorency'/ [Unnamed regent of Cambridge to Richard Nix], 31 May 1531, SP 1/66 f.19. The correct sender and recipient seem to be an unnamed regent of the University of Cambridge writing to Richard Nix, which can be ascertained from the letter contents, which asks the Bishop of Norwich to give the newly appointed interceptor of divinity, Nicholas Shaxton, a licence to preach in his diocese.

(meaning the year of writing only was supplied in 7.7%); and 4,045 letters are given a month-long window (meaning a year and month only were supplied in 3%). In these cases no further precision is possible, and so we need to work with a level of ambiguity in the temporal dimension of our data. A further 5,198 letters (3.9%) have a date of composition that spans a ten-day window. This is due to the transition from the Julian to the Gregorian calendar, which was 'only adopted in Protestant Europe by fits and starts' after its propagation in 1582.[31] At this date, the two Calendars were ten days out of alignment, which became an issue when letters crossed borders where dating protocols varied—accounting for 3.9% of letters in our dataset. Most western European countries shifted the first day of their numbered year to 1 January even before they adopted the Gregorian calendar. However (and conversely), following the reform the year starting on 25 March was called the Civil or Legal Year. It was not uncommon for a date between 1 January and 24 March to be written as '1556/57'. Where Calendar editors did not impose the proleptic Gregorian new year of 1 January, we were able to check that the slash formulation of the date was translated correctly into the machine-readable metadata fields, thanks to work undertaken for us by undergraduate research assistant, Emily Shah. While 97.6% of letters have fixed dates, or date windows relating to standard causes, the remaining 2.4% mostly comprise undated letters. In these cases the workers adding metadata entries to SPO created temporal windows of varying sizes—some with discernible logic, others without. In total there are date windows of 338 different durations, from a single day to 400 years (in this case due to a typographical error); but only 913 have a window larger than thirty years. Ruth manually checked these, providing narrower time windows (or occasionally exact dates) where possible, by using letter descriptions, scans of the original letters, and contextual information. We undertook a similar task for large temporal gaps in an individual's correspondence, manually reviewing the 596 individuals for which there was a gap of twenty years or more between letters sent.

Further corrections to the various metadata fields followed piecemeal during the analysis of the dataset, as small errors or overlooked examples emerged by studying in detail the local networks of individuals, rather than looking at aggregated data. Future users of this dataset will undoubtedly find further errors, or be able to suggest further improvements, which could be re-deposited as a new version of the dataset.

Transformation

This final transformation of this archive, therefore, was a significant piece of work. It was undertaken using two custom-built computational interfaces (the Disambiguation Engines for people and places) and a series of further custom-designed algorithms (such as the checks involving mapping chains and loops, date windows, and velocities),

---

[31] Miranda Lewis, Arno Bosse, Howard Hotson, Thomas Wallnig, and Dirk van Miert, 'Time', in *Reassembling the Republic of Letters*, pp. 97–118.

developed by Sebastian, for the curation of the person and place metadata. This infrastructure needed to be developed before the cleaning could even begin. The cleaning itself took around eighteen months of full-time labour, four months of which were contributed by research assistants Jose Cree and Lotte Fikkers, several hours of extra data checking undertaken by the Stanford undergraduates Tani Thomsen and Emily Shah, and the remainder undertaken by Ruth.[32] In connecting this labour with the long afterlife of the letters, we seek to suggest the value of data cleaning as a contribution in and of itself, and part of the long history of care work undertaken by those previous keepers and editors.[33] We can quantify this work not just in hours spent, but in the number of changes wrought: 37,101 name labels were resolved to a list of 20,566 unique individuals; each was assigned a gender label; and ~16% were provided with linked open data, associating them with authority files.[34] 7,981 place names were resolved to 5,409 unique geographic locations, and each was geocoded.

The value of such work, however, is not intrinsic, but rather evidenced in the transformation that it enables. The 20,566 individuals become the nodes in our network,[35] connected by letters, and located in time and space.[36] As an abstract framework, the network radically reframes how we can conceptualise and navigate historical data: the relation of the individual within their social and political contexts; the interplay of national and international relations; and how historical events play out temporally. These are the broad frameworks within which we frame history and, broader still, human experience. More specifically, with regards to this specific dataset, we will show in the following chapters how this remix of the data permits us to identify information hubs in our networks (Chapter 2); identify the brokers and bridges between epistolary communities (Chapter 3); find individuals with similar correspondence patterns (Chapter 4); model the role of women in mediation (Chapter 5); plot 'trending topics' in letter contents and trace their dissemination through the network (Chapter 6); and identify people who were in the same place at the same time, and whether they mentioned one another in their letters (Chapter 7). Such methods do not provide answers to complex historical questions on their own, but they do help us to *ask* a different kind of question, and to proceed in a different mode. They permit

---

[32] See Acknowledgements for further details.

[33] Katherine Bode has made a similar argument, suggesting that the creation of a dataset is analogous to a scholarly edition in *A World of Fiction: Digital Collections and the Future of Literary History* (University of Michigan Press, 2018), introduction.

[34] Chapter 2 will explain further the reasons for the low percentage, but in brief this is because ~68% of people only correspond with one person, whereas only ~16% correspond with more than ten people. The former group are hard to provide with LOD either because they are not historically 'significant' enough to have their own authority file (e.g. petitioners), or because the lack of information makes it difficult to make a definitive identification.

[35] We made the decision to leave councils and other institutionalised groups as entities with their own URIs. The most prominent example, and where our decision has the most impact, is in the case of the Privy Council.

[36] The process of disambiguation and deduplication results in the assignment of a unique identifier (ID) for each unique individual. It is therefore straightforward to extract a table in which each row represents a letter, and in which the columns give the sender and recipient IDs, the date range of writing (in the form of two 'YYYYMMDD'-formatted dates), the manuscript reference, a unique ID for the place of writing, and the XML filename. In this tabular form the data can easily be read by an algorithm written in Python or pretty much any other programming language.

researchers to retrieve data in a way that differs from results returned by the search box, the index, and the temporally ordered Calendar; and this mode of retrieval enables researchers to iteratively hone their questions and queries.[37]

The way in which the remixing of the data helps to ask questions in a different way can be grasped by the interactive visualisation of our data designed by our collaborator Kim Albrecht. The homepage of this visualisation provides a macro view of the whole archive, representing as nodes all people who exchanged letters with two or more people, arranged chronologically by the average date of their correspondence.[38] As shown in Figure 1.2, this page simulates random walks through the network which appear as dynamic bursts of blue (letters received) and red (letters sent) radiating out from individuals to their correspondents. This entrance page is designed to let people glean some first insights about the archive, its modulations in size over time, and the dominance of key correspondence hubs. Those already familiar with the archive might rightly guess that the two main bulges over the century correspond with Thomas Cromwell and William Cecil, Lord Burghley's respective periods in office as Principal Secretary. From the front page, users can then navigate—via search or by clicking one of the nodes—to a specific individual's correspondence which can be viewed either temporally or spatially.

The temporal view of an individual's correspondence allows users to grasp the volume of their correspondence and the breadth of their epistolary social network. The example of Sir Francis Vere, a soldier who served in the Low Countries, can be seen in Figure 1.3. His fourteen correspondents are represented as yellow circles, sized by the volume of letters they exchanged with Vere: the largest is Burghley, followed by the Privy Council and Robert Devereaux, the Earl of Essex. Lines connect each correspondent to their individual items of correspondence. Letters sent by Vere are represented as a red dot, received ones as blue; and each dot can be clicked to see the Calendar description of the letter. This bird's-eye view reveals at a glance that Vere mostly appears in the State Papers as an author of letters, rather than as a recipient (due to his military activities abroad he was a key provider of foreign intelligence); and that all the letters were written between the very late 1580s and the end of Elizabeth's reign, with a fairly even distribution over the entire period, but at a modest volume.

The spatial view by comparison enables users to see the locations from which an individual sent and received letters. Figure 1.4 shows the geographical spread of the correspondence of Sir Thomas Smith, who served both as a Principal Secretary and diplomat. Red dots show the origin of all the letters he sent, and blue the locations from which he received letters; they are sized by the volume written from that location. The lines represent a rough-hewn, inferred itinerary based on the time ordering of

---

[37] For a similar argument, see Jo Guldi, 'Critical Search: A Procedure for Guided Reading in Large-Scale Textual Corpora', *Journal of Cultural Analytics* 3:1 (2018), <https://doi.org/10.22148/16.030>.

[38] The website as a whole takes all individuals into account, including those who only communicate with one other person.

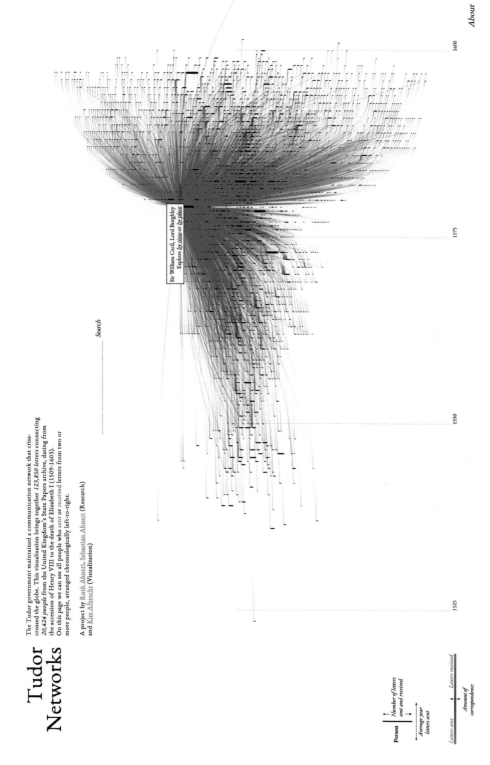

Figure 1.2 Front page of the Tudor Networks visualisation (https://tudornetworks.net/), with a freeze frame of William Cecil, Lord Burghley's interactions. Letters sent appear in red, and letters received in blue. Image credit: Kim Albrecht.

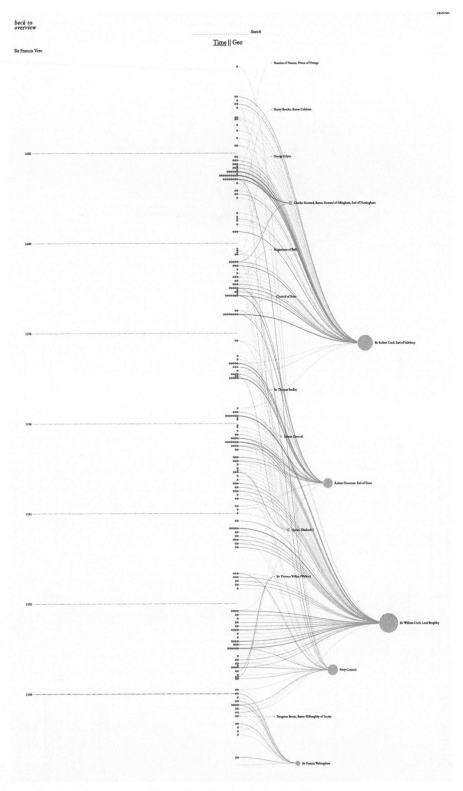

Figure 1.3 Temporal view of Sir Francis Vere's correspondence in the Tudor Networks visualisation (http://tudornetworks.net). Image credit: Kim Albrecht.

Sir Thomas Smith

Figure 1.4 Geographical view of Sir Thomas Smith's correspondence in the Tudor Networks visualisation (http://tudornetworks.net). Red dots mark locations from which the individual sent letters, and the lines between them show the temporal sequence, thus creating an approximate itinerary. The blue dots mark locations from which letters were received by the individual. Image credit: Kim Albrecht.

the places from which he wrote. It necessarily misses out stops that are not evidenced in the letters contained in the State Papers. Nevertheless it gives a sense of the travel necessitated by his diplomatic missions, which are dominated by his periods as ambassador to France. Once again by clicking the dots, users can navigate to the Calendar descriptions of the letter contents.

The interactive visualisation, then, is a digital aid to discovery, rather than digital analysis. Nevertheless it does provide users with an intuition about the contours of the data and allows them to begin asking questions that are suggested by those contours. It invites users to notice differences between the temporal and spatial profiles of individuals' correspondence, or between different categories of correspondent in ways that foreshadow the more powerful analytics we employ in the following chapters. By browsing enough individuals one can begin to appreciate that the volume of correspondence in which individuals are implicated varies by orders of magnitude.

We can observe that different types of people have a very different balance of incoming and outgoing correspondence. For instance, in the temporal view of the principal secretaries the items of correspondence are predominantly blue, meaning that most of their correspondence is incoming (which makes sense in light of the history of the archive outlined above); conversely diplomats and soldiers have a lower volume of correspondence that is mostly red, because the archive has more of their outgoing correspondence. The statistical breakdown of this balance is discussed more in Chapter 2.

We can also think of the differing geographical profiles of correspondents. In Figure 1.5 we show a comparison of Henry VIII's Principal Secretary, Thomas Cromwell, and Francis Walsingham, who held this office in the reign of Elizabeth I. It shows that Walsingham had a much larger network of correspondents in Europe and beyond, as shown by the spread of blue dots across the map. Users can also observe the stark difference between the static profile of Cromwell and the more mobile profile of Walsingham (shown by the limited spread of the red dots, denoting the location from which they wrote), who also served on embassies. We can see a different set of divergences between the geographic profiles of Walsingham and Smith (Figure 1.4). Smith, like Walsingham, also served both as Principal Secretary and diplomat: the distribution of red dots is very similar, but the network of Smith's contacts in blue is much sparser, suggesting that Smith left behind a much smaller body of correspondence from his period in office as Secretary. These are differences that we probe more quantitatively in Chapter 2.

Beyond person-to-person comparison, visualisation can also help us to begin to see what we might be able to ask about the character of the archive in the aggregate. Moving now beyond the affordances of the interface, in Figure 1.6 we visualise each letter in our dataset that provides information about their place of composition or sending (82,479 or 62.1% of the total). These various letter origins tell us where the Tudor government had eyes, revealing the spread and density of coverage of their diplomatic and intelligence networks, as well as the gaps in those networks. In other words, these origins form a view of the early modern world from the perspective of the English government. The obvious way to 'see' that view might be to mark each geo-coordinate (assigned to each place during our data preparation) as a point on an existing map. But there is another more visually powerful option: to place that point onto a blank canvas as we do in Figure 1.6. The result is striking. It shows that we do not need an underlying map; this excerpt of the data provides a pointillist impression of England and continental Europe. England is densely filled, with slightly less coverage in Scotland, Ireland, and Wales, whilst continental Europe is more sparsely described but still discernible, with highest densities in France, the Netherlands, and the Holy Roman Empire. It shows immediately the extent and the limits of the Tudor world-view: the detail reduces markedly in Spain and Portugal and in Eastern Europe. But we are also beginning to glimpse the way that voyage and discovery was expanding that world-view: at the very bottom of the figure we see isolated points in Northern Africa, and—if we were to pan out further still—we would glimpse more still in

Thomas Cromwell, Earl of Essex

Sir Francis Walsingham

Figure 1.5 Comparison of the geographical reach of Thomas Cromwell and Francis Walsingham in the Tudor Networks visualisation (http://tudornetworks.net). Image credit: Kim Albrecht.

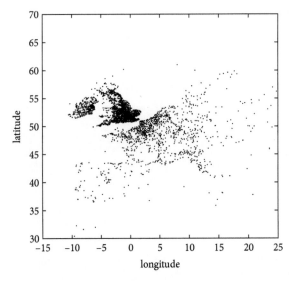

Figure 1.6 Excerpt of the geo-coordinate place metadata (longitude and latitude), plotted on a blank canvas. Each point marks a place of writing. The density of data points is such that the outlines of Europe are clearly visible. There are additional places of writing outside this geographical region in the Americas, Africa, the Middle East, and Asia, but these are comparatively few, and are discussed further in Chapter 8.

North, Central, and South America, the Ottoman empire, Sub-Saharan Africa, India, and East Asia. We provide a breakdown of this picture, and explore some of the journeys that led to these far-flung letters in Chapter 7.

Conclusion

The foregoing visualisations provide preliminary sketches of the data—as is natural for an introduction. However, they give a clear sense of the power unlocked by the process of cleaning and restructuring the data, which yields new value and insights from the historical archive. Most importantly, as we will explore more in the next chapter, the visualisations help us to trace the contours of our data, and to understand how these contours shape the outcomes of our analysis. Moreover, by examining this archive through the abstract framework of the network, and by adding geolocations, we allow patterns to emerge from the data that can give rise to new research avenues.

Of course visualisation is not a neutral act; it is, rather, a layer that invites certain kinds of interpretation, and reveals and occludes different aspects of the data.[39] For example, in choosing to only represent people with two or more correspondents on

---

[39] On the rhetoric of network visualisation, see Ruth Ahnert, Sebastian E. Ahnert, Catherine N. Coleman, and Scott B. Weingart, *The Network Turn: Changing Perspectives in the Humanities* (Cambridge University Press, 2020), chapter 4.

the website homepage, we exclude 68% of correspondents from this particular view. But this was for good reason: rough drafts of the visualisation revealed that including all correspondents would have rendered the visualisation too complex to navigate intuitively. One must be attuned to the rhetoric of the chosen mode of visualisation as one develops questions. In the pages that follow visualisation plays a relatively limited role, at least as a means of *discovery*; visualisations are used primarily to *communicate* our findings. In the following chapters we move to more advanced quantitative measures, building first from standard off-the-shelf algorithms to bespoke methods, which more powerfully harness the potential of the new dataset created from this ancient collection of papers.

The purpose of this introductory chapter is to call attention to the value of the dataset in its own right, as a distinct contribution from the book, or perhaps more accurately, the foundation on which the book is built. While the following pages explore a series of experiments and paths through this network, our hope is that the dataset as an entity will have its own afterlife. To that end, we have chosen to make our data and methods openly available for the reuse of others. As well as releasing the interactive visualisation, our data is published as a dataset on an institutional repository.[40] Similarly, the methods (including the code for the tools we developed for our data-cleaning process) are made available via an openly accessible code repository on GitHub, complete with documentation.[41] This is in line with the values of open research. But, perhaps more importantly in terms of the long afterlives of the letters, it is in keeping with the actions of the long lineage of their caretakers, who have sought to ensure the future of the collection by rendering it navigable not only for their future selves but also for other users. We believe that this dataset therefore offers an important—and potentially transformative—contribution to the evolving field of knowledge surrounding the State Papers. Never before has anyone had such full, complete, and correct information about the entire epistolary holdings of the Tudor State Papers archive. A vast number of research questions can be explored using this material. We hope the following pages of this book give a suggestion of just some of the ways in which this data might be used by those interested in answering historical research questions through quantitative analysis.

By positioning ourselves within this long afterlife, we also acknowledge the labour that will continue after our contribution. This kind of work is never truly over. Despite all our best efforts, there will be small errors, and new knowledge will come to light that will render the decisions we made outdated. By making this data available we allow other scholars to continue to iteratively improve upon it, to augment it, and reuse it in ways we cannot yet foresee. There are particular opportunities, for those with more time and different research questions, for example: to think further about the peripatetic nature of 'the Court', which is not a static location but rather an entity

---

[40] <https://doi.org/10.17863/CAM.99562>.
[41] <https://github.com/tudor-networks-of-power/code>.

that travels with the monarch;[42] how we might tease apart bodies and groups like the Privy Council, who are usually invoked as an entity, but are made up of a changing roster of individuals who varied widely in their level of involvement over time; or unpicking letter bundles. This ongoing iteration, within a community of scholars with different kinds of expertise, is the best possible outcome for such work.

[42] A useful resource for thinking further about this is Marion E. Colthorpe, *The Elizabethan Court Day by Day,* available at: <https://folgerpedia.folger.edu/The_Elizabethan_Court_Day_by_Day>.

2

The Shape of the Archive

In this book we employ network analysis and other computational methods to navigate between distant views of our data and close readings of its constituent documents. This chapter provides the most distant of our views. The metaphor of aerial photography and its utility in modern archaeological research, which we have proffered elsewhere, is useful for positioning its aims: our contention is that before we begin archaeological excavation we need to understand the whole landscape.[1] Aerial archaeology has enabled the discovery of hundreds of previously unknown archaeological sites, but it has also helped to make sense of known, clearly visible prehistoric landscape features, such as the Nazca lines in Peru, which form a large-scale pattern that only makes sense when viewed from a great height.[2] This is an apt metaphor for this chapter: while researchers will have grasped aspects of the features of the State Papers archive, their cumulative impact on the shape of this dataset is impossible to appreciate without quantitative approaches. This chapter represents that preparatory survey of the land, which, like the aerial photograph, sacrifices resolution for the ability to find large-scale patterns. In the following chapters, as we focus on specific areas of the letter archive and more specific questions, we employ more sophisticated algorithms, combinations of algorithms, and bespoke methods. Here, however, our aim is to draw a coarse-grained picture on a large scale by employing foundational network measures.

The issue that faces researchers as they encounter the archive—whether that be through traditional or digital methods—is how to disentangle the question of what happened in the past from what survives from the past. As we discovered in the previous chapter, the various steps in the long history of the State Papers, and the hands of the caretakers through which they passed, have each impacted the contours of this dataset in complex ways. Its origin as the working papers of the Principal Secretary determined the manner and scope of the materials originally collected. However, conscious destruction, loss, and archival scattering have led to patchy survival; and, of the surviving documents, what and how it has made its way into our data has been determined both by the editorial decisions of nineteenth- and twentieth-century archivists and editors, and the scope and ambition of the twenty-first-century project *State Papers Online*. The letters in the State Papers dataset, therefore, constitute a very particular

---

[1] Ruth Ahnert, Sebastian E. Ahnert, Catherine N. Coleman, and Scott B. Weingart, *The Network Turn: Changing Perspectives in the Humanities* (Cambridge University Press, 2020), chapter 6. Available at: <https://doi.org/10.1017/9781108866804>.

[2] For a similar metaphor, but used to make a countervailing argument, see Bruno Latour, 'Anti-Zoom', <http://www.bruno-latour.fr/sites/default/files/P-170-ELIASSON-GBpdf.pdf>.

Tudor Networks of Power. Ruth Ahnert and Sebastian E. Ahnert, Oxford University Press. © Ruth Ahnert and Sebastian E. Ahnert 2023. DOI: 10.1093/oso/9780198858973.003.0002

world-view, which in turn has been imperfectly and incompletely mapped. It is vital to survey these in order to fully contextualise the more focused analyses of the following chapters. Moreover, this aerial view also provides an important framework for approaching the historiography of this period that has used the archive as its primary evidence. While digital scholarship has sometimes been critiqued for lapsing into uncritical positivism,[3] histories of Tudor administration have also been shaped by an over-emphasis on what is present in the archives, attesting to the exceptional nature of the statesmen whose papers have passed down to us most intact—leading in turn to the comparative marginalisation of those whose papers survive only partially.

The aerial view of the epistolary network is delivered via a handful of foundational network metrics. As in the following chapters, we only supply metrics as they are needed by the reader, when we are able to immediately explain the payoff by providing the results. The chapter begins with the metric of 'degree' (or 'degree centrality') which shows the number of people a given person wrote to and received correspondence from. It reveals the huge order of magnitude over which these numbers stretch, from the vanishingly small number of people who corresponded with thousands of people, to the thousands who corresponded with just one person. The network hubs correspond broadly with the centre of the Tudor government. These include both the symbolic hubs of the monarchs and the administrative hubs of the principal secretaries—the latter of whom constitute the true centre of this archive, as its constituent makers.

Thereafter we introduce the concepts of weighted and directed networks, which underpin a set of network measures that quantify the volume of incoming and outgoing correspondence for each individual. As we show below, charting the balance of incoming and outgoing correspondence is a simple yet effective way of understanding some of the different correspondent types within the archive. The people with the largest bodies of correspondence associated with their name, the 'government hubs', are marked by much higher levels of incoming correspondence than outgoing. Their counterparts, with the inverse distribution, are mostly diplomats, military leaders, and other foreign agents. In other words, those posted to outposts have the highest outgoing correspondence. Of course, this is not because diplomats actually wrote more letters than they sent. It is in these cases where the survey is vital because it helps us understand where the fact of what survives (as opposed to what once existed) can become a useful feature in our analysis. If we had complete correspondence records, these imbalances would be much less pronounced. The value of the incompleteness of the record is that it precisely points towards the processes of the archive's creation. As we suggest below and in several of the following chapters, there are often correlations between the role an individual served in relation to the Tudor government and the profile of what letters survive. The inverse pattern of secretaries and

---

[3] See, for example, Tom Eyers, 'The Perils of the "Digital Humanities": New Positivisms and the Fate of Literary Theory', *Postmodern Culture: Journal of Interdisciplinary Thought on Contemporary Cultures* 23:2 (2013). On the opportunities of post-positivism, see James Smithies, 'Digital Humanities, Postfoundationalism, Postindustrial Culture', *DHQ* 8:1 (2014).

diplomats points to their interdependence in the international trade of information required for effective foreign policy. Similar kinds of imbalance point us towards other means by which principal secretaries sought to expand their world-view, including letter interception and the seizure of personal papers.

There are of course different kinds of survival and loss, as we explore in the final section of this chapter. This is perhaps most obvious from an exploration of the hubs. While the biggest hubs all tend to be principal secretaries or monarchs, not all principal secretaries are hubs. Using the suite of metrics introduced earlier in the chapter, this final section seeks to show how this archive can be characterised as a set of very particular viewpoints, or what Gabriel Tarde and after him Bruno Latour would describe as the monad: 'not a part of a whole, but a point of view on all the entities taken severally and not as a totality'.[4] Through it we show which secretaries' papers form the State Papers, and which secretaries are merely present in our archive by virtue of being captured through the communications of the dominant hubs. Through this framework we seek to grasp the different and partial viewpoints from which our histories are constructed, what kinds of voices they encompass, and what has been lost or excluded.

Hubs and Peripheries

We begin our exploration with one of the simplest network metrics, 'degree'. The degree, or 'degree centrality', of a node is the number of connections of that node, calculated as the total of its incoming and outgoing connections. The degree is the most obvious measurement of a node's infrastructural significance in the network, and in this case it helps to reveal the hubs that created and dominate the structure of the archive. As we might expect, the people with the highest degree tend to be the monarchs, their principal secretaries, and the Privy Council. In Henry's reign the person with the highest degree is Henry's Principal Secretary and later Lord Privy Seal Thomas Cromwell (with a score of 2,137), followed by Henry himself (1,128). In Edward IV's reign the top scoring nodes are: the Privy Council (200); Lord Protector Edward Seymour, who effectively ruled in Edward VI's stead in the early years of the reign (189); Secretary William Cecil (188); and, in fourth place, Edward VI (118). In Mary I's reign the three nodes with the highest degree are: Mary herself (326); the Privy Council (91); and King Philip II, Mary's husband (77). And in Elizabeth's reign the three people with the highest degree are Elizabeth's Principal Secretary and, later, Lord Treasurer, William Cecil, Lord Burghley (4,127); his son and last Principal Secretary of Elizabeth's reign, Robert Cecil, Earl of Salisbury (2,458); and Elizabeth herself (2,220).

---

[4] Bruno Latour, Pablo Jensen, Tommaso Venturini, Sébastian Grauwin, and Dominique Boullier, '"The whole is always smaller than its parts": A Digital Test of Gabriel Tardes' Monads', *The British Journal of Sociology* 63 (2012), 590–615 (p. 598).

In a sense the monarch and the Secretary can be considered as a paired epistolary super-hub. This is because in terms of early modern government correspondence the monarch was often a symbolic hub: their mailing address was (in most cases) the desk of the Principal Secretary, who had also drafted much of their outgoing correspondence. The distinction between the monarch as personal author and institutional symbol is even more pertinent when we consider the reign of Edward VI. Lasting just five and a half years, until his death at the age of 15, Edward's 'rule' was overseen by his councillors, who constructed his kingship on his behalf. While the State Papers do contain personal correspondence to and from the monarch, such as the famous examples of Henry VIII's love letters to Anne Boleyn (which include the sensitive confession of 'having been more than a year wounded by the dart of love'),[5] the majority are bureaucratic missives in service of government business. Grants are perhaps the clearest example of this, such as the formulaic document issued in Elizabeth I's name to Richard Morley, Michael Peniston, and Christopher Porter in 1585 granting them permission to measure linen cloths, thereby challenging the perceived corruption in the trade of imported cloth.[6] Clearly the monarch would not have troubled herself personally with the wording of such a minor directive.

In the other direction—letters addressed to the monarch—the case is even clearer. Just because a letter was addressed to the king or queen does not mean that it reached their eyes. Much of the monarch's correspondence would have been handled by their secretaries. In an Elizabethan account of the office of Secretary, written in 1592 by Robert Beale, a long-serving Clerk of the Council, the weight of correspondence with which they dealt is described: 'the keeping of all lettres, minutes of lettres to and from the king for the counsaill, instruccions and other suche other writings as shalbe treated vpon by the counsaill'.[7] In Henry VIII's time it had been common for a letter to the king to be enclosed in a covering note to the Secretary, to be passed on only with the latter's approval.[8] It was regarded as improper to write directly to the monarch uninvited, a form of etiquette that Edward Courtenay, the Earl of Devon, was reminded of by James Basset (Lord Chancellor Stephen Gardiner's Secretary):

> Your lettres were thankfully accepted of the kinges and quenes highness and thei lyked, it was good advyse bothto wryt unto them and also to sende your letres to Master Secretary Petre to deliver them [...] whensoever you wryte to their majesties you shold evermore sende your letters to him to be delivered for yt is the ordinarie way and wylbe best taken[.][9]

---

[5] Henry VIII to Anne Boleyn, 1527, *LP Volume 4: 1526–1528*, 23218.   [6] BL Lansdowne Vol/44 f.95.

[7] Robert Beale, 'Treatise of the Office of a Counsellor and Principal Secretarie', printed in Conyers Read, *Mr Secretary Walsingham and the Policy of Queen Elizabeth*, 3 vols. (Clarendon Press, 1925), vol. 1, pp. 423–43.

[8] C. S. Knighton, 'The Principal Secretaries in the Reign of Edward VI: Reflections on Their Office and Archive', in *Law and Government Under the Tudors: Essays Presented to Sir Geoffrey Elton Regius Professor of Modern History in the University of Cambridge on the Occasion of His Retirement*, ed. Claire Cross, David Loades, and J. J. Scarisbrick (Cambridge University Press, 1988), pp. 163–76 (p. 165).

[9] 27 May 1555, SP 11/5 f.86.

This reminder stresses this practice was both the usual administrative practice and one that recognised that access to the monarch was reserved for the lucky few.

The measure of degree, then, is a basic metric for understanding the power structures as they were expressed through government habits of correspondence; it helps us to highlight both symbolic hubs and administrative ones. But it can also help us understand the shape of the archive and viewpoints it represents if we analyse the distribution of degree scores across all people in the dataset. In a field-defining study for the establishment of network science as a discipline, Albert-László Barabási and Réka Albert showed that a wide variety of seemingly heterogeneous real-world networks—such as power grids, social networks, and the World Wide Web—exhibit nearly identical distributions of connectivity, and offered an elegant model that explained how these distributions might arise. Specifically they showed that these networks reveal a highly skewed degree distribution, with a small number of dominant high-degree nodes ('hubs') and much larger numbers of poorly connected nodes.[10]

We find this same skewed distribution in our letter network, as shown in Figure 2.1, which shows a plot of the degree scores of all correspondents for each reign. It is important to acknowledge that while graphs like this will be familiar to scholars conversant in network analysis, they are far from intuitive; but with some unpacking, they are rich in what they reveal about the archive. What we might notice about the four distributions shown in Figure 2.1 is that they all lie along similar diagonal lines, representing what is known as a 'power-law distribution'.[11] This term, taken from the field of statistics, describes a distribution that spans several orders of magnitude and is therefore normally plotted on logarithmic axes (here rising by factors of 10). On these axes a power-law distribution appears as a straight diagonal line, meaning that whether we look at the network as a whole or just within a specific region, we will always find a few relatively well-connected 'hubs' (people with a disproportionately large number of connections) and a very large number of nodes with a relatively small number of connections. The reason we use logarithmic scales—instead of the more usual and intuitive linear scale—is that the numbers cross several orders of magnitude, making it nearly impossible to plot within the normal proportions of the printed page.

For example the overall distribution of degree scores for Henry's reign (Figure 2.1a) reveals that Cromwell and Henry VIII are in fact the only two people in the network to have thousands of connections; the next closest person is Sir Thomas Wolsey with 672. In fact, out of 5,718 people in the Henrician letters network, only 17 (0.3%) people have a degree over 100, 34 (0.6%) have a degree over 50, and 119 (2.1%) have a degree over 20. By comparison, 5,262 (92%) people have five or fewer connections, and 3,888 (68%) have only one. This long tail holds across all four reigns: the proportion of nodes with a degree of one is 68.8% in Edward's reign, 67.4% in Mary's reign, and 66.2% in Elizabeth's (a variation of only 2.6%).

---

[10] Albert-László Barabási and Réka Albert, 'Emergence of Scaling in Random Networks', *Science* 286 (1999), 5439.

[11] This means that the number of nodes $P(k)$ of a given degree k is proportional to k^m, i.e. that degree to a constant power m (which is negative).

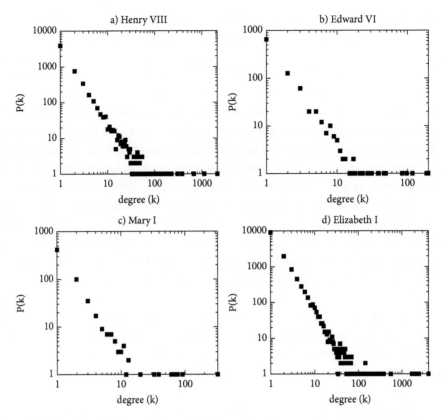

Figure 2.1 The distributions of degree (total number of connections) in the State Papers correspondence networks for the four Tudor reigns: (a) Henry VIII, (b) Edward VI, (c) Mary I, and (d) Elizabeth I. These closely follow a power law in all cases.

This is a very long tail of one-time correspondents, made up of many different kinds of people, from minor administrators to petitioners writing to the Principal Secretary seeking favour or aid. The latter are implicated in this network merely because they want something from the government: they are represented often by a single letter, usually directed to the Principal Secretary, seeking favour or aid of some kind. For example, a haberdasher from London named Robert Ingulson wrote to Cromwell in 1536 asking to be made one of his servants with livery and wages.[12] Other requests suggest a greater level of desperation. One is from John Feylde, a prisoner in the Counter prison, who also writes to Cromwell in 1536 pleading that since he has 'vnderseruyngly suffered long and grevous imprisonment by the space of iii yeres' that it may be 'diminished in time and greffe.'[13]

---

[12] SP 1/113 f.158r. On the form of the letter of petition, see James Daybell, *The Material Letter in Early Modern England: Manuscript Letters and the Culture and Practices of Letter-Writing, 1512–1635* (Palgrave Macmillan, 2012), p. 70.

[13] Feylde to Cromwell, 26 November 1536, SP 1/111 f.231r. For further discussion of letters of petition, see Chapter 6.

This overview is a powerful starting point for analysis. One might be tempted to argue that these findings are obvious, or just confirm what we already knew: that the top 0.3% of the network— the monarch and their secretaries and key statesmen— dominate the archive, and that the majority of correspondents are in fact peripheral. But that is not necessarily a given. As Matthew Lincoln has persuasively argued, scholars 'are particularly susceptible to confabulating these post-facto rationalizations with the idea that we somehow knew the results of this quantitative work already (and, implicitly, that we didn't need to waste our time doing it)'. Rather he is keen to stress the difference between what 'in retrospect sounds reasonable' from 'what we actually knew before'.[14] It is important to recognise that the power-law distribution that we observe is far from intuitive. Indeed while the paper is now over twenty years old, Barabási and Albert's observation of the power-law degree distribution of many real-world networks was an entirely different pattern of connectivity from that which most scientists would have expected at the time. Similarly, before the monumental data-cleaning task behind this project it was not possible to compute the total number of correspondents (at the most basic level), let alone the distribution of communications between those correspondents. It is highly likely, for example, that estimates of the total number of people in the archive corresponding with only one person would have been wrong by a factor of ten.

Grasping the highly skewed distribution of connections allows us to look at the archive from two different perspectives. The first, more standard, view considers the archive as a record of the government's purview, and is supported by the statistical dominance of figures like Cromwell. As the Principal Secretary to Henry, Cromwell was one of the very figures who created this archive through his personal and professional record keeping, and allows us to reconstruct his administrative reach and the extent of the information he marshalled through these administrative structures. We have his papers so fulsomely because, at his arrest in 1540, all his papers were seized from his files and have stayed in government hands ever since. But looking at the statistics another way, we can see the extent to which Cromwell and others mentioned above are outliers. Rather, the truly dominant category of correspondents are those who correspond with only one person. People like the petitioners Ingulson and Feylde are implicated in this network merely because they need something from the government. They are structurally peripheral to the network. We might think of these 13,729 correspondents (across the whole Tudor period), as forming a giant fringe around the edge of the network. Network analysis provides a way of asking the data to show us all the people who constitute this giant fringe by returning a list of all these one-time correspondents. This allows us to harness the archive to tell different kinds of stories, about ordinary people in the sixteenth century and the things that concerned them: their legal standing, their property, income, or freedom. In fact, their pleading letters may be the only evidence that they ever lived, apart perhaps from entries of their

---

[14] Matthew Lincoln, 'Confabulation in the Humanities', available at: <https://matthewlincoln.net/2015/03/21/confabulation-in-the-humanities.html>.

births, marriages, and deaths in a parish register. It also helps to remind us that histories most often reconstructed through the study of the State Papers represent less than 10% of all the people implicated in this archive; and most focus on the 0.3%. Network analysis can therefore have a powerful democratising influence, allowing us to uncover the histories of people at the peripheries of the government's purview and thereby inverting the usual ways in which the archive is used.

We see the dataset as an invitation for more work in this area. For our part, we touch on this giant fringe at intervals throughout the book: the peripheral victims of letter interception in Chapter 4, the language of petition in Chapter 5, and the geographical fringe of communications in Chapter 7. And as we suggest through methods proposed in Chapter 4, one way of pulling these fringe figures into the centre of scholarship may be to think about them at the meso-scale, by finding categories of correspondent who share attributes. However, the category of nodes that we engage with most frequently in this book are neither the hubs, nor this giant fringe, but rather the intermediate class of nodes that appear in the centre of the diagonal lines in Figure 2.1: the ~6,000 people (around one-third of the archive) with between 2 and 100 connections. These people are the bread and butter of the approach in our book, the minor and overlooked figures of the less famous ambassadors, agents, 'intelligencers', spies, conspirators, female mediators, couriers, and adventurers. Their interest as objects of study emerges when we leverage more nuanced metrics and bespoke methods in the following chapters. Here they are revealed to be structurally vital to the function of the government and its archival afterlife, playing an important role in the transmission of intelligence in the early modern information economy. Sometimes they are significant in their own right; in other cases (as we argue in several places) they gain their significance as *categories* of nodes. The approach through which we draw this statistical middle ground of the data into the foreground is motivated by a wish to correct for the centralised power structures of the archive. It is an attempt to read against the grain by digitally excavating figures whose oeuvre may largely be lost due to the hub-focused structure of the archive's creation.

Weighted and Directed Networks

To begin the process of teasing apart the data, we need to gain a more granular perspective than is possible by looking simply at degree; this section introduces the facets of *direction* and *weight*. A relationship marked by only one unreciprocated letter is quite different from a mutual correspondence of several dozen or hundreds of letters. The former might be a petitioner like Feyle or Ingulson, seeking favour from the government, usually by addressing the Principal Secretary (which were rarely met with replies within the State Papers archive); the latter a long-term friendship or business association. In order to understand the role that different people played in the transfer of information across the network we need to know the direction in which letters moved, and how many of them there were.

Those not familiar with the State Papers archive or patterns of epistolary survival might assume that most people in the network would send and receive roughly the same amount of correspondence. Contemporary letter-writers themselves thought this a reasonable expectation: as Gary Schneider has shown, there was a strong cultural expectation that all letters, however banal, would receive a response as a basic form of civility.[15] This expectation seems to have transcended both rank and position. In the State Papers archive letters frequently open with queries about whether the author's previous letters have been received. So strong was the expectation of a reply that the lack of one caused writers to fear their correspondence was lost, mis-delivered, or intercepted—or else that it denoted a loss of favour. For example, on 31 October 1514 Thomas Dacre, Baron Dacre of Gilsland, wrote to Wolsey 'mervailing gretly seing I stond charged with the borders that I had no lettres fro the kinges grace ne from you my lordes of the most honorable councale sens the iij daye of august considering that sens that time I haue written two tymes'.[16] Dacre had just become the Warden of the Marches, an office in the governments of Scotland and England responsible for the security of the border between the two nations. However, it appears that his letters to the king and his Council had not met with replies. One can imagine his concern at being physically removed and left in command without news or direction for almost three months.

Given the social pressure of reciprocity, then, we can safely assume that the majority of letters sent to and from the Tudor government—with the exception of petitions and certain news bulletins from agents posted abroad, especially military reports—would have received a reply. What survives in the archive, however, presents a very different picture, highlighting the difficulty of understanding epistolary practice through a single archive. However, while superficially this might seem like a problem for scholarship, quantitative measures suggest that differences in survival rate can also offer powerful indicators about the economy of information in which the Tudor principal secretaries traded. The fact (as we shall see) that the people with the very highest degrees have more incoming letters than outgoing tells us something crucial about how information was managed by the hubs in this network.

Correspondence networks are an example of network data that is both weighted and directed. In general networks can be directed, meaning that every connection has a directionality, such as that defined by senders and recipients of letters. They can also independently be weighted, meaning that every link is associated with a numerical value, for example the number of letters that passed from a particular sender to a particular recipient. In order to measure the extent to which the archive deviates from our expectation of reciprocity, we can compare the number of incoming letters ('in-strength' in network terms) and the number of outgoing letters ('out-strength') for each correspondent in the network. In each of the four graphs in Figure 2.2 (a–d) the

---

[15] Gary Schneider, *The Culture of Epistolarity: Vernacular Letters and Letter Writing in Early Modern England, 1500–1700* (Newark, DE: University of Delaware Press, 2005), pp. 61–3.

[16] SP 1/9 f.119r.

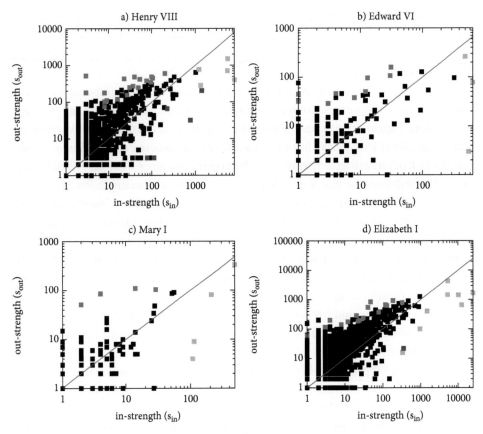

Figure 2.2 Comparison of in- and out-strength for the reigns of (a) Henry VII, (b) Edward VI, (c) Mary I, (d) Elizabeth I. The red line shows equality between the two metrics. The green, blue, and red points highlight categories of people discussed in the text. Green nodes represent government hubs including the monarch, their council, and principal secretaries, and other secretarial figures. Blue nodes represent figures whose letters entered the archive through seizure. The red nodes are those of diplomats and other categories of 'intelligencer'.

x-axis (horizontal) represents the in-strength and the y-axis the out-strength. Once again, those axes are logarithmic. The diagonal line in red represents a perfect balance between the number of letters sent and the number of letters received (suggesting epistolary reciprocity has been maintained).

Once again the aerial view offered by these graphs is so abstract that they are tricky to intuit at face value; but with some excavation they bear some rich insights. Immediately we can see that the greatest difference between the four graphs is the density of data points. Due to the relatively short reigns of Edward VI and Mary (in addition to other factors, discussed below), we have smaller collections of documents for these periods. Despite this superficial difference in terms of density, however, we can see a clear trend that is consistent across all the graphs. Crucially, there is signifi-cant variation on either side of the diagonal 'reciprocity' line, and in each case the distribution is denser above the diagonal in the lower reaches. However, at the very top of the scale the outliers appear below the diagonal. What this leads us to observe is that, in the surviving State Papers archive, the majority of people (75.6%) sent more letters than they received.

However, the people with the very highest degrees have more incoming letters than outgoing. These are the green points in Figure 2.2 a–d. In Henry's reign they include: the king, the Privy Council, Cromwell, Wolsey, William Paget, and Arthur Plantagenet, Viscount Lisle. In Edward's: Protector Somerset, the Privy Council, William Cecil (later Lord Burghley). In the following reigns the majority of these are made up of the same categories of people: the monarch (with the exception of Edward's reign, where the Protector seems to occupy this position in the graph), their council, and principal secretaries (William Paget, William Petre, William Cecil, later Lord Burghley, his son Robert Cecil, and Francis Walsingham).

This emphasis on incoming information at the very top end of strength distribution is a product of the activities of the principal secretaries, as intelligence-gathering hubs. Incoming intelligence was necessary to their success on the domestic and foreign stage. Conversely, we have relatively few outgoing missives from the monarch and their Secretary because outgoing mail was only filed in the secretaries' papers if a draft or duplicate copy was made, or if the recipient filed and kept them, and their papers also made their way into the archive. We also see this tendency more weakly expressed for other secretaries such as Thomas Fanshawe (out-degree 100; in-degree 961), and Michael Hicks (out-degree 16; in-degree 332) who both appear in Figure 2.2d highlighted in green, but further towards the bottom left quadrant of the graph than the principal secretaries. Hicks was one of Burghley's two secretaries at the time Burghley was the queen's chief minister. As mentioned in the history of the archive in Chapter 1, the so-called Burghley papers (which form a significant portion of the data underlying SPO) were in Hicks's possession and stayed in his family until about 1682 when they went to a London stationer called Richard Chiswell.[17] As the Queen's Remembrancer, Fanshawe's primary duty was to keep records of the taxes, paid and unpaid.

There are also administrative reasons for the imbalance between incoming and out-going correspondence from other hubs in the networks. For instance, the reason we have so much of the incoming correspondence of the Privy Council is because it 'leaked into the Secretarial archive'; the rest, sadly, was burnt in the Whitehall fire of 1619.[18] In many other cases the reason for this imbalance is the seizure of personal archives. We have a massive quantity of Wolsey's incoming correspondence due to the confiscation of his papers by the government when he came under suspicion. This is also the way that Cromwell's papers entered the archive, and why they survived in such quantities; unlike other secretaries whose letters passed into private collections

---

[17] Stephen Alford, 'State Papers of Edward VI, Mary I and Elizabeth I', SPO, available at: <https://www.gale.com/intl/essays>.

[18] David J. Crankshaw, 'The Tudor Privy Council, c.1540–1603', SPO, available at: <https://www.gale.com/intl/essays>.

of their families, these letters were recovered before they suffered the vicissitudes of time. This was not just the case for secretaries. Highlighted in blue in Figure 2.2 are some of the figures outside the central government whose papers were seized. Lord Lisle, Lord Deputy of Calais (out-strength 204; in-strength 1,391), and his wife Honor Plantagenet (37; 773) both appear prominently in Figure 2.2a because his archives were seized when he was imprisoned in the Tower of London on suspicion of treason, on the charge of plotting to betray Calais to the French. Similarly, John Johnson has a significant representation in the archive because the letters of this mercantile family were gathered by the Privy Council in 1553 as evidence in bankruptcy suits in the Admiralty Court.[19] Similarly, in Elizabeth's reign Nicholas Williamson (out-strength 7; in-strength 137) appears in this position because a substantial sub-collection—the 'Williamson Papers'—was folded into the archive that became the State Papers. In this instance it appears all the letters in his family's keeping, including personal missives and accounts, were seized because he was suspected of complicity in Catholic plots against the throne after going to Antwerp, where he resorted with known traitors, and from where he was sent into Scotland by the Jesuit William Crichton.

By examining the balance of in-strength and out-strength, then, we can begin to sketch out the process by which the State Papers came into being, and the way that process affects the shape of the epistolary network we are able to construct. A high concentration of in-strength not only signals the archiving process of secretaries, but also seizure and Victorian editorial policy. But these in-hubs have a counterpart in the network; there are also important outliers who sent many more letters than they received. These figures can tell us important things about where, and from whom, the Tudor government gathered their intelligence.

Outposts and Out-Strength

The figures with the largest relative out-strength are those who were dispatched, in different capacities, to outposts. Returning to Figure 2.2, these are the people highlighted in red. In Henry VIII's reign (Figure 2.2a) these are Eustace Chapuys, Stephen Vaughan, Robert Wingfield, Tommaso Spinelli (discussed further in Chapter 3), James V of Scotland, Cuthbert Tunstall, later Bishop of London, Ralph Sadler, Edmund Harvel, John Husee, Sebastian Giustinian, Richard Pace, Richard Wingfield, Edward Carne, Thomas Legh, William Sandys, 1st Baron Sandys, Edward Lee, later Archbishop of York, Richard Croke (discussed in Chapter 6), Pedro Ortiz, and Miguel Mai. This list is dominated by those who served on diplomatic missions; only James V and John Husee do not fulfil this role (Husee, Lord Lisle's servant, is there due to the seizing of the Lisle letters). Four were foreign ambassadors (Chapuys and Giustinian,

---

[19] James Daybell, *Women Letter-Writers in Tudor England* (Oxford University Press, 2006), p. 35.

Ortiz, and Mai), and the remainder were men sent on diplomatic missions by the Henrician government.

The inverse distribution of the diplomat and the Principal Secretary is not an accident; their roles are complementary. Diplomats were sources of intelligence from foreign locations, and the secretaries are the main recipients and archivers of this intelligence. For example, of 486 outgoing letters, Vaughan sends 184 to Lord William Paget (all from the period of his secretaryship), and 95 to Cromwell; and of Robert Wingfield's 419 outgoing letters, 196 are sent to Wolsey and 165 to Henry VIII. The vital interplay between centre and periphery in Tudor administration has been argued by Steven Ellis.[20] On a smaller scale, it also explains Husee's position: he effectively acted as Lisle's agent, reporting information back to Calais.

The same trend is borne out in the reigns of Edward and Mary although the numbers are lower.[21] But if we look at the Elizabethan period we see a broader range of people emerging in these outlying positions. This change correlates not only with the specific concerns and geographic territories at the heart of Elizabethan foreign policy, but also a shift in the personnel used by Elizabeth's secretaries.[22] As in the previous reigns, we see the appearance of several royal agents, including Thomas Randolph, Henry Norris, 1st Baron Norreys, and Christopher Mont, George Gilpin, Robert Sidney, Edward Stafford, Noel de Caron, Edward Barton, and Francis Vere (all highlighted red in Figure 2.2d). We also see large volumes of correspondence coming from military and political leaders positioned in outposts of national interest, in Scotland and Ireland. These communications were crucial to what Jane Dawson has described as 'the British dimension' of Elizabethan foreign policy.[23] In the first half of her reign we see a high volume of outgoing correspondence from William Drury, the Marshal and Deputy-Governor of Berwick-upon-Tweed, who became a close observer of the affairs of Mary Queen of Scots, and kept in near-constant communication with Lord Burghley; and William Maitland, who the diplomatic community apparently came to regard 'as a sort of Scotch [William] Cecil'.[24] The increased interest in Scotland was due in part to the political instability that followed the marriage of Mary Queen of Scots to Henry Stuart, Lord Darnley. Some further notable outliers (above the

---

[20] Steven Ellis, 'Centre and Periphery in the Tudor State', in *A Companion to Tudor Britain*, ed. Robert Tittler and Norman Jones (Blackwell, 2004), 133–50; Ellis, *Tudor Frontiers and Noble Power: The Making of the British State* (Clarendon, 1995).

[21] In Figure 2.2b these figures are Sir Richard Morison, Pietro Vanni, Andrew Dudley, Thomas Chamberlain, Thomas Thirlby, Bishop of Westminster, and Sir Philip Hoby. Others in that peripheral region can also be explained: William Grey, 13th Baron Grey de Wilton, and Thomas Wharton, 1st Baron Wharton, were both serving in a military capacity on the borders of Scotland during this period; John Brende wrote meticulous reports during 1548 and 1549 on the Scottish war. Military leaders and soldiers serve an analogous function to diplomats in terms of information movement regarding foreign relations; as figures with the best intelligence on military developments, they also needed to be in frequent contact with the monarch and Privy Council. With Mary's reign the pattern is even clearer: the four biggest outliers in Figure 2.2c—Nicholas Wotton, John Mason, Carne, and Vanni—were all diplomats.

[22] For an overview, see Susan Doran, *Elizabeth I and Foreign Policy, 1558–1603* (Routledge, 2002).

[23] Jane E. A. Dawson, 'William Cecil and the British Dimension of Elizabethan Foreign Policy', *History* 74 (1989), 196–216.

[24] Mark Loughlin, 'Maitland, William, of Lethington (1525×30–1573)', *ODNB*, <https://doi.org/10.1093/ref:odnb/17838>.

diagonal line in Figure 2.2d are members of the government placed by the English in 'hir land' of Ireland: Henry Wallop, a member of the Irish Council; Geoffrey Fenton, Secretary to the Lord Deputy of Ireland, Lord Grey de Wilton, and by 1603 himself Principal Secretary of State, and Privy Councillor, in Ireland; and Edward Waterhouse, private Secretary to Henry Sidney, the Lord Deputy of Ireland, Chancellor of the Exchequer of Ireland.

The Elizabethan outliers, however, not only show key areas of geographical interest, but also a changing strategy in the methods of intelligence gathering during this reign. In the graph for Elizabeth's reign we see four names that are notably different from those listed above: Niccolo Stoppio, William Stallenge, Thomas Stokes, and Christopher Perkins. Stoppio has been described as 'a new type of intermediary' that appeared in the second half of the sixteenth century: 'courtiers and members of the lower nobility or patricians who supplied princes, high ranking clergymen and the urban elites with news, art objects, exotic articles and books'.[25] Stoppio is best known as an art dealer, who worked for Albert V, Duke of Bavaria; but during the 1560s he sent the diplomat John Mason and William Cecil (later Lord Burghley) regular letters containing the latest news from Rome and Constantinople arriving in Venice along with the goods in which he traded. This was a period, according to Gary M. Bell's *A Handlist of British Diplomatic Representatives 1509–1688*, when there was no diplomat resident in Venice and he seems to have supplied particularly useful intelligence on Turkish fleets and peace negotiations.[26] The use of mercantile networks for intelligence gathering is more evident in the archive as the reign progresses. We also see the names of two merchants amongst the outliers: Thomas Stokes and William Stallenge. Like Stoppio, Stallenge and Stokes seem to have used their position to pass on the news items that arrived with ships. From 1580 to 1584 Stokes provided Walsingham with regular intelligence reports from Bruges; and, located at the new Plymouth haven, from 1595 until the end of the reign, Stallenge collected intelligence for Robert Cecil from Brittany, Spain, and Portugal.[27] The role of such men within the broad and heterogeneous group of 'intelligence producers' identified by William H. Sherman is discussed in more detail in Chapter 4.[28]

Perkins points to yet another shift in the intelligence-gathering strategies of the principal secretaries. In the early 1590s Perkins served on numerous diplomatic

---

[25] Renate Pieper, 'Trading with Art and Curiosities in Southern Germany before the Thirty Years' War', in *Markets for Art, 1400–1800*, ed. Clara Eugenia Núñez (Universidad de Sevilla, 1998), pp. 87–101 (p. 87). See also Mario Infelise, 'From Merchants' Letters to Handwritten Political avvisi: Notes on the Origins of Public Information', in *Correspondence and Cultural Exchange in Europe*, ed. Francisco Bethencourt and Florike Egmond (Cambridge University Press, 2007), pp. 41–2.

[26] See, for example, the following letters to Cecil: SP 70/100 f.8, SP 70/101 f.12. Bell's *Handlist* (Royal Historical Society, 1990), p. 289, indicates there was no resident ambassador between the end of Pietro Vanni's tenure in 1557 and the beginning of Sir Anthony Standen's in 1603.

[27] On the use of more informal networks of intelligence gathering, see Marika Keblusek and Badeloch Vera Noldus, eds., *Double Agents: Cultural and Political Brokerage in Early Modern Europe* (Brill Publishers, 2011); Noldus Badeloch, Marika Keblusek, and Hans Cools, eds., *Your Humble Servant: Agents in Early Modern Europe* (Uitgeverij Verloren, 2006).

[28] See William H. Sherman, 'Research Intelligence in Early Modern England', *Studies in Intelligence* 37:5 (1994), 95–104.

missions: special ambassador to Poland, Denmark, and the Hanse cities.[29] This appointment, however, is interesting because of his earlier affiliations: after studying at the University of Oxford, Perkins entered the Society of Jesus in Rome (1569) and, following a period first at the Jesuit College in Rome and then Dillingen in Germany, he was ordained priest in 1572. In 1580 Perkins was assigned to the Jesuit mission to England: a project ultimately aimed at returning the nation to the Catholic fold.[30] By 1588, however, he was communicating with Walsingham and serving as his inform-ant. In the space of ten years, then, Perkins went from being a religious enemy of the state to being a representative of the queen's interests abroad. Such a trajectory, whilst unusual, is not without precedent. The process by which Perkins was first recruited as an informant was probably very similar to the stories of the various Catholic double agents working for Walsingham, Burghley, and Robert Cecil in the 1580s and 1590s. The second half of Elizabeth's reign was a tense period, where threat was perceived on all sides: European Catholic powers joined forces with recusant exiles in repeated attempts to dethrone the Protestant queen. In response, the Tudor government recruited spies, double-agents, and code-breakers to discover and defeat these plots. The peculiar case of Perkins is discussed further in Chapter 7 through his overlapping journeys with another lesser-known agent, called Seth Cocks.

By simply comparing two basic network measures, then, we can begin to describe the shape of the State Papers archive. It is a coarse-grained aerial view, but neverthe-less it allows us to say a number of things. Firstly, the majority of the people in the archive have more outgoing correspondence associated with them than incoming let-ters. Secondly, the people with the largest bodies of correspondence, the 'government hubs', are marked by much higher levels of incoming correspondence. Thirdly, their counterpoints, the outliers with relatively high levels of outgoing correspondence, are mostly diplomats and other 'intelligencers'. Fourthly, these patterns are interdepend-ent: the most frequent recipients of letters by diplomats and intelligencers are the monarchs' principal secretaries. Finally, these out-strength outliers also reveal the key locations in which the government was interested (Scotland, Ireland, etc.), and the strategic ports at which they required informants (Venice, Plymouth). While these *general* patterns will not be news to anyone familiar with the State Papers archive and the process of its composition, what may be surprising is that this could in principle be statistically detected by someone altogether unfamiliar with the archive. Moreover, it is extremely important that the method confirms what we already know. That means it works, and that we can put some trust in it when it draws attention to things we might not have observed before. Already in the overview outlined above we are seeing the emergence of names that have been largely overlooked in the histories constructed from this archive, such as Stoppio, Stallenge, and Stokes. In the final pages of this chapter we want to suggest how we can gain a more fine-grained understanding of the

---

[29] Thomas M. McCoog, 'Perkins, Sir Christopher (1542/3–1622)', *ODNB*, <https://doi.org/10.1093/ref:odnb/21968>.

[30] See Michael L. Carrafiello, 'English Catholicism and the Jesuit Mission of 1580–1581', *Historical Journal* 37 (1994), 761–74.

relative significance of the secretarial hubs, and what this can tell us about the viewpoints that dominate the archive and the histories that we can write using it.

The Principal Secretary and the Monad

The aerial picture allows us to see that the making of the archive can create particular network profiles. From this vantage point it also becomes apparent that the varied survival of the papers of the principal secretaries—over several orders of magnitude—creates an uneven portrayal of their administrative and historical 'significance'. This is not just a problem for the quantitative analysis of letter networks; it has also fundamentally affected the existing Tudor historiography. It is hard to disentangle the scholarly claims for the exemplarity of Cromwell and Burghley from their fulsome and detailed paper trails.

To fully understand this unevenness, and its impact on the history we are able to reconstruct, it is important to not view the State Papers as a single archive, but instead as a series of overlapping epistolary 'perspectives'. This approach brings to mind Bruno Latour's definition of the monad, which builds on Gabriel Tarde's idea that everything is a society (i.e. that the world is made up of composite and relational entities). Latour writes: 'A monad is not a part of a whole, but *a point of view on all the entities* taken severally and not as a totality' (added emphasis).[31] The method Latour describes is distinct from the one used in this book. Whereas the data we have captured is available as a whole, he describes a process of building up the network by crawling through it, edge by edge. Nevertheless, his observations about the resulting structure remain pertinent as they could arguably describe the process of the archive's making:

> It begins as a dot, a spot, and it ends (provisionally) as a monad with an interior encapsulated into an envelope. Were the inquiry to continue, the 'whole world', as Leibniz said, would be 'grasped' or 'reflected' through this idiosyncratic point of view.[32]

The State Papers archive as crystallised in SPO can therefore be described as a series of overlapping monads. Each of those monads can be traced back to a particular 'dot': the secretaries, the Privy Council, the monarch, and those letter-writers whose archives were seized by the state. The 'whole' archive could thus be more accurately described as the sum of those various idiosyncratic points of view. This leads to a very complex system that has areas of high granularity, areas that are much sparser in terms of data, and, of course, many absences.

Although secretaries make up a large number of those 'dots', not all secretaries have their own monad. We can establish this fact even without knowing the history of this

---

[31] Latour et al., 'The whole is always smaller', p. 598.
[32] Ibid., p. 599.

archive, simply by looking at the ranking of all of the secretaries for their degree (the total number of connections)[33] and in-strength (total number of incoming letters) during their tenure. As we might recall from the analysis above, the figures with the highest scores for these two measures were all principal secretaries. However, not all principal secretaries have high scores for these metrics. In the table below we give a list of the degree and in-strength for each secretary, and their rank amongst their contemporaries in regard to these two measures (and the top percentage in which that places them). By looking only at their period in office, and focusing on rank (as opposed to raw numbers), we can compare those who held their office for only one year (e.g. Nicholas Wotton) with those who were in office for fourteen years (e.g. William Cecil, Lord Burghley) on a similar footing. What we want to know is whether they received the largest amount of incoming correspondence in that period, or wrote to the largest number of people, compared to all of their contemporaries. If a secretary's papers were folded into the archive we would probably expect them to rank in the top five for in-strength and degree (along with the monarch, Privy Council, and other secretaries with whom they held the post concurrently). Because of the scale-free nature of degree distribution discussed above, and the limitation to their period in office, anyone who ranks far outside the top twenty individuals is likely to only be present in the archive because they appear in the overlapping correspondences of intersecting monads, rather than because they themselves constitute one of the idiosyncratic points of view.

Focusing on the numbers in brackets in the final two columns of Table 2.1 we can see that a number of secretaries rank first for degree and in-degree: Cromwell, William Cecil, Lord Burghley, and his son Robert Cecil, each rank top in both measures for their period in office. Trailing only a little behind is Walsingham (ranking second for degree and first for in-strength), Sir William Paget (third and second respectively), and William Davison (third for both). By contrast, others rank suspiciously low, including Knight, Wootton, and Herbert, whilst Cheke is absent altogether for the epistolary network during his period in office. This indicates that their personal archives did not make their way into the State Papers.

The four top ranking figures are not surprising. These are also the secretaries whose careers have received the most scholarly attention, and the claims of their political dominance are inextricably tied up with their paperwork practices.[34] In *The Tudor Revolution in Government*, G. R. Elton contends that Cromwell was instrumental in the introduction of a number of financial and administrative innovations that can be seen as the birth of the modern bureaucratic state system, and which replaced the medieval model of government that was overseen from the royal household, where most of the administration was done by the king's servants rather than by separate state offices. Burghley kept a vast political archive for which we

---

[33] Calculated as the total of the incoming and outgoing connections.

[34] See, for example, Norman Jones, *Governing by Virtue: Lord Burghley and the Management of Elizabethan England* (Oxford University Press, 2015).

Table 2.1 Degree (column 3) and in-strength (column 4) scores, rankings, and top percentage for each Principal Secretary (column 1) during their period in office (column 2)

Name	Dates in office	Degree (rank/top %)	In-strength (rank/top %)
Thomas Ruthall	1500–1516[a]	14 (22/3.3%)	17 (24/3.6%)
Richard Pace	1516–1526	41 (8/0.8%)	90 (6/0.6%)
William Knight	1526–5 August 1529	6 (47/7.2%)	1 (112/17.1%)
Stephen Gardiner	5 August 1529–April 1534	12 (21/1.5%)	14 (24/1.7%)
Thomas Cromwell	April 1534–April 1540[b]	1,736 (1/0.03%)	6,149 (1/0.03%)
Thomas Wriothesley	April 1540– January 1544	47 (5/0.7%)	66 (13/1.9%)
Sir Ralph Sadler	April 1540–23 April 1543	21 (12/2.0%)	26 (20/3.4%)
Sir William Paget	23 April 1543–April 1548	179 (3/0.2%)	1,350 (2/0.16%)
Sir William Petre	January 1544–March 1557	72 (13/0.6%)	361 (7/0.3%)
Sir Thomas Smith	17 April 1548–15 October 1549	25 (7/1.8%)	34 (5/1.3%)
Nicholas Wotton	15 October 1549–5 September 1550	1 (69/14.1%)	0 (164/33.5%)
Sir William Cecil	5 September 1550–July 1553	136 (1/0.22%)	441 (1/0.2%)
Sir John Cheke	June 1553–July 1553	—	—
Sir John Bourne	July 1553–April 1558	10 (17/1.7%)	8 (22/2.8%)
John Boxall	March 1557–November 1558	10 (10/1.8%)	31 (5/0.9%)
Sir William Cecil	November 1558–13 July 1572	1,037 (1/0.04%)	7,905 (1/0.04)
Sir Thomas Smith	13 July 1572–March 1576	24 (14/1.3%)	117 (7/0.7%)
Sir Francis Walsingham	20 December 1573–April 1590	1,690 (2/0.03%)	10,090 (1/0.02%)
Thomas Wilson	12 November 1577–16 June 1581	32 (12/0.8%)	195 (6/0.4%)
William Davison	30 September 1586–February 1587	61 (3/0.47%)	116 (3/0.47%)
Lord Burghley	5 July 1590–July 1596[c]	1,285 (1/0.03%)	6,364 (1/0.03%)
Sir Robert Cecil	July 1596–24 May 1612	2,223 (1/0.02%)	10,925 (1/0.02%)
John Herbert	(10 May 1600–9 July 1617)[d]	11 (30/1.4%)	6 (62/2.8%)

[a] The measures are only counted from Henry VIII's accession. Where dates are imprecise (e.g. a full calendar year) we have start dates as 1 January and end dates as 31 December.

[b] Principal Secretary 1534–6 and Lord Privy Seal 1536–40. There were no principal secretaries during this latter period.

[c] Acting Secretary.

[d] Here we are counting only letters dating from before the death of Elizabeth.

know he had special indexes, and he preserved these by leaving his papers to his son Robert, who replicated some of his father's systems; and Walsingham also organised his official papers systematically, as discussed in Chapter 1 with regards his 'table book'. But their survival is also down to some degree of luck: Cromwell's and Walsingham's were both seized, and the Cecil papers passed through the hands of various fastidious caretakers, making it hard to separate exceptionality in office from exceptionality of survival.

The relatively low scores of other secretaries are also due to a combination of administrative practice and survival rates. One cause of the much lower scores for Cromwell's predecessors can be attributed to changes to the nature of the job during Cromwell's tenure. Stephen Gunn argues that the Secretary had risen in political importance through the late fourteenth and fifteenth centuries. The secretaries of Richard III and Henry VII wielded substantial influence, but they were often absent on embassy, as were Henry VIII's early secretaries. It was not until Cromwell's period in office that the Secretary organised the Council's work.[35] It is tempting to read the paucity of his predecessors' letters as further evidence for that shift. But, with the exception of Pace, their scores are so low we must assume that the majority of their correspondence must have been lost: Ruthall received just sixteen letters in the first seven years of Henry's reign; Knight just one letter in three years; and Gardiner thirteen in five years. Indeed, the only reason we have a relatively large quantity of Pace's correspondence (ninety letters over the period of his decade in office, placing him in the top 0.8% and 0.6% for degree and in-strength respectively) is due to another act of seizure: rumours of undiplomatic disclosures resulted in Pace and some of his servants being committed to the Tower of London, and his papers and books confiscated.[36]

In fact, the only reason these early secretaries have any presence in the archive is due to their overlap with the dominant monads in Henry's reign: Cromwell and, before him, Wolsey, whose papers occupy more than eighteen volumes of SP1 due to their seizure following his arrest. The story of seizure is a constant one. As James Daybell has commented, 'the State Papers Foreign and Domestic consist almost entirely of official letters or papers confiscated by the government.'[37] Crucially, Wolsey's tenure overlaps with three of the four secretaries that preceded Cromwell, and as a result his papers document a wide range of epistolary relationships.

Table 2.2 attempts to quantify the extent to which these early secretaries are, to use Latour's metaphor, 'encapsulated' within the 'envelope' of the larger epistolary hubs. This table has two columns. The first provides three network statistics for their period in office: the total volume of correspondence (total strength), the number of outgoing letters (out-strength), and number of incoming (in-strength). The second column provides the top three ranking figures for total strength during their period in office, which are likely to contain the name of the monads within which the secretaries' letters have been encapsulated.

What we see is that Wolsey and/or Cromwell are at or near the top of the rankings for each of the four secretaries preceding Cromwell. Of these four, Pace is the only one to appear in the top ranking three for total strength, whereas the others occupy lower ranks during their period in office (indeed their numbers look inconsequential next to those top ranking statistics). However, even in the case of Pace part of the reason

[35] Steven Gunn, *Early Tudor Government, 1485–1558* (Palgrave, 1995), p. 53.
[36] See Cathy Curtis, 'Pace, Richard (1483?–1536)', *ODNB*, <https://doi.org/10.1093/ref:odnb/21065>.
[37] James Daybell, *Women Letter-Writers in Tudor England* (Oxford University Press, 2006), p. 35.

Table 2.2 Strength scores for Henrician secretaries prior to Cromwell (column 1) compared to the three top-ranking figures for total strength during their period in office (column 2)

Secretary (tenure) and strength scores (rank and top %)	Top-ranking nodes for total strength (score in brackets)
Ruthall (1500–16; statistics for 1509–16)	(1) Henry VIII (1,137)
Total strength: 25 (48/7.6%)	(2) Wolsey (917)
Out-strength: 8 (62/9.8%)	(3) Margaret of Austria, Duchess of Savoy (274)
In-strength: 17 (24/3.8%)	
Pace (1516–26)	(1) Wolsey (4,029)
Total strength: 409 (3/0.3%)	(2) Henry (1,409)
Out-strength: 319 (2/0.2%)	(3) Pace (409)
In-strength: 90 (6/0.6%)	
Knight (1526–4 August 1529)	(1) Wolsey (1994)
Total strength: 46 (27/3.9%)	(2) Henry (550)
Out-strength: 45 (19/2.7%)	(3) Cromwell (164)
In-strength: 1 (114/16.3%)	
Gardiner (5 August 1529–April 1534)	(1) Cromwell (1,591)
Total strength: 40 (24/1.9%)	(2) Henry VIII (604)
Out-strength: 26 (21/1.6%)	(3) Emperor Charles V (427)
In-strength: 14 (23/1.8%)	

for his high-ranking position is not that he is the biggest hub of *in-coming* intelligence (unlike the pattern observed of the most prominent secretaries, discussed above), but rather his high *out-strength*: in fact, he sends three times more letters than he receives. And if we look in detail at his correspondence, the vast majority of his outgoing letters from this period are to our hubs: 278 out of 343 are to Wolsey, and 13 to Henry VIII. Those dating from before the end of 1517 are all from his Imperial embassy when he visited the Emperor in southern Germany, as well as visiting Swiss cantons, and the Regent Margaret in the Low Countries; and throughout his tenure there were special embassies to the German States, the Low Countries, and to Rome and Venice, from where he sent back diplomatic reports.[38] The 3:1 ratio of out- to in-strength gives him a profile closer to the diplomats and other agents seen in Figures 2.2a–d, and it is by this mechanism he appears so prominently in the archive: as the information-bearing counterpoint to Wolsey's intelligence hub. It shows clearly how it is only thanks to the extensive bodies of Cromwell's and Wolsey's surviving papers that we can glimpse the epistolary activities of the first four secretaries of Henry's reign; but our perception of their epistolary reach is shaped by the idiosyncratic perspective of these two exceptional men. This bias is perhaps even more pertinent in the

---

[38] For a full list of Pace's embassies, see Gary Bell, *A Handlist of British Diplomatic Representatives 1509–1688* (Royal Historical Society, 1990), E5, E8, F18, G1, IT6, LC11 LC15, LC17, SWZ1–3, V2.

case of Pace given that Wolsey may have played an active part in removing Pace from power.

But what of the secretaries *following* Cromwell's period in office? After Cromwell's fall and execution in 1540, there is another factor affecting the prominence of secretaries in the network: the division of the secretaryship by Cromwell into two separate jobs.[39] The intention of this division seems to have been to have one Secretary permanently in attendance on the king, and the other on the Lord Privy Seal. The suggestion has been made that Cromwell proposed this change to make sure that his successors could not eclipse his power: 'Two parallel Secretaries with ostensibly identical duties and powers naturally could not dominate the administration as Cromwell had, and as William and Robert Cecil were to do.'[40] Returning to Table 2.1, it does help us understand the statistical change in 1540, when Wriothesley and Sadler took over. But this division is not the only reason for their lower ranks. Even if we count the shared office as a single node, we see that their combined in-strength during the period April 1540–April 1543 only amounts to 89 (which would place them joint rank 42nd). The statistics are very similar to earlier holders such as Gardiner and Knight.

A better sense of the true power of Wriothesley, however, can be gleaned by looking at the period directly preceding his appointment. As Elton noticed, 'the promotion of these two men [Wriothesley and Sadler] made no difference to their spheres of action', as Clerk of the Signet, and as Cromwell's Secretary respectively. During the period 1536–40 (i.e. immediately prior to Wriothesley's promotion and when Cromwell had already become Lord Privy Seal), Wriothesley's network ranking is actually higher than in his period as Secretary. He has a degree of 155 (rank 4), and in-degree 237 (5), and in terms of the latter measure he is only outranked by Cromwell, Henry VIII, and Lord and Lady Lisle (whose letters, as we know, form their own monad). This is because one whole volume of the State Papers (SP 7) comprises letters addressed to Thomas Wriothesley 1536–40 as Clerk. By making this comparison with his earlier correspondence, we have a clear indicator of what we are not seeing for Wriothesley's period as Secretary, and why direct comparison between office-holders is so difficult.

In some cases the low ranks are not simply due to loss, but rather due to active destruction. The numbers of letters received by secretaries other than William Cecil during Edward VI's reign are strikingly low. This is a direct result of the deliberate destruction of papers of the protectorate on the eve of Somerset's fall.[41] In the surviving archive, Cheke and Wotton receive no letters during their tenure, and Smith only 34. Petre does receive 361, but this is over the whole period of his office

[39] G. R. Elton, *The Tudor Revolution in Government* (Cambridge University Press, 2010), p. 312.

[40] Ibid., p. 315. For further discussion, see Caitlin Burge, 'Letters, Networks of Power, and the Fall of Thomas Cromwell, 1523–1547' (unpublished doctoral thesis, 2022), pp. 208–18, available from: <https://qmro.qmul.ac.uk>.

[41] C. S. Knighton, 'The Principal Secretaries in the Reign of Edward VI: Reflections on Their Office and Archive', in *Law and Government Under the Tudors: Essays Presented to Sir Geoffrey Elton Regius Professor of Modern History in the University of Cambridge on the Occasion of His Retirement*, ed. Claire Cross, David Loades, and J. J. Scarisbrick (Cambridge University Press, 1988), pp. 163–76 (p. 169). See also Dale Hoak, 'Re-habilitating the Duke of Northumberland: Politics and Political Control, 1549–53', in *The Mid-Tudor Polity, c.1540–1560*, ed. Jennifer Loach and Robert Tittler (MacMillan, 1980), pp. 29–51 (pp. 34–5).

(January 1544–March 1557); if we isolate the Edwardian period it drops to just 57. From such a depleted Edwardian archive, and one that specifically seems to bias against Cheke, Wotton, Smith, and Petre, it seems perhaps an unfair conclusion on the part of Elton (and C. S. Knighton following him) that amongst this cohort it was only Cecil who 'exercise[d] the Secretaryship in much the way that Cromwell had done'.[42] We have a similar paucity of evidence for Mary's reign: Secretary Petre only receives 114 letters during his period of office under Mary, but this is enough to rank him third for in-strength over the entire reign (after Mary with 483 in-letters and the Privy Council with 211). He far outstrips his two companions in office, Bourne and Boxall, who receive just 8 and 27 letters apiece.

Coming to the end of this monadic overview, and the bottom of Table 2.1, we encounter again the biggest archive of all, that of Burghley. In order to fully grasp its effect on our understanding of Elizabethan politics, it is perhaps most helpful if we look beyond his long tenure as Secretary (when we expect him to dominate) to the period following his promotion to Lord Treasurer in July 1572. Alford argues that 'in a sense the State Papers become from this point on the archives of Cecil's successors as Secretary like Sir Thomas Smith and Sir Francis Walsingham'.[43] While this holds true for the figure of Walsingham, all other secretaries who served during his lifetime are largely overshadowed by the behemoth of the Burghley archive. In Smith's period in office, for example, his in-strength (113) is surpassed by Burghley (with 2,019 letters), Walsingham (371), the Privy Council (325), Elizabeth I (288), Sir William Fitzwilliam, Lord Justice and later lord Deputy of Ireland (274), and the royal favourite Robert Dudley, Earl of Leicester (119). The result is similar for Secretary Wilson. However, thanks to the presence of the Davison papers in the State Papers archive (recovered from the collector Ralph Starkey's house by Wilson's nephew, also Thomas, after obtaining a warrant in 1619 to search his house), Davison provides an important view of the network despite his short period in office. During the four and a half months Davison was in office, he received 114 letters (compared to Walsingham's 265 and Burghley's 244). Davison's impact, however, was curtailed when he was blamed for allowing Mary Stuart's signed death warrant to be sent to Fotheringhay Castle without the queen's knowledge, and he was imprisoned in the Tower of London; following this, his final years were spent in relative obscurity. The only real competing views that we gain of the Elizabethan period are those of Walsingham and Burghley's son Robert.

In summary then, almost without fail the secretaries studied and praised for their administrative prowess are those who left behind large archives. While administrative skill and fulsome files may be correlated, it is problematic to build a comparative case on relative absence. Moreover, the size of their separate archives, or monads, means that their immediate world is so fulsomely documented that scholars going into the

[42] Elton, *Tudor Revolution*, pp. 354–5; Knighton, 'The Principal Secretaries', p. 167.
[43] Stephen Alford, 'Politicians and Statesmen II: William Cecil, Lord Burghley (1520–98)', *State Papers Online, 1509–1714* (Thomson Learning EMEA Ltd, 2007). Available at: <https://www.gale.com/intl/essays>.

archive are forced to interpret the period from their perspective. But what are we to do with the knowledge of archival unevenness, of paucity, and absence?

We must interpret quantitative results in light of archival history and, conversely, use quantitative results to shed light on the biases of the archive. If we are to write histories from the perspective of the hubs, then they must be constructed with a keen sense that they are privileged viewpoints, and that other 'voices' are refracted through the network reach and collection policies of these individuals. Moreover, a quantitative description of where those viewpoints originate also gives us pause to examine which figures might not have been given the attention that they deserve. One such example is Sir William Paget, who held the post of Secretary 23 April 1543–April 1548.[44] If we revisit Table 2.1, we can see that he had a degree of 179, placing him rank 3 (top 0.27%, outranked only by Henry VIII and the Privy Council) and received 1,350 letters, placing him in rank 2 (top 0.27%, outranked only by Henry VIII). We have, then, an undeniable picture of the correspondence network from his 'idiosyncratic point of view', and he is also asserted to have gained the confidence of the king during the final years of Henry's reign. His entry in the *History of Parliament* states that: '[a]part from his five embassies, he was rarely permitted to go far from the court. Contemporaries observed the growth of his influence and increasingly directed their letters to him [... and] eventually Henry came to use Paget as the main intermediary not only between himself and the Council, but also between himself, the court and the kingdom'.[45] But although Paget tends to be identified as one of the key figures in the transition of power from Henry VIII to Sir Edward Seymour, Earl of Hertford when Edward VI ascended the throne, it is notable that he has not attracted the same kind of scrutiny: just one book-length study has been written about him.[46] Given his exceptional quantitative profile, we would strongly suggest that his personal and epistolary networks deserve a reassessment.

Conclusion

Our aerial view of the archive has emphasised the extent to which it provides us with a history from the perspective of the powerful few. Hubs, we discover, are vanishingly rare amongst the 20,560 correspondents, totalling less than 0.3%. Rather, the majority of people found in this dataset (~68%) represent a giant fringe, connected to just one other person (often via a petition to the Principal Secretary). However, while hubs make up the minority of nodes in our epistolary network, they dominate its structure.

---

[44] Burge comes to the same conclusion about Paget in her analysis of our dataset. See Burge, *Letters, Networks*, pp. 208–18.

[45] A. D. K. Hawkyard, 'PAGET, William (by 1506–63), of Beaudesert Park and Burton-upon-Trent, Staffs., West Drayton, Mdx., and London', *The History of Parliament: The House of Commons 1509-1558*, ed. S. T. Bindoff, 1982. Available at: <http://www.histparl.ac.uk/volume/1509-1558/member/paget-william-1506-63>.

[46] Samuel Rhea Gammon, *Statesman and Schemer: William, First Lord Paget, Tudor Minister* (David & Charles, 1973). An edition of his letters was published the following year: *The Letters of William, Lord Paget of Beaudesert, 1547–63*, ed. Barrett L. Beer and Sybil M. Jack, Camden Fourth Series, vol. 13 (1974).

Other influential nodes, such as diplomats, agents, and military figures, appear in the archive as a complementary category of nodes within an intelligence economy focused on these hubs: they are the providers of intelligence that form the material connections and information that enable the Principal Secretary's engagement in foreign policy. The interdependence of their network attributes—the Secretary as the largest hubs with predominantly incoming correspondence, and intelligence providers as small but sizeable nodes with predominantly outgoing correspondence—reveal two key facets of the archive's making.

The first is that we must reverse-engineer the making of the archive and determine who is responsible for the presence of each document and each person in the archive; and to understand from whose idiosyncratic point of view we are grasping the significance of these individuals and the worlds of information they have helped to create. As we show, not all principal secretaries were made equal; some loomed much larger than others, due in large part to the role played by seizure, as well as the care taken over the afterlife of the Cecil Papers. These are the creators of the evidence we have for networks of power, and it is therefore unsurprising that the evidence points back to their centrality.

The second insight yielded by the interdependence of the Secretary-hubs and their intelligence providers is how the patterns of partial survival can reveal links between the role of correspondents and how their correspondence was archived. These correlations will form a key component of the methods introduced in some of the following chapters (especially in Part II) in which we construct profiles for different categories of correspondent. Chapter 3, for example, explores diplomacy via one specific measure called 'betweenness centrality'; and in Chapter 4 we build a more complex method for characterising epistolary profiles, using a combination of eight network metrics to create a kind of network 'fingerprint'. These approaches allow us to quantitatively describe different types of power and influence. The kinds of power that emerge as part of these activities arise from the ability of individuals to bridge different social worlds or communities.

In sum, the message of this chapter is that the first step in analysing digitised collections is to fully understand the power structures that created them. Only in doing so can we grasp their distorting nature, and how we should proceed in order not to reinscribe them through our analyses.

PART II
STRUCTURE

3

'Betweenness'

The previous chapter employed some foundational network metrics to identify the hubs of the information network. We saw that certain principal secretaries received vast numbers of letters, which document in extensive detail the requests and tasks submitted to the holders of this office, their professional networks, and the information they needed to master in order to carry out their duties. Their success as administrators, however, relied on a whole economy of information. In this chapter, therefore, we move from the centres of power to the fibres that connected the secretarial hubs to disparate communities and distant locations, the kinds of people that Mark Granovetter characterised as 'weak ties'.

In his highly influential 1973 paper 'The Strength of Weak Ties' Granovetter argued that people's social worlds tend to be made up of strong and weak ties, but that weak ties are much more important for the transmission of information. He considered a random sample of people who were employed in professional, technical, and managerial positions in the Italian community of the West End in Boston, Massachusetts, and who had recently changed jobs. Granovetter asked those who found a new job through personal contacts how frequently they were seeing the contact around the time they learnt about the job. He used this contact frequency as a measure of tie strength.[1] What he observed was that information about job opportunities predominantly travelled along weak ties. Because our close friends tend to move in the same circles that we do, the information they receive overlaps largely with what we already know. Acquaintances, by contrast, are more likely to know people that we do not, and therefore provide access to novel information. This means that

> whatever is to be diffused can reach a larger number of people, and traverse greater social distance (i.e. path length), when passed through weak ties rather than strong. If one tells a rumor to all his close friends, and they do likewise, many will hear the rumor a second and third time, since those linked by strong ties tend to share friends. If the motivation to spread the rumor is dampened a bit on each wave of retelling, then the rumor moving through strong ties is much more likely to be limited to a few cliques than that going via weak ones; bridges will not be crossed.[2]

---

[1] Mark S. Granovetter, 'The Strength of Weak Ties', *American Journal of Sociology* 78 (1973), 1360–80 (p. 1371).
[2] Ibid., p. 1366.

Tudor Networks of Power. Ruth Ahnert and Sebastian E. Ahnert, Oxford University Press. © Ruth Ahnert and Sebastian E. Ahnert 2023.
DOI: 10.1093/oso/9780198858973.003.0003

Granovetter's study showed that weak ties are vital to ensuring that information circulates outside closed communities, and over distance. One of the attributes that made this work so influential in the field of sociology (and, later, network science) was that it connected micro-observations about an individual's relationships to information at the scale of the city region, allowing Granovetter to make generalisations about community structures.

But how can we make use of this work, which relied on qualitative assessment, when working with information about a network of over 20,000 people? This chapter explores how we can find the people in the State Papers who have access to novel information—the 'weak ties' between communities—by using simple quantitative measures. Numerous studies have proposed ways of measuring brokerage in networks based on Granovetter's classic work. Thomas Valente and Kayo Fujimoto's 2010 paper followed his micro-macro approach by developing a node-based measure of brokerage that considered the entire network structure;[3] and in their 2016 paper, 'Bridging, Brokerage and Betweenness', Martin G. Everett and Valente modified this work by using an algorithm called 'betweenness centrality' as an underpinning concept.[4] We are not seeking to adapt their method wholesale in this chapter. Rather, we will introduce the concept and the usefulness of betweenness centrality as a way for thinking about bridges and brokerage between communities. Betweenness centrality was first defined quantitatively by Linton Freeman in 1977. For any two nodes in a network, there is a shortest path between them, and betweenness tells us how many of these shortest paths go through a given node. In other words, it can show us how central a particular node is to the network's organisation, and how important it is in connecting other people.[5] For this reason betweenness has been used by scholars to think quantitatively about the influence a node may have on the flow of information across the network.

However, the metric finds two distinct kinds of people that act as short paths in the transferral of information across a network: hubs and bridges. Hubs are frequently highlighted by the measure of betweenness because they have a disproportionately high number of edges and therefore make the world of the network much smaller. This is the premise underlying the concept of 'six degrees of separation', the theory that any two people in the world are separated by no more than five mutual acquaintances. This idea, first posited by the Hungarian novelist Frigyes Karinthy in a short story called 'Chain-links', was subsequently tested by Michael Gurevich, and then Stanley Milgram, whose famous paper 'The Small World Problem' suggested that US citizens seemed to be connected by approximately three friendship links, on average.[6]

---

[3] Thomas W. Valente and Kayo Fujimoto, 'Bridging: Locating Critical Connectors in a Network', *Soc. Networks* 32:3 (2010), 212–20.

[4] Martin G. Everett, and Thomas W. Valente, 'Bridging, Brokerage and Betweenness', *Soc. Networks* 44 (2016), 202–8.

[5] Linton C. Freeman, 'Set of Measures of Centrality Based on Betweenness', *Sociometry* 40 (1977), 35–41.

[6] Jeffrey Travers and Stanley Milgram, 'An Experimental Study of the Small World Problem', *Sociometry* 32 (1969), 425–43. For an overview of the history of small-world theory, see Barabasi, *Linked*, chapters 2–4. See our discussion of small-world networks and six degrees of separation in Ruth Ahnert, Sebastian E. Ahnert,

In his popular book, *The Tipping Point*, Malcolm Gladwell argues that the small-world phenomenon is dependent on a few extraordinary people ('connectors') with large networks of contacts and friends: these hubs then mediate the connections between the vast majority of otherwise weakly connected individuals.[7] In the Tudor period, by accessing the network of a queen, emperor, pope, or doge you could propel information across the network very rapidly.

But hubs are not the only reason that networks can be small worlds. Duncan Watts and Steven Strogatz showed in 1998 that a very small number of long-range connections can turn a network that is only locally connected (with a large degree of separation between most of its nodes) into a small-world network in which every node can reach every other node in a small number of steps. This is equivalent to the small number of members in a given secondary school class who move abroad after graduating, and thus indirectly connect their old classmates to sets of people that would otherwise be far removed. These are the definition of Granovetter's 'weak ties'.[8] Such bridging figures do not necessarily need many links to put them on a shortest path across the network; rather, their significance and their high betweenness derive from the ways they span different communities or geographical spaces. This chapter examines the kinds of people found in the State Papers who embody this kind of bridging connectivity—diplomats, international intellectuals, bishops and reformers, merchants, military leaders, and soldiers—but also how the government sought to institutionalise these weak ties through diplomatic postings and more specifically through the establishment of the role of the resident ambassador. The chapter provides an overview of the kinds of people appointed to these posts, and how this evolved over the duration of the Tudor reigns.

Who Has High Betweenness?

One can begin to gain a sense of what betweenness centrality reveals about the organisation of information by looking at the ranked list of the figures with the highest scores for this metric during the first decade of VIII's reign:[9]

(1) Henry VIII, (2) Cardinal Thomas Wolsey, (3) Desiderius Erasmus, (4) Pope Leo X, (5) James IV of Scotland, (6) Ferdinand II of Aragon, (7) Richard Pace, (8) Leonardo Loredan, Doge of Venice, (9) Francis I of France, (10) Margaret of Austria, (11) William Warham, (12) Privy Council, (13) James V of Scotland, (14) Louis XII of France, (15) Margaret Tudor, (16) Cuthbert Tunstall, (17) Silvestro de Gigli, (18) Thomas Dacre, Baron Dacre of Gilsland, (19) Thomas Darcy, Baron Darcy of Darcy,

Catherine N. Coleman, and Scott B. Weingart, *The Network Turn: Changing Perspectives in the Humanities* (Cambridge University Press, 2020), pp. 19–21.

[7] Malcolm Gladwell, *The Tipping Point: How Little Things Can Make a Big Difference* (Little, Brown, 2000).

[8] On the connection between small worlds and weak ties, see Damon Centola and Michael Macy, 'Complex Contagions and the Weakness of Long Ties', *American Journal of Sociology* 113 (2007), 702–34.

[9] To calculate betweenness we apply the Python NetworkX *betweenness_centrality* function.

(20) Emperor Maximilian I (21) Catherine of Aragon, (22) Sir Edward Poynings, (23) John Stewart, Duke of Albany, (24) Robert Wingfield, (25) Patrick Paniter, (26) Pope Julius II, (27) Sir Richard Wingfield, (28) Tommaso Spinelli, (29) William Blount, 4th Baron Mountjoy, (30) Thomas Ruthall, Bishop of Durham.

These rankings include both hubs and bridges. Hubs include secular rulers and leaders (numbers 1, 5, 6, 8, 9, 10, 13, 14, 15, 20, 21, 23), leading statesmen, secretaries of state, and Privy Council (2, 12, 25) and the pope (4, 26). There are also 13 people in the top 30 nodes for betweenness who fulfil the definition of a bridge.

The most obvious bridges are the diplomats Pace, Poynings, Spinelli, Robert Wingfield, and Richard Wingfield. There is a good reason why betweenness would help to highlight diplomats: the correspondence network of the State Papers is international and the shortest paths across it are likely to pass through figures who are physically travelling between geographically removed locations, and actively involved in mediation between different powers. Dacre, Darcy, and Mountjoy are military and administrative equivalents of the diplomats. Throughout Henry VIII's first decade on the throne, Dacre was Lord Warden of the Marches, a post that required him to oversee the security on the border between England and Scotland, a task which required military action; he also served briefly as a special ambassador to Scotland in 1512.[10] Darcy was sent on a number of foreign expeditions, first to Spain in 1511 to serve as admiral to Ferdinand II of Aragon, and then subsequently in other military capacities on the Scottish border and in France (although after the period at which we are looking he would become a rebel).[11] Mountjoy also found himself in Spain and France: after attending the court of Spain in 1513, he was put in charge of transport for the war against France, travelling to Calais with a force of 500 men and then, following the capture of Tournai, acting lieutenant, bailiff, and, in January 1515, governor of the city.[12] Like the role of diplomat, such positions required regular communication with the central government. Dacre, Darcy, and Mountjoy needed to prove good intelligence on security, provisions, territory, and military action, and to evaluate the best strategy on the ground; but their assignments were ultimately at the behest of the government.

Alongside Dacre, Darcy, Mountjoy, and the diplomats, we should also consider most of the church leaders appearing in the list above (numbers 2, 11, 16, 17). The employment of church leaders in early Tudor diplomacy is well documented, although there was a 'precipitate decline' in their use throughout Henry VIII's reign.[13] If we look at the biographies of the church leaders in the ranking, and examine their epistolary output during this period, we can see that the majority of them undertook diplomatic missions that left an international paper trail. Silvestro de Gigli, the royal

---

[10] Gary Bell, *A Handlist of British Diplomatic Representatives, 1509–1688* (Royal Historical Society, 1990), SC4.

[11] R. W. Hoyle, 'Darcy, Thomas, Baron Darcy of Darcy (b. in or before 1467, d. 1537)', *ODNB*. Available at: <https://doi.org/10.1093/ref:odnb/7148>.

[12] James P. Carley, 'Blount, William, fourth Baron Mountjoy (c. 1478–1534)', *ODNB*. Available at: <https://doi.org/10.1093/ref:odnb/2702>.

[13] David Potter, 'Mid-Tudor Foreign Policy and Diplomacy, 1547–63', *Tudor England and Its Neighbours*, ed. Glenn Richardson and Susan Doran (Macmillan, 2005), pp. 106–38 (p. 110).

chaplain, was commissioned as the king's special representative at the Fifth Lateran Council, and he was a royal English orator at the Roman curia (the central government of the Catholic Church). Around the same time that he was appointed archdeacon of Chester in 1515, Cuthbert Tunstall was called upon by Wolsey to serve as an envoy to the young Charles, Duke of Burgundy, to join in negotiations to maintain the trade treaties that had been agreed during the reign of Henry VIII. Thomas Ruthall (Bishop of Durham and Principal Secretary 1500–16, as discussed in Chapter 2), accompanied the king to France in 1513 with a hundred men, but was sent back to England when James IV of Scotland threatened war. Ruthall took a leading part in preparing the defences of the borders, superintending the fortifying of Norham Castle, before being appointed keeper of the privy seal in 1516, an office that required close work with Wolsey in the conducting of foreign affairs.[14] Finally, we might add Wolsey to this list. Although he acts as a hub if you consider his career as a whole and the volume of correspondence that we have due to the seizure of his papers in 1529 (see Chapter 2), he also proved his diplomatic value to Henry VIII in military negotiations with European powers.

The final person to consider in our ranking of the people with the highest betweenness is Erasmus. Erasmus was a Dutch philosopher and theologian who is considered one of the greatest scholars of the northern Renaissance. He is perhaps one of the first great international intellectuals. He seems anomalous in the ranked list of high betweenness figures above because he is neither a monarch, nor a statesman.[15] The reasons for his presence, however, are illuminating for our understanding of what the measure of betweenness highlights. His high betweenness derives both from his 'hubbishness', and the ways that he connects diverse communities and locations.

Anyone familiar with the Erasmian oeuvre will know that he was an intellectual hub: his contacts were numerous and wide-ranging. For the first decade of Henry's VIII's reign we have 209 outgoing letters to 70 different correspondents, and 85 incoming letters from 33 people. He therefore has the metrics of a hub, appearing in the top five people (0.6%) during this period for all the statistics we encountered in the previous chapter (in-degree, out-degree, in-strength, and out-strength). However, he is also a bridging figure, spanning the courtly world of his patron Baron Mountjoy, government hubs such as Wolsey, the intellectual humanistic community around Thomas More (who was also Lord High Chancellor of England from October 1529 to May 1532), the university world of Cambridge and its associated scholars, and the episcopal sphere via friends and patrons, including John Colet, Richard Fox of Winchester, and John Fisher of Rochester. Moreover, the travels occasioned by the printing of various works written during this decade meant that he created

[14] Cecil H. Clough, 'Gigli, Silvestro (1463–1521)', *ODNB*, <https://doi.org/10.1093/ref:odnb/10671>; D. G. Newcombe, 'Tunstal, Cuthbert (1474–1559)', *ODNB*, <https://doi.org/10.1093/ref:odnb/27817>; and Margot Johnson, 'Ruthall, Thomas (d. 1523)', *ODNB*, <https://doi.org/10.1093/ref:odnb/24359>.

[15] His papers appear in the *Letters and Papers, Foreign and Domestic, of the Reign of Henry VIII* because of the editorial policy of John Sherren Brewer and his associates, which sought to include papers by those connected with English state affairs.

international links with leading European humanists (including, amongst others, Pieter Gillis, Ulrich von Hutten, Marcus Laurinus, and Beatus Rhenanus), and diplomats (including Richard Pace, Pietro Vanni, and John Yonge).[16] In other words, Erasmus's high betweenness was the result of the short paths he created in this network by connecting diverse and dispersed communities, both through his intellectual breadth and his physical movement. He shows how the high betweenness associated with weak ties is strongly correlated with movement and travel. But, perhaps more importantly, his presence on this list shows how the networks of the Tudor state were densely interwoven with intellectual networks, as well as military ones.

Following this brief unpacking of the people with the top thirty betweenness rankings for the first decade of Henry VIII's reign, we can see its use as a way of identifying the weak ties in our epistolary network—*once* we subtract the impact of the hubs (i.e. those with high degree—see Chapter 2). Of the thirteen non-hubs in the ranked list above, ten undertook diplomatic missions. This is not just an anomaly of the first decade. Testing this finding for subsequent decades we can see very similar results. For the 1520s, Erasmus appears again, nine figures served on diplomatic missions (Gian Matteo Giberti, Bishop of Verona, Thomas Magnus, Cardinal Lorenzo Campeggio, Sir Thomas More, Pace, James Beaton, Richard Croke, Stephen Gardiner, and Thomas Boleyn, Earl of Wiltshire and Ormond), and three were military leaders stationed abroad or on the borders (Darcy and Dacre once again, and Henry Percy, Earl of Northumberland). In the 1530s the total is also 12: eight posted on diplomatic missions (Thomas Cranmer, Eustace Chapuys Thomas Wriothesley, Pedro Ortiz, Edmund Bonner, Charles Brandon, 1st Duke of Suffolk, Jean du Bellay, Bishop of Paris, and Cardinal Rodolfo Pio), and four on military missions (Lord Lisle, Darcy, Henry Clifford, 1st Earl of Cumberland and George Talbot, 4th Earl of Shrewsbury).

Betweenness also captures different acts of international mediation and bargaining. One example is the appearance of Philip Melanchthon (ranking twelfth for betweenness in the 1530s). Unsurprisingly for someone primarily occupied with scholarly and literary matters his correspondence network is largely made up of continental reformers, but it also includes communications with Henry VIII and English religious leaders, which reveal his involvement in negotiations between England and the Schmalkaldic league of Lutheran princes. England had common ground with these states in their rejection of papal authority, having broken with Rome through a series of acts passed in 1532–4. As John Schofield has remarked, 'the Lutheran Schmalkaldic League offered diplomatic advantages and military security to a schismatic king at enmity with the pope and in danger of isolation.'[17] In a 1535 letter from Martin Luther, Melanchthon is asked to meet with the two English ambassadors ('legates ambobus'),

---

[16] On the impact of Erasmus's travels on his network, see Chapter 8.

[17] John Schofield, *Philip Melanchthon and the English Reformation* (Ashgate, 2006), p. 60. See also Rory McEntegart, *Henry VIII, the League of Schmalkalden, and the English Reformation* (Boydell and Brewer, 2002), pp. 26–76.

and to act as a worthy comrade and disputer.[18] The two ambassadors are presumably Christopher Mont and Nicholas Heath because, of the four diplomats sent to Germany, these are the ones to whom Melanchthon writes. Melanchthon subsequently writes to Henry on matters both religious and diplomatic: he commends his religious zeal, recommends a friend (John Stratius) for diplomatic service, comments on the appointment of Francis Burchardt as ambassador, encourages Henry to purge England of heresy, and upbraids him for the superstitious rites that still remain.[19] Through these letters we can see how Melanchthon makes use of England's isolation following its break with Rome to establish an epistolary relationship with the English monarch, and thereby to negotiate for religious reform.

More broadly, Melanchthon's case shows how the position of mediator bestows a particular kind of power, a strategic advantage that allows the holder to leverage connectivity for favour. For the remainder of this chapter we will focus on how betweenness can therefore help us to understand the diplomatic network profile, and in both this and the next chapter we will examine how this profile evolved over the sixteenth century.

Institutionalising Weak Ties

Diplomatic practice seeks to institutionalise the kind of long-range 'weak ties' explored by Granovetter, Watts, and Strogatz, which facilitate the movement of information between discrete communities. A diplomat, most simply put, is a person appointed by a state to conduct negotiations with one or more other states; their role is premised upon transmitting information between their host nation and their home state. It is about overcoming not only geographic and ideological gaps, but also lacunae in information. The idea of lacunae is important: Ronald Burt's research reformulated Granovetter's thesis of weak ties by arguing that what is of central importance is not so much the ties, but rather the 'structural holes' that they bridge.[20] When these structural holes are bridged there are benefits for the network, which translates to a benefit for the individual: insofar as they constitute the only route through which information or other resources may flow from one network sector to another, these nodes achieve a strategic advantage. Empirical studies suggest that people who fill structural holes in corporations or other organisations have more successful careers. This analogy has a clear relevance to the role of royal agents abroad, for whom such missions could provide a route into the higher echelons of Tudor government.

---

[18] See Melanchthon to Mont, 4 October 1535, BL, Lansdowne Vol/1 f.218; to 'the English ambassador', 1535, Lansdowne Vol/1 f.218; and Melancthon to Heath 1 April 1539, 'Letters and Papers: April 1539, 1–5', in *Letters and Papers, Foreign and Domestic, Henry VIII*, vol. 14 Part 1, January–July 1539, ed. James Gairdner and R. H. Brodie (Longman, Green, Longman, & Roberts, 1894), pp. 330–48. *British History Online* <http://www.british-history.ac.uk/letters-papers-hen8/vol14/no1/pp330-348>.

[19] LP VIII 384; LP IX 223, 224, 918, 1003, 1068; BL, Cotton Cleopatra E/VI f.339; Cotton Cleopatra E/V f.251, f.254, f.256; LP XIV, ii, 444; LP XV 231.

[20] Ronald S. Burt, *Structural Holes: The Social Structure of Competition* (Harvard University Press, 1992).

Table 3.1 Edges ranked by strength 1509–1519

Rank	Sender	Recipient	Strength
1	Tommaso Spinelli	Henry VIII	171
2	Richard Pace	Thomas Wolsey	167
3	Robert Wingfield	Henry VIII	155
4	Tommaso Spinelli	Wolsey	140
5	Sebastian Giustinian	Leonardo Loredan, Doge of Venice	119
6	Sir Richard Wingfield	Wolsey	78
7	Emperor Maximilian I	Margaret of Austria	77
8	Pope Leo X	Henry VIII	73
9	Silvestro de Gigli	Wolsey	72
10	Cuthbert Tunstall	Henry VIII	71
11	Sir Richard Wingfield	Henry VIII	64
=12	Richard Sampson	Wolsey	57
=12	Giustinian	Council of Ten	57
14	Tunstall	Wolsey	53
15	Charles Somerset, Earl of Worcester	Henry VIII	49
16	John Yonge	Henry VIII	47
17	Thomas Boleyn, Earl of Wiltshire and Ormond	Henry VIII	45
18	Leo X	Wolsey	44
19	Matthäus Schiner, Cardinal of Sion	Wolsey	43
=20	Charles Brandon, Duke of Suffolk	Wolsey	42
=20	Margaret of Austria	Henry VIII	42
=20	Robert Wingfield	Wolsey	42

In order to fully comprehend the network profile of the diplomat, it is helpful to momentarily separate the issues of network structure and diplomatic identity. Thinking in a purely structural sense, how can we test the algorithm of betweenness? How can we prove that our betweenness rankings are really showing us the best routes through the networks? One way is to see how the names in a ranked list of those with the highest betweenness correspond with the 'edges' with the highest traffic—in other words turning our attention to the nature of the tie. We want to see if the edges connected to our identified bridges (people with 'weak' ties) also have the highest traffic (strength), thereby measuring the strength of weak ties. Table 3.1 is a list of edges (relationships marked by letters) dating from the first decade of Henry's reign, ranked by strength (the number of letters passing between them).

There are several things to note about this list of weighted edges. The list of recipients (column 3) is dominated by hubs. The people to appear in the list of senders (column 2), however, seem heterogeneous, including rulers and leaders, courtiers, bishops, and a cardinal. However, there is a uniting theme: 18 of the 22 edges with the highest weights originate with figures serving in a diplomatic function—our weak ties or bridges. Giustinian (ranked 5th and =12th) was the Venetian ambassador to England 1515–19.[21] Sampson (=12th) amongst other missions was assigned to an embassy to treat with Lady Margaret at Brussels in September 1514, and appointed to the famous trade commission to Burgundy with Sir Thomas More, Cuthbert Tunstall (ranked 10th and 14th), and others in May 1515.[22] Yonge (16th) was sent on several diplomatic missions by Henry VIII, including one from 16 May 1512 to April 1513, when he was sent on a long mission to the Low Countries accompanied by Sir Thomas Boleyn (17th).[23] All of the forty-nine letters sent to Henry VIII from Somerset (15th) are from his diplomatic missions, including those concerning the surrender of Tournai.[24] Some of the letters from Brandon (=20th) to Wolsey concern the 'jousting embassy' to France to celebrate the marriage of Louis XII to Henry's sister Mary in the autumn of 1514, and the mission to escort Mary to him again after his death (although this turned into an opportunity for the illicit marriage of her and Brandon).[25] Schiner (19th), as papal legate for Italy and Germany, was appointed commander of a Swiss and Venetian army, and in 1516 raised another army with the aid of England; his correspondence with Henry concerns relations with the Swiss and the emperor, and details frequent contact with Pace (2nd), including use of his servants as couriers.[26]

By cross-referring this list of the edges with the highest epistolary traffic with the betweenness rankings we can see two things. Firstly, there is a strong overlap in the identities. Of the senders in Table 3.1, 15 out of 20 featured in the top 30 for betweenness, and of the recipients, all bar one recur. This suggests that the shortest paths across the network (identified by high betweenness) coincided with those that were most heavily used. The difference between the two columns also reiterates the complementary relationship between diplomats and central government in the model of information flow described in the previous chapter: here we can see how valuable information from a variety of sources and locations comes together to inform central government and to populate its archives. Betweenness, then, provides a statistical way of modelling information flow and the infrastructural significance of the diplomat. What this tells us is that 'ambassador' is not just a job; it is a *function*. That function was sometimes performed by figures that we do not think of when we consider the idea of a diplomat, by bishops or zealous reformers. More importantly, it is a function that manifests itself as a certain network position within a flow of information.

Betweenness therefore provides a way of thinking about the status and identity of the diplomat. As if to prove this, a number of scholars, completely unaware of either

[21] Barry Collett, 'Giustinian, Sebastian (1460–1543)', *ODNB*, <https://doi.org/10.1093/ref:odnb/70789>.

[22] Andrew A. Chibi, 'Sampson, Richard (d. 1554)', *ODNB*, <https://doi.org/10.1093/ref:odnb/24594>.

[23] Ronald H. Fritze, 'Yonge, John (1466/7–1516)', *ODNB*, <https://doi.org/10.1093/ref:odnb/30227>.

[24] Jonathan Hughes, 'Somerset, Charles, first earl of Worcester (c.1460–1526)', *ODNB*, <https://doi.org/10.1093/ref:odnb/26004>.

[25] S. J. Gunn, 'Brandon, Charles, first duke of Suffolk (c.1484–1545)', *ODNB*, <https://doi.org/10.1093/ref:odnb/3260>.

[26] See, for example, SP 1/11 f.178, BL, Cotton Vitellius B/XVIII f.238, SP 1/12 f.41, SP 1/12 f.147, and Cotton Vitellius B/XIX f.21.

the language or methods of network analysis, have utilised the word 'betweenness' to think about the practice of early modern diplomacy. Ellen McClure writes that 'diplomacy, essentially, is a matter of betweenness, of dialogue'.[27] Timothy Hampton is speaking about Tasso's *Il Messaggiero* (or *The Messenger*), a dialogue on the role of the diplomat written in the early 1580s, when he writes: 'The dialogue opens with the poet in a position of "betweenness", reminiscent of the position of the legate. We see him wavering between sleeping and waking, as he is visited by the spirit at dawn.'[28] A legate is a personal representative of the pope to foreign nations, a variety of diplomat. Hampton suggests that the 'betweenness' of the diplomat is both structural and ideological. Tasso's own words make that double betweenness clear:

> If the one who brings together minds is the go-between between those whose minds he brings together, it does not appear that he should be more on the side of one than on the side of the other. For a mediator always participates equally in both sides. But on the other hand this seems most inconvenient since the ambassador belongs completely to the one whom he represents, and not to the one in whose court he resides. Hence his goal should be rather to carry out negotiations to the satisfaction of the prince his master, with no regard for the usefulness or honour of the other.[29]

This passage distinguishes between the action of the 'mezzanino'—nicely captured in the translation as 'go-between'—and the concept of mediation. Tasso suggests that the structural betweenness contains a paradox, which can be explained by Roger V. Gould and Roberto M. Fernandez's highly cited 1989 paper on the 'Structures of Mediation'. The paper identifies and visually represents five brokerage relationships shown in Figure 3.1.[30] A true mediator should neither take the part of the one whom he represents, nor the one in whose court he resides, aiming instead to help those parties to meet in the middle, thereby exemplifying Gould and Fernandez's fifth category of brokerage, which they call 'liaison'. However, 'since the ambassador belongs completely to the one whom he represents' he carries the burden to bring his host to the position of his prince, making him the definition of the 'representative' (brokerage type 4). The diplomat's professions of betweenness, therefore, are merely a posture. In this context betweenness can be interpreted as a janus-faced doubleness. As Catherine

---

[27] Ellen M. McClure, *Sunspots and the Sun King: Sovereignty and Mediation in Seventeenth-Century France* (Chicago University Press, 2006), p. 140. See also Brian Lugioyo, *Martin Bucer's Doctrine of Justification: Reformation Theology and Early Modern Irenicism* (Oxford University Press, 2010), p. 8.

[28] Timothy Hampton, *Fictions of Embassy: Literature and Diplomacy in Early Modern Europe* (Cornell University Press, 2009), p. 54.

[29] *Se ciascuno, che unisce gli animi è mezzano fra color gli animi de' quali unisce, non pare che più debba esser d'un principe che de l'altro; perché sempre il mediatore egualmente partecipa de gli estremi; ma da altra parte ciò pare molto inconveniente, perché l'ambasciatore è tutto di quel principe la cui persona rappresenta, non di quello appresso cui risiede; laonde dovrebbe esser più tosto il suo fine di trattare i negozi a pro ed a sodisfazione del principe suo signore, senza aver alcun riguardo a l'utile, ed a l'onor de l'altro.* Torquato Tasso, *Prose*, ed. Ettore Mazzali (Ricciardi, 1959), p. 69; translation, Hampton, *Fictions of Embassy*, pp. 54–5.

[30] Roger V. Gould and Roberto M. Fernandez, 'Structure of Mediation: A Formal Approach to Brokerage in Transaction Networks', *Sociological Methodology* 19 (1989), 89–126.

the five types of brokerage relation

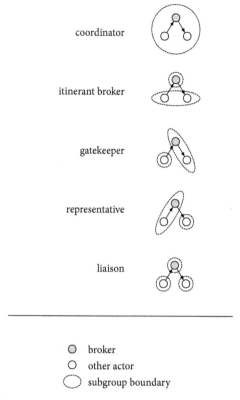

coordinator

itinerant broker

gatekeeper

representative

liaison

○ broker
○ other actor
⬭ subgroup boundary

Figure 3.1 Gould and Fernandez's taxonomy of brokerage relationships.

Fletcher notes, the nature of the role and (often tense) political context gave the diplomat good 'reason to simulate and dissimulate'.[31]

The need to consider the tensions between the structural and social aspects of diplomacy can be linked to the professionalisation of the ambassador in the late fifteenth and early sixteenth centuries. Medieval diplomatic messengers gradually gave way to ambassadors acting in the ongoing interests of sovereign states. And as the nature and personnel of diplomacy evolved, a branch of literature emerged that interrogated the very concept of embassy.[32] In the words of Joanna Craigwood: 'The introduction of the permanent embassy is symptomatic of this transition from a series of communications to an art and practice of representation'.[33] The story of the rise of the resident ambassador was described in detail in the classic 1955 study of Renaissance diplomacy by Garrett Mattingley, and has more recently been nuanced in the work of

---

[31] Catherine Fletcher, *Diplomacy in Renaissance Rome: The Rise of the Resident Ambassador* (Cambridge University Press, 2015), p. 2.

[32] On this tradition, see Hampton, *Fictions of Embassy*; and William Rossiter and Jason Powell, eds., *Authority and Diplomacy from Dante to Shakespeare* (Ashgate, 2013).

[33] Joanna Craigwood, 'Sidney, Gentili, and the Poetics of Embassy', in *Diplomacy and Early Modern Culture*, ed. Robyn Adams and Rosanna Cox (Palgrave Macmillan, 2011), pp. 82–100 (p. 82).

Douglas Biow, Daniela Frigo, and Catherine Fletcher.[34] The resident ambassador, as the title implies (and his letter of credence explained), was sent to reside. He had no particular mission to fulfil and remained in the court where he was accredited for an indeterminate period. Though discrete, short-term missions continued, more envoys were dispatched to be resident at the court of a foreign power. This system allowed governments to keep themselves abreast of local news, and especially of the possibility of secret and hostile alliances, in order to foresee problems and opportunities. As Fletcher comments: 'while individuals came and went their office was increasingly assumed to be permanent'.[35] What mattered was that a prince had eyes and ears at the courts of rival powers; whose they were, did not.

A comparison of the lists of diplomats that appear in the top thirty for betweenness during the first years of Henry VIII's reign and the middle of Elizabeth I's (1580–9) reveals telling changes in the composition of the diplomatic corps. Of the eleven figures who undertook diplomatic missions in the former period only one—Spinelli— might be called a 'professional' diplomat, as the second resident ambassador to ever be appointed by the English throne. As we have gleaned in the previous pages, the others served on missions on top of their everyday jobs in Tudor administration, ecclesiastical posts, or military postings. By comparison, the top thirty in terms of betweenness during the period of 1580–9 contains eight figures who undertook diplomatic missions during this period.[36] Five are English diplomats posted abroad (William Davison, William Brooke, 10th Baron Cobham, Thomas Wilkes, Thomas Randolph, Sir Edward Stafford), and three are foreign diplomats resident in England (Michel de Castelnau, Sieur de la Mauvissière, Bernardino de Mendoza, and Archibald Douglas). Unlike the cohort from 1509–19, most of these men might be called professional or career diplomats in that they spent most of their careers on embassies with the exceptions of Davison (who combined his embassies with his role as secretary to Queen Elizabeth I) and Cobham (whose primary roles were Lord Warden of the Cinque Ports, and member of the Privy Council). Only Douglas held an ecclesiastical post, compared to the four men in the list from 1509 to 1519.

The disappearance of the ecclesiastical diplomats is directly linked to the professionalisation of diplomacy. The job required a certain set of skills that, until the latter part of the fifteenth century, princes had clearly felt the clergy were best qualified to fulfil. This is something noticed by Étienne Dolet, the former secretary to the French ambassador to Venice (1528–9) and author of an early treatise on diplomacy, *De Officio Legati* (1541):

---

[34] Garrett Mattingly, *Renaissance Diplomacy* (Houghton Mifflin, 1955); Douglas Biow, *Doctors, Ambassadors, Secretaries Humanism and Professions in Renaissance Italy* (University of Chicago Press, 2002); Daniela Frigo, *Politics and Diplomacy in Early Modern Italy: The Structure of Diplomatic Practice, 1450–1800* (Cambridge University Press, 2002); and Fletcher, *Diplomacy in Renaissance Rome*.

[35] Fletcher, *Diplomacy in Renaissance Rome*, p. 36.

[36] While the total number of diplomats returned in the top thirty has decreased from the total returned during the first decade of Henry's reign, in addition to these eight diplomats another kind of foreign policy is captured: the Tudor conquest of Ireland is represented via the five military leaders and statesmen posted to Ireland that appear in the top thirty (Sir John Perrott, Sir William Fitzwilliam, Sir Nicholas Malby, Sir Henry Wallop, and Arthur Grey, 14th Baron Grey de Wilton).

Up to the present time, however, it has been the prevalent practice among kings and other princes to employ men of ecclesiastical rank on embassies, I suppose either because of their reputation for letters and learning, or because they think that in view of their holy character they will be in less danger of personal injury.[37]

Dolet focuses here on the qualifications for embassy in terms of learning and moral character. Following this passage, he continues by observing that the clerical or secular status of a proposed ambassador made little difference now that the nobility took the study of letters seriously. This observation suggests that the change is due in part to the rise of humanist education. The increase in lay ambassadors is not unrelated to the rise of the resident ambassador. As Fletcher notes, special embassies were large and splendid to convey the wealth and status of the prince or republic they represented, and '[t]heir size meant they could combine all manner of expertise': sociable noblemen, humanists, doctors of law, bishops. By contrast, in selecting a resident ambassador, who may be the sole representative of his prince, choices had to be made.[38] Increasingly a lay ambassador was chosen.

To understand the professionalisation of the role, we can look to one of the earliest examples of the lay resident ambassador: Tommaso Spinelli. He can tell us much about the network of such a figure. As demonstrated above, Spinelli not only has one of the highest betweenness values for the period up to the end of 1519 (rank 28th), he is also the source node for two of the edges with the highest epistolary traffic in this period: in rank 1 is the edge he shares with Henry VIII, along which Spinelli sent 171 letters; and in rank 4 his edge with Wolsey, which is marked by 140 letters in this period. Despite his quantitative exceptionality, however, he has neither an entry in the *ODNB* nor a page on Wikipedia, and he is mentioned in passing in just a handful of books on early modern diplomacy through references that are almost completely reliant on a single article by Betty Behrens dating from 1933.[39] A re-examination of his career within the context of network metrics, however, reveals some important insights into the network benefits of the resident ambassador—both to the holder and to the Tudor government—as well as the strong potential it created for mistrust.

Tommaso Spinelli

Tommaso Spinelli (b. 1471) was one of the very earliest resident ambassadors for England, preceded only by John Stile.[40] While Stile has relatively little surviving correspondence (25 incoming letters, one outgoing), we have 434 letters sent by Spinelli and 23 letters addressed to him before his death in 1522. These letters, and the

---

[37] Quoted by Fletcher, *Diplomacy in Renaissance Rome*, p. 83.   [38] Ibid., p. 81.
[39] Betty Behrens, 'The Office of the English Resident Ambassador: Its Evolution as Illustrated by the Career of Sir Thomas Spinelly, 1509–22', *Transactions of the Royal Historical Society* 16 (1933), 161–95.
[40] Mattingly, *Renaissance Diplomacy*, p. 159.

network they describe, tell us not only about the development of Spinelli's individual career, but also the development of the profile of the professional diplomat more generally. As detailed above, special ambassadors were sent to foreign courts for specific negotiations and would leave as soon as the requirements of their commission were met; their success relied upon their negotiation skills. By contrast the resident ambassador's success was built upon his networks of information, his structural (and sometimes moral) betweenness.

Spinelli's first surviving letter, dated 26 June 1509, is addressed to Henry VIII and references an earlier missive, now lost, in which the king thanked Spinelli for his services, and asked to retain them. Along with his confirmation of ongoing service, Spinelli sent an extract of the news written by the emperor to Margaret of Austria eight days before.[41] According to Behrens, at this time Spinelli was acting as an 'agent' for Henry VIII at the court of Margaret of Austria, who had been made governor of the Low Countries and guardian of her young nephew Charles (the future Charles V, Holy Roman Emperor) in 1507.[42] The term agent, however, tells us relatively little about the formality of the relationship. It was some years until he would be formally appointed as an ambassador: in a letter to Henry VIII dated 4 August 1517 he writes, 'Your Grace had deputyd me, Thomas Spinelly, to be your ambassatour resident in his [Charles V's] court and to go in his company into Spaine.'[43] Rather the provision of news in this early letter suggests that Spinelli's primary service in 1509 may have been that of 'intelligencer'—an extra-diplomatic source of news.

Spinelli's value, like a number of other resident ambassadors appointed in this period, was derived from his social network. Fletcher writes: 'In a mutually beneficial relationship the employing prince would gain access to his envoy's personal networks, while the envoy's family and friends gained valuable contacts with potential patrons in the European courts.'[44] This perfectly describes Burt's contention, that when structural holes are bridged there are benefits for the network, which translates to benefits for the node. And Spinelli clearly fulfilled this kind of strategic appointment: he hailed from an eminent Florentine merchant family: he was a nephew of Filippo Gualterotti, head of one of the largest banking houses in the Low Countries, with establishments in Bruges and Antwerp and an important English connection, and he had a brother who was chamberlain to the pope. Philip Jacks and William Caferro's work on the Spinelli family asserts that, by his early twenties, Tommaso was engaged in international grain trading for his uncle's firm in Bruges, although he eventually gave this up for his diplomatic career.[45] His mercantile background is not insignificant. It meant that he was embedded in local networks in the Low Countries by the end of the fifteenth century, but also more generally highlights the important link between early

---

[41] SP 1/1 ff.35r–37v.   [42] Behrens, 'The Office of the English Resident Ambassador', p. 168.

[43] BL, Cotton MS Galba B. V. f.298. See Behrens, 'The Office of the English Resident Ambassador', p. 175. For a surviving example of a credential, see Henry VIII's letter to Charles V, dated 2 April 1520, appointing Spinelli resident in the Imperial Court on the recall of Cuthbert Tunstall (BL, Cotton Vespasian F/I f.79).

[44] Fletcher, *Diplomacy in Renaissance Rome*, pp. 118–19.

[45] Philip Jacks and William Caferro, *The Spinelli of Florence: Fortunes of a Renaissance Merchant Family* (Penn State University Press, 2001), p. 261.

modern diplomacy, commerce, and news. The strategic location of trading ports—at the intersection of vast regional and international information networks—put merchants at a structural advantage in news gathering. Long before the Tudor period, merchants were trading information alongside goods, and Andrew Pettegree suggests that the medieval commercial correspondence, the 'varied digests of news presented in the merchant correspondence', should be seen as the 'true ancestors of the newspaper'.[46] Spinelli's structural advantage derived from his familial and commercial network and his status as a foreign agent for England. Figures like Spinelli, with local knowledge, could access intelligence that was otherwise unobtainable to special ambassadors and commissioners sent on short missions.

Spinelli's structural advantage derives from the quality of the contacts he had on the ground. Within the State Papers archive we have letters by Spinelli addressed to eight people:

Cardinal Thomas Wolsey (249 letters), Henry VIII (172), Sir Brian Tuke (6), Christopher Bainbridge, Archbishop of York (3), Charles Somerset, Earl of Worcester (1), Sir Gilbert Talbot (1), Louis Maroton (1), Privy Council (1).

And there are twenty-three surviving letters addressed to Spinelli, from sixteen people:

Wolsey (5), Henry VIII (2), Anthoine (2), Tunstall (2), Charles Somerset, Earl of Worcester (1), Robert Wingfield (1), Filippo Gualterotti (1), Petrus Alamire (1), Raphael de Medicis (1), Nicholas West, Bishop of Ely (1), William FitzWilliam, 1st Earl of Southampton (1), Jean, Seigneur de Berghes (1), Antoine I de Lalaing, 1st count of Hoogstraten (1), Louis Maroton (1), Simon de Taxis (1), and Simon von Reischach (1).

The correspondence addressed to Henry, Wolsey, and the postmaster Tuke comprises the majority of the documentation surrounding Spinelli due to the nature of the archiving process, as discussed in Chapter 2. Although the edges shared with his other correspondents do not have the strength of these aforementioned associations, they go some way to demonstrating the quality of Spinelli's associations and sources of intelligence. De Berghes was head of one of the most powerful houses in the Low Countries and a member of the Margaret of Austria's council, who attended her wherever she resided.[47] De Lalaing was another influential member of this council.[48] Von Reischach was Chancellor of Friesland, and member of the Saxon embassy to London negotiating a renewal of the trade agreement between England and Friesland.[49] The

---

[46] Andrew Pettegree, *The Invention of News: How the World Came to Know About Itself* (Yale University Press, 2014), p. 72. See also Mario Infelise, 'From Merchants' Letters to Handwritten Political *avvisi*: Notes on the Origins of Public Information', in *Correspondence and Cultural Exchange in Europe*, ed. Francisco Bethencourt and Florike Egmond (Cambridge University Press, 2007), pp. 41–2.

[47] H. G. Koenigsberger, *Monarchies, States Generals and Parliaments: The Netherlands in the Fifteenth and Sixteenth Centuries* (Cambridge University Press, 2001), p. 93.

[48] Ibid., pp. 174–7.

[49] *The Correspondence of Erasmus: Letters 1122 to 1251, 1520 to 1521*, tr. R. A. B. Mynors and annotated by Peter G. Bietenholz (University of Toronto Press, 1988), p. 353.

Taxis family, with the help of the governments concerned, ran a postal service over the greater part of northern and central Europe; and Simon de Taxis was nephew to the Maistre des Postes at this time, François de Taxis.[50] Petrus Alamire was a merchant of manuscripts, chaplain, singer, and instrumentalist, but between 1515 and 1518 he acted as a spy for Henry VIII against the pretender to the English throne, Richard de la Pole (although later he was discovered to be a double agent).[51] Spinelli was also in touch with other special and resident ambassadors, English and foreign, at the centre of their own intelligence networks: Bainbridge, Robert Wingfield, Tunstall, Worcester, West, Southampton, and Moraton. Taken together, we can see that Spinelli had contacts within the government of his host state, agents in key positions at other European courts, and perhaps most importantly at the communication centre: the post office of the Taxis family. In addition Spinelli had direct access to the regent Margaret and Charles V respectively, as both his letters and theirs to Henry VIII readily attest. But even when we read through his letters, we perhaps only see part of his network of informants and couriers, such as the woman he paid to carry news 'to Lysle'.[52] Presumably the names were redacted to protect his sources, and the woman used to avoid suspicion.[53]

The letter network, then, shows us not only the extent of Spinelli's betweenness, with long-range links between key information centres, but also the *quality* of the nodes with whom he shared edges. In Spinelli's first letter to Henry we see him advertising both his structural advantage and the strength and quality of his contacts, where he describes the 'neueu du maistre des postes', Simon de Taxis, as 'mon grant amy'.[54] The structural advantage, however, created a wider benefit as Spinelli seemingly used his position to improve epistolary infrastructure. In a letter from François de Taxis to Henry's Privy Council on 4 January 1513, he informs them that the previous July, at the order of Spinelli, he laid two additional posts (beyond the six) from the court in Mechelen to Calais.[55]

Spinelli's position at the intersection of trade routes, formal postal routes, and gossip is the foundation of his value in his first years as an agent, especially before the grant of his credential. His primary correspondence was with Henry and Wolsey. As was common in this period, the lengthy itemised lists of news were addressed to the king. On its arrival its contents might be deciphered, translated, filtered, and summarised by a secretary before reaching the king's hands. We see that many of the letters in cipher were deciphered by Tuke. Spinelli's correspondence to Wolsey is often much

---

[50] On the place of the Taxis family within the wider history of early modern postal networks, see Nikolaus Schobesberger, Paul Arblaster, Mario Infelise, André Belo, Noah Moxham, Carmen Espejo, and Joad Raymond, 'European Postal Networks', in *News Networks in Early Modern Europe*, ed. Joad Raymond and Noah Moxham (Brill, 2016), pp. 19–63.

[51] Eugene Schreurs, 'Petrus Alamire: Music Calligrapher, Musician, Composer, Spy', in *The Treasury of Petrus Alamire: Music and Art in Flemish Court Manuscripts 1500-1535*, ed. Herbert Kellman (Ghent Ludion, distributed by the University of Chicago Press, 1999), pp. 15–27.

[52] Spinelli to Wolsey, 1 April 1514, SP 1/7 f.271r.

[53] On the use of women as informants and couriers, albeit for a slightly later period, see Nadine Akkerman, *Invisible Agents: Women and Espionage in Seventeenth-Century Britain* (Oxford University Press, 2018).

[54] SP 1/1 f.36r.   [55] Cotton Galba B/III f.68r.

briefer, and refers him to the longer missives sent to the king ('by a lettre that I writt vnto the king your grace shalbe advertised of all the newes'), which suggests the news-letters were imagined to be held in common.[56] His success is closely linked to the quality and frequency of the news he sent to the crown (explaining the high out-strength typical of diplomats). Almost every missive opens with a statement of when the post had arrived from a given destination: for example, on 27 July 1512 he writes that although he last wrote on the 24 July, since then 'laposte dallemaygne' has arrived advertising Margaret of Austria of news from Italy. With his covering letter he sends three other documents.[57] The first is an original letter from Simon de Taxis, reporting information from Maroton. The second is titled 'Extractum litterarum ex Blesis data-rum die iij. Augusti, ad magistrum postarum ex Italico in Latinum translatum': the extract of the letter from Blois to the Master of the Posts, translated out of Italian and into Latin containing the news that the Spaniards have taken Pampeluna, and the Duke of Bourbon has been sent to resist them. The third is a copy of a letter from Margaret of Austria to Andrieu Andries, 'rentmaistre de Bewesterscelt', commanding him to apprehend Robert Barton and other pirates from Scotland entering the ports of Zealand for pillaging English merchants and others. The practice of bundling together the items of intelligence is common throughout Spinelli's correspondence, particularly news received by Margaret during his residence in her court. Spinelli also frequently mentions that he has enclosed letters from Robert Wingfield.[58] The example from 27 July 1512, however, is particularly striking because four documents, in three different hands, were bundled together in a single packet, and are now filed as one in the State Papers archive. We might thus see this packet as an embodiment of part of Spinelli's network: three sources of news, meeting in the person of Spinelli, and forwarded to the English crown.

While this structural betweenness effectively functioned to elevate Spinelli from the role of merchant to professional diplomat, it also had the effect of trapping him in one particular role. Spinelli met the need of local intelligence that special ambassadors could not provide, but the Tudor government continued to send special commission-ers and ambassadors into the Low Countries for negotiations, to which Spinelli was not made privy. These ambassadors and the government clearly imagined a division of labour. For example, in 1512 Richard Wingfield, Sir Edward Poynings, Dr John Yonge, and Sir Thomas Boleyn were commissioned as special ambassadors to the Low Countries to treat with the regent Margaret of Austria, the pope, the emperor Maximilian, and Ferdinand II of Aragon for the formation of a holy league in support of the church and against France. In letters from this mission the special ambassadors repeatedly stated that 'as touching all such newes [...] your grace shalbe aduertised by Thomas Spynelles lettres', while they proceeded with the negotiations.[59] This division of labour does not seem to have bothered Spinelli at first, but in later letters we see

[56] See SP 1/12 f.171r.   [57] SP 1/2 ff.147r–150v.

[58] For example, Cotton Galba B/III ff.130r–135v contains a digest of news sent 'by my Lady of Savoy un[to Thomas] Spinelly which she hath understonde of the [ambassador] of Aragon'.

[59] Cotton Galba B/III f.43r. See also Cotton Galba B/III f.45r.

him petitioning Wolsey to be treated in the same way as the other ambassadors. In one letter dating from 16 October 1515 he writes: 'I humbly beseche you [...] that I may be entreatyd as your others ambassadors and commissioners that haue promocions besydes'.[60] It is not clear whether his concern is his career trajectory or the low wages he received. More usually his petitions regarded his need for better or more regular payment and complaints that he has been forced to borrow money. However, in a letter dated 16 February 1516 we see a similar expression of frustration: 'If I am not intreatyd as others [...] it is vmpossible for me to contenew heere'.[61] Whether his concerns were addressed or not is unclear, but he nevertheless continued in post. Despite this appeasement, however, it is clear that his fellow ambassadors did not view him as an equal. In a letter from Aragon dated 4 May 1518, he describes a meeting with the special ambassadors John Kite, Bishop of Armagh and John Bourchier, Lord Berners. He had received the king's letter dated 25 February, approving his services and commanding that he should be taken into communication with them. On appearing before the ambassadors, however, they made it clear that he 'shulde not be present to any of theyr comunyquacions'.[62] He experienced the same fate when Tunstall was dispatched as special ambassador to Charles V in 1520, a further disappointment which led Spinelli to ask for his discharge.[63]

Whether the reasons for this exclusion were based on snobbery or mistrust is difficult to tell; in the case of Tunstall it is most likely the latter. Spinelli's allegiances were repeatedly brought into question, and most often by Tunstall. In 1514 Wolsey seems to have become suspicious of his agent because, according to a report from Brian Tuke, the Master of the Posts, Spinelli had been accused of making sinister reports to Margaret of Austria against him.[64] Spinelli of course denied that accusation, stating it would have been a 'grette Ingratitude' and 'very grete vtercuydaunce' (the French 'outrecuidance', meaning impertinence); and two other diplomats at Margaret's court, Knight and Richard Wingfield, also defended Spinelli, stating their faith in his fidelity.[65] However, later the following year, Tunstall wrote to Wolsey informing him that Charles V's councillor, William II de Croÿ, Lord of Chièvres, had a design to obtain leave for Spinelli to come to England to obtain a loan from the king. Tunstall, however, advised that this leave must not be granted, and marvelled how they could 'for shame desire any such friendship by the King's grace to be unto them, seeing their dulness and doubleness in the King's affairs'.[66] The word doubleness here is interesting because of its connection with the structural attributes of betweenness. As Behrens writes: 'the very factors which made him invaluable as an informant—his foreign origin and his continuous residence in the Netherlands—made, equally, his honesty a matter of doubt'.[67]

---

[60] SP 1/11 f.141r.   [61] SP 1/13 f.8r.   [62] Cotton Vespasian C/I f.141r.   [63] SP 1/21, f.55r.
[64] See Spinelli to Wolsey, 1 April 1514, SP 1/7 f.271r, and Knight to Wolsey, 3 April 1514, Cotton Galba B/III f.163r.
[65] SP 1/7 f.275r   [66] Cotton Galba B/III f.299r.
[67] Behrens, 'The Office of the English Resident Ambassador', p. 175.

Behrens's statement reveals the double bind that governments found themselves in: the best-qualified individuals, those with the highest structural betweenness, often also exhibited a kind of moral betweenness. Fletcher writes: 'The foreign-born ambassadors were not only able to pretend that they were acting on behalf of other princes, or in a private business capacity, but could also give the impression they were acting for themselves [...] while envoys of any national origin could switch between official and unofficial personae, foreign state servants were peculiarly able to walk the stage in masks'.[68] Referring back to Gould and Fernandez's taxonomy of brokerage relationships, we see that this describes what they call the itinerant broker (see Figure 3.1). Spinelli never fully escaped from Wolsey and Tunstall's suspicion: having asked to be made privy to Tunstall's negotiations with Maximilian I, regarding the defence of Verona in 1516,[69] Wolsey wrote to Tunstall saying that he must keep his discussions secret because Spinelli was believed to have had intelligence with Chièvres, and spread the report that an agreement had been arrived at between Maximilian and the French.[70] Throughout their communications on this matter, Tunstall and Wolsey maintained their decision to keep them hidden from Spinelli.[71]

Wolsey's policy appears to have been to exploit Spinelli's structural betweenness for maximum information, whilst assigning him the minimum trust. While this approach may have suited English interests, it was unacceptable to Charles, as the newly instated ruler of the Holy Roman Empire. Following his visit to England in 1520 an agreement was reached that a resident English ambassador at the imperial court would thereafter be a condition of the Anglo-Imperial alliance. Spinelli, however, clearly did not fulfil the requirement that the latter should be a person with whom all matters might be discussed. In the end the matter was fudged; two resident ambassadors were appointed—the other being Richard Wingfield. Wingfield wrote to Wolsey that the emperor was less than pleased, but he believed that he would ultimately content himself 'considering that you have not, on this side the sea, the choice of personages to be sent hither of such qualities as they desire'.[72] It was in this role that Spinelli would die the following year, having climbed further than he ever could have expected in his mercantile upbringing, but also never fully gaining the acceptance within the ambassadorial inner sanctum that he so desired.

Conclusion

The position that Spinelli attained, as one of the first English resident ambassadors, is instructive: it reveals how the Tudor government negotiated the benefits and dangers posed by such figures posted permanently abroad. Moreover, the particularities of

---

[68] Fletcher, *Diplomacy in Renaissance Rome*, p. 91.
[69] See SP 1/14 f.57r, where Tunstall describes Spinelli's repeated requests for inclusion.
[70] Cotton Galba B/VI f.109r.
[71] See, for example, Cotton Galba B/IV f.264r and Cotton Galba B/V f.21r.   [72] SP 1/23 f.126r.

Spinelli's role, his status, and reputation perfectly illustrate why a measure such as betweenness centrality should be effective in detecting diplomats. It is not just a lucky coincidence, but rather the diplomat's structural and ideological position—betwixt and between the interests of two courts—that accounts for the correlations noticed above.

It is worth reflecting, therefore, just how far we can get with a single off-the-shelf algorithm. By applying betweenness centrality to nodes (people) in the network, we can understand the figures best placed to facilitate the movement of information, and that these are both central government hubs and bridging figures. With manual sorting of the hubs from the bridges we quickly ascertain that the 'weak ties' are a heterogeneous body of figures who served diplomatic functions, both formal and informal, including international intellectuals, bishops and reformers, merchants, military leaders, and soldiers. However, an analysis of the strongest edges (the relationships between pairs of individuals) shows us even more persuasively that these weak ties were the lifeblood of the government's information system: eighteen of the twenty-two edges with the highest weights originate with figures serving in a diplomatic function. Furthermore, the ranked list of nodes with the highest betweenness—i.e. on the shortest path through the network—correspond with many of the edges with the greatest weight of letters passing along them through this first decade of Henry VIII's reign. This shows us that these weak ties really were the strongest not just in terms of novel information, but in volume of information too.

The reasons that our finding above focuses primarily on the first decade of Henry VIIIs reign is not merely to serve as a proof of concept; rather, as we began to show by comparing our results with a decade from Elizabeth I's reign, it is important to disaggregate our data over time because of the changing nature of the diplomatic corps during the Tudor period. As we will explore more in the following chapter, these changes are twofold. Firstly, as suggested above, the role of ambassador became professionalised, as more resident ambassadors were appointed and lay figures (rather than church men) were increasingly appointed to these roles. The second cause is that the data would suggest (and scholarship has attested) that the principal secretaries and other key statesmen working for Elizabeth I marshalled a much larger network of informal agents, intelligencers, spies, and double agents.

To more accurately chart this evolution in the management of international intelligence networks we need to move beyond a single algorithm. The manual sorting of hubs from bridges in our results above works on the smaller scale, but it also shows us that a single metric is rarely a good proxy for the specific cultural attributes or phenomena a scholar is interested in. To find the nodes or individuals of particular interest, or to develop more nuanced research questions, the measures typically need to be combined with other quantitative or qualitative approaches. In the next chapter, therefore, we introduce a more complex method for quantitatively describing certain epistolary behaviours in terms of a 'network profile'.

4

Network Profiles

The position and connectivity of each person in a network is unique. In a correspondence network, such as the one we are studying, it is determined by a myriad of factors: how many people a given correspondent wrote to or received letters from; the volume and the balance of incoming and outgoing correspondence; their position either at the centre of communities, between communities, or at the network's peripheries; and their proximity to power and influence. No one metric can capture all of these factors. However, what we can ascertain is each individual's network *profile*.

The concept of the network profile was first introduced in our article 'Metadata, Surveillance, and the Tudor State'.[1] The article offers an approach for mapping the unique network 'fingerprint' of each person in the network based on a combination of eight metrics. We have already observed how certain categories of correspondent can be quantitatively described using one or two metrics. Chapter 2 showed how principal secretaries are hubs that have an anomalously high number of incoming and outgoing connections (in-degree and out-degree), and that they are also characterised by a much higher volume of incoming correspondence than outgoing (in-strength versus out-strength). Diplomats and intelligencers, by contrast, have a much higher volume of outgoing correspondence. Chapter 3 then extended our understanding of the diplomatic function by showing that diplomats have high betweenness centrality due to the way they bridge otherwise separated communities. Because each of the previous metrics only captures one aspect of a correspondent's epistolary behaviour, the likelihood of any single measure being a reasonable proxy for the specific cultural attributes or phenomena a researcher might be looking for is minimal. However, when these metrics are layered up, we can begin to create a profile that describes the unique network position of a given correspondent, which in turn allows us to ask more complex research questions.

In addition to the seven metrics introduced in previous chapters (in-degree, out-degree, total degree, in-strength, out-strength, total-strength, and betweenness) the network profile that we implemented employs one further measure that provides a good quantitative proxy for proximity to power and influence—eigenvector centrality. A node that has a high eigenvector score is one that is adjacent to nodes that are themselves high scorers: as Stephen Borgatti puts it, 'the idea is that even if a node influences just one other node, who subsequently influences many other nodes (who themselves influence still more others), then the first node in that chain is highly

---

[1] Ruth Ahnert and Sebastian E. Ahnert, 'Metadata, Surveillance, and the Tudor State', *History Workshop Journal* 87 (2019), 27–51.

Tudor Networks of Power. Ruth Ahnert and Sebastian E. Ahnert, Oxford University Press. © Ruth Ahnert and Sebastian E. Ahnert 2023.
DOI: 10.1093/oso/9780198858973.003.0004

influential'.[2] By combining these eight networks we map individuals' behaviour in a higher-dimensional space, more clearly demarcating and measuring the subtle and manifold differences between our correspondents. However, our aim with the development of this approach is not to stress the differences between our correspondents, but to better understand what it means when they share similarities. The value of this approach is in the way that these unique fingerprints can be compared in multidimensional space. Once we understand the dimensions of potential difference, it provides us with a structural way of understanding the similarity between two people that bypasses human-assigned labels and taxonomies, looking directly at their behaviours and functions within the network.[3] Of course no two fingerprints can be identical, but they may share what Ludwig Wittgenstein described as family resemblances—a set of overlapping similarities.

This chapter begins by exploring the family resemblance of those employed through the diplomatic wing of the government. By returning briefly to Tommaso Spinelli we show how this early example of the resident ambassador can be used as a yardstick against which to measure the evolving profile of the diplomat in the sixteenth century. Specifically, he shows us how his network profile is more similar to other Henrician diplomats than it is to Elizabethan diplomats, who become more like small hubs in their own right. Within the Elizabethan period, by contrast, Spinelli is more similar to the widening cohort of 'intelligence producers' employed to inform the government:[4] a body of agents and informants that supplement the information obtained through formal embassy. These are no longer the anonymous murky sources cited in ambassadors' letters, but a distinct and identifiable class of informants who used their skill for their own personal and professional advancement. This chapter provides an extended account of one such intelligencer, called Pietro Bizzarri. We selected Bizzarri because he seems in many ways to be an edge case—he is an exceptional figure as a travelling scholar who experiences at least one dramatic adventure. However, while the specifics of his story may be unique, his network behaviours are in fact highly typical of the intelligencers marshalled in the Elizabethan period by Francis Walsingham, William Cecil, Lord Burghley, his son Robert Cecil, and, to a lesser extent, Robert Devereux, 2nd Earl of Essex. By understanding these commonalities, we can move beyond the histories of exceptional men to understand the collective structures needed to supply the diplomatic needs of the Tudor government.

More broadly, we can think about the utility of the method—of measuring fingerprint similarity—for thinking about categories of nodes and shared epistolary behaviours. The adaptability of the method for gleaning first insights into a dataset can be seen by turning to another facet of the intelligence strategy utilised by early modern governments: the interception of correspondence. There are several reasons that the

---

[2] Stephen P. Borgatti, 'Centrality and Network Flow', *Social Networks* 27 (2005), 55–71 (p. 61).

[3] A similarity score can be calculated in several ways. Our approach was to use the Euclidean distance between the eight-dimensional points defined by the logarithms of an individual's ranks for the different measurements. See <https://github.com/tudor-networks-of-power/code>.

[4] William H. Sherman, 'Research Intelligence in Early Modern England', *Studies in Intelligence* 37:5 (1994), 95–104.

similarity method might be useful in approaching this practice. Firstly, it provides a rough-hewn way of finding examples, which are hard to discover at scale within the dataset because they are rarely labelled as acts of interception in the Calendars of State Papers. Indeed, estimates of the proportion of papers that entered the State Papers archive through interception varies widely. By beginning with known subjects of interception, the ranked list of most similar people contains a high number of individuals that were also objects of interception and surveillance. This is a great example of the utility of such a method. Results may initially look heterogeneous, containing foreign monarchs, diplomats, Catholic conspirators, and church leaders. However, by thinking about similarity as something structural we can foreground similarities that might not be immediately apparent, or indeed pull against the categories and taxonomies into which we are more used to sorting people. As we will suggest below, the reason for the success of this method is that it identifies both the epistolary habits of people sending intelligence or secret missives and the patterns created in the data by acts of interception. Again, therefore, our methods encourage us to be attentive to the way in which our archive was created and the impact that this has on what we can know.

The Changing Diplomatic Profile

As discussed in the previous chapter, the characteristics of diplomatic personnel changed over the duration of the sixteenth century, from a group that was dominated by church leaders to a more lay contingent, who occupied the role in a professional capacity. Tommaso Spinelli was part of the change, and therefore he is a useful starting point for examining the network profile. His eight network measures for the reign of Henry VIII are provided in Table 4.1.

So, for his in-degree we can see that sixteen separate people write to Spinelli, giving him a ranking of 70, and placing him in the top 1.2% of people in the period 1509–47. If we think back to the nature of scale-free distribution discussed in Chapter 2, and the high differentiation in the top 2% of nodes, we can see that Spinelli has relatively high degree, very high strength, and even higher out-strength. His out-degree

Table 4.1 Tommaso Spinelli's network metrics

Metric	Score	Rank position	Top % of people
Total degree	24	92	1.6
Out-degree	8	163	2.8
In-degree	16	70	1.2
Total strength	457	23	0.4
Out-strength	434	11	0.2
In-strength	23	132	2.3
Eigenvector centrality	0.0377104239347	89	1.6
Betweenness centrality	0.000452362035105	128	2.2

(the number of people to whom he writes) and in-degree differ by a 1:2 ratio. But this is dwarfed by the divergence between his outgoing and incoming mail as it survives in the State Papers, which is approximately 19:1. More importantly, he has high betweenness centrality (which points towards his diplomatic bridging function) and even higher eigenvector centrality. As suggested above, this metric is a useful proxy for measuring proximity to power, and we can see that here it captures the fact that Spinelli's main correspondents are Cardinal Thomas Wolsey and Henry VIII. The table thus gives a concise summary of the epistolary behaviours of a resident ambassador, and structural advantages it can beget.

The concept of the network profile or fingerprint is that it allows us to measure in eight-dimensional space the people most similar across these metrics. There are two separate ways we can compute this. Our first approach calculates a fingerprint for a given individual by considering their ranks for the eight metrics and taking the logarithm of each.[5] The distance between two individuals is then simply the Euclidean (i.e. 'straight-line') distance between the two corresponding points in this eight-dimensional space. The second approach is to do the same with the additional step of *normalising* the fingerprint, meaning that we only consider (the logarithms of) the ranks for each network measure relative to each other for a given individual. For example, if one individual ranks high for in-degree, low for out-degree, medium for strength, etc., another individual for which all of these ranks are much lower but still display the same *relative* pattern (i.e. much higher in-degree than out-degree rank, with strength ranking in between, etc.) will *not* be regarded similar using the first approach, but *will* be if we use the second. The second approach is useful if we are comparing individuals over longer time scales across which total letter volumes in the archive may vary substantially. The approaches reveal subtly different things about what it means to be 'like' Spinelli. If we begin with *absolute* similarity for the reign of Henry VIII (1509–47), the twenty people with the most similar profiles (in rank order of most similar to least) can be found in Table 4.2.

With the exception of Rowland Lee, all the people in Table 4.2 served on diplomatic missions during the reign of Henry VIII (95%). If the aim of this kind of method was discovery of other diplomats, that would be a good result. But there are easier ways of finding other diplomats from the period.[6] More importantly it allows us to quantify the extent to which certain roles correspond to certain epistolary behaviours, that are in turn manifested in a particular network fingerprint. In this case, we can see that Henrician diplomats often have a moderately large network (degree), a large number of outgoing letters, but relatively few incoming (high out-strength, relatively low in-strength). In fact, as we know from the in-depth examination of Spinelli in the previous chapter, the majority of that high letter traffic tends to pass along only two edges: to the monarch and Principal Secretary.

---

[5] This last step reflects the highly skewed 'Zipfian' distribution of these measurements—rank 10 differs from rank 100 about as much as rank 100 does from rank 1,000.

[6] For example, via reference works like Gary M. Bell, *A Handlist of British Diplomatic Representatives 1509–1688* (Royal Historical Society, 1990).

Table 4.2 Ranked list of people with the most similar
(absolute) network profile to Tommaso Spinelli, 1509–47

Rank	Name
1	Sir Richard Wingfield
2	Edward Lee, Archbishop of York
3	John Clerk, Bishop of Bath and Wells
4	Stephen Vaughan
5	Rowland Lee, Bishop of Coventry and Lichfield
6	Robert Wingfield
7	Cardinal Girolamo Ghinucci
8	Nicholas Wotton
9	Sir Edward Carne
10	Christopher Mont
11	Cardinal Lorenzo Campeggio
12	William Knight
13	Sir William Lord Sands
14	Maximilian I
15	Richard Pace
16	Anthony Sentleger
17	Charles de Marillac
18	Sir Gregorio Casale
19	Charles Somerset, Earl of Worcester
20	Thomas Boleyn, Earl of Wiltshire and Ormond

This method can also help us to see if the diplomatic network profile changed over time. We might expect that widening our search period from Henry VIII's reign to the whole period of study would bring diplomats across the Tudor period to the fore. In fact, of the twenty most similar figures to Spinelli for the period 1509–1603, fifteen recur from the previous list, and two further people that are new to the list also served as diplomats during the Henrician period: Rodolfo Pio da Carpi, who was papal Nuncio at the court of Francis I 1535–7 before being made a cardinal, and François van der Delft, who was Imperial ambassador to the court of Henry VIII 1545–50. In other words Spinelli's surviving correspondence gives him a network profile that makes him much more similar to other diplomats from Henry's reign than diplomats from later reigns.

This result could be attributed, in part, to the varying survival rates of correspondence between the different reigns, as discussed in Chapter 2. The comparatively low survival rates of the secretaries' archives in reigns of Edward and Mary, compared to Henry's reign, and the proliferation of documentation in the Elizabethan period due to large surviving archives of Burghley, Walsingham, and Robert Cecil, mean that the reigns have internal cohesions that make comparisons between reigns more difficult. Nevertheless, the cross-period similarities where they arise are illuminating. Along with the seventeen diplomats from the Henrician period, there are three correspondents dating from the Elizabethan period: Sir Edward Barton, Sir Henry Neville, and Ottywell Smith. The former two follow the trend of the Henrician period in being formal diplomats: Barton was ambassador to the Ottoman Empire, and Neville was appointed Ambassador to France and attended the Court of Henri IV. Smith, by comparison, was an English merchant based in Dieppe who supplied intelligence to the government—what contemporaries would have called an 'intelligencer'.[7]

In fact, the function that Smith served is very similar to the kind of service that Spinelli provided early in his career. Of course, Spinelli too came from a mercantile family. As described in Chapter 3, there is an important relationship between early modern diplomacy, commerce, and news. Sanjay Subrahmanyam described the role of merchants as 'privileged intermediaries. The in-between class [...] inhabiting inter alia the meeting grounds created by European expansion'.[8] Smith was an English merchant based in Dieppe who communicated heavily with Robert Cecil (170 letters) and to a lesser degree, Francis Walsingham (36) and Robert Devereux, the Earl of Essex (11), providing valuable information regarding Henri IV's so-called 'Conquest of the kingdom' (1589–93).[9] Following his accession in 1589, the French king was not recognized by many of his Catholic subjects, and he was forced to fight against a Catholic League, aided by Spain. Smith's case is instructive: his value as an intelligencer was directly entangled with his role as a merchant. He had previously been driven out of Rouen with other merchants by the Leaguers, and was a firm supporter of the idea of besieging Rouen, a position which he advised both in his contact with Henri and in the letters he dispatched to Walsingham and Robert Cecil. Smith's access to the king seems to derive from his ability to supply what Henri needed: in a letter from the king dated 16 February 1590, he asks Smith to send him 'powdre pour mon armée' (powder for my army) within twelve days.[10] Smith encloses the letter in a report to Walsingham, detailing how the king had summoned all forces to join him before the end of the month, and asking how he should proceed.[11] On 10 October 1590 the king sent for Smith and told him that he would gladly besiege Rouen if he had 200,000 crowns to pay his strangers. Smith reportedly replied that the king should write to Elizabeth asking to borrow the amount from the merchants from London, Lancashire, Yorkshire, Devonshire, and Wales, who had a vested interest because by Rouen 'doth stand all the trade and utterance of all the cloth that is made in those quarters'.[12] This made economic sense: there was a real threat that lack of sales could drive these merchants into debt, which would not only affect their personal livelihoods but also the English economy, with lost customs on goods moving out and in. The intelligence Smith shared both with Henri and the Tudor government was inflected by the role he understood trade to play in international relations. Such trade should be understood both in the metaphorical sense of trading allegiances, faith, and personal credit, and in the most material terms.

---

[7] The uncertainty of what to call Smith has led to him being described, amongst other things, as an 'unofficial agent'. See Wallace T. MacCaffrey, *Elizabeth I: War and Politics, 1588–1603* (Princeton University Press, 1994), p. 157.

[8] Sanjay Subrahmanyam, 'Introduction', in *Merchant Networks in the Early Modern World*, ed. Subrahmanyam (Variorum, 1996), p. xiii.

[9] See R. J. Knecht, *The French Civil Wars, 1562–1598* (Longman, 2000), chapter 12.   [10] SP 78/21 f.83.

[11] SP 78/21 f.79.

[12] *List and Analysis of State Papers, Foreign Series: Elizabeth I*, ed. Richard Bruce Wernham, 6 vols. (HM Stationery Office, 1964–89), vol. 1, Analysis 470. See also R. B. Wernham, *After the Armada: Elizabethan England and the Struggle for Western Europe, 1588–1595* (Clarendon Press, 1984), p. 262.

Table 4.3 Ranked list of people with the most similar
(relative) network profile to Tommaso Spinelli, 1509–1603

Rank	Name
1	William Stallenge
2	Sebastian Giustinian
3	Thomas Stokes
4	Otwell Johnson
5	Richard Wingfield
6	Robert Wingfield
7	Clerk
8	Rowland Lee
9	Georges Fremyn
10	Pace
11	Miguel Mai
12	Pietro Bizzarri
13	Sir Ralph Winwood
14	Eustace Chapuys
15	Vaughan
16	Ghinucci
17	James Hudson
18	Pedro Ortiz
19	William Knight, Bishop of Bath and Wells
20	George Lawson
21	Richard Johnson
22	Richard Camarden
23	Anthony Cave
24	John Hilsey, Bishop of Rochester
25	Katherine Bertie, Duchess of Suffolk
26	Stafford
27	Sir John Hackett
28	Richard Clough
29	William Lyly
30	Leonard Grey, Lord Deputy of Ireland

The Smith correlation is not an anomaly. Figures like Smith come to the fore more
frequently when we use *relative* similarity, our second approach, which will group
together fingerprints that share the same relative pattern of ranks. If we search the
whole period of study for the most similar figures to Spinelli using this relative similarity measure, the top thirty results returned are (in rank order of most similar to
least) found in Table 4.3.

The ranked list lacks the homogeneity of that produced using *absolute* similarity.
Like the previous ranking, the list is dominated by diplomats (2, 5, 6, 7, 10, 11, 13, 14,
15, 16, 18, 19, 26, and 27) and royal agents (17 and 24),[13] but they are joined by seven
merchants, a captain, a historian, and a personal servant to an ambassador. Despite

---

[13] John Hilsey acted as an agent for the promotion of Henry VIII's reformation, and James Hudson acted as
resident agent for James VI of Scotland in London (but, as demonstrated by the content of his numerous letters
to Robert Cecil and Walsingham, also provided intelligence for the English government). Thompson, 'Hilsey,
John (d. 1539)', *ODNB*, <https://doi.org/10.1093/ref:odnb/13325>. Hudson only receives passing reference in
scholarship. See, for example, Paul E. J. Hammer, *The Polarisation of Elizabethan Politics: The Political Career of
Robert Devereux, 2nd Earl of Essex, 1585–1597* (Cambridge University Press, 1999), p. 168.

this explicit variation, however, what we observe from the letters is a striking continuity of *function*. In the previous chapter we argued that ambassador is not a job but a function. Similarly, this diverse group of men is dominated by figures marshalled by the government to keep abreast of intelligence abroad.[14] Of the seven merchants in this list—Stallenge, Stokes, Otwell Johnson, Richard Johnson, Camarden, Cave, Clough—four seem to have been regular intelligencers (the exceptions being the Johnsons and Cave). The dominance of this group is even more striking when we add that (like Spinelli) Vaughan and Hackett both began as merchants before becoming royal agents, and then diplomats.[15] The other identified intelligencers on this list include: Fremyn, a French captain, later governor of Saftingen, who was a regular correspondent and intelligencer for Walsingham;[16] Bizzarri, a historian and intelligencer for William Cecil, Lord Burghley, Francis Walsingham, and also the Elector August of Saxony (discussed further below); and Lyly, personal servant and agent to Stafford, resident ambassador to France, who was entrusted with some of the ambassador's 'most critical intelligence functions'.[17] Of the top thirty, then, at least twenty-four served as intelligencers.

If we are to compare the success of the two models for finding people who are similar in terms of job description, the absolute measures are slightly better than the relative measures (95% versus ~87%). If our aim was simply to find a predictive model for finding diplomats and intelligencers, we would choose the former. However, if we wanted to ask questions about the profile of the diplomatic corps over time, from the beginning of the period of this study until its end, the relative measure might be more useful. The absolute measure found relatively few Elizabethan examples (just two), whereas the relative measures included people with a comparable distribution across the reigns of Henry and Elizabeth, with a few letters dating from the reigns of Edward and Mary too. However, that greater distribution is due to the presence of merchants and intelligencers in the list: of the sixteen diplomats and royal agents identified by the relative measure, only Winwood, and Hudson did not serve during the Henrician reign; and the heterogenous body of intelligencers made up of merchants, captains, historians, and servants are all Elizabethan. This may imply that the diplomatic network profile changed over the period of the sixteenth century, becoming less like

---

[14] Those that do not include Rowland Lee (discussed above), a Lord Deputy of Ireland (Grey), an administrator in Yorkshire (Lawson), a patron and devout Protestant (Duchess of Suffolk), and two merchants (the Johnsons). Of course, communication such as that produced by Grey and Lawson functions, like foreign intelligence reports, to communicate information across the government's administrative arms, and therefore produces a similar network profile.

[15] Vaughan was an active member of the Merchant Adventurers. See W. C. Richardson, *Stephen Vaughan, Financial Agent of Henry VIII: A Study of Financial Relations with the Low Countries* (Louisiana State University Press, 1953), and Ian Blanchard, 'Vaughan, Stephen (b. in or before 1502, d. 1549)', *ODNB*, <https://doi.org/10.1093/ref:odnb/28146>. On Hackett, who began as an Irish wool merchant, see *The Letters of Sir John Hackett, 1526–1534*, ed. Elizabeth Frances Rogers (Morgantown, West Virginia University Library, 1971).

[16] *The Correspondence of Sir Philip Sidney*, ed. Roger Kuin, vol. 1 (Oxford University Press, 2012), pp. xlii–xliii. On the wider role of soldiers and other military figures for intelligence, see Nina Lamal, 'Communicating Conflict: Early Modern Soldiers as Information-Gatherers', *Journal of Medieval and Early Modern Studies* 50 (2020), 13–31.

[17] See Dennis Flynn, *John Donne and the Ancient Catholic Nobility* (Indiana University Press, 1995), p. 150. Lyly was also the subject of considerable suspicion due to his fraternisation with leading figures within the exiled Catholic community, which will be discussed further in the following chapters. See also Alan Haynes, *Walsingham: Elizabethan Spymaster & Statesman*, e-book (The History Press, 2007), chapter 10.

Spinelli's. Considering this possibility, what is striking is that the person with the most similar profile is William Stallenge, a merchant located at the new Plymouth haven, who collected intelligence for Robert Cecil from Brittany, Spain, and Portugal from 1595 until the end of the reign. Indeed, of the top four, three are merchants.[18]

What could it mean that Spinelli is more 'like' the merchant-intelligencers of the Elizabethan era than the special ambassadors of his own era in terms of his network profile? It is not a coincidence that Spinelli is a transitional figure. As discussed in the previous chapter, in this period we see the rise of the resident ambassador who, in Alan Stewart's words 'is split between two essential tasks: acting as an ambassador, with all the court entertainment and protocol that entailed, and acting as an intelligence gatherer and disseminator of news'.[19] Before Spinelli there had been a distinct division of these tasks; as we saw, he petitioned Wolsey to be entrusted with negotiation, but for most of his career Spinelli was stuck in the role of the news disseminator. A better term might be an information funneller: his network is limited in size and the vast majority of intelligence passes almost exclusively in one direction, outwards, towards Wolsey and the king.

We can see how these roles became more integrated by looking at a resident ambassador from the middle of Elizabeth's reign. We came to Spinelli by observing his high ranking for betweenness in the first decade of Henry's reign. If we look at a figure of similar *ranking* (as opposed to raw score) for betweenness in the 1580s, we find another resident ambassador at around the same rank position: Robert Bowes (ranking 35th, compared to Spinelli at 29 for the period 1509–19). Bowes was resident ambassador in Scotland during the years 1577–83, after having served as Treasurer of Berwick, and his diplomatic career can be traced through the many letters to and from him that survive.[20] He sent 894 letters to 57 people, and received 468 letters from 63 people, giving him the scores for the decade 1 January 1580–31 December 1589 shown in Table 4.4.

Table 4.4 Robert Bowe's network metrics

Metric	Score	Rank position	Top % of people
Total degree	42	27	0.5
Out-degree	15	30	0.6
In-degree	27	26	0.5
Total strength	408	12	0.2
Out-strength	300	10	0.2
In-strength	108	16	0.3
Eigenvector centrality	0.0801268780027	17	0.3
Betweenness centrality	0.00116855121318	35	0.7

[18] <http://www.historyofparliamentonline.org/volume/1558-1603/member/stallenge-william-1545> (accessed 15/05/2020).

[19] Alan Stewart, 'Francis Bacon's Bi-literal Cipher and the Materiality of Early Modern Diplomatic Writing', in *Diplomacy and Early Modern Culture*, ed. Robyn Adams and Roseanna Cox (Palgrave Macmillan, 2011), pp. 120–34 (p. 121).

[20] See C. A. McGladdery, 'Bowes, Robert (d. 1597)', *ODNB*, <https://doi.org/10.1093/ref:odnb/3059>.

While the ranking for betweenness is similar to Spinelli's, however, we can see that Bowes's raw scores are much higher, and that he is in a higher percentage bracket for every score (within the top ~0.7% or higher). He has many more connections than Spinelli (total degree of 42 as compared to 23), but perhaps more important is the difference in the ratio between his out- and in-strength, which is approximately 3:1 (compared to Spinelli's ~19:1). While the hub-like nature of Bowes can be in part attributed to the volume of his correspondence that survives, deposited in the Cottonian and Harleian Collections in the British Library,[21] it also seems to suggest that Bowes more successfully integrated the two essential tasks described by Stewart: as ambassador and news disseminator. If successfully managed, the role of resident ambassador could form a powerful stepping-stone into the most important administrative office of the period: many principal secretaries served for a period as resident ambassadors (several of them in France), before or after their period in office, including Stephen Gardiner, Ralph Sadler, Thomas Smith, Nicholas Wotton, Francis Walsingham, and William Davison.[22]

The increasing hubishness of the resident ambassador, however, has a corollary. The more the role became institutionalised, the less likely the holder was to be embedded in local informal intelligence networks. It is therefore unsurprising that the institutionalisation of the resident ambassador should coincide with the rising prominence of informal intelligencers in our data for the Elizabethan period, as they could supply some of the structural function of figures like Spinelli. It implies an expansion and diversification of the diplomatic corps in the Elizabethan period, one that recognised the necessary differences, both in terms of acceptability and lawfulness, between 'diplomacy and illicit intelligences'. As Filippo de Vivo notes, these were 'mutually necessary activities, and the growth of the former entailed an increase in the latter'.[23] Various studies have shed light on the more dramatic stories of espionage and counter-espionage that the Elizabethan archives yield. But what we are seeing here is the emergence of a particular body of intelligencers from the shadows. In Spinelli's letters we read about the (often anonymous) network of informants that supplied his information on the ground. But the Elizabethan secretaries increasingly sought to cut out the middleman, communicating directly with these kinds of informants, who in turn sought to use their skill for their own personal and professional advancement.

In the next section of this chapter we will look at the history of Pietro Bizzarri—one of the informants shown to be 'similar' to Spinelli (ranked 12th). His case usefully illustrates how different kinds of people became assets to the Tudor government due to their location or travel, and how that confluence of aims (in his case scholarship and intelligencing) often became densely interwoven. In focusing on a single case study we also wish to make a point about the relationship between the use of

---

[21] See *The Correspondence of Robert Bowes, of Aske, Esquire, the Ambassador of Queen Elizabeth in the Court of Scotland*, ed. Revd J. Stevenson (J. B. Nichols and Son, 1842).
[22] See Bell, *Handlist*, E42, F58, F75, F86, F100, F117–18, F121–2, LC36, LC67, SC23.
[23] Filippo de Vivo, *Information and Communication in Venice: Rethinking Early Modern Politics* (Oxford University Press, 2007), p. 75.

quantitative approaches, which can allow us to understand abstract aggregate patterns about the structural similarity of intelligencers, and close study of contingent and particular histories. While the particularity of Bizzarri's colourful biography seems to defy reduction to a simple data point, we can begin to see how the features of his narrative and letters make him structurally almost indistinguishable from the merchants, the captain, and the servant alongside whom he was ranked.

Pietro Bizzarri's 'Knowledge Transactions'

The intelligencers highlighted by our method for finding similar network profiles constitute just a handful of the army of informants marshalled in the Elizabethan period by Walsingham, Burghley, Robert Cecil, and, to a lesser extent, the Earl of Essex. They were merchants, soldiers, servants, and another sub-category, which Lisa Jardine and William Sherman dubbed 'the scholarly reader'. These scholars were offering what Jardine and Sherman call 'knowledge transactions': information in exchange for paid service in the employ of key political leaders, career advancement, or simply permission to travel.[24] This category has received some limited attention: Elizabeth Williamson has highlighted the role of the educational traveller in the intelligence corps in the final decades of the sixteenth century;[25] and Will Tosh has shown that '[a]s continental travel became more popular amongst elite young men in the sixteenth century, permission to depart increasingly came with a condition: well-connected travellers were expected to send home intelligence from foreign countries'.[26] While the examples highlighted by Jardine, Sherman, Tosh, and Williamson largely date from the 1580s and 1590s, we can see evidence of this kind of knowledge transaction occurring as early as the 1560s in the case of Bizzarri.

Bizzarri was born in 1525, probably in Sassoferrato in Umbria, Italy, and was educated in Venice, where he converted to Protestantism. As a result of his reformist faith, he travelled to Germany, and then to England and Scotland, where he spent time in Cambridge as a fellow, and subsequently at the courts of Edward VI, Elizabeth I, and Mary Stuart with his friend and patron Francis Russell, hoping to 'build a career as a poet and courtier'.[27] His relevance to this study, however, emerges when in 1564 he sought to leave England to pursue a career as a writer, and proposed a 'knowledge transaction' with Elizabeth's Principal Secretary, William Cecil.

---

[24] Lisa Jardine and William Sherman, 'Pragmatic Readers: Knowledge Transactions and Scholarly Services in Late Elizabethan England', in *Religion, Culture and Society in Early Modern Britain: Essays in Honour of Patrick Collinson*, ed. Anthony Fletcher and Peter Roberts (Cambridge University Press, 1994), pp. 102–24.

[25] Elizabeth Williamson, '"Fishing after News" and the Ars Apodemica: The Intelligencing Role of the Educational Traveller in the Late Sixteenth Century', in *News Networks in Early Modern Europe*, ed. Noah Moxham and Joad Raymond (Brill, 2016), pp. 542–62.

[26] Will Tosh, *Male Friendship and Testimonies of Love in Shakespeare's England* (Palgrave Macmillan, 2016), p. 10.

[27] Kenneth R. Bartlett, 'Bizzarri, Pietro (b. 1525, d. in or after 1586)', *ODNB*, <https://doi.org/10.1093/ref:odnb/2487>. The fullest biography of Bizzarri's career can be found in Massimo Firpo, *Pietro Bizzarri, esule italiano del cinquecento* (Giappichelli, 1971). See also Nicolas Barker, 'The Perils of Publishing in the Sixteenth Century: Pietro Bizari and William Parry, Two Elizabethan Misfits', in *England and the Continental Renaissance: Essays in Honour of J. B. Trapp*, ed. Edward Chaney and Peter Mack (Boydell and Brewer, 1990), pp. 125–42.

In a letter dated 12 June 1564, we learn that he is in receipt of a prebend worth £20 a year, which he would like to continue to receive with an increase while he travels to Venice or Lyons to oversee the printing of his writings. His justification for why he should be subsidised for furthering his own writing career is: 'because I think there is no place in Europe, and no better time, to gain knowledge of affairs that are beneficial to kings and princes, as experience shows us daily'.[28] In other words, he proposes to Cecil that he be permitted to pursue his literary career with the security of a stipend, while the government would gain from the intelligence he is able to gather in these locations. From the government's perspective his literary career is beside the point: what he is offering is information for money.

The government clearly saw the benefit of his proposal, for in the second letter we have from Bizzarri to Cecil he is already en route to Venice.[29] Whether it was Bizzarri or Cecil who decided on the location as opposed to Lyons is unclear, but the choice has a strategic benefit for the Tudor government because, at that time, there was no official diplomatic presence in Venice.[30] Bizzarri therefore presented a key opportunity to fill a knowledge vacuum. Moreover, Venice was a location of strategic importance for the movement of regional and international news in the early modern period. It occupied a position of trading centrality, with a pivotal role in three areas of trade: cloth with London and Bruges, wool with Spain, and cotton and spices with Egypt and the Levant. This fact shows too why merchants like Spinelli, Cuthbert Vaughan, Hackett, Stallenge, Stokes, and Clough provided such valuable assets for the government. The betweenness of Venice, however, was not only geographic, but also political and religious: Filipo de Vivo notes that, '[l]ocked between opposite blocks—Bourbons and Hapsburgs, Catholics and Protestants, Christians and Turks—Venice became an arena for espionage not wholly unlike central European capitals during the Cold War'.[31] The added benefit for Cecil was that Bizzarri was an Italian native who had been educated in Venice, giving him access to local networks that an English ambassador would have been unlikely to be able to penetrate.

As soon as he arrived in Venice, by the beginning of March 1565, Bizzarri began producing regular intelligence communications, which were sent on a weekly basis to coincide with the dispatch of the Imperial Post (leading to his relatively high out-strength of 202 letters).[32] The very format of these newsletters shows the valuable infrastructural position of Venice in the trade of news. Bizzarri's first letter from Venice contains a one-page digest of news of the affairs of Venice, Turkey, Spain, Naples, Mantua, Genoa, and Transylvania. In later letters, these bulletins become more detailed and take on a format we are more accustomed to seeing in early newspapers, or *avvisi*. The form of the *avviso* had emerged out of merchant letters and

---

[28] '*Et auidem existimo nullum esse in europa locum qui sit magis aptus et opportunus rebus cognoscendis, quam uero istud omnibus Principibus ac Regibus perutile sit, quotidiana experientia testatur*', SP 15/12 f.23r.

[29] Bizzarri to Cecil, 24 November 1564, SP 70/75 f.96.   [30] See Bell, *Handlist*, p. 289.

[31] De Vivo, *Information and Communication in Venice*, p. 74.

[32] On Imperial Post, see Nikolaus Schobesberger, Paul Arblaster, Mario Infelise, André Belo, Noah Moxham, Carmen Espejo, and Joad Raymond, 'European Postal Networks', in *News Networks in Early Modern Europe*, ed. Noah Moxham and Joad Raymond (Brill, 2016), pp. 19–63.

been, in Mario Infelise's words, 'gradually perfected' during the late fifteenth and early sixteenth centuries until it reached a format that would remain consistent for several decades: 'one or more sheets with news organised according to the place where it had been collected rather than the place where the event recorded had in fact taken place'.[33] Bizzarri's letters took a near identical form. For example, in his letter to Cecil on 27 May 1565 we can see that news is grouped under headings that detail the geographic origin of the news, and the date on which it was dispatched from that location: 'Da Roma li 19 di Maggio'; 'Da Madrile li 29 di Aprile'; 'Da Genoua li vi di Maggio'; 'Da Genoua li xi di Maggio'; and 'Di Vienna li xvii di Maggio'.[34] The headings illustrate Bizzarri's position at the intersection of these converging communication networks, and thus the value of his position in Venice—the perfect embodiment of his betweenness.[35] The change of format from his first letters might suggest he was influenced by the form of the intelligence he received. We know, from the large number of *avvisi* surviving in the Elizabethan state papers, that diplomats and intelligencers not only received *avvisi secreti* (confidential handwritten newsletters) but also *avvisi publici* (handwritten and printed newsletters to which it was possible to subscribe), from which they collated selected items. Bizzarri clearly participated in this news market.

The contents of Bizzarri's communications contain a significant focus on the progress of wars. His reports on Turkish battles at sea and on land must have been valuable; news from Turkey was rarer than, for example, news from Antwerp. The military minutiae detailed in these letters makes for dry reading, but between these items we occasionally find fascinating stories and events that seem more akin to myth than documentary such as news from the Imperial Camp in Hungary, which comprises a narrative strikingly reminiscent of the biblical story of Daniel in the lion's den.[36] Such news is passed on without commentary; neither does Bizzarri provide analysis of the battles. Bizzarri's primary function, then, is as a news-forwarding service. In this way, then, his function is very typical of the extra-diplomatic intelligencer, and this is manifested in his network metadata, and the way it closely resembles Spinelli's: two edges shared with government hubs, with very high traffic, and a handful of weaker edges. Bizzarri's principal correspondent before 1576 is Cecil (to whom he sends 128 letters); and thereafter it is Francis Walsingham (65 letters). The other people in the correspondence network described in the state papers archive are William Davison, at

---

[33] Mario Infelise, 'From Merchants' Letters to Handwritten Political *avvisi*: Notes on the Origins of Public Information', in *Cultural Exchange in Early Modern in Europe*, vol. 3, *Correspondence and Cultural Exchange in Early Modern Europe, 1400–1700*, ed. Francisco Bethencourt and Florike Egmond (Cambridge University Press, 2007), pp. 41–2 (p. 40).

[34] Bizzarri to Cecil, 27 May 1565, SP 70/78 f.104.

[35] They also suggest the relative distances and time it took for news to travel from those locations. The news from Madrid, for example, had taken almost an entire month to reach Bizzarri's news digest, whereas the news from Vienna was only ten days old. For an analysis of what this paragraph structure (origins and dates) can reveal about how information travelled, see Yann Ciarán Ryan, '"More Difficult from Dublin than from Dieppe": Ireland and Britain in a European Network of Communication', *Media History* 24 (2018), 458–76.

[36] A letter to Walsingham dated 4 August 1576 (SP 70/139 f.71) informs the reader that, on the order of 'Bassa Budensis' (the Bassa of Buda), an Arian soldier had been tied to the stake and a fierce lion let loose on him. The lion, after he had torn off his shoes without injuring the soldier, tore his own keeper to pieces; the bystanders interceded for the captive, because of his miraculous escape, and the Bassa consented to set him at liberty.

that time Walsingham's secretary (to whom he wrote 3 letters); Elizabeth I (to whom he wrote 2); the diplomat Robert Beale (2), his friend the Earl of Bedford (1), and one John Sheres, a gentleman who also furnished Cecil with news from Venice, amongst other places (1). Bizzarri also receives two letters from della Roche, the informant Bizzarri left in his place when he left Venice for Lyons in 1568.

However, while the structure of Bizzarri's network might be very standard for intelligencers, his personal history is more unique, and explains why he has been the subject of a book-length history (in Italian) by Massimo Firpo. From the government's perspective the knowledge transaction they had entered into with Bizzarri was a stipend in exchange for intelligence; but Bizzarri also hoped that his service would be rewarded with literary patronage. The pairing of intelligence reports and petitions for patronage was a strategy he also employed with Augustus Elector of Saxony, for whom he also acted as an intelligencer (although that material falls outside the purview of this current archive).[37] This had no material effect on the shape of his network, but it meant that along the edges that his news reports travelled, we can also trace the passage of new writings, often dedicated to their recipients. In a letter to Cecil, dated 2 June 1565, he informs him that he had published his treatise *De principe tractatus*, dedicated to Her Majesty, and *De bella et pace*, dedicated to Mary I of Scotland, along with some other works, one of which is inscribed to Cecil.[38] On 1 August he sends a copy of the former, along with three copies of *Petri Bizzari Poemata* (for Cecil, Lord Dudley, and John Ashley), which contain poems in praise of Cecil's wife and sisters, and of the chancellor, and asks Cecil to be his patron and Mecænas (*'mihi Patronum et mecoenatem praebeas'*).[39] Mecænas was the ally, friend, and political adviser to Octavian as well as being an important patron for the new generation of Augustan poets, including Horace. In thus addressing Cecil he is requesting him to act as a broker between himself and the queen. On the same date he also sent a copy of *De principe tractatus* to the queen, with a copy of his Latin poems.[40] The combined aim of these two letters is clear: to secure royal patronage, and to enjoy the publicity that such an endorsement brought with it. Bizzarri's petitions for Tudor endorsement continued throughout his career, with his final letter on 23 November 1586 entirely devoted to the promotion of his writings.[41] Royal patronage, of course, was the aim of many writers, and the strategy of dedication was standard.[42] It was less often coupled, however, with intelligence gathering.

---

[37] Bizzarri served as an intelligencer for Augustus, Elector of Saxony, after proposing a similar knowledge transaction to that he proffered to Cecil. With the help of Hubert Languet, he dedicated to Augustus the new Latin translation of his history of the Hungarian war (previously composed and published in Italian), and then offered his services as an intelligencer. While he appears to have been quite open about his dual intelligencing role with Cecil and Walsingham (we find mentions of this relationship especially in Bizzarri's later letters), we cannot capture the extent of this German network because the newsletters to the elector fall within another archival jurisdiction. For further discussion, see Firpo, *Pietro Bizzarri*.

[38] SP 70/78 f.125.   [39] SP 70/79 f.85.   [40] SP 70/79 f.83.   [41] SP 84/11 f.8.

[42] On literary patronage, see Richard Anthony McCabe, *'Ungainefull Arte': Poetry, Patronage, and Print in the Early Modern Era* (Oxford University Press, 2016); Heidi Brayman Hackel, *Reading Material in Early Modern England: Print, Gender, and Literacy* (Cambridge University Press, 2005); and Jason Scott Warren, *Sir John Harington and the Book as Gift* (Oxford University Press, 2001).

The fact that the networks that Bizzarri used for the funnelling of news coincided with those he sought to utilise for literary patronage suggests that we should see Bizzarri's dual activities as more integrally connected than has been previously acknowledged. The small body of scholarship that has focused on Bizzarri has tended to place an emphasis on *either* the political aspect of his career or his literary output.[43] However, their entanglement can be demonstrated by one of the more colourful episodes from Bizzarri's travels. Following the publication of his Persian history 1583, which he had dedicated to the Elector of Saxony, Bizzarri sought passage with a merchant boat travelling to Cologne so that he might present a copy to his patron in person. However, his ship was captured on the Rhine by Catholic soldiers serving Charles de Ligne, 2nd Prince of Arenberg (a leading aristocrat of the Habsburg Netherlands), and Bizzarri was robbed, imprisoned, and then brought before the general. In a letter dated 31 March, he describes this meeting to Walsingham, and how he sought to use his literary activity as a cover, saying he was 'neither trader, nor soldier, nor gentleman, but only a poor wayfarer, and that I devoted myself to studies, as one of the correctors of the press to Mr. Christopher Plantin'.[44] However, one of the Walloons interjects that Plantin had printed many books in favour of the Prince of Orange, and in dispraise of the king, Philip II, to which Bizzarri responds that he was not a regular corrector: but only for a Latin work of his own, entitled *Historia Rerum Persicarum*, which he says he was going to sell at the Frankfurt Fair (eliding his intention to visit the Elector).[45] Upon hearing this the general and other bystanders ask to see this book, which Bizzarri informs them had been in the hold of the boat with his other writings. However, as we learn from a subsequent letter written from Antwerp, Bizzarri was very fortunate that all these writings had been destroyed by his captors, who tore them up and threw the pages into the Rhine. Crucially, amongst those books was a recently completed manuscript of a long verse 'exhortation' to the 'states of this country' (the provinces of the Netherlands and specifically the Southern Catholic provinces that remained loyal to Phillip II) recounting the tyrannies of the Spaniard and the bad government of the French, and adjuring them to abandon France and Spain, and put themselves under the protection of England and Denmark. Had such a text been discovered and read it would have placed Bizzarri in extreme danger: he writes that he would have been straightway reduced to dust and ashes ('*polvere e cenere*') if they had been found.[46]

The description of this lost work points to a strong continuity between the intelligence forwarded in Bizzarri's newsletters and his literary output. While Bizzarri's

---

[43] See Barker, 'The Perils of Publishing', p. 125. Barker distinguishes between the 'political aspects of Bizari's career', which is the focus of his chapter, and the literary aspects, which he says is the focus of Firpo's monograph on Bizzarri. Aside from the *ODNB* article, the Firpo and Barker pieces have been the only focused studies we have been able to find; other scholarship touching on Bizzarri tends to mention him only in passing as the source of information regarding other people or events.

[44] '*non era ne mercante, ne soldato, ne gentil-huomo, ma solamente un pouero viandante, et [sic] che attendena agli studi, con esser uno de correttori della stampa de M. Christoforo Plantino*'. For the full account see Bizzarri to Walsingham, 31 March 1583, SP 83/18 f.106.

[45] '*non era correttori ordinario: ma solamente d'una mia opera Latina intitolata Historia rerum Persicarum*'.

[46] Bizzarri to Walsingham, 5/15 July 1583, SP 83/19 f.155.

works are normally classed as histories, this example shows the contemporaneity of this work and so many of the other writings he published: these events were part of the ongoing Dutch Revolt, which would play out over eighty years.[47] Moreover, Bizzarri makes it clear that his account had a clear political and religious point of view, siding with the northern provinces who had rebelled against Spanish rule, and who, under the rule of the Calvinist-dominated separatists, gradually converted to Protestantism. It was not a disinterested account but rather an active piece of political propaganda that had a particular end in mind. As if to underline the pressing relevance of these verses, Bizzarri describes how, in being captured by the very Catholic forces against whom he had been writing, he finds himself part of this unfolding history, and is saved only by God's favour.

In this account we can, therefore, see how Bizzarri's access to the most recent and accurate intelligence not only allowed him to fulfil his obligations to the Tudor government and Elector August, it also provided material for his commercial literary output. His privileged access in Venice to information on Turkish military developments prompted the composition of *Historia della guerra fatta in Ungheria* in 1566, which follows the events of the (then current) Turkish-imperial confrontation in Hungary, and has been described by Kenneth R. Bartlett as being written in an 'almost journalistic style'.[48] Similarly, when *Cyprium bellum* was published in 1573, Cyprus had just been conquered by the Turks, and Bizzarri was communicating the latest news on these events from Augsburg.[49] The common emphasis on information and contemporaneity in both of Bizzarri's roles shows how the efforts he took to serve the Tudor government affected his literary activity. The role of intelligencer in the first instance may well have been opportunistically seized by Bizzarri to help him facilitate his literary ambitions with a stipend, but his literary and intelligencing roles gradually converged. To describe this continuity of interests, we might think about the modern use of the word 'correspondent', as one employed by a journal or news outlet to contribute news and other materials.[50] While such a role had not been fully conceived of in this period, Bizzarri might be argued to function as a proto-correspondent.[51]

By focusing on Bizzarri's narrative we gain a sense of the exceptionality of his life: the drama, the prolific literary output, the religious and political aspirations of those writings, and his value as an intelligencer to two courts. But Bizzarri's access to the material for his literary outputs is a direct result of his embeddedness within an established information economy: his access to novel information relied on pre-existing news networks, on travelling along existing trade routes, and being stationed in places

---

[47] Further analysis of Tudor intelligence on the Dutch Revolt is undertaken in Chapter 5.

[48] Bartlett, 'Bizzarri, Pietro (b. 1525, d. in or after 1586)'.

[49] See, for example, SP 70/127 f.59r–v and SP 70/127 f.105r–v.

[50] The first usage of the word 'correspondent' in the *OED* to mean one who contributes letters to a newspaper or journal—specifically, one employed by a journal to contribute news and other material to its columns from some particular place—is dated 1711.

[51] Scholarship on the history of the news recognises how closely intertwined is the history of early modern postal networks and epistolary culture. See, for example, Schobesberger et al., 'European Postal Networks', and Nicholas Brownlees, '"Newes also came by Letters": Functions and Features of Epistolary News in English News Publications of the Seventeenth Century', in *News Networks*, ed. Moxham and Raymond, pp. 19–63, and 394–419.

at the centre of unfolding events. In those ways his network looks largely indistin-guishable from those of soldiers and merchants fulfilling the same function. As such we should consider that structural similarity in tandem with the exceptionality of individuals who made up this diverse cohort of intelligence producers. There is an important extent to which different experience and skills were linked to the different needs that the government had in terms of the supply of domain-specific information. For example, Sherman's taxonomy of Elizabethan intelligence producers attempts to lay out the breadth of their occupations: scholars, secretaries/clerks, merchants, lawyers/antiquaries, architects/surveyors, military men, ecclesiastical leaders, and foreign intelligence.[52] It is true that the intelligence service was compiled of these various men, and that the intelligence they produced corresponded with the particular kinds of access and specialist skills. However, what we can see by thinking about the struc-tural similarities between Spinelli, Bizzarri, and merchant-intelligencers identified above is that such labels can act to mask important parallels in the way that informa-tion was funnelled to the Tudor government. This emphasises what a number of scholars have come to agree on recently: that is, as Robyn Adams has put it, the 'elastic and fluid nature of information gathering and exchange' in early modern England.[53] Stephen Alford writes: 'there was no kind of distinction between the gathering of intelligence at home or abroad or between intelligence, security work and counter-espionage. The secret reports on Walsingham's desk in the 1580s could range from letters by diplomats to the reports of informants working close to English Catholic families.'[54]

Against Taxonomies

By developing methods to examine the level of similarity between different corres-pondents' communication habits, we can in a sense measure the amount of flex in that 'elastic and fluid nature' that Adams describes. In doing so we can begin to see that these are not bounded categories, but rather that information exchange occurred across a greyscale of subtle and often obscure differentiation: formal diplomacy shades into more informal intelligence networks, which in turn shade into the murky terri-tory of double agents and conspirators. We can begin to see those gradations by com-paring the most similar people to Spinelli with the cohort of figures that most resemble Bizzarri. For example, the fifteen people most similar (by the absolute measure) to Bizzarri in the Elizabethan period are ranked in Table 4.5.

From the ranked list in Table 4.5 emerges a diverse cast including military leaders (7, 8, 10, 13, 14), men in the service of diplomats (1, 4, 15), merchants (3, 5, 15),

---

[52] Sherman, 'Research Intelligence', p. 100.

[53] Robyn Adams, 'A Most Secret Service: William Herle and the Circulation of News', in *Diplomacy and Early Modern Culture*, ed. Adams and Cox, pp. 63–81 (p. 64).

[54] Stephen Alford, 'Some Elizabethan Spies in the Office of Sir Francis Walsingham', in *Diplomacy and Early Modern Culture*, ed. Adams and Cox, pp. 46–62 (p. 48).

Table 4.5 Ranked list of people with the most similar (absolute) network profile to Pietro Bizzarri, 1558–1603

Rank	Name
1	Lyly
2	Edmund Palmer
3	Stokes
4	Roger Aston
5	Stallenge
6	Sir Ferdinando Gorges
7	Sir William Browne
8	Georges Fremyn
9	Thomas Copley
10	Captain Cockburn
11	Sir Dennis O'Roughan
12	John Lee
13	Sir Edmund Uvedale
14	Cuthbert Vaughan
15	Edward Grimeston

priests, and other 'agents'. As we look carefully at their letters, however, we can observe that all but one (Copley) of these fifteen men are involved in reporting to the government. For example, Edmund Palmer, described in the Calendar of State Papers as a priest, was a double agent located mainly in Saint-Jean-de-Luz, a port on the French–Spanish border, and sent intelligence reports on the Spanish to Walsingham (9 letters), Burghley (18), and his son Robert Cecil (24).[55] Sir Dennis O'Roughan was a double-agent Catholic priest, first used by the Lord Deputy of Ireland Sir John Perrott as a priest-catcher, and then by Perrott's successor, Sir William Fitzwilliam, to accuse Perrott of being a crypto-papist Spanish spy, on which topic he wrote 36 letters to Burghley and 3 to Elizabeth I.[56] And John Lee was an agent in Antwerp, posted there perhaps first in a military capacity, who sent reports to Burghley (38 letters) and his son Cecil (12) on the activities of the English exiles.

What is also notable about this list of fourteen intelligencers is that only six of them have any kind of biographical record, either in the *Oxford Dictionary of National Biography*, or *The History of Parliament*, or even in *Wikipedia*: Aston, Stallenge, Gorges, John Lee, Uvedale, Vaughan. Lacking biographical entries does not, of course, mean that figures are unknown to historians, but in addition these other eight men are almost absent from scholarship apart from the occasional passing reference, normally following the formulation: '[Person] sent a letter to [Walsingham/Burghley/Cecil] with the information that…'.[57] The focus is on the events reported by these

---

[55] *List and Analysis of State Papers, Foreign Series: June 1591–April 1592*, vol. 1 (HM Stationery Office, 1980), p. 402. See also passing mentions of Palmer in Alan Haynes, *The Elizabethan Secret Services*, e-book (The History Press, 2011).

[56] See Hiram Morgan, 'The Fall of Sir John Perrot', in *The Reign of Elizabeth I: Court and Culture in the Last Decade*, ed. John Guy (Cambridge University Press, 1995), pp. 109–25 (p. 111).

[57] See, for example, the reference to Stokes in Mack P. Holt, *The Duke of Anjou and the Politique Struggle during the Wars of Religion* (Cambridge University Press, 1986), p. 199; to Fremyn in Peter C. Mancell, *Hakluyt's Promise: An Elizabethan's Obsession for an English America* (Princeton University Press, 2010), p. 62; or to Grimeston in

men, rather than on the men themselves and their intelligence roles. However, while individually these men may not be deemed worthy of their own histories, we would contend that, when considered as a group, they are. By using the similarity score we are encouraged to understand the commonalities between those men, and how they constitute a category of extra-diplomatic intelligencers. A call to write a collective history of this extra-diplomatic category, if answered, would allow us to extend, and problematize, the existing scholarship on early modern diplomacy.

The discussion of taxonomies brings us to a more general, and perhaps more important point: that we might need to think more capaciously about what it means for two people to be similar. Our tendency is to want to create bounded categories with labels, and ontologies, and to think about similarity in those terms. This, however, can be counterproductive when thinking about people. Individuals can hold multiple official or unofficial roles in the network through time or simultaneously; the definition of roles may change (and may not even be consistent at a given time); and roles may overlap. What two people may have in common may not be a role at all, but a function, or a shared way in which their data was collected. By instead thinking about similarity in terms of network properties rather than human-assigned categories we can begin to understand group identity in more abstract ways. In the final section, therefore, we move to an application of the method that foregrounds a structural commonality shared by those who were subjects of surveillance and letter interception. The subjects of this practice varied widely: indeed, seeing a list of those whose letters were intercepted without contextual information (such as letter metadata), it might be very difficult to determine what connects them. What the similarity measure is able to pick up, however, is that such acts of seizure left behind a very specific signal in the network data.

Interception and the Case of Edward Courtenay

Early modern governments are known to have frequently exploited the mechanics of the early modern postal system. The structures of the post route and its protocols were such that secrecy was virtually impossible. Gary Schneider writes that 'epistolary management, besides the withholding and suspending of letters, also included actions such as intercepting letters; secretly opening, deciphering, and copying letters; and employing and infiltrating secret post channels'.[58] The Tudor government actively

---

John Nichols, *The Progresses and Public Processions of Queen Elizabeth: Volume III: 1579 to 1595*, ed. Elizabeth Goldring, Jayne Elisabeth Archer, and Elizabeth Clarke (Oxford University Press, 2013), p. 546, n. 94.

[58] Gary Schneider, *The Culture of Epistolarity: Vernacular Letters and Letter Writing in Early Modern England, 1500–1700* (University of Delaware Press, 2005), p. 91. Those communicating sensitive material therefore used a variety of precautions to protect their letters' contents. These included methods to confound interceptors, such as the use of a cipher, or invisible ink (e.g. orange juice), which would only appear if held over a candle; crafty modes of conveyance, such as a private courier, the concealment of letters in the lining of clothes or, in the famous case of Mary Queen of Scots, in a cask; or misleading directions, such as a false address on the address leaf, or an address that served as a pick-up location for the true recipient. Other modes of protection may not

participated in these practices: the archive is littered with references to interception. For example, in a letter to Cardinal Thomas Wolsey dated 23 June 1516, Tommaso Spinelli discusses his commission to intercept the letters of Richard de la Pole—a pretender to the throne from the House of York, at that time in exile in Metz. Spinelli speaks of the difficulty of the task and the payment he will need. But, following a conversation with the servant of the Master of the Posts, he adds a postscript offering a better solution: that the servant will intercept the letters from Francis I, King of France to de la Pole for 'C. gowlden gyldens' paid in hand 'and C.C. when he delyuere the sayd lettres'.[59] This letter shows how the postal system could be exploited by a government for a relatively small price. Evidence of more general surveillance directives can be found in a letter from John Bourchier, Lord Berners, to Henry VIII dated 14 March 1523, in which he encloses copies of two letters taken from a fellow of Canterbury coming to England, in response to a recent order to intercept messages to and from English gentlemen in France.[60] The aim of interception was twofold: it not only provided a way of tapping into communication channels that may be beneficial to the government, it also sought to disrupt foreign networks. For example, William Maitland's letter from the Camp near Leith to William Cecil on 17 May 1560 describes how the Council there were minded to intercept all intelligence whereby the French may receive any comfort.[61] In other words, the intention there was not simply to access and copy the contents of the letters, but also to prevent foreign powers from gaining the information they needed.

While it is fully appreciated by historians that interception was used by the Tudor government as part of its intelligence strategy, the *extent* of the practice is not yet fully grasped. Estimates regarding the proportion of correspondence that entered the State Papers archive via interception vary widely. For example, James Daybell suggests that 'the State Papers Foreign and Domestic consist almost entirely of official letters or papers confiscated by the government, which promotes an event-based crisis-ridden form of historical narrative'.[62] While this statement conflates seizure of Secretaries papers, with acts of interception, it is notable that Stephen Alford's estimate—that 'dozens' of letters were intercepted while 'passing between England's enemies on the roads of mainland Europe'—differs by orders of magnitude.[63]

One of the reasons for this discrepancy is that the calendaring project which began in the Victorian period—which, as described in Chapter 1, reordered, catalogued, and described the State Papers—hardly ever uses the specific label or designation 'intercept copy'. Rather, it is a judgement that must be reached by amassing information. The Calendars do provide valuable insights in support of such judgements in terms of whether a letter is a holograph or copy, by whom it was endorsed, and sometimes even in whose hand it was written. The most important characteristic of interception,

---

prevent information being leaked, but it could alert the recipient that their letter had been tampered with: one example is the use of innovative letter-locking methods.
[59] Cotton Galba B/IV f.102.   [60] SP 1/27 f.122.   [61] SP 52/3 f.224.
[62] James Daybell, *Women Letter-Writers in Tudor England* (Oxford University Press, 2006), p. 35.
[63] Stephen Alford, *The Watchers: A Secret History of the Reign of Elizabeth I* (Penguin, 2012), p. 1.

of course, is that it involves a third party without consent from the sender and/or recipient (as distinct from forwarding or enclosing letters with consent, which was common early modern practice).[64] Sometimes evidence can be derived from what would have formed the covering letter for a packet of intercepted missives, making clear the element of consent. Other evidence is apparent in the material appearance of the letters where a cryptographer may have been used to crack a cipher. But in other cases an educated guess will be required.

Because there is no simple 'intercept' label on which to search our data it remains challenging to find intercept letters, and even more so to uncover examples at scale. In a recent study undertaken with Rachel Midura on the Elizabethan State Papers Foreign, we developed a method precisely to find candidates and to assign a confidence estimate for whether they were likely to have been intercepted. Using this approach we not only uncovered examples to close read, but were able to posit that at least 4.6% of non-government communications found in this subset of the State Papers archive were intercept letters.[65] However, our question here is what distinguishes the network profiles of those found in this archive as a function of interception from those who were formally part of the Tudor governments' epistolary intelligence network.

Of course, while the label is rarely used, we do know about various subjects of interception due to scholarship on more sensational examples, such as Mary Queen of Scots and her associates (discussed further below). Moreover, there are a small handful of letters in the Calendars that are labelled as 'intercept copies', including the letters of Edward Courtenay, the Earl of Devon, thanks to the archival work of C. S. Knighton, who updated the Calendars for the reign of Mary I. Devon's network fingerprint (during the reign of Mary I) is provided in Table 4.6. What Table 4.6 clearly shows is that Devon is in the top six (top ~1%) for all measures except eigenvector centrality, for which he ranks 176th, which only places him just inside the top 29%. That eigenvector score is very low for someone with such a high degree. To understand his case as a

Table 4.6 Edward Courtenay, Earl of Devon's network metrics

Metric	Score	Rank position	Top % of people
Total degree	62	5	0.8%
Out-degree	40	3	0.5%
In-degree	22	5	0.8%
Total strength	138	4	0.7%
Out-strength	86	5	0.8%
In-strength	52	6	1%
Eigenvector centrality	0.0436660925801	176	28.6%
Betweenness centrality	0.0385787605966	6	1%

---

[64] James Daybell, *The Material Letter in Early Modern England* (Palgrave Macmillan, 2012).

[65] Rachel Midura, Sebastian E. Ahnert, and Ruth Ahnert, 'Shadow Networks: Intercept Letters in the British State Papers, 1580–1603', in *Network Analysis and the Early Modern Archive*, ed. Ruth Ahnert, Philip Beeley, Esther van Raamsdonk, and Yann Ryan, as a special issue of *Huntington Library Quarterly* (forthcoming).

point of departure, however, it is useful to understand the earl's history and the possible role of interception in this network profile.

Those ranking highest for measures such as degree and strength tend to be monarchs, principal secretaries, and leading statesmen; those who ranked highest for betweenness are leaders and diplomats. Devon, by comparison and despite a noble birth, spent most of his life in prison. He was great-grandson of Edward IV, and therefore the paternal second cousin to Edward VI, Mary I, Elizabeth I, and James V of Scotland, but the young Devon was imprisoned at age 12 in 1538, following his father's involvement in the Exeter conspiracy—the plot to depose Henry VIII and replace him with the Yorkist and Catholic Henry Courtenay. He remained in the Tower for fifteen years because of his own dynastic claim and the fear he would become a Catholic figurehead. After Mary's accession, however, he was set at liberty and there followed a short period of favour, during which he was mooted as a possible spouse for the new queen. But as the likelihood of this match decreased, and following her marriage to the son of the Holy Roman Emperor, Philip of Spain, Devon appears to have been approached by other groups—notably Protestants and anti-imperialists—seeking to make him the focus of a coup. Subsequently he was implicated in the Wyatt rebellion of 1554, although in the spring of 1555 he was released on condition that he left England to prevent him becoming the figurehead of further domestic conspiracies. He would remain in exile for the rest of his life, dying in Italy on 18 September 1556 aged only 30.

Knowledge of Devon's background, therefore, shows him to be an anomaly within the top ranking figures in the network. His high ranking position is instead caused by an unexpected burst in activity. Prior to his exile Devon received just one letter that survives in the State Papers archive, but from the period he was in Europe (sixteen and a half months until his death) we have 139 letters. This wealth of data is caused by a sudden increase in interest in his correspondence: over 85% of those sent by him are classified in the Calendars of State Papers as 'intercept copies', made by English or Imperial postmasters or spies; and many of the remainder of the letters entered the archive when they were taken by Mary's government after his death. The interception began as soon as Devon left England around Easter 1555. The first letters he wrote, on 8 May 1555, to his mother Gertrude, Marchioness of Exeter, his aunt Lady Catherine Berkeley, and James Basset (an MP, whose stepfather Lord Lisle was a relative by marriage to Courtenay) are all copied together on one sheet, with imitation signatures under each one.[66]

The reason that Devon was placed under surveillance is clear: the very status that had made him a potential suitor for the queen also cast him as a direct threat to her. Devon's claim to the throne offered validation and security to the first female monarch. But the domestic conspirators behind the 1554 rebellions, and the foreign

---

[66] SP 11/5 ff.73r–75v. The resulting document appears, interestingly, like a letter. It is on one large sheet, first folded in two as was the common practice, with the contents copied onto the recto of the first sheet; the page then seems to have been folded into a letter package with the following words written on the address leaf (the verso of the second sheet): 'To my Ladye, my Ladye Berkley, and Master Bassat from Callie this viijth of May, 1555'.

powers who sought to partner with them, also saw him as a powerful figurehead for their own efforts to unseat the Catholic monarch by marrying Devon and Princess Elizabeth and placing her on the throne. Removing him from the public eye in England limited the threat he posed in one respect. He continued, however, to be of interest to foreign powers and the many religious and political exiles that found themselves in Europe following Mary I's accession. The Imperial powers would come to regard him as a growing threat, whereas the French king would seek to recruit him to an international conspiracy against Mary and Philip. As a result, Devon was being watched by several governments: he is the subject of numerous letters found not only in the State Papers archive, but also in the papers relating to English diplomacy in the Spanish and Venetian archives.[67] From the English side, it seems most likely that the Principal Secretary William Petre oversaw this process (supported by the fact that neat copies of the hasty intercept transcriptions can be found in a hand very similar to that of one of Petre's secretaries), and that the directive for surveillance came from Mary I's husband, Philip. As discussed by Kenneth Bartlett amongst others, Philip was almost certainly behind a plot to have Devon assassinated.[68]

Our concern here is to understand the extent to which Devon's network profile, presented in Table 4.6, can be attributed simply to the interception, and to what extent it is caused by other factors. The simple answer is that these 'causes' are intimately connected. One might conclude at this stage that, because surveillance provides lots of extra data on Devon, it has created a statistical anomaly that makes him look more important than he is. But this is false logic. Rather, the inverse is true: it is his peculiar social network that caused his monitoring. When we turn to the letters they reveal a complex picture of his social standing during his exile, and allows us to see that his network profile makes him at once a very valuable enemy of the state and a figure that deserved close surveillance. Devon's high strength, for example, is a result of all of the extra data created through interception. And the combination of interception and archival seizure accounts for why there is a relative balance between his in- and out-degree, and in- and out-strength. What it cannot account for is the extent of the correspondence network he maintains (his degree), the betweenness of his position, or the surprisingly low eigenvector centrality ranking he has despite such high scores in all other measures.

Devon corresponds with fifty-one unique people—a high number given the short period of time that his body of correspondence covers. These can be broken down into six partially overlapping groups: (1) Devon's family, (2) Mary and Philip and influential figures with access to the monarchs, (3) those overseeing Devon's finances and material provision, (4) diplomats and agents abroad, (5) Devon's servants, or

---

[67] For further scholarship on Devon, see: Anne M. Overell, *Italian Reform and English Reformations, c.1535–c.1585* (Routledge, 2008), pp. 61–80; Overell, 'A Nicodemite in England and Italy: Edward Courtenay, 1548–56', in *John Foxe at Home and Abroad*, ed. David Loades (Ashgate, 2004), pp. 117–35; A. L. Rowse, 'Edward Courtenay, last Earl of Devon of the Elder Line', in *Court and Country: Studies in Tudor Social History* (University of Georgia Press, 1987), pp. 61–101; and Kenneth R. Bartlett, '"The misfortune that is wished for him": The Exile and Death of Edward Courtenay, Earl of Devon', *Canadian Journal of History* 14 (1979), 1–28.

[68] See Bartlett, '"The misfortune that is wished for him"'.

those seeking service, and (6) men with suspect affiliations. In this latter group are a group of men who had been associated with the Protestant rebellion against Mary's Catholic marriage led by Thomas Wyatt, and others who may have been sympathetic to Devon's claim to the throne because of religious motivations.[69] It is Devon's maintenance of a broad range of contacts, as well as his reliance on servants, agents, and other intermediaries, that accounts both for his high degree and his high betweenness: he nurtured links with various different, and potentially opposed, parties. It was a pragmatic response in the circumstances. Following his exile to the Imperial court regular scuffles between Spaniards and members of Devon's household led Andrea Badoer, the Venetian ambassador there, to report that the earl was in great fear ('molto dubioso') of his life.[70] If these threats came from the Habsburg party, Devon must have suspected Philip's involvement. In such an environment it is understandable that the earl may have sought support from other quarters.

Devon's resort to these suspect contacts did not go without remark: a letter from Secretary Petre dated 23 November 1555 warns Devon: 'in your journayes, companyes, and choyce of places, use thatt forsyght thatt no occasion may be given to the ill men to speak ill, whereof might follow any impayrment of the good opinion the queenes mate hath conceyved of you'.[71] This warning seems to be a direct response to Devon's reported activities in the preceding weeks when, following leave to travel to Italy, he travelled to Louvain where he planned to meet two known conspirators: Sir Philip Hoby and Peter Carew. Interestingly, the information we have about his meeting with Carew comes from Devon's own account, supplied in a letter to Petre:

> I spoke with him and find him such a one for his bodie redie to the service of the kinge and Queenes [...] as you shall never repent the frendshippe and the favour you have shewed him. But touching his conscience led by his religion although I haue thereabout had a good effect with hym yet there resteth in that point a piece of work for you to bringe him to a more perfection.[72]

In this passage we see that Devon attempts to turn what could be damning evidence of his fraternisation with a rebel into a demonstration of his dedication to Mary and Philip. He styles himself as their agent abroad, appealing to Carew's conscience to turn away from his enmity towards the king and queen, but also his false Protestant belief.[73] This self-presentation as an agent is interesting in light of the earlier part of this chapter, and Chapter 3, which both show the link between high betweenness and diplomatic activities and intelligence gathering. A government asset with Devon's network profile would be invaluable. The difference between Devon and the agents discussed in the previous chapters, however, is that Devon's true allegiances were never

---

[69] These men include: George Brooke, Baron Cobham, and Sir Gawain Carew, Sir Thomas Chamberlain, Thomas Aldersay, Sir Philip Hoby, Humphrey Michell, Thomas Harvey, Francis Hastings, Earl of Huntingdon, and Francis Peto.
[70] CSP Venetian, VI, 123.   [71] SP 11/6 f.104r.   [72] 23 November 1555, SP 11/6 f.97r.
[73] For further discussion, see Overell, 'A Nicodemite in England and Italy', p. 128.

resolved. In the absence of evidence to prove his innocence, the only sensible response for the Tudor government was to suspect Devon: to place him under surveillance, and perhaps to take the ultimate step of having him assassinated.[74]

The most interesting aspect of Devon's network profile, however, is his surprisingly low eigenvector centrality. A node that has a high eigenvector score is one that is adjacent to nodes that are themselves high scorers. Hubs benefit from this measure, but so do nodes with few connections, as long as they are well placed in the network. For example, an edge shared with a monarch or Principal Secretary will ensure a high eigenvector centrality score. Because of the nature of this archive, which is constructed from the perspective of the Principal Secretary, we can see eigenvector centrality as a rough indicator of distance from central government.

When we think about the mechanism of government interception, the correlation with low eigenvector centrality makes sense. Interception brings into the network communication lines that might otherwise be separate from official government intelligence networks. Inclusion of these letters might boost the degree of individuals by adding data, and it may uncover connections between sub-communities in the network that might otherwise have been hidden. However, the centres of those communities are still, necessarily, distinct from the crown. Interception of diplomatic correspondence being sent to foreign courts might implicate a foreign monarch in the network, but that monarch is necessarily distant from the centre of this network, both from a geographic perspective and an archival one; in their own country's archives they would form a central hub, but in the English State Papers archive they should only really appear in direct correspondence with the Tudor monarch and their leading statesmen. Where diplomatic correspondence may have contained material that would have been dangerous in the hands of another government, correspondents would have actively sought out security measures, such as the use of ciphers and trusted couriers. The aim—even though we can see this was not always achieved—was to keep these letters as far away as possible from the eyes of the Tudor government. Such methods were not dissimilar to those used by conspirators, but the risks posed by such communication led to ever more intricate means of maintaining secrecy—and thus separation from the formal correspondence network infrastructure.[75]

Devon's network profile, therefore, provides a useful starting point for thinking about what a high profile target of surveillance might look like. In this case part of his profile has been shaped by the targeted destruction of part of his archive by Venetian authorities.[76] But there is good reason not to be concerned about the impact on the

---

[74] On the case for interpreting his death as suspicious, and the likely role of Philip II, see Bartlett, '"The misfortune that is wished for him"', pp. 23–4.

[75] Indeed, this idea of 'distance' from the Tudor State apparatus is one that formed a central plank of our method developed with Rachel Midura for identifying likely examples of interception. See Midura et al., 'Shadow Networks'.

[76] Following Devon's death the diplomat Pietro Vanni requested the rector of Padua Piero Morosini to sequester the earl's letters and writings in a sealed casket. However, on 16 November 1556 the Council of Ten (the governing body of Venice) intervened and instructed a carpenter to open the box and remove the contents in such a way as to be able to reseal it perfectly. The Council then read the documents carefully, and marked with a cross all of those to be removed. Subsequently the casket was resealed by the carpenter, returned to Padua, and

network profile. Firstly, work Sebastian has done with Yann C. Ryan has shown that network analysis is surprisingly robust in the face of missing data.[77] More importantly, there is a good argument for seeing incompleteness as part of the intercept profile. This can be seen by looking at the most similar correspondents to Devon.

Predicting Interception

While interception is only one of the features that determines the network profile of Devon, the use of the fingerprint similarity method is surprisingly successful at finding examples of other correspondence that does not 'belong' in the State Papers archive. It usefully narrows down candidates, as well as helping us to identify confusing signals in the metadata supplied by the Victorian calendaring projects.

In Table 4.7 we show the thirty most similar profiles to Devon's using the relative similarity function, to try and capture people with profiles of the same shape, while allowing for different volumes of material. The list is heterogeneous in nature, but we can observe two dominant patterns in these results. The first is a presence of people in high-profile positions who would have been sending or receiving information that would be highly valuable for the Tudor government, including foreign leaders (1–5, 9, 13, 16, 18, 21–3), their key administrators (19, 24, 25), and diplomats (27–9). These figures are united by their access to, or ownership of, intelligence that was at a structural remove from the Tudor government. Foreign policy was directed by the aim of bringing all these sources of intelligence into the ambit of the government, through the interception of letters and the infiltration of networks privy to plans against the English nation. We also note an over-representation of Henrician correspondence: 18 out of the top 30 results (1, 2, 3, 4, 6, 8, 9, 10, 11, 14, 15, 23, 24, 25, 27, 28, 29, 30, in Table 4.7).

There are overlapping reasons for these patterns. Interception is one, as neatly emphasised by the appearance of Mary Queen of Scots in the results (rank 5 in Table 4.7), as she was famously brought down by the interception of her correspondence. Mary had been the focus for a number of conspiracies to remove the Protestant Queen Elizabeth from the throne and replace her with the Catholic Mary; but until 1586 it had proved impossible to confirm her involvement. From 1568 Mary was effectively held under house arrest and moved frequently between residences, making undetected communication almost impossible. Moreover, the July 1584 decree by Queen Elizabeth following the Throckmorton Plot prevented all communication to

---

made to look as if it had never left. Only then was Vanni told he might collect Devon's effects. No letters with crosses survive in the archive, suggesting these plans were successfully carried out. In the process the Venetian authorities may also have removed the evidence that would have proved whether the surveillance of Devon was justified. See Cal. Span., XI, 12, Cal. Ven., VI, 716 (20 November 1556), Cal. Ven., VI, 729 (26 November 1556), and Cal. Ven., VI, 729–31 (26 November 1556).

[77] Yann C. Ryan and Sebastian E. Ahnert, 'The Measure of the Archive: The Robustness of Network Analysis in Early Modern Correspondence', *Journal of Cultural Analytics* 6:1 (2021), <https://doi.org/10.22148/001c.25943>. See also Matthew Peeples, 'Network Science and Statistical Techniques for Dealing with Uncertainties in Archaeological Datasets', <http://www.mattpeeples.net/netstats.html>.

Table 4.7 Ranked list of figures with the most similar
(relative) network profile to the Earl of Devon

Rank	Name
1	John Stewart, Duke of Albany
2	James IV
3	Catharine of Aragon
4	Ferdinand II of Aragon,
5	Mary, Queen of Scots
6	Thomas Dacre, 2nd Baron Dacre of Gilsland
7	John Daniell
8	Sir Thomas More
9	Pope Leo X
10	Reginald Pole
11	Thomas Darcy, Baron Darcy of Darcy
12	William Carnsew
13	Henri IV, King of France
14	Sir Thomas Heneage
15	William Popley
16	Emperor Rudolf II
17	Thomas Fitzherbert
18	Alessandro Farnese, Duke of Parma
19	Claude Nau de la Boisselliere
20	Henry Foljambe
21	Valentin Pardieu de la Motte
22	Charles of Lorraine, Duke of Mayenne
23	Louis XII, King of France
24	Patrick Paniter
25	James Beaton
26	Christopher Nugent, Baron Delvin
27	Thomas Magnus
28	Gian Matteo Giberti
29	Giovanni Battista Sanga
30	Hugh Latimer

and from Mary. However, Gilbert Gifford established a system whereby Mary's personal letters could be carried out of Chartley, her current residence, hidden in a beer barrel. As a double measure, these letters were ciphered. Gifford had, in fact, been recruited as one of Walsingham's spies, and so each of the letters was intercepted and decoded, including the letter in which Mary consented to the assassination of Elizabeth. The evidence led to the execution of Mary and the network of conspirators in 1587.[78]

The second mechanism is seizure, which is distinct from the piecemeal process of interception in that the papers enter the archive en masse, but it leaves a similar epistolary fingerprint to interception focused on key individuals over an extended period. Subjects of seizure in Table 4.7 include the MP William Carnsew (rank 12), whose family archives, containing legal, family, and business papers, were requisitioned and form the Carnsew Papers, SP 46/71. Many of Thomas More's (rank 8) papers and

---

[78] John Bossy provides a nearly day-by-day account of the espionage operations of 1583–5 leading to that pivotal moment. John Bossy, *Giordano Bruno and the Embassy Affair* (Yale University Press, 1991).

books were confiscated following his arrest, although—perhaps with foresight—he had destroyed the official papers from his period in office as royal secretary and Lord Chancellor. Henry Foljambe (rank 20) appears here because he is a frequent correspondent with Nicholas Williamson, an English lawyer and Catholic recusant whose personal archive was seized when he was arrested in 1595. And the case of John Daniell (rank 7) shows that, as well as entering the archive through repeated petitions to the crown, his papers appear to have been seized as part of his trial before the Star Chamber in 1601, under accusation of blackmailing Frances Devereux, Countess of Essex (discussed further in Chapter 5).

The third mechanism accounts for the large number of results from Henry VIII's reign: the editorial decisions of John Sherren Brewer, James Gairdner, and R. H. Brodie, the editors of the multi-volume *Letters and Papers, Foreign and Domestic, of the Reign of Henry VIII*. As Brewer wrote in his Preface to the first volume:

> This Catalogue, of which the first volume is now submitted to the reader, differs in some important respects from the Calendars of State Papers which have already appeared under the sanction of the Master of the Rolls. They relate to documents contained in single departments of the State; this embraces an abstract of all Letters and Miscellaneous Papers, illustrative of the reign of Henry VIII., foreign or domestic, printed or in manuscript, preserved either in the different departments of the Great National Depository, or in the British Museum, the Bodleian and the Lambeth libraries, or the colleges of Oxford and Cambridge. It has further been found necessary, from the peculiar nature of the work, to include in it a complete index and summary of the French, the Scotch, the Patent and the Parliament Rolls, the Signed Bills and Privy Seals, the army, navy, ordnance, and wardrobe accounts of the same period, not omitting the transcripts made by the late Record Commission from foreign archives, for the new edition of Rymer's Foedera.[79]

Brewer outlines a much more comprehensive policy of inclusion than that employed by the editors of the Calendars of the later reigns. Notably the inclusion of material from foreign archives explains why more material that one would expect to be outside the natural purview of the Henrician government is found in our correspondence records for this period. It is through this mechanism that we have a pair of highly sensitive letters that Catherine of Aragon (rank 3 in Table 4.5) and her chaplain Thomas Abell wrote to her nephew Emperor Charles the V on 9 January 1529. In the emperor's keeping was a brief concerning the bull of Pope Julius II that would provide valuable evidence against Henry VIII's case for the annulment of his marriage to the queen. Knowing that the emperor would not send the document to Henry, Catherine was forced under duress to write to her nephew asking him to send her this document. However, following its dispatch Catherine sent another missive in the keeping of her servant Juan de Montoya and Abell, which requests that Charles does not,

---

[79] *LP*, vol. 1, p. vii.

under any circumstances give up the brief, notwithstanding that the other letter earnestly requested it, and confirming that she was compelled under oath to write in that
manner. Abell and de Montoya travelled by sea to Fuenterrabía strictly in order to
avoid spies, and ensured that the messengers sent by the king were delayed, so that
they might reach Charles first.[80] The letters were successful precisely because they
were not intercepted, and Henry's ambassadors were outmanoeuvred. We have these
letters in the current dataset because they were included from the Simancas archive in
Spain by Brewer and his colleagues.[81]

What this means is that we are detecting overlapping signals in the results for
Henry's reign—one caused by interception and seizure and another caused by the editorial inclusion of material from foreign archives—and these are hard to separate at
scale. Reginald Pole's oeuvre (rank 10) is a good demonstration of this. Pole was certainly a candidate for surveillance. As a close relative of Henry VIII (Pole was great-
nephew to Edward IV and Richard III), he had been offered the Archbishopric of York
or the Diocese of Winchester if he would support the annulment of Henry's marriage
to Catherine. But Pole had not only withheld his support but also gone into self-
imposed exile, from where he became the focus of various efforts to counter Henry's
agenda—to seek an annulment from his wife, which in turn heralded a separation
from the Church in Rome. It was suggested to Emperor Charles V that Pole marry
Henry's daughter Mary and combine their dynastic claims; he was involved in supporting the Pilgrimage of Grace (a popular uprising against Henry's break with
Rome); and he was implicated in the Exeter conspiracy—which had led to the execution of Devon's father and his own long imprisonment. For the latter, Pole was
attainted *in absentia*. Much of Pole's correspondence during his exile was thus of great
interest to Henry's government. It enters the *Letters and Papers* partially through the
editors' inclusion of the eighteenth-century edition of Pole's correspondence by
Angelo M. Quirini, which gathered his papers from scattered locations across
Europe.[82] But alongside this are other letters that entered the State Papers through
interception, such as the letter he received from his mother denouncing his behaviour
and beseeching him to take another way and serve the king, 'as thy bounden duty is to
doo oneless thou will be the confusion of thy mother'.[83] As James Daybell has argued,
these letters were written knowing that they would be read by the Privy Council, and
should therefore be seen as an opportunity for the countess to provide 'proof of loyalty to the crown' both to 'the intended and apparently "unintended" audiences'.[84]

---

[80] On this manoeuvre see Geoffrey de C. Parmiter, *The King's Great Matter: A Study of Anglo-papal Relations 1527–1534* (Barnes & Noble, 1967), p. 83.

[81] *LP*, vol. 4, p. 5154.

[82] A. M. Quirini, ed., *Epistolae Reginaldi Poli S. R. E. Cardinalis et aliorum ad ipsum*, 5 vols. (Brescia: Bavarian State Library, 1744–57). On the partiality of this effort, see Thomas F. Mayer's edition of Pole's correspondence, *The Correspondence of Reginald Pole, Volume 1 A Calendar, 1518–1546: Beginnings to Legate of Viterbo* (London: Routledge, 2002), pp. 1–37.

[83] Countess of Salisbury to Reginald Pole, 1536, SP 1/105 f.65.

[84] James Daybell, *Women Letter-Writers in Tudor England* (Oxford University Press, 2006), pp. 143–4.

Therefore, our method for measuring fingerprint similarity—when applied to Devon—is good at detecting communications that should be 'distant' from the Tudor government's communication channels, but it is blind to the reasons for this distance. When applied to examples dating from after 1547, however, the confusion created by Brewer's editorial policy is removed. Of the twelve post-Henrician examples in Table 4.7, we can deduce by examining the letters that all were subject to requisitioning, seizure, and interception - including the aforementioned subjects of requisitioning and seizure, Carnsew, Daniell, Foljambe, and More.[85] The subjects of interception can be divided into two camps. The first are the foreign leaders who would have been sending or receiving information that would be highly valuable for the Tudor government, including Henri IV, Emperor Rudolf II, Alessandro Farnese, Duke of Parma, Valentin Pardieu de la Motte (governor of Gravelines), and Charles of Lorraine, Duke of Mayenne. The other category is those suspected of conspiracy against Elizabeth I, including Mary Queen of Scots, her confidential secretary Claude Nau de la Boisselliere, the English Jesuit Thomas Fitzherbert, and Sir Christopher Nugent, Baron Delvin, an Irish nobleman and writer arrested on suspicion of treason against Elizabeth.

However, this is not simply about the ability of the fingerprint similarity to find examples of interception, but what understanding the network profile helps us to grasp. In this case the conflation of seizure and interception tells us something useful. Because we began with Devon, who was subject to systematic surveillance, we are finding people who were also subject to more sustained and focused attention. This is even more apparent if we try the process again with Mary Queen of Scots and focus our temporal window. For example, the ranked list of the 40 most similar people to Mary in the decade beginning 1580—that is, the period from the beginning of the Jesuit missions until the death of 'spy-master' Walsingham—contains twenty-five people who were subject to at least one instance of interception or seizure.[86] These include: Rudolf II, Nau, Sir Francis Englefield, Nicholas Leclerc, Sieur de Courcelles, Henri IV, Thomas Paget, Philip II, Francis, Duke of Anjou, Bernardino de Mendoza, the Company of Merchant Adventurers, Pedro de Zubiaur, Thomas Morgan, George Gordon, Marquess of Huntly, Michel de Castelnau, Sieur de la Mauvissière, Gilbert

---

[85] Acts of interception can be verified or deduced from a combination of features. The central feature is where neither sender nor recipient is a member of the Tudor state and it has entered the state's hands without their permission. Letters may also be described as 'copies' in the Calendar descriptions, and be endorsed by a principal secretary or one of their clerks, or they bear marks of having been deciphered. For example, one of the letters that Alessandro Farnese, Duke of Parma, received from Philip II, dated 20/30 January 1590, is described as 'Decipher, with some gaps and corrections' (SP 94/3 f.131).

[86] The full list in rank order is: (1) Carnsew, (2) Farnese, (3) Rudolf II, (4) Nau de la Boisselliere, (5) Sir Francis Englefield, (6) Sir John Perrott, (7) Nicholas Leclerc, Sieur de Courcelles, (8) Henri IV, (9) Thomas Paget, (10) King Philip II of Spain, (11) Francis, Duke of Anjou, (12) Bernardino de Mendoza, (13) Edward Fiennes de Clinton, Earl of Lincoln, (14) Robert Devereux, Earl of Essex, (15) Company of Merchant Adventurers, (16) Pedro de Zubiaur, (17) Gerard Prouninck van Deventer, (18) Thomas Morgan, (19) George Gordon, Marquess of Huntly, (20) Sir Thomas Leighton, (21) Michel de Castelnau, Sieur de la Mauvissière, (22) Robert Cecil, (23) Francis Knollys, (24) Gilbert Gifford, (25) Sir William Stanley, (26) Sir William Catesby, (27) James Golde, (28) Sir Roger Williams, (29) Thomas Mills, (30) Francis Milles, (31) Charles Arundel, (32) William Allen, (33) Pope Sixtus V, (34) Anthony Babington, (35) Arthur Atey, (36) Sir Henry Bagenal, (37) James VI of Scotland, (38) Guillaume de l'Aubespine, Baron de Châteauneuf-sur-Cher, (39) Sir Nicholas Malby, (40) Charles Paget.

Gifford, Sir William Stanley, Sir William Catesby, Charles Arundel, Cardinal William Allen, Pope Sixtus V, Anthony Babington, James VI, Guillaume de l'Aubespine, Baron de Châteauneuf, and Charles Paget. At least seventeen of the figures are associated with Catholic plots, or are correspondents of known conspirators. What is perhaps interesting about that commonality is that, of those seventeen, all bar two were directly connected to one another via correspondence, and all seventeen are within two degrees of one another (meaning they share a correspondent).

When we compare these results with those found using the fingerprint similarity above, the fact of connectivity is new. It is not due simply to the narrower temporal window, but to the *programmatic* nature of the surveillance of this network. By tapping into the network at various points, and sustaining the surveillance, the government acquired a lot of data on each individual and their associates, which allowed them to successfully uncover the size and breadth of the network that coupled its interests to those of the imprisoned Queen Mary. The causes which sought to free the queen, depose Elizabeth, and put the Catholic monarch in her place were both religious and political, and came from Scotland, France, and Spain, as well as the exile community (both religious and lay). As Stephen Alford has suggested, the level of perceived threat created a kind of circular logic, or self-fulfilling prophecy: 'the heightened vigilance of Queen Elizabeth's advisers was in fact potentially corrosive of the security they craved. The more obsessively a state watches, the greater the dangers it perceives.' From our analysis of the network above, we can see the level of vigilance from the multiple points of entry to this network. As Walsingham and others traced the lines of connection into what network scientists would call a 'giant connected component', they gained a picture of a coordinated affront. It is easy to understand how such evidence would have raised alarm and led to a doubling down on a policy of surveillance. What we are seeing in the list of results for the most-similar network profiles to Mary is the network fingerprint of that particular style of surveillance. The network fingerprint, therefore, always points in two directions: both to the behaviours of the correspondents and to the ways in which the government collected information on them.

Conclusion

The chapter offers interventions on two fronts. The first is methodological: it proffers our own mathematical definition of similarity based on network structure and metrics. The utility of the method is not just in the way that it helps to 'find' people with similar roles and functions in the network, but also in the way that it facilitates different ways of thinking about what it means for two things to be similar. Our process of examining and evaluating the results of such a mathematical process—seeking to uncover the features and epistolary behaviours that make two individuals similar—brings to light the conceptual borderlands and fuzzy boundaries between our human-constructed categories and labels.

The second contribution of the chapter derives from the application of this method. Broadly we have been able to elucidate the activities and personnel that constituted the information wing of the Tudor government in the sixteenth century. It helps us to see that with the professionalisation of the role of ambassador came a need for informal networks of informants, which were supplied by movable types such as merchants, military figures, and travelling intellectuals, as well as those embedded in strategic locations. As such we show how early modern diplomacy was not a role or a profession but a function—a set of network behaviours. By recasting the information-gathering part of government in these terms we can better understand the similarity between diplomats like Perkins and Spinelli, scholar-intelligencers like Bizzarri, and merchants like Ottywell Smith. In fact, their epistolary behaviour can be charted on a continuum that connects resident ambassadors or diplomats on special embassies with those of other kinds of agents, intelligencers, double agents, or (beyond the scope of this chapter) agents provocateurs, triple, or re-doubled agents. It makes clear how individuals might move along this continuum, or slip back and forth over time.

The chapter also explores how the method can be deployed for a range of different research questions. In applying it to the practice of letter interception and more systematic surveillance—another intelligence strategy of the Tudor government—we show once again that the method is particularly suitable for identifying structural similarities that may not be apparent from the biographies or other obvious labels we might associate with a set of individuals. The subjects of interception may have very little in common apart from their correspondence being opened, read, and copied without their consent. The method therefore helps to foreground these latent parallels. Specifically, we are here detecting the fingerprint left behind by government surveillance, showing us once again that quantitative methods always ultimately direct our attention to the manner in which data has been collected.

This brings us to the bigger point: that the method has the benefit of turning the apparent problem of an incomplete archive to our advantage. As we outlined in Chapters 1 and 2, the history of the Principal Secretary's office, and the afterlives of the letters that passed through it, can help us to understand the gap between what survives and that which once existed. Usually those gaps are lamented in terms of what they occlude. However, the application of this method and the results it is able to deliver suggest that those archival gaps are not a bug but a feature. The value of the incompleteness of the state record is precisely that it points towards the processes of the archive's creation. As we have shown here, there are strong correlations between the role an individual served in relation to the Tudor government and the resulting network profile created by the letters that survive. An intelligencer has a high out-strength and low in-strength because they sent a steady stream of letters to the Principal Secretary but their own incoming correspondence would have been in their personal papers, which—*if* they survived the vicissitudes of time—would have landed in another archive or collection. Intelligencers' incoming letters would only have ended up in the archive if seized, leading to a very different network profile, more like that of the Lisles (discussed in Chapters 2 and 5) and Carnsew (mentioned above).

Therefore, while in many cases incomplete data presents a disadvantage in data-driven work, we can also work with the contours of the data to show what it can reveal not only about the different roles and functions of the individuals documented in this archive, but also the process by which they were documented. Perfect survival, by contrast, would obscure the processes of documentation—the information-gathering strategies of secretaries, and the accretive formation of the state archive.

5

Women

Petitioning, Power, and Mediation

The worlds of diplomacy and conspiracy into which the last few chapters have delved are dominated by men. The main women to enter the scene have been female monarchs: Mary I, Elizabeth I, and Mary Stuart. In network terms, we have been narrating a history in which women were at once the central hubs—the foci of power and intrigue—and relegated to its peripheries. This is borne out by basic statistical analysis of the network: Elizabeth I is ranked fourth and Mary I twelfth for their degree centrality—the key metric for determining hubs. However, the network contains only 857 women in total, which corresponds to just 4% of all people; and while 15,519 (around 11%) of the letters in the archive were either written or received by a woman, this total drops to just 4,833 (under 4%), if we exclude the correspondence of the Tudor queens.

This is perhaps unsurprising given the political nature of the archive: aside from monarchs and formal court positions, women could not hold political office. Women's letters entered the archive only if they wrote to the government, or if their family papers were folded into the State Papers archive. This might happen if the woman was related to one of the principal secretaries (especially if the secretary's private papers were mixed in with his working papers), if family papers were seized for investigation (as in the case of Honor Plantagenet, Viscountess Lisle), or if their letters were intercepted (as with Jane Suárez de Figueroa's correspondence). But while these factors explain the low representation of female writing in the State Papers, it does not account for similar levels in other databases. Interestingly the figure of 4% is not far from the percentage that women made up in the first iteration of the *Six Degrees of Francis Bacon* Project, which sought to map the early modern social network by inferring social connections from the co-occurrence of names in entries of the *Oxford Dictionary of National Biography*, and then verifying and adding to these connections through expert crowdsourcing.[1] The structural biases of the *ODNB*—with only 11% of all entries focusing on women, and only 6% in the period 1500–1700—mean that the project subsequently sought to drive up the representation of women in its database with targeted 'edit-athons'. A solution to a similar under-representation of women in *Early Modern Letters Online* was proposed by the spin-off *Women's EMLO*

---

[1] <http://www.sixdegreesoffrancisbacon.com/>. See Christopher N. Warren, Daniel Shore, Jessica Otis, Lawrence Wang, Mike Finegold, and Cosma Shalizi, 'Six Degrees of Francis Bacon: A Statistical Method for Reconstructing Large Historical Social Networks', *Digital Humanities Quarterly* 10:3 (2016), available at: <http://digitalhumanities.org/dhq/vol/10/3/000244/000244.html>.

Tudor Networks of Power. Ruth Ahnert and Sebastian E. Ahnert, Oxford University Press. © Ruth Ahnert and Sebastian E. Ahnert 2023. DOI: 10.1093/oso/9780198858973.003.0005

(WEMLO), although the result of this is still only just over 7% representation in the database.[2] The reasons for these low levels of representation derive from a complex set of causes and biases that it is almost impossible to separate: from lower literacy and education rates in women, to uneven survival of archives, and traditional scholarly attitudes to female epistolary output, as well as other structural biases in scholarship. As James Daybell summarises, these causes have converged as a 'long-term prejudice against women's letters' as 'of no importance'—a prejudice that he and other literary historians working on women's correspondence in recent years have sought to correct.[3]

Finding strategies to engage with the archiving practices of the past, especially when developing data-driven approaches, is a pressing intersectional issue. In their recent book *Data Feminism*, Catherine D'Ignazio and Lauren F. Klein seek to highlight 'the risks incurred when people from dominant groups create most of our data products', noting that it 'is not only that datasets are biased or unrepresentative, but that they never get collected at all'.[4] This statement could as easily have been written about archives; and it has strong connections with the scholarship around archives as sites, and sources, of tacit narratives of power. Elizabeth Yale has provided a vital overview of recent scholarship that has sought to understand archives and their collections as 'crucial sites for the exercise of political power'.[5] Eric Ketalaar writes that 'social, cultural, political, economic and religious contexts determine the tacit narratives of an archive'.[6] Our problem is that, if quantitative approaches merely reinforce the narrative that women's letters are a minority object, marginal political discourse, or 'of no importance', then they are not fit for purpose.

As such, in this chapter we take a series of approaches that allow us to attend to the relevant parts of the archive, and at a scale appropriate to the subject matter. Moreover, we seek to adapt methods that are sensitive to power dynamics and how they are encoded in historically contingent social relations, and the ways in which the records arising from those relations were created and archived. The chapter begins with a discussion of the method we used to identify all writers and recipients of letters who were women: to find out that just 4% of the names in our dataset were women's, we needed first to develop a method for identifying gender. Thereafter, the chapter proceeds with a simple analysis of the letter descriptions between men and women, showing the marked disparity between the language used to describe women's letters to men, compared to men's letters to women: while the former are more frequently associated with petition and request (seeking to *receive* something), men's letters more often narrate how they are *giving or sending*. This suggests a very general power

---

[2] These statistics are from the back-end interface of EMLO, and provided kindly by Miranda Lewis.

[3] James Daybell, *Women Letter-Writers in Tudor England* (Ashgate, 2006), p. 8.

[4] Catherine D'Ignazio and Lauren F. Klein, *Data Feminism* (The MIT Press, 2020), chapter 1 (available open access at <https://data-feminism.mitpress.mit.edu/>).

[5] Elizabeth Yale, 'The History of Archives: The State of the Discipline', *Book History* 18:1 (2015), 332–59 (p. 333). More broadly, see Antoinette M. Burton, ed., *Archive Stories: Facts, Fictions, and the Writing of History* (Duke University Press, 2005); Michel-Rolph Trouillot and Hazel V. Carby, *Silencing the Past: Power and the Production of History* (Beacon Press, 2015).

[6] Eric Ketalaar, 'Tacit Narratives: The Meanings of Archives', *Archival Science* 1:2 (2001), 131–41 (p. 137).

differential that we seek to further understand within their immediate network structures through a process of excavation and contextualisation, in which the scale of reading narrows accordingly.

Rather than taking an approach which prioritises the running of metrics across the entire network we rather sought to isolate a particular network 'motif' known as a 'triad' (three nodes forming a triangle of communication). These are building blocks of social networks that have been studied in depth by social scientists because of the varied dynamics of social interactions they can display. We then explicate a method to quantify the extent to which women appear in different positions within these social micro-structures. This positionality is merely a heuristic device, but it allows us to think about how women used letters to manage or signal their social standing. By directing us to the level of individual interaction, the process allows us to reconstruct the particular stories of women's lives and how they found themselves in the position of petitioner or mediator, and how they manoeuvred themselves into positions of structural power. In this way, the method encourages us to be attentive to women's individual stories, allowing us to recentre female narratives and the contexts that both empowered and limited them.

Women's Words

We began our analysis of women's letters by tagging all our senders and recipients of letters with attributes of male or female. We found the women in our dataset by searching our name entity fields for appearances of female titles or roles (e.g. Abbess, adulteress, Baroness, coheiress, Countess, daughter, Dowager, Duchess, godmother, governess, heiress, Lady, maiden, Mademoiselle, Maid of Honour, Marchioness, Marquess, Mistress, Mme, mother, mother of maids, Mrs, niece, nun, Prioress, Princess, shepherdess, sister, Queen, Viscountess, wife), or containing one of the given names extracted from a resource providing Tudor women's biographies.[7] The list of women that was thereby extracted from the dataset was then manually checked by two research assistants, who went through each name and checked that it really was a woman, either by using the linked biographical data that had already been mapped to women (where available), or inferring it from the letter descriptions.[8] Care was needed especially around ambiguous names such as 'Anne', which was a common French man's name (e.g. Anne de Montmorency). While some men's names slipped into the list of women's (and were then removed at the manual cleaning stage), the quality

---

[7] See <https://github.com/tudor-networks-of-power/code>. Miriam Posner describes another way of automatically identifying gender in this tutorial: <https://github.com/miriamposner/derive_gender/blob/master/derive-gender-from-a-column-of-first-names.md>.

[8] Thanks to Tani Thomsen and Emily Shah who undertook this data checking, and to Stanford Humanities Center and the Center for Spatial and Textual Analysis (CESTA) for funding these undergraduate research assistantships.

of the lists used meant that virtually no women ended up in the men's list.[9] The addition of male/female labels means that we are able to do focused queries that distinguish by gender.

A basic, but revealing, query was to find and order the most common words in the Calendar descriptions of letters written by women to men (7,053 letters) and by men to women (7,564 letters) by their statistical deviation from one another. While, sadly, full transcriptions of the State Papers do not exist at this time, the dataset contains a field deriving from the Calendars of State Papers that describe the contents of the letters. As discussed further in Chapter 6, these summaries are a decent proxy for the language of the letters: the most active editor, Anne Everett Green (née Wood), determined that 'all the significant contents of a letter would be mentioned and key phrases might be printed verbatim; the summary of the rest would follow the structure of the original, trimmed of its superfluities'.[10]. Using this field, we wanted to see which words are frequently used in descriptions of the contents of letters by women, and comparatively little by men to see if there is a particularly female lexicon, and vice versa. Because we wanted to explore the roles of women other than the monarchs, we removed letters from and to Elizabeth I, Mary I, and Mary Queen of Scots for this analysis, leaving 1,840 letters from men to women and 2,130 from women to men. The ranked list of most dominant words used by women (to men) has some lexical consistency. Indeed, the top-ranking words were dominated by two lexical sets that we might label 'familial relations', and 'the language of petition'. The former group include the words 'husband' (which is the fifth most common word compared to 108th for letters from men to women), 'son' (6th versus 57th), 'children' (98 v. 649), 'brother' (29 v. 178), and 'father' (75 v. 194). The language of petition includes words such as 'favour'/'favor' (78 v. 478; 383 v. 652), 'beg'/'begs' (186 v. 343; 45 v. 248), 'trouble' (177 v. 669), 'suit' (103 v. 376), 'help' (137 v. 408), 'desires' (51 v. 155), 'justice' (398 v. 946), 'grant' (231 v. 512), and 'pray' (143 v. 387).

The identification of the latter group of words with the process of petition and request can be demonstrated by examining examples of these words in context. For example, the description of a 1601 letter from Anne White to Robert Cecil contains several of these petition words: 'My duty remembered to you, my cousin William, your son, and my cousin Frances, your daughter, giving you thanks for the favour showed to my son Welby and my daughter when they were at London in their suit and trouble, by means of the suretyship and bonds he came in for his brother Adam.'[11] Checking the context is especially important with more ambiguous words, like 'pray', which could refer to the religious act of prayer, or a request to a temporal being. However, when we look at the context in which it appears we observe that, while it

---

[9] We also developed code to work out likely spouses and to extract the network of people they spoke to together. In the event this method was not used in this chapter, but the code can be found. See <https://github.com/tudor-networks-of-power/code>.

[10] Ibid.

[11] A[nne] W[hite] to Sir Robert Cecil, 21 October 1601, 'Cecil Papers: October 1601, 21–31', in *Calendar of the Cecil Papers in Hatfield House: Volume 11, 1601*, ed. R. A. Roberts (HMSO, 1906), pp. 440–65. *British History Online* (BHO), <http://www.british-history.ac.uk/cal-cecil-papers/vol11/pp440-465>.

was occasionally used in the religious sense, it more commonly occurred in letters addressed to the Principal Secretary requesting personal favours, money, or information.[12] For example, the description of the 1544 letter from Margaret Shelton to Sir John Gates contains the following summary: 'Pray move Mr. Denny instantly that deeds of feoffment be made now before Mr. Shelton's going in the King's affairs; and to sue a recovery of all Mr. Shelton's lands mentioned in the indentures.'[13] To this lexical set of petition words we can also add the words 'lands' (134 v. 748), 'land' (274 v. 641), and 'house' (53 v. 232), as these were the frequent subject of legal suits and petitions to the secretaries, most often by widows.

The language of petition is not, however, entirely separate from the language of familial relations. When we examine the descriptions of letters mentioning husbands and sons especially, we frequently find that they are coupled by a request on their behalf—either for patronage or for help. The prevalence of the language of petition in the corpus of women's letters to men will not be surprising to those familiar with female epistolary habits in this period. Daybell has asserted that letters of petition, suitors' letters, or letters of request account for almost one-third of early modern women's letters, based on his survey of more than 3,000 manuscript letters from the period 1540–1603.[14] Our basic statistical survey therefore highlights a dominant mode of writing that specialists in the field have previously identified through exhaustive work on the surviving archives. While the method does not reveal anything new in this instance, it is significant that a piece of code that took a few hours to write can reveal something that previously necessitated years in the archive. Moreover, the similarity of the findings suggests we can place some trust in these new methods.

If we return to the ranked list of words that are used most commonly in men's letters to women (but relatively little in women's letters to men) we gain a broader sense of the ways in which letters can help us reconstruct the power structures surrounding women. Women's letters more often contain words in which they are asking to *receive* something; by comparison, men's letters more often narrate how they are *giving or sending* something. These words include: 'send'/'sends'/'sending' (which is the 25th most common word compared to 42nd for letters from women to men; 133 v. 206; 282 v. 604), 'remembrance' (626 v. 925), 'money' (74 v. 140), 'despatch' (434 v. 878), 'things' (166 v. 504), 'token' (315 v. 929), 'cost' (296 v. 932), and 'news' (91 v. 348). The word 'send' and its variants appears most often in letters that accompany goods, and while men and women both engaged in the exchange of goods, men outrank women. They sent women all sorts of objects from books (e.g. Sir Richard Sackville to

---

[12] In letters from men to women, by contrast, the word was used in a religious sense more often: of 28 letters sent to Lady Lisle including that word, at least 21 instances referred to prayers to God.

[13] Margaret Shelton to John Gates, 29 April 1544, SP 1/244 f.208.

[14] Daybell, *Women Letter-Writers*, p. 229. For scholarship on the practice of petitioning in the period from c.1570 to 1800, see the AHRC-funded project 'The Power of Petitioning in Seventeenth-Century England' (AH/S001654/1), <https://petitioning.history.ac.uk/>, which transcribed and published the texts of more than 2,500 petitions, including *Petitions in the State Papers, 1600–1699*, ed. Brodie Waddell, BHO, <http://www.british-history.ac.uk/petitions/state-papers>.

Lady Throckmorton),[15] to quails (Otwell Johnson to Sabine Johnson).[16] The word 'remembrance' occurs in forty-six letters from men to women, and most usually denotes a token of remembrance, either in an abstract or concrete form, including letters, gifts (e.g. 'cramp rings', or barrels of herring), or more occasionally remembrance of cause or matter. The words 'money' and 'cost' frequently co-occur with references to such goods, often detailing the price of goods sent when they have been acquired for trade purposes (rather than as gifts). News is a more abstract offering, but still implies a transaction. Like the giving of gifts and sourcing of goods, the way that men represent themselves as bringers of news seems to place them in a position of power. As with physical goods, it represents a resource that men had access to and that women did not, and which they could bestow as a sign of their favour.

Taken as a whole, the coarse-grained picture created by the dominant forms of language exchanged between men and women is one of a gendered economy in which men had power, information, and goods, and women were placed in a position where they must ask for them. This provides a simple, but overly schematic, picture of social (as well as economic) capital in the early modern period. The sense of women being impoverished in terms of social capital is seemingly supported by the prominence of a specific word in women's letters: 'poor'. This word has one of the highest discrepancies in usage between letters written by women to men, versus men to women: it is the 81st most common word in the former, occurring in the description of 171 letters, versus 546th in the latter. When we look at the context in which the word 'poor' appears, we see that it occurs most frequently in letters of petition addressed to principal secretaries, and that it frequently co-occurs with words such as 'favour' and 'help'. For example, in a later from one Mary Tomlynson to Cromwell dated 29 December 1533, she first informs him of her situation as a 'poer wydoy [widow]' of Robert Tomlynson, 'lat merchaunt of the Staple of Calyce [Calais]'; and then asking that 'by yower goode help his [her late husband's] vnrasonable seyssement by the Staple may be reformyd and mytygatyde accordyng to good conscyence or elles I shall nother be able to pay his dettys nor bryng vp hys childryn and myne accordyng vnto hys well'.[17] In this context, the poor condition of the letter's author is both the motivation and the justification for her plea for help.

But it is difficult to separate biographical fact here from rhetorical posture. As Daybell has noted, probably the most frequent trope in women's letters of petition is 'the depiction of themselves and other women as objects of pity, victims of poverty and suffering'.[18] In representing themselves as worthy of pity, women drew on conventional petitioning strategies advocated in epistolary manuals such as Erasmus's *De conscribendis epistolis*. However, these tropes of pitiful womanhood also situate the letters in a longer tradition of female petitioning dating back to the middle ages.[19]

---

[15] Sir Richard Sackville to Lady Throckmorton, 11 July 1560, SP 15/9/2 f.43.
[16] Otwell Johnson to Sabine Johnson, 2 June 1545, SP 46/5/1 f.131.   [17] SP 1/81 f.51r.
[18] Daybell, *Women Letter-Writers*, p. 249.
[19] See, for example, W. Mark Ormrod, *Women and Parliament in Later Medieval England* (Palgrave Macmillan, 2020), introduction (pp. 1–24).

In fact, the tradition suggests that women had a particular benefit over men making their petitions heard. This in turn explains why we see women not only petitioning for themselves but also on behalf of their male relatives, friends, and servants. We can observe a general pattern by looking at the use of the word 'favour'/'favor', which is employed most usually in requests for different kinds of help or patronage, and some-times for favours already bestowed. Of 292 letters from women to men using this word, 101 made those requests for themselves (or their family as a whole), 10 were requests on behalf of another woman, 120 asked for favour on behalf of a man (normally a male family member, servant, or letter bearer), and the remainder used the word favour in a non-petitioning context. This appears to be representative: women using the language of petition were seeking help for themselves in less than half of all cases (here 44%). More often, they were positioning themselves as mediators in the case of another, writing letters of recommendation or intercession. The suits brought in letters for family were similar to those that women pursued for themselves, suits con-cerning land, inheritance, judicial trials, and imprisonment. But Daybell estimates that over a quarter of women's letters of petition were penned on behalf of groups outside the immediate and extended family: servants, tenants, neighbours, friends, and clients.[20]

Therefore, while the role of petitioner may seem to cast women in a position of powerlessness, there are two ways in which it could be used to acquire social capital. Firstly, women wielded certain tropes of female weakness as part of a 'linguistic strat-egy' or 'cultural script' that could be employed to their advantage to gain the desired outcomes in the suits they brought.[21] Secondly, by positioning themselves as medi-ators in the suits of other people—usually men—they assumed what scholars of social networks would describe as a brokerage position. As briefly mentioned in Chapter 3 (and depicted in Figure 3.1), Roger V. Gould and Roberto M. Fernandez's classic 1989 study identified five structurally distinct types of broker, which follow from a parti-tioning of actors into non-overlapping subgroups.[22] We might observe that the struc-ture underlying each of the categories of brokerage is what is known as an 'open triad': that is, A is in contact with B, and B is in contact with C, but A is not in direct contact with C. Therefore, B acts as a broker between A and C, bridging what Roland Burt described as a 'structural hole'.[23]

Triads are a local phenomenon within social networks, or what is known as a network motif. Motifs are semantically meaningful 'subgraphs' that serve as building blocks for complex networks. The study of network motifs was pioneered by Paul W. Holland

---

[20] Daybell, *Women Letter-Writers*, p. 237.

[21] See Lynne Magnusson, 'A Rhetoric of Requests: Genre and Linguistic Scripts in Elizabethan Women's Suitors' Letters', in *Women and Politics in Early Modern England, 1450–1700*, ed. James Daybell (Taylor and Francis Group, 2004), pp. 51–66 (pp. 55, 63); and Daybell, *Women Letter-Writers*, p. 249. See also Caroline Bowden, 'Women as Intermediaries: An Example of the Use of Literacy in the Late Sixteenth and Early Seventeenth Centuries', *History of Education* 22 (1993), 215–23.

[22] Roger V. Gould and Roberto M. Fernandez, 'A Formal Approach to Brokerage in Transaction Networks', *Sociological Methodology* 19 (1989), 89–126 (pp. 92–3).

[23] Ronald S. Burt, *Structural Holes: The Social Structure of Competition* (Harvard University Press, 1992).

and Samuel Leinhardt.[24] Triadic motifs can help us to better understand women's social standing and influence with the epistolary network. At the scale of the entire network, so often their role is dwarfed. But by extracting these sub-graphs for analysis we can begin to find patterns in how women used letters to manage their social worlds. Specifically, the model of brokerage gives us ways of thinking about how women might have been involved in the practice of petitioning. Firstly, it allows us to see how petitioning, and the required model of mediation, can be understood through several different forms of brokerage relationship illustrated in Figure 3.1. For example, an estranged husband and wife may require the wife (A) to appeal to an *itinerant broker* (B) to gain financial support from her spouse (C). A woman (B) might approach the Principal Secretary (C) with an appeal as a *representative* of her family. Or an individual (A) might approach one of Elizabeth I's ladies-in-waiting (B) seeking the queen's favour, positioning that lady-in-waiting as a *gatekeeper*. One might also imagine a nobleman or noblewoman being approached as a *liaison*, if they were believed to have a useful route to power. Secondly, these theoretical scenarios allow us to see that women could occupy any of the three positions within these triads, as a petitioner, mediator, or holder of power. In the following section we examine how we can automatically extract all triads involving women from our data to understand the extent these structures can help us to understand women's structural access to power.

'Triads'

We find 1,369 triads in the network that include at least one woman other than the monarchs Elizabeth I, Mary I, or Mary Queen of Scots. These triads involve 184 women. Within this list of triads, some women dominate: Honor Plantagenet, Viscountess Lisle is part of 168 triads; Mary of Guise in 160 triads; Catherine de'Medici, Queen consort of France in 98; Mary of Austria, Queen consort of Hungary and Bohemia in 82; Catherine of Aragon and Katherine Parr each appear in 79; Eleanor Fitzgerald, the Countess of Desmond in 78; and Margaret Tudor, Queen consort of Scotland in 76. The involvement in triads therefore correlates with traditional power structures. Queens consort were born to wealthy or royal families, and consolidated their social position by marrying monarchs; they were the rare kinds of women who would have been the *recipients* of petitions, or functioned as mediators because of their access to (absolute) power.

But the number of triads intersecting on an individual is not the only way of ascertaining their relationship to power. Their *position* within each triad is also a crucial factor. If we look at Figure 5.1 we can see that the 1,369 triads that include at least one woman (other than Elizabeth I, Mary I, or Mary Queen of Scots) can be broken down into 35 different subtypes. That variety of forms is due to the fact that triads can be

[24] Paul W. Holland and Samuel Leinhardt, 'The Statistical Analysis of Local Structure in Social Networks', *NBER Working Papers 0044*, National Bureau of Economic Research (1974).

(a)   35 distinct types of triad involving at least one woman*

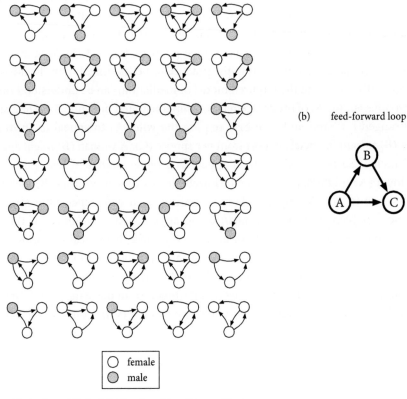

(b)   feed-forward loop

| ○ | female |
| ◉ | male |

*) who is not Elizabeth I, Mary I, or Mary Queen of Scots.

Figure 5.1 (a) The 35 distinct types of triad present in the network in which at least one individual is a woman who is not Elizabeth I, Mary I, or Mary Queen of Scots. (The three monarchs can still appear in the triad if there is at least one other woman present.) (b) A general feed-forward loop. Position A can be regarded as an input node, e.g. a petitioner, B as a mediator or moderator, and C as an output node. Of the 35 types of triads only two (the first in the second row and the first in the last row) do not contain a feed-forward loop.

either open or closed triads, can have differing numbers of women, and each edge can be marked by three different directions (A to B, B to A, or reciprocal). However, for the purposes of our inquiry into petitioning and mediation, we were interested in extracting a particular subset of these triads that resemble the underlying structure of brokerage relationships. These are known in network analysis as simple feed-forward loops. In its basic form, a feed-forward loop consists of only three nodes: an input, a moderator, and an output node (see Figure 5.1b). Importantly, the feed-forward loop underpins the majority of the triads depicted in 5.1a; of the thirty-five types of triads depicted, only two (the first in the second row and the first in the last row) do not contain a feed-forward loop.

This motif—the feed-forward loop—is studied in many real-world networks, such as gene regulatory networks.[25] In the specific context of social networks, and the history of their study in the social sciences, these structures are known as transitive triads and have been studied for several decades.[26] The idea underpinning transitivity is that, given a link from node A to node B, and a link from node B to node C, then a link from node A to node C should also be forged. If we can compare Figure 5.1b to Gould and Fernandez's brokerage models we can see that the feed-forward loop or transitive triad has an additional edge that is absent from the brokerage diagrams, even though it is implicitly sought: i.e. node A approached node B precisely because they want something from node C. However, in some cases, it may benefit node B if the triad stays open. This is the basic precept of Burt's theory of structural holes: by focusing on absent ties, Burt generalises Mark Granovetter's key insight that valuable information tends to flow across weak ties (discussed in Chapter 3). For Burt, a tie becomes valuable if it 'bridges' across previously unconnected groups, thus spanning a structural hole. The influence pertains the longer the final edge is not closed. In the case of gatekeeping, we can see how the relationship is specifically managed to avoid direct access between nodes A and C. However, an act of petition could lead to the edge subsequently being closed if the petition was successful.

In this case we are using the feed-forward loop to explore how women positioned themselves in relation to power. We are using the positions that a woman occupies within the feed-forward loop as a rough-hewn proxy for her social position, based on an assumption (following early modern epistolary etiquette) that a person of lower social standing or greater vulnerability would seek to approach someone above them in the hierarchy through a mediator figure, whose own social standing might usefully bridge those of nodes A and C. There are of course many cases where this will not pertain, but it holds in enough places to be a useful heuristic in the first exploratory stages of this investigation into women's relationships.

Of the 1,369 triads involving at least one woman (other than the three female monarchs mentioned above), 1,349 triads contain feed-forward loops. Tables 5.1a–c show sections from a ranked list of the 184 women involved in these feed-forward loops, ordered by their average position; those shown are involved in 4 or more triads but the rank position takes into account those women involved in less than 4. The tables enumerate how often these women found themselves in positions A, B, or C (as shown in Figure 5.1b), the average position, and also gives the total number of triads in which they were involved.[27] Those who spent most time in position A will have an average

---

[25] See, for example, Shai S. Shen-Orr, Ron Milo, Shmoolik Mangan, and Uri Alon, 'Network Motifs in the Transcriptional Regulation Network of Escherichia coli', *Nature Genetics* 31:1 (2002), 64–8.

[26] See, for example, Anatol Rapoport, 'Spread of Information through a Population with Socio-structural bias: I. Assumption of Transitivity', *Bulletin of Mathematical Biophysics* 15 (1953), 523–33; Paul W. Holland and Samuel Leinhardt, 'A Method for Detecting Structure in Sociometric Data', *American Journal of Sociology* 76 (1970), 492–513.

[27] Note that it is possible for the position counts to exceed the total number of triads, as the position counts are done using the directed feed-forward loop, and there are two ways in which an individual can occupy each of the given positions A, B, or C, and both of those ways can be realised for the same (undirected) triad.

Table 5.1a Solely petitioners

Rank	Name	Pos. A	Pos. B	Pos. C	Average position	Total triads
3	Isabel Manners, Countess of Rutland	14	0	0	1.00	10
4	Lady Margaret Hawkins	20	0	0	1.00	10
5	Mabel Fitzgerald (née Browne), Countess of Kildare	18	0	0	1.00	10
6	Charlotte De La Marck	19	0	0	1.00	10
7	Anne Fiennes, Baroness Dacre	12	0	0	1.00	7
8	Lady Bridget Norris	9	0	0	1.00	5
9	Lady Anne Hungerford	5	0	0	1.00	4
10	Marie de Brimeu (Princess of Chimay)	7	0	0	1.00	4
11	Françoise de Bourbon, Duchess of Bouillon	5	0	0	1.00	4
12	Eleanor Zouche	8	0	0	1.00	4

Table 5.1b Mixed fortunes

Rank	Name	Pos. A	Pos. B	Pos. C	Average position	Total triads
88	Frances Devereux, Countess of Essex	33	1	0	1.03	22
89	Elizabeth Howard, Duchess of Norfolk	6	1	0	1.14	6
90	Dorothy Percy, Countess of Northumberland	16	3	0	1.16	9
91	Louise, Princess of Orange	21	4	0	1.16	11
92	Lady Ursula Walsingham	9	2	0	1.18	7
93	Mary Wriothesley, Countess of Southampton	11	3	0	1.21	9
94	Anne Dudley, Countess of Warwick	16	5	0	1.24	10
95	Agnes MacDonald, Lady of Dunnyveg	6	2	0	1.25	5
100	Lady Penelope Rich	9	4	0	1.31	9
101	Anne Howard, Countess of Arundel	10	5	0	1.33	8
102	Lady Thomasina Malbie	6	3	0	1.33	6
112	Anne Boleyn	32	15	3	1.42	25
117	Lady Anne Fitzwilliam	6	4	1	1.55	5
118	Princess Cecilia of Sweden	5	3	1	1.56	4
119	Elizabeth Talbot, Countess of Shrewsbury	45	25	11	1.58	42
120	Marguerite de Navarre	4	6	0	1.60	9
121	Anne Williamson	2	3	0	1.60	4
122	Lady Elizabeth Cromwell	2	3	0	1.60	4

position close to 1, those who spent most time in position B will be closer to 2, and those primarily in position C will have an average position that approaches 3. The tables break down the filtered results into three regions, which correspond broadly to the position they most often occupy in petitioning relationships. Those near the top (shown in Table 5.1a) are almost always the petitioners, those at the bottom (Table 5.1c) are often in a position of power and influence. In between these extremes we find

Table 5.1c Ladies of power

Rank	Name	Pos A	Pos B	Pos C	Average position	Total triads
124	Mary Princess of Castile	18	12	7	1.70	20
125	Margaret of Parma	11	9	4	1.71	15
126	Margaret Douglas, Countess of Lennox	19	15	8	1.74	25
127	Catherine de'Medici, Queen consort of France	104	85	49	1.77	98
128	Jeanne III, Queen of Navarre	21	17	10	1.77	18
129	Lady Elizabeth Russell	15	13	7	1.77	21
130	Anne of Denmark	4	4	2	1.80	4
131	Eleanor Fitzgerald, Countess of Desmond	85	72	56	1.86	78
132	Princess Catherine de Bourbon	14	14	9	1.86	16
133	Margaret Tudor, Queen consort of Scotland	102	86	77	1.91	76
134	Queen Katherine Parr	65	62	52	1.93	79
135	Queen Mary I*	44	49	35	1.93	55
136	Mary of Austria	74	74	60	1.93	82
137	Mary of Guise	125	120	102	1.93	160
138	Catharine of Aragon	62	58	54	1.95	79
165	Mary Queen of Scots*	17	19	18	2.02	32
166	Queen Elizabeth I*	153	178	185	2.06	197
167	Julian Penn	2	4	3	2.11	4
168	Jane Suárez de Figueroa, Duchess of Feria	2	3	4	2.22	5
171	Honor Plantagenet, Viscountess Lisle	16	135	198	2.52	168
172	Sabine Johnson	0	7	11	2.61	8
176	Isabella of Portugal, Holy Roman Empress	0	6	13	2.68	7
177	Mildred Cooke Cecil, Lady Burghley	0	0	8	3.00	5

useful examples of mediation (Table 5.1b). Note that the ranking given in the first column denotes the individual's position within the 184 total women found in feed-forward loops (even though we are only listing the subsample of 51 women to appear in more than 4). As such, the ranking provides a useful way of orienting us towards large scale patterns of communication, as well as individual case studies that can be reconstructed.

Petitioning

Tables 5.1a–c show the fifty-one women (of 184 total) who were involved in four or more triads. In Table 5.1a we find a wide range of women who are always found in position A in the feed-forward loop; and the first half of Table 5.1b contains women who are predominantly in position A. We can quickly see, by examining their titles, that these are not low-ranking women. But nevertheless their letters reveal that they were consistently placed in the role of petitioner. This coincides with what Daybell noted in his lengthy trawl through the archives: that the majority of female writers of letters of petition that he encountered were well connected and of high birth, operating within a relatively wide social ambit (though a small proportion of letters derived from women of the professional and middling classes, the wives and widows of lawyers and merchants).[28] His analysis of the epistolary conventions and linguistic tropes used in such letters of petition suggest that they were 'coded according to early modern social hierarchies'.[29] However, to be able to identify this genre simply from these women's position within feed-forward loops is exciting because it not only offers a new way to discover these roles, but shows that these coded social hierarchies were embodied not only in the language these women adopted, but in the way that they navigated their epistolary networks to meet their needs. In other words, they are coded in the *structure* of their social networks.

One of the dominant categories of writer that appears in position A (in Tables 5.1a and 5.1b, and elsewhere in the ranking) is the widow. This prominence is perhaps unsurprising: Daybell has suggested widows were responsible for over 50% of letters containing personal suits and over 35% of letters written on behalf of third parties.[30] In particular these letters are concerned with their changed circumstances, requesting aid for legal or financial concerns, or for the support of their children. For example, Isabel Manners, Countess of Rutland (Table 5.1a) sent 8 letters, which implicate her in 14 overlapping feed-forward loops (contained in 10 undirected triads),[31] in each of which she occupies position A. Each of these missives dates from after her husband's death, and each is a petition treating the negotiations surrounding his will. Her first letter, dated May 1587, is one to the new Earl of Rutland asking him to discharge a recognizance of £4,000, and the administration of the will of the late earl.[32] As they had no sons, the Rutland title had passed to the earl's brother, Roger Manners, but their daughter Elizabeth kept the title Baroness Ros. Elizabeth was the subject of another letter of petition, in which her mother complains to Lord Burghley that she has had communications with Sir Thomas Cecil, respecting Elizabeth's jointure, but that Cecil had required that the lands should be charged with his debts, to which she objects.[33]

Other widows in Table 5.1a include Lady Margaret Hawkins and Lady Bridget Norris, and in Table 5.1b we find Dorothy, Countess of Northumberland. Hawkins's letters place her consistently in position A. Her first letter in the State Papers, dated 12 December 1595 and addressed to Robert Cecil, provides news from her husband, Admiralty official Sir John Hawkins, on the events of his voyage via the Canary Islands, asking for it to be passed onto the queen. Whilst a request of sorts, the fact that she is in receipt of news that she can share gives her a certain status. However, when she writes again seven months later, we see her adopting the role of petitioner to the queen, sharing news of the admiral's death, and the cause of her suit: that on the death of her late husband, amongst other debts, she is left owing the crown £2,000 from his 'late vnfortunate voiage'. As was common in such letters, the language underscores the pitiable and desperate position of the widow: 'Yf it shalbe your highenes

---

[28] Daybell, *Women Letter-Writers*, p. 238.   [29] Ibid., p. 243.   [30] Ibid., p. 239.

[31] Note again that there can be up to twice as many directed feed-forward loops as undirected triads.

[32] Dowager Countess of Rutland to Roger Manners, Earl of Rutland, May 1587, SP 12/201 f.88.

[33] SP 12/231 f.55.

pleasure to impose this charge vppon mee, I muste and will sell all that euer I possesse, leaue my selfe a beggar, putt awaye my servaunts and soiourne w[i]th my frendes, rather then leaue it vnperformed and haue yo[u]r dyspleasure.'[34] The language is designed to arouse pity, but also shows the often dramatic changes in fortune that widows experienced following a husband's death.

The letters of Lady Norris, wife to Sir Thomas, a soldier later made Lord President of Munster, once again position her consistently in position A (with no exceptions). They bear similar motifs to the previous widows, but her correspondence is also instructive for her conscious use of mediating figures. Like the Countess of Rutland, all her letters in the State Papers appear following the death of her husband on 20 August 1599, who was fatally wounded during a skirmish in Munster.[35] Her letter to the Lord of the Council on 25 September is a petition for the monies due to Sir Thomas.[36] And a letter to Sir Robert Cecil dated 13 November encloses a note of the value of Moyalloe—the castle her husband had been undertaking to build in Munster, upon which he had expended £5,000—and a petition to tender the property to the queen in order that she might have a pension for her maintenance and to bring up her child.[37] Lady Norris emphasises her need by detailing the £1,000 of debt with which she is threatened, and which prevents her from laying 'her dear husband in the earth in any honourable sort'. However, her failure to secure immediate relief led her to try a range of alternative avenues, specifically via female mediators. In a letter to Robert Cecil in 1599 she asked him to peruse an enclosed letter, which she had procured from her friend to plead on her behalf, due to her 'present unfitness to plead for my distressed self', and asking his leave 'to remember your Honour of the reward for me and my distressed infant's relief'.[38] The interest here is not only the use of a (presumably female) mediator, but the effect of claiming to be in too much distress to plead on her own behalf.

A more orchestrated attempt to leverage a female mediator is employed in 1600 when she writes to Lady Elizabeth Ralegh—a communication that is highlighted by Daybell because of its layered manoeuvres. It includes an enclosure that comprises minutes for a letter she wished Cecil to write to the Lord Deputy of Ireland. The letter also entreats Lady Ralegh to enlist the help of her husband, Sir Walter Ralegh, in the letter's composition: 'I haue framed the effect of a letter that I desire to Haue derected to the Deputy [of Ireland] from Mr secretarie. I trust yf S[i]r Walter Raleighe will take the paines to polishe them he shall also preuaile in the subscribing therin.'[39] The minute itself concerns the granting of a warrant to Lady Norris to remove any captain lodging on her lands, and to place there the company in the leading of her overseer; that there should be only so many men left in the castle as should be fit to secure it from any sudden violence, being a place of very great importance in the time of war.

---

[34] Cecil Papers, 42, f.48 (Daybell's transcription).
[35] Judith Hudson Barry, 'Norris, Sir Thomas (1556–1599)', *ODNB*, <https://doi.org/10.1093/ref:odnb/20285>.
[36] SP 63/205 f.333.
[37] 'Cecil Papers: November 1600, 1–15', in *Calendar of the Cecil Papers in Hatfield House: Volume 10, 1600*, ed. R. A. Roberts (HMSO, 1904), pp. 371–84. BHO, <http://www.british-history.ac.uk/cal-cecil-papers/vol10/pp371-384>.
[38] Cecil Papers, BHO, <http://www.british-history.ac.uk/cal-cecil-papers/vol9/pp413-440>.
[39] Cecil Papers, 83, f.28 (Daybell's transcription).

The example of Ladies Norris and Ralegh is useful because it allows us to see how this method can help us identify not only the position of female petitioners, but also those of female brokers and mediators: while she does not appear in the tables because she is only involved In two triads, Lady Ralegh appears in position B in two feed-forward loops (see full table in supplementary material[40]), and an analysis of letters shows her petitioning on behalf of her husband for support to go to sea, and on behalf of her kinsman Mr Brett.[41]

As well as widows, amongst our results in Table 5.1a we also find a woman seeking help due to another kind of bereavement. Charlotte de La Marck would seem to be beyond the need for letters of petition given that she was the ruling Princess of Sedan, and a Duchess of Bouillon in her own right between 1588 and 1594. However, her brother's death in 1588 (by which she came to this title) led to a period of unrest in the Principality of Sedan. As Mark W. Konnert writes, 'under the rule of Huguenot La Marcks, Sedan developed into a significant centre of Huguenot strength in an otherwise strongly Catholic region'.[42] Following her brother's death, Duke Charles of Lorraine led an attack against Charlotte, laying siege to Jametz in January 1588. It is in this context that she writes two letters to Elizabeth I. The second, on 10/20 August 1588, asks the queen to move the States of Holland to allow that her name might be put in the letters and passport originally granted to her brother, the late duke. This would have provided some relief in her affairs and accommodated her subjects with regard to their exports. She writes that she is in urgent need of money to avert the imminent danger to God's church in her small state, and asks Elizabeth for the loan of 15,000 or 20,000 crowns.[43] The troubles detailed in the Duchess's letter are of a different scale and nature to those in the widows' letters; it is, rather, a state emergency.[44] However, the strategy bears some close resemblance to Lady Norris seeking the mediation of an influential woman to gain help. She approaches Elizabeth both directly and through Elizabeth's closest associates, Burghley, Walsingham, and Robert Dudley, the Earl of Leicester (placing Elizabeth in position C).

Bereavement was not the only cause of female vulnerability and petitions, of course. We see women petitioning on behalf of husbands and friends for other kinds of trouble. For example, Table 5.1a shows that Mabel Fitzgerald, the Countess of Kildare, appears in position A in eighteen feed-forward loops, petitioning on behalf of her husband Gerald (the 11th Earl of Kildate, known as 'the wizard earl') to the Privy Council, Burghley, and Walsingham in the 1560s, 1570s, and 1580s, but especially in

---

[40]   See <https://github.com/tudor-networks-of-power/supplementary>.

[41]   See Lady Ralegh to Sir Robert Cecil, 7 April 1595; and Lady Ralegh to Sir Robert Cecil, 25 July [1595]. See Cecil Papers, BHO, <http://www.british-history.ac.uk/cal-cecil-papers/vol5/pp161-173>, and <http://www.british-history.ac.uk/cal-cecil-papers/vol5/pp281-297>. On Lady Ralegh's role as a mediator, see Karen Robertson, 'Negotiating Favour: The Letters of Lady Ralegh, in *Women and Politics in Early Modern England, 1450–1700*, pp. 99–113.

[42]   Mark W. Konnert, *Local Politics in the French Wars of Religion: The Towns of Champagne, the Duc de Guise, and the Catholic League, 1560–95* (Taylor and Francis, 2017), p. 183.

[43]   SP 78/18 f.313.

[44]   We might compare here the case of Louise de Coligny, Princess consort of Orange. Although her husband dies, and Elizabeth writes with commiserations, she is not seeking support. See, for example, Princess of Orange to Elizabeth I, 5/15 1585, SP 84/1 f.54.

the four years before he died in 1585 (after which we see a couple of classic widows petitions).[45] Her ongoing petitions were required due to the frequent accusations of treason against Kildare, and his imprisonment, first in Dublin Castle and later in the Tower of London. His survival was perhaps due to her calls for favour, but also to the regard in which he was held by Elizabeth, who twice dismissed the charges of treason against him.

Treason also plays into the intriguing case that connects two further women, Frances Devereux, Countess of Essex (Table 5.1b) and Jane Daniell (who is only involved in three triads—see supplementary material[46]). Some of the Countess of Essex's earlier petitions in 1595 were on behalf of John Daniell, Jane's husband. Daniell had entered Robert Devereux the Earl of Essex's service in the 1580s, following a period in the household of Thomas Butler, the 11th Earl of Ormond. It was through his service to Essex that Daniell met Jane van Kethull, a religious exile from Flanders who had become lady-in-waiting to Frances following the death of the countess's first husband and before her marriage to Essex in 1590. Jane and John were married in the winter of 1595/6. Around the same time the countess sent a number of letters petitioning the Lord Chancellor, the Lord Keeper, and the Chief Baron for John Daniell to be compensated for the loss of profits and tithes (presumably on his lands in Cheshire) and to be allowed to enjoy his lease.[47] In these letters, then, the countess was using her status to petition on behalf of her servants, with whom she appears to have been on good terms: the Daniells had named one of their children Deveraux after the earl. The next we hear of the Daniells in the countess's letters, however, is in 1601 following the famous Essex rebellion—during which Essex tried to raise the support of Londoners to seize the queen and force her to dismiss Cecil amongst others. Following his subsequent trial, she writes to the Lord Keeper, the Lord Treasurer, the Lord Admiral, and Cecil concerning John Daniell's 'cozening' (deception), and a plea for payment of £2,000.[48]

The nature of the cozening is worth laying out in a little detail. On 10 October 1599 the countess had entrusted a locked casket of letters to the safekeeping of her lady-in-waiting Jane. With her husband under house arrest (due to returning from Ireland without permission, and having failed to suppress the long-running revolt of the Catholic Earl of Tyrone) she presumably felt that the letters were too sensitive to fall into the hands of the authorities. How sensitive they truly were is hard to gauge as none of them now survive. As Andrew Gordon remarks, given the trouble they would subsequently cause, it is likely that they were destroyed by the earl or countess.[49]

---

[45] See especially Mabel, Countess of Kildare to Walsingham, 1 February 1581, SP 63/80 f.143; 3 April 1581, SP 63/82 f.7; 26 March 1584, SP 63/108 f.153; and 26 October 1584, SP 63/112 f.113. David Finnegan, 'Fitzgerald, Gerald [Garret, Gearóid], eleventh earl of Kildare (1525–1585)', ODNB, <https://doi.org/10.1093/ref:odnb/9557>.

[46] See <https://github.com/tudor-networks-of-power/supplementary>.

[47] See SP 46/52 f.43, SP 46/52 f.44, and SP 46/52 f.45. On the life of the Daniells, see Andrew Gorden, 'Recovering Agency in the Epistolary Traffic of Frances, Countess of Essex and Jane Daniell', in Women and Epistolary Agency in Early Modern Culture, 1450–1690, ed. James Daybell and Andrew Gordon (Routledge, 2016), pp. 182–206. For Jane and John's own autobiographical accounts see TNA HAD D/F/TYS 71/9, 'Danyells Dysaster" and HAD D/F/TYS 71/9, 'Misfortunes of Jane Danyell'.

[48] 'Cecil Papers: December 1601, 26-31', in Calendar of the Cecil Papers in Hatfield House: Volume 11, 1601, ed. Roberts, pp. 531–88. BHO, <http://www.british-history.ac.uk/cal-cecil-papers/vol11/pp531-588>.

[49] Gordon, 'Recovering Agency', p. 190.

However, when the casket was subsequently returned, a number of letters were missing. According to the narrative that can be reconstructed from the legal proceedings, and from John and Jane's own autobiographical accounts, John realised that they contained evidence somehow damaging to Essex, and he intended to present them to the queen. John employed a scrivener, Peter Bales, to make copies of these letters, and then demanded £3,000 for the return of the letters, arguing that something was owed to him in lieu of Jane's dowry which had never been paid—essentially blackmailing the countess. In April 1600 the countess paid the Daniells £1,720, having raised the money by selling her jewellery. Essex's trial brought to light John's blackmail and he was called before the Star Chamber on 17 June 1601. The scrivener Bales testified against him, claiming that he had been asked to imitate Essex's handwriting closely when copying the letters, suggesting that John was making forgeries rather than just copies. John was fined £3,000 and imprisoned in the Fleet. The countess's letter, mentioned above, sought £2,000 of that fine because, like many of the widows discussed above, her husband's debt was causing her great hardship.[50]

The State Papers, however, also allow us to see the other side of this case through the feed-forward loops we see associated with Jane Daniell. Looking at the larger correspondence of both Jane and John Daniell shows that the pair were serial petitioners, with more than 100 submitted by the couple over their lifetime.[51] From 1601 onwards, these touch on the Essex affair and the long-term impact of the case on their finances. For example, in December 1601 she wrote to the queen directly complaining that she was:

> dailie afflicted by the Countesse of Essex, whom I have served most faithfullie (as my saviour is my witnesse), and yet because we are not able to paie her Ladyship 2,000l. of your Majesties said fine so speedelie as she would, therefore by her frends she hath [...] found meanes to cause my poore children to be turned out of the Personage of Hackney [...] and so to leave them in danger of beggarie.[52]

She also complained both to the Council and Elizabeth in late 1601 and early 1602 about the financial implications of the misvaluation of their property and goods. She claimed that the sheriff and other officers had valued the Hackney parsonage and the goods, worth £2,000 at £700, to the loss of £1,300—an amount which would have satisfied both Her Majesty and the Countess of Essex.[53] Thus, as the wife of an incarcerated and indebted husband, Jane Daniell's situation was not too dissimilar from that of a widow, and Gordon argues that she was a shrewd negotiator: it was to Jane that

---

[50] For another letter of petition following her husband's execution, see Countess of Essex to Sir Robert Cecil, 3 April 1601, 'Cecil Papers: April 1601, 1–15', in *Calendar of the Cecil Papers in Hatfield House: Volume 11, 1601*, ed. Roberts, pp. 153–65. BHO, <http://www.british-history.ac.uk/cal-cecil-papers/vol11/pp153-165>.

[51] See <https://petitioning.history.ac.uk/investigating-petitioners/1601-1610-jane-and-john-daniell-pester-the-authorities-with-many-petitions/>.

[52] SP 12/283 f.41.

[53] Jane Daniell to Council, 13 December 1601, SP 12/283 f.40; Jane Daniell to the queen, January 1602, SP 12/283a f.43.

the secretary to Lord Treasurer Buckhurst, Robert Bowyer, wrote to arrange her husband's submission to the countess—a key stipulation of the settlement.[54] John eventually obtained his release from the Fleet in 1604, after the accession of James I. His and Jane's subsequent petitions largely constitute appeals for the restoration of his lands and bonds. Lady Essex's portion of the fine had not been paid by 1607, when the balance was granted to her new husband, the Earl of Clanricarde.

Another sub-category within our results is separated and estranged wives. Examples in Table 5.1a include Lady Anne Hungerford, and in Table 5.1b Elizabeth Howard, Duchess of Norfolk, Dorothy, Countess of Northumberland, and Anne Williamson. The Duchess of Norfolk appears in six feed-forward loops in position A, including different configurations of the duchess, Henry Stafford, Lord Stafford, Ralph Neville, Earl of Westmorland, Thomas Cranmer, Archbishop of Canterbury, Cardinal Thomas Wolsey, and Thomas Cromwell. In all but one case Cromwell or Wolsey occupy position C and the other men act as intermediaries. One person she does not correspond with, however, is her husband. She had married Thomas Howard, then Earl of Surrey (and later 3rd Duke of Norfolk), at some point before 8 January 1513, when she was only 15 years of age. She accompanied him to Ireland in 1520–2 when he was posted there. Through birth and marriage, she was very well connected. But in around 1527 Norfolk took a mistress, Bess Holland, the daughter of his steward. He began to live with her openly at Kenninghall and resolved to separate from the duchess, which he finally did in 1534. Before this date the Duchess of Norfolk had used her position as a wife of a noble to petition for help or patronage for others, as we see in a 1524 letter to Wolsey in which she thanks him for accomplishing her petition for Jaks Darnell and her other suits, or in the 1533 letter from Cranmer addressing her request for the benefice of Cheving to go to her chaplain, Mr Molinex. However, following the separation from her husband, which resulted in her dispatch to Redborne, all her letters are concerned with the management of her position; rather than using the position of her husband, she writes letters that triangulate between Cromwell, her brother Stafford, and her brother-in-law Westmorland (to whom she had also been betrothed), which demonstrate her utter reliance on the mediation of others and her helplessness when such aid was not forthcoming.

The triads between the duchess and these three men all leave her in position A in the feed-forward loop. She sends a series of eight letters to Cromwell, which are well targeted not only because of his influence as Principal Secretary, but also because of his close professional relationship with Norfolk, who was uncle to the new queen Anne Boleyn. These letters provide an account of her treatment at the duke's hands: that she was held in a state of virtual imprisonment with a meagre annual allowance of only £200, and that she was abused by the duke, his mistress, and their servants. For this she seeks redress, refusing the wishes of others for them to reconcile, or her husband for divorce, but rather petitioning for fair financial settlement so that she might

---

[54] See Gordon, 'Recovering Agency', p. 194.

'haff ha bat er leffene' (have a better living).[55] She asks Cromwell to treat both with the king and with her husband to bring this about.[56] The only surviving letter to her brother merely asks for her niece Dorothy to be sent to her (presumably to act as a servant).[57] The request, while not explicitly relating to her marriage, is concerned with the comfort of her living, and its pleading tone seems to have arisen from her brother's previous refusal to take her side in the breakdown of her marriage, or offer any kind of support. Her brother's lack of help is documented on the other side of the triad in the communication between Cromwell and Stafford. On 13 May 1533 Stafford sends Cromwell an answer to a letter (now lost), in which he appears to have asked Stafford to intervene to restore 'tranquility' between Norfolk and the duchess. Stafford refuses, writing: 'the redresse of this standythe not in the aduertysement of her kynne, wherof she hathe had sundry tymes great plentye [...] praing her to call to remembrance the great honor she is come to by that noble and her husband, and in what possibilitie she was yn to do all her frendes good if she had folowed the Kinges highnes pleasure.'[58] In another letter written on the same day to Norfolk, he also refuses the duke's request to take his sister into his house, stating his inability to stop her 'wild language'.[59]

Taken together we see how Stafford is being pushed by Cromwell and Norfolk into the role of mediator, and also his absolute refusal to accept it. He has no sympathy for his sister, blaming the duchess's behaviour for the rift between the couple. It is unclear if he thinks her claims are lies, but he certainly believes that she should overlook any ill treatment for the benefits she gains by virtue of being so well married, and those it would bestow on her family and friends by placing her close to the crown. The implication here is that he resents the way that his sister has given up her own status as a powerful mediator, able to bestow aid and patronage through her connections. Here, then, the duchess's loss of social capital places her in a position with very little leverage. The relationships that Stafford, Cromwell, and Norfolk have with one another are valuable and not worth risking for a marital dispute: they pre-existed the contact with the duchess, and it was clearly imagined that they would outlast it. The major topics of the correspondence that passes between the three concern government business and personal petitions for lands; and so we never see that triangle between the Duchess and Duke of Norfolk closed. Of her correspondents the only one who seems to have materially helped the duchess is Westmorland, whom she thanks for his troubles in 1540.[60]

What this example shows is that however well positioned a woman may have been during her marriage (including any powers of mediation that her position gave her), once separated she was in the lowest possible position in the hierarchy within the triad. With only the language of weakness on her side, she needed a mediator to take that petition to her husband, or to a higher power if the husband refused to respond to such counsel. We see this same pattern in the letters of Lady Hungerford and Anne

---

[55] Cotton Vespasian F/XIII f.151.   [56] See SP 1/106 f.219r and BL, Cotton Titus B/I f.388.
[57] Duchess of Norfolk to Lord Stafford, 1537, Cotton Titus B/I f.162.   [58] SP 1/76 f.39.
[59] SP 1/76 f.38.   [60] SP 1/158 f.201.

Williamson. Anne Williamson wrote a pitiful letter to Cecil on 6 November 1598 complaining that following twelve years of marriage, her husband was committed to the Tower for reasons to which she was never made privy; but, now 'being released from thence, he utterly rejects my company'. She states that she has tried the mediation of friends without avail, and he yields her no 'relief', although at his request she sold and conveyed away her jointure without assurance of any other living. What became of Anne is hard to reconstruct, but it seems her husband served Cecil as an agent following his release from prison. The evidence suggests positive outcomes from the petitions of deserted wives were rare, and that their best recourse was their own networks.

This was the case for Lady Anne Hungerford (née Dormer), who was sister to Jane, Duchess of Feria. In 1558 Anne had become the second wife of Walter Hungerford, but in 1568 Walter sued for divorce, alleging that his wife had tried to poison him some years earlier, and that she had committed adultery and had an illegitimate child with William Darrell. Lady Hungerford's correspondence forms five feed-forward loops with her in position A, two of which are pertinent to the divorce proceedings. The first is the triad connecting Lady Hungerford to Darrell and Walsingham. From these letters we can see Lady Hungerford's affair with Darrell was true, although the attempt on Walter's life is more uncertain: the letters make the affair explicit and say that it must be kept secret, and she even swears to marry Darrell if her husband dies.[61] The second triad that is pertinent is that formed between Lady Hungerford, Dorothy Essex (lady-in-waiting to her sister the Duchess of Feria), and Darrell. It is in this feed-forward loop that we see Lady Hungerford actively petitioning. It is notable that she does not seek help from the traditional power structures represented by key statesmen and principal secretaries, to which we saw widows resorting; rather, she chose to utilise her female networks. Her letters of petition are to her sister and her sister's lady-in-waiting. The letters to these women are written five days apart and concern similar topics, including her lack of friends, her poverty, her children's rejection of her, and the refusal of her husband Walter to pay her £250 in costs as the court had directed, preferring to lie in the Fleet prison rather than give her a penny.[62] Essex's value as mediator here is twofold: not only is she asked to speak on Lady Hungerford's behalf with the Duchess, but there is also the opportunity for her to intercede with Darrell due to a familial connection. Essex writes to Darrell on three occasions (all undated), which form the B→C edge in the triad with Lady Hungerford. These letters mostly concern news about common friends and other intimacies, but one refers to 'my ladi hungerfordes matter which I think ys nether strang[e] to yowr years [ears] mor over I beleav her self writes to you thereof'.[63] While Essex makes no direct plea on behalf of Lady Hungerford, by invoking the matter to Darrell, she acts to remind him, and stand in solidarity with her mistress's sister. Darrell did not

---

[61] See SP 46/44 f.188, SP 46/44 f.196, SP 46/44 f.186, SP 46/44 f.190, SP 46/44 f.194.

[62] Anne Lady Hungerford to the Duchess of Feria, 20 March 1570, SP 15/18 f.50; and Hungerford to Dorothy Essex, 25 March 1570, SP 15/18 f.62r.

[63] SP 46/44 f.174v.

honour this relationship; and ultimately Lady Hungerford's relationship with Essex turned out to be more valuable. Unlike the use of male mediators, which often only function in times of crisis, we see Anne's female relationships crystallising following her separation from Walter; she ultimately moves to be near her sister in Belgium, where she remained for the rest of her life.

Sorting the feed-forward loops by the women's average position also helps us to identify a case in which the estranged wife appears in position B. Dorothy, Countess of Northumberland (Table 5.1b) appears sixteen times in position A within feed-forward loops, and three times in position B. We can see in her letters some clear examples of petition, such as her letter to the queen following the death of her first husband Sir Thomas Perrot in 1597, which has much in common with the letters written by widows discussed above.[64] However, she is also the recipient of two letters from her brother, the Earl of Essex, which situate him in position A and her in position B in three separate feed-forward loops (with Elizabeth, Burghley, and Robert Cecil in position C). In these letters he upbraids her for 'the breach' between her and her second husband, Henry Percy, 9th Earl of Northumberland, and pleading with her to write Northumberland a letter expressing her desire of reconcilement, and showing her 'constancy of your purpose to live with him hereafter [as] a wife should do with her husband'.[65] While the Earl of Essex's letters would not formally be viewed as a petition, he is nevertheless trying to initiate and manage a piece of communication with a third party (Northumberland) which would be to his family's reputational and social benefit. Daybell and Gordon discuss the textual evidence for a ghosted draft copy (in the hand of Essex's servant, Edward Reynolds), which shows the attempts of male family members like Essex to orchestrate the relationships of their female relations.[66] But the countess had the power to act or not, and it is unclear whether the letter was ever sent.

The example of the Countess of Northumberland shows that while many of the women discussed above are implicated exclusively in letters of petition, which place them consistently in position A, women's epistolary positioning within hierarchies could change according to circumstances. If we look at the lower half of Table 5.1b and Table 5.1c we can see that some women occupy positions B and C to a considerable extent. Where one interaction may require a letter of petition, others might position a woman as a mediator, or even someone empowered to bestow favours and grace. Examples of women who occupied both petitioning and mediating roles include Anne Dudley, Countess of Warwick (Table 5.1b), who was a lady-in-waiting and close friend of Elizabeth I. Whilst on the one hand we see her occupying position A in her petitions to Burghley, Walsingham, Sir Julius Caesar, and Roger Wilbraham, it is worth noting that these letters of petition are in fact on behalf of others (although

---

[64] See Cecil Papers, BHO, <http://www.british-history.ac.uk/cal-cecil-papers/vol14/pp31-49>.

[65] Essex to the Countess of Northumberland, 7 March 1600, 'Cecil Papers: 1600', in *Calendar of the Cecil Papers in Hatfield House: Volume 14, Addenda*, ed. E. Salisbury (HMSO, 1923), pp. 126–59. BHO, <http://www.british-history.ac.uk/cal-cecil-papers/vol14/pp126-159>.

[66] Andrew Gordon and James Daybell, 'Living Letter: Re-reading Correspondence and Women's letters', in *Women and Epistolary Agency*, ed. Daybell and Gordon, pp. 1–20 (pp. 3–4).

no prior letters from those individuals to the countess survive): a letter to Burghley forms a request to stay the suit of the Countess of Leicester and her husband for the lease of certain lands in Gloucestershire, which have been extended for the late Earl of Leicester's debts;[67] and her letter to Sir Julius Caesar and Roger Wilbraham, despite placing her in position A, is in fact a petition on behalf of 'a distressed gentlewoman' named Elinor Sampson.[68] In some cases, however, the prior letters asking for her mediation do survive and these place Warwick in position B, as in the case of Peter van Heile (position A) in which he asks her to move the queen for a protection for Giovanni Darcuero from his debtors.[69]

A similar case can be seen with Lady Ursula Walsingham (Table 5.1b). Whilst following the death of her husband Sir Francis we see the usual petitions of a widow (topics such as favour for her children and permission to purchase land), her earlier letters show how her marriage to the Principal Secretary positioned her as a mediator.[70] For example, her cousin Thomas Copley was a Roman Catholic exile who wrote a steady stream of petitions to the Tudor government: he wrote to Lord Burghley (30 letters), Walsingham (11), the other Principal Secretary, Thomas Wilson (5), and the queen herself (3), desiring pardon and permission to return to England and to enjoy his estates, but always maintaining his adherence to the Catholic faith. His letter to Lady Walsingham is on the same topic, asking for her to help him by 'friending me to your husband', in the hope that he can induce Her Majesty to answer his suit to be restored to his living.[71]

Taken together, then, the feed-forward loops method is a useful heuristic for understanding how epistolary activities place women in different power relations to their correspondents. It is effective at identifying relationships in which petitioning is likely to be happening, the places in which women move from petitioner to mediator, and the gradations that should be noted within that distinction, as seen with the Countess of Warwick (petitioning, but on behalf of others). The benefit of taking this approach is that we can think about the way that women's positions changed in response to their circumstances and the people with which they corresponded. But how useful is this framework for helping us think about the opposite end of the scale of power and influence?

Power

In Table 5.1c are the women with the very highest average position in the feed-forward loop. They are of interest because they occupy more triads in positions B and C than A,

[67] Anne Countess of Warwick to Lord Burghley, 28 November 1590, SP 12/234 f.40.
[68] Anne Countess of Warwick to Dr Caesar and Mr Wilbraham, 3 October 1602, SP 12/285 f.52.
[69] Peter van Heile to the Countess of Warwick, August 1596, SP 46/125 f.236.
[70] For examples of her petitions, see Lady Walsingham to Lord Burghley, 3 June 1591, Lansdowne Vol/67 f.104, and 24 October 1591, Lansdowne Vol/67 f.106.
[71] Thomas Copley to Lady Walsingham, 3 January 1582, SP 15/27/1 f.91.

suggesting they most often occupy brokerage or power roles within these local interactions. If we look at the correspondence of these women, we can see the kinds of power they wield varies considerably. It includes, of course, the indubitable power of female monarchs. Elizabeth I, for example, appears almost at the very bottom of the table as we might expect. The few women outranking her do not send as many letters, but do have a slightly higher proportion of feed-forward loops in which they occupy position C. Note again that, due to their exceptional position in the government, the monarchs Elizabeth I, Mary I, and Mary Queen of Scots are here only considered if the triad also contains another woman, which is why the number of triads is relatively modest. Without these restrictions they would be part of 5,789, 951, and 542 triads respectively, instead of 197, 55, and 32. Despite the divergence in the scale of data, however, the average positions for each of these monarchs are rather similar with and without restrictions—2.03, 1.82, and 1.77 compared to 2.06, 1.93, and 2.02. The reason the monarchs do not appear even more often in position C is likely because they send many orders—corresponding to outgoing edges—to subordinates at various levels, which increases their counts in positions A and B.

For these reasons, hubs like Elizabeth are less interesting to look at. Once we look beyond them we can see more clearly that feed-forward loops can help us to explore the kinds of power and influence open to women of rank. Some of the more obvious examples are noble figures such as the Duchess of Feria (rank 168) and Isabella of Portugal, Holy Roman Empress (rank 176). Their status is due not only to their proximity to power, but also their status in their own right as recipients of news, information, and pleas.

Isabella was wife to Charles V, and her correspondence is largely included as a result of the editorial policy behind *Letters and Papers, Foreign and Domestic, of the Reign of Henry VIII*, which sought to include papers from other European state archives where they touched on English affairs (as discussed in Chapter 4). In this case the papers are included because they discuss Henry VIII's campaign to have the dispensation to marry his brother's widow Catherine of Aragon (granted in 1509) overturned so that he might be free to remarry, and the attempts of the emperor—who was Catherine's nephew—to intervene (discussed further in Chapter 6). These epistolary exchanges place her exclusively in positions B and C (6 loops and 13 respectively), an indication of power which is supported by her biography: Isabella was appointed as regent and governor of Spain during her husband's absences on military campaigns and to attend the administration of his other territories, especially between 1529–33 and 1537.[72] In this way Isabella acts as a kind of second body for the emperor: or what Gould and Fernandez would describe as a 'representative' role (see Figure 3.1). We see this demonstrated structurally by the fact that he co-appears in every feed-forward loop with Isabella bar one. This shows a triangulation of contacts between the two, an effective strategy for working together.

---

[72] Fabien Montcher, 'Politics and Government in the Spanish Empire during the 16th Century', in *A Companion to the Spanish Renaissance*, ed. Hilaire Kallendorf (Brill, 2018), pp. 61–87 (p. 68).

The contents of the letters show Charles's trust in Isabella to conduct important international affairs. In a letter dated 31 July 1531 he informs her how the proceedings in the case of Catherine of Aragon made it necessary to examine the treaties made about the queen's marriage, and requests Isabella to make a search for them, giving details of whom to consult and where to travel, before sending them on to his ambassador Miguel Mai in Rome. On other military matters he writes to her on 10 March 1531 that he has paid much attention to what she has written about procuring provisions in England for his fleet which is to sail to Africa.[73] But perhaps more importantly, completing those triads between her and Charles, we see her in direct receipt of intelligence from ambassadors, including Ortiz (from whom she received 50 letters), Jean Hannaërt, sieur de Liederkerke, viscount of Lombeck (7 letters), Miguel Mai (3), Lope Hurtado de Mendoça (2), and Chapuys (2). Ortiz's letters, which make up the majority, provide intelligence on English affairs, focusing amongst other things on Henry's 'great matter', the treatment of Princess Mary, the execution of Anne Boleyn, and the suppression of the monasteries; other figures offer news from other European locations, such as Mendoça's missive which touches on 'the enterprise of the Turks against Christendom'.[74] These, then, were highly political intelligences rather than the more domestic kinds of news in which early modern women more commonly traded.

Similarly, we see how the receipt of intelligence is linked to positions B and C in the feed-forward loops in which the Countess (later Duchess) of Feria is implicated. Jane Dormer was an English lady-in-waiting to Mary I who, after the queen's death, married Gómez Suárez de Figueroa y Córdoba, the Count (and later Duke) of Feria—a close confidante of Philip II of Spain and his first ambassador to Elizabeth I's court. After her marriage to Feria, she went to live in Spain, and it is from this period that all her letters date. Several items appear to have entered the archive through surveillance and letter interception, due to her focal position within the network of English Catholic exiles—'although she was never clearly linked with conspiracy'.[75] Before leaving England the Count of Feria had petitioned Elizabeth, with some difficulty, to remove over sixty of the most prominent Catholic members of Mary I's court from England, which over the coming years would 'reassemble around Jane'.[76]

The countess's epistolary network as evidenced in the State Papers is represented in Figure 5.2. These communications place her more frequently in positions B and C (three and four loops respectively) than position A (just twice). These positions of

[73] 'Henry VIII: July 1531, 16–31', in *Letters and Papers, Foreign and Domestic, Henry VIII, Volume 5, 1531–1532*, ed. James Gairdner (Longman, Green, Longman, & Roberts, 1880), pp. 160–77. BHO, <http://www.british-history.ac.uk/letters-papers-hen8/vol5/pp160-177>.

[74] Lope Hurtado de Mendoza to the Empress, 4 May 1532, LP, BHO, <http://www.british-history.ac.uk/letters-papers-hen8/vol5/pp459-470>.

[75] Albert J. Loomie, *The Spanish Elizabethans: The English Exiles at the Court of Philip II* (Burns and Oates, 1965), p. 96. On the role of interception in the shaping of the State Papers, see Rachel Midura, Sebastian E. Ahnert, and Ruth Ahnert, 'Shadow Networks: Identifying Intercepted Letters in the Elizabethan State Papers Foreign', in *Network Analysis and the Early Modern Archive*, ed. Ruth Ahnert, Philip Beeley, Esther van Raamsdonk, and Yann Ryan as a special issue of *Huntington Library Quarterly* (forthcoming).

[76] See Hannah Leah Crummé, 'Jane Dormer's Recipe for Politics: A Refuge Household in Spain for Mary Tudor's Ladies-in-Waiting', in *The Politics of Female Households: Ladies-in-Waiting Across Early Modern Europe*, ed. Nadine Akkerman and Birgit Houben (Brill, 2013), pp. 51–71 (p. 58).

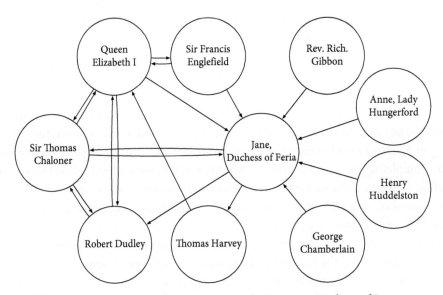

Figure 5.2 The network surrounding Jane Suárez de Figueroa, Duchess of Feria.

potential influence can be understood in different ways. If we examine her times in position B, we can see that in all cases the people occupying positions A and C are both representatives of Elizabeth's court, while she—an outsider, held in some suspicion—is poised between them. The two loops in which she triangulates between Elizabeth's court (Elizabeth and Leicester) and Sir Thomas Chaloner are especially interesting. Chaloner was Elizabeth's ambassador in Spain, and thus acted as a channel of information from the Tudor court to the duchess, as well as as a source of international intelligence. For example in a letter dated 25 March 1563 he apologises that the last news from England contained only parliamentary matters not yet at a point, and then gives a summary of various topics: that the grant of the subsidy is passed; the suit of the Commons about the succession has good hopes given; Havre de Grace is still kept by the English for some further parlance for Calais; and that peace is concluded between the contrary parts in France.[77] As with the case of Isabella, we might note that these are serious political notices, rather than familial or domestic news. Such news necessarily imparts power, as it is something the countess could trade: Hannah Leah Crummé has argued that her hospitality to and correspondence with figures like Chaloner gave her access to information that eventually made her one of the advisers of Philip II of Spain.[78] Conversely, looking at the edges between Chaloner and the court in these loops we can see his dispatches to Elizabeth and Dudley

---

[77] It is worth noting that Clarence H. Miller has commented that he was not the best source of news because 'the queen, Cecil, and his friends did not keep him posted on the latest news and this lack of information caused him serious embarrassment. The most important political struggles at this time were in France, and most of the news Chaloner wrote has more anecdotal than historical value'. See Clarence H. Miller, 'Chaloner, Sir Thomas, the elder (1521–1565)', *ODNB*, <https://doi.org/10.1093/ref:odnb/5040>, and Tracey A. Sowerby, 'Elizabethan Diplomatic Networks and the Spread of News', in *News Networks in Early Modern Europe*, ed. Joad Raymond and Noah Moxham (Brill, 2016), pp. 305–27.

[78] Crummé, 'Jane Dormer's Recipe for Politics', p. 62.

(as well as others at court, such as William Cecil) are marked by information about the Feria household.

The receipt of intelligence can also be attributed as the cause of the countess's appearance in position C in the feed-forward loops. These are not just from Chaloner but also from Sir Francis Englefield, a former privy councillor to Mary I who became a close associate of exiled Catholic leaders William Allen and Robert Persons, and was in receipt of a pension from Philip II during the last twenty years of his life. As his associations might suggest, he was a source of quite different intelligence from Chaloner. Writing from Antwerp in 1570, where he had recently landed with other English Catholic refugees, he passes on information about those gathered with him in Antwerp, personal news pertaining to her family and closely associated Catholic families such as the Dacres, news of Mary Queen of Scots, and intelligence regarding the activities on the borders of Scotland.[79] In this letter he also acts as an additional mediator speaking on behalf of her sister Anne Hungerford (discussed above, with regards her estrangement from her husband), saying that he has asked her to 'come hither', and requests Jane to speak with their father. Compared to Chaloner, then, his letters are much more personal. Part of that personal dimension is betrayed by his more frank expressions of sympathy for Mary Queen of Scots, and hope that there will be a provision passed by Parliament to tolerate the Catholics to use their religion.[80] For this reason he warns her to take care of his letters, for 'though there be no treason, yet is the worst there, and more than I say to any other, or were meete to come to other's eyes'. Englefield's letters are illustrative of how the countess's correspondence situated her between the networks of Elizabeth's court and those of Catholic exiles—and here we might note that beyond the feed-forward loops in Figure 5.2 we see many more communications between the countess and exiled Catholics. These, like the communications with Engelfield, all presumably entered the State Papers archive through interception. Her position between these communities could be interpreted as a source of influence and power, allowing her to bridge structural holes. This positioning has been commented on. The author of her *ODNB* entry remarks, somewhat dismissively, that she 'found herself at the centre of political intrigues whose complexity and international dimensions often eluded her.'[81] One wonders if such a judgement would have been levied if she were a man. By contrast, Crummé has argued that the influence Jane asserted as an adviser of both English and Spanish monarchs, 'paired with the soft diplomacy of her role as the hostess of English ambassadors in Spain, allowed her both to perpetuate and develop Catholic culture in England, even while

---

[79] Sir Francis Englefield to the Duchess of Feria, 20/30 April 1570, SP 15/18 f.117.

[80] Englefield to the Duchess of Feria, 12 November 1574, BL, Cotton Caligula C/III f.513.

[81] M. J. Rodriguez-Salgado, 'Suárez de Figueroa [née Dormer], Jane, duchess of Feria in the Spanish nobility, (1538–1612)', *ODNB*, <https://doi.org/10.1093/ref:odnb/7836>. Albert J. Loomie has also suggested (despite describing her as a 'leader' within the community of what he dubs Spanish Elizabethans) that she was manipulated by the 'confidence man' Thomas Morgan and her sister Anne Hungerford (Loomie, *Spanish Elizabethans*, pp. 115–121).

she lived abroad.[82] Her influence, then, is agreed in scholarship—even if the level of her control and premeditation is debated.

Elsewhere in Table 5.1c we can see that others associated with positions of power were wives of influential statesmen. In these cases there is something to be said about the opportunities provided by such a role, and how different women chose to use that power. The wives of this kind who appear near the bottom of the table (with the highest ranking) were also remarkable in their own right. Maybe the clearest examples of this are Mildred Cecil (later Lady Burghley), and Honor Plantagenet, Viscountess Lisle.

Mildred Cecil famously benefited from the fact that her father Sir Anthony Cooke provided his five daughters with an education equal to that afforded to his sons, and she undertook various translation work (although none of it was published in her lifetime).[83] Cecil is the only woman involved in more than four triads and solely at position C in all feed-forward loops: she is eight times in this position, as shown in Figure 5.3 by the denser cluster of men on the right-hand side of the network. We know that it was 'incumbent upon upper-class women as mistresses of the household to further the interests of servants and retainers, to mediate in their affairs and to forward their suits' and that 'numerous women took charge of patronage interests during

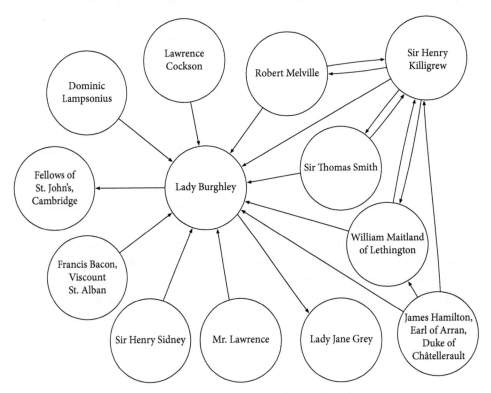

Figure 5.3 The network surrounding Mildred Cecil, Lady Burghley.

[82] Crummé, 'Jane Dormer's Recipe for Politics', p. 51.
[83] See Caroline Bowden, 'The Library of Mildred Cooke Cecil, Lady Burghley', *The Library: Transactions of the Bibliographical Society* 6 (2005), 3–29.

the absence of husbands'.[84] But as well as dealing with petitions, Mildred Cecil's actions stretch into the political sphere. This is particularly evident in the six feed-forward loops featuring James Hamilton, Duke of Châtellerault, 2nd Earl of Arran (formerly regent of Scotland), William Maitland (secretary to Mary of Guise), and Robert Melville (diplomat). The three men had, at the time of writing to her, taken the side of The Lords of the Congregation, a group of Protestant Scottish nobles who mounted a successful rebellion against Mary of Guise (in Maitland's case, acting as a double agent against the regent). The letters Mildred Cecil received from the three concerned the Treaty of Edinburgh of 1560, drawn up between the Commissioners of Elizabeth I with the assent of the Scottish Lords of the Congregation and the French representatives of King Francis II of France, to formally conclude the wars of the congregation. Her husband, William Cecil, was at that point urging the queen against her inclinations to commit herself to military involvement in Scotland. As Caroline Bowden has commented, 'The letters were couched in terms indicating that Mildred Cecil had a considerable knowledge of the issues under discussion and could influence her husband in the attempt to secure English support against the French presence in Scotland'.[85] Maitland's situation at this time was particularly precarious, and his letter to Mildred Cecil dated 19 July 1560 contains a petition for her help 'in the matter whereunto she knows he most earnestly presses'.[86] Bowden argues that Mildred Cecil's correspondence thus demonstrates that she 'was not afraid to give advice even on public affairs at a high level', and this is borne out by her structural position in these triads.

The case of Lady Lisle illustrates another kind of exceptionality. It derives in part from the voluminous archive she leaves behind due to the seizure of the Lisle family papers when her second husband, Arthur Plantagenet, Viscount Lisle, was imprisoned in the Tower of London on suspicion of treason (see Chapter 2). It is a hugely valuable source for understanding the ways in which women of such stature managed their households, from the quotidian topics of ordering meat, through to the soft diplomacy required to shore up political esteem. The plentiful records mean that we are able to minutely reconstruct her epistolary relationships, and she appears in hundreds of feed-forward loops—predominantly in positions B and C (135 and 198 loops respectively, as opposed to only 16 in position A). This positioning has several causes. It is due in part to her being at the centre of her own archive, and in part to her beneficial marriage: after the death of her first husband, Sir John Basset of Umberleigh, Devon, she married Lord Lisle. Her marriage placed her in an international and noble network, with strong links to the royal family. She moved to Calais in 1533 when Lord Lisle was appointed Lord Deputy of Calais, which located her at an important geographical hub: as merchants kept headquarters there, ambassadors passed through

[84] Daybell, *Women Letter-Writers*, pp. 236 and 237.

[85] Caroline M. K. Bowden, 'Cecil [née Cooke], Mildred, Lady Burghley (1526–1589)', *ODNB*, <https://doi.org/10.1093/ref:odnb/46675>.

[86] William Maitland to Lady Cecil, 19 July 1560, Cecil Papers, BHO, <http://www.british-history.ac.uk/cal-cecil-papers/vol1/pp243-256>.

on their missions, and, because the French continually sought to reclaim this land, an English garrison and naval presence were maintained there. Barbara A. Hanawalt observes, 'had Honor remained the wife of a West Country gentleman, her network would have been limited to her relatives and other similarly situated families'.[87] However, we should not underestimate her gift for social networking: Lady Lisle's social skills benefited Lord Lisle's social standing as much as his status benefited her.

This mutual benefit is demonstrated in the way that the couple triangulated on the same contacts, Lady Lisle shoring them up with her hospitality, gifts, and favour. If we begin looking at the 135 times that Honor appears in position B, we can see that in almost all cases it is Lord Lisle (78 times) or Thomas Cromwell (44 times) who appear in position C; the four exceptions to this are Edward Seymour, 1st Earl of Hertford (later Duke of Somerset) who appears nine times, Thomas Thirlby, Bishop of Westminster and Ely (three times), and Anthoinette De Saveuses (once). The relationship with Cromwell was perhaps the most vital, next to that with Henry VIII, to foster and buttress. A good relationship with Cromwell was of primary importance because, as the king's *locum tenens* in Calais, Lord Lisle was required to enact the king's will, which was conveyed primarily through communications from his Principal Secretary. Lady Lisle's four letters to Cromwell cover a range of topics. Two early letters, from before her departure to Calais, thank him for their good supper on All Hallows Day, and for various other kindnesses, including the loan of £20; in thanks she sends with her letters two cheeses and wildfowl.[88] The niceties continue after her arrival in Calais; but the underlying concern is laid bare by a letter from Cromwell to Lady Lisle dated 20 November 1534. It clearly arrives in response to a letter, now lost, expressing her concern about a rumour that she has fallen out of the secretary's favour. He writes reassuring her that 'I knowe no cause wherefor I should so be' and that, if she continues to act as he hears, she will 'fynd me as redy to do you any pleasure that may lye in me to do as any frynd that ye have'.[89] Such concerns clearly continued as we can see in the feed-forward loops containing William Popley in position A (who has been described as Cromwell's 'principal man of business'),[90] Lady Lisle in B, and Cromwell in C. In a letter to Lady Lisle dated 16 October 1535 he replies to a letter of hers complaining of a report made to his 'master' (Cromwell) that she does 'intermeddle' much in Lord Lisle's business concerning the king's causes.[91] Popley reassures her of Cromwell's continued regard for Lord Lisle, but the accusation here is interesting. It suggests that the unnamed person regarded Lady Lisle as wielding too much influence. However some scholars have dismissed her political influence: for example, David Grummitt (in his *ODNB* entry for her husband) writes, that she 'was active in maintaining Lisle's links with the court, but her priorities, in common with those of

---

[87] Barbara A. Hanawalt, 'Lady Honour Lisle's Network of Influence', in *Women and Power in the Middle Ages*, ed. Mary Erler and Maryanne Kowaleski (University of Georgia Press, 1988), pp. 188–214 (p. 193).

[88] Lady Lisle to Cromwell, 22 November 1532, SP 1/72 f.53; and 6 December 1532, SP 1/72 f.100.

[89] Cromwell to Lady Lisle, 20 November 1534, SP 3/10 f.144.

[90] I. S. Leadham, *Selden Society: Select Cases before the King's Council in the Star Chamber*, vol. 2 (B. Quaritch, 1903–11), p. 262.

[91] Popley to Lady Lisle, 16 October 1535, SP 3/13 f.65.

most other aristocratic women of the time, appear to have been the running of her household and provision for the education and marriage of her children'.[92] However, this assessment overlooks the structural benefits that work in this area might bestow on a family's political standing; thinking in terms of feed-forward loops allows us to see this better.

An example of how these 'domestic' concerns provide structural benefits to the Lisle's family network can be seen in the feed-forward loops involving Seymour. The single communication that places Lady Lisle in position B to Seymour's nine-time position C concerns a previous petition to his family to place Lady Lisle's daughter, Katherine Basset, in his household. The request for patronage of this sort was designed to flatter the recipient, cement the social relationships between the families, and, if granted, it would have placed the daughter favourably, allowing her to develop her own network. However, as Lady Lisle's letter reveals, although the Seymours granted her request, her daughter Katherine ultimately decided to stay with Lord and Lady Rutland (where she resided at that time). Perhaps to smooth over the embarrassment of this change of plan, Lady Lisle sends along with the letter her own prized bird to replace the bird she had previously sent as a gift, and which had been killed by a cat.[93] The entire negotiation was clearly designed to heal rifts: in the preceding five years the Lisles and Seymours had clashed in two land disputes.[94] It was, then, more than a domestic concern. Moreover, it is clear that Lord Lisle understood the broader importance of good education for their children, because he did not leave its negotiation alone to his wife; rather, the pair's communications triangulate frequently on the men and women tasked with educating their children, shown by them appearing interchangeably in positions B and C (often in both) with those individuals. On the education and placement of Lady Lisle's sons, John, George, and James Basset, we see the pair communicating with Richard Norton, the abbot John Capon, the priest John Atkinson, the President of the Parliament Paris Guillaume Poyet, scholars Antony Barker and John Berkensaw, the merchant Guillaume le Gras, and the priest Jehan des Gardins. It appears that while Lord Lisle took it upon himself to oversee the programme of his stepsons' education, Lady Lisle managed the particulars. Efforts to place Lady Lisle's daughters also went through both Lisles, as documented in their correspondence with Anne Rouaud Madame de Bours, Jenee de Saveuses Madame de Riou, Anthoine (or Adriane) de Noyelle, Abbess of Bourbourch, and John Husee. Husee was a London merchant and Lord Lisle's business agent in England who acted as a letter courier, kept Lord Lisle informed of political events at court, sourced them merchandise, oversaw the placement of Lady Lisle daughters into the service of Queen Jane Seymour (just before her death), Eleanor Lady Rutland, and Mary Countess of Sussex. This labour, then, positioned their broader family into households of power and influence,

---

[92] David Grummitt, 'Plantagenet, Arthur, Viscount Lisle (b. before 1472, d. 1542)', *ODNB*, <https://doi.org/10.1093/ref:odnb/22355>.

[93] Lady Lisle to the Earl of Hertford, 10 May 1539, SP 1/151 f.123.

[94] M. L. Bush, 'The Lisle-Seymour Land Disputes: A Study of Power and Influence in the 1530s', *Historical Journal* 9 (1966), 255–74.

as Husee's letter to Lady Lisle on 1 September 1537 makes clear, when he mentions that, by the other letters from Lady Sussex, she will find that the queen (i.e. Jane Seymour) wishes to see her daughters as soon as possible.[95]

Lady Lisle also served the standard role accepted by wives of men in high office, as an alternative point of access for petitions. Just as ladies-in-waiting received the petitions of those desiring the queen's favour, here we see Lady Lisle acting both as a 'representative' and 'gatekeeper' of her husband (to return to the roles identified by Gould and Fernandez's brokerage taxonomy, see Figure 3.1). The Lisles received requests for official posts and employment, for financial relief for those in distress, as well as the everyday requests for them to reward the carriers of letters. Hanawalt shows that the volume of requests for patronage increased considerably after the Lisle's move to Calais, and we might imagine that Lady Lisle's involvement was required to manage this. Lord Lisle was the one with the authority to make appoint-ments, so more of these requests were addressed to him in the first instance, but Lady Lisle was often contacted to ask for support in these suits. One such example are the two triads involving Lord Edmund Howard (at that time Controller of Calais), Lord and Lady Lisle (with the couple alternately in positions B and C). He wrote to Lady Lisle in 1535 regarding her efforts to place one of his sons, who has now been placed with a good living elsewhere, and requesting Lady Lisle to 'move my Lord for the grant' for another of his sons or servants.[96] What is notable about this exchange is that there are no letters to Lord Lisle on this topic, suggesting either they were lost, that the two men had discussed these employment options in person, or that the arrange-ments were directed entirely through Lady Lisle. On numerous occasions we see suits first sent to Lord Lisle then raised with Lady Lisle, presumably when a positive response, or perhaps even a reply, failed to emerge. Other examples, however, suggest Lady Lisle was influential in her own right, and had powers to grant certain petitions that need not pass though her husband. Stephen Gardiner corresponded with both husband and wife, but when he sought to gain help for a widow in a letter dated 20 June 1534, he wrote to Lady Lisle alone (she appears in multiple feed-forward loops with Gardiner, but always in a position 'above' him). After first asking if he might make 'bold to recommend this widowes cause', he makes it clear that he writes 'neyther to your husband [...] ne to any others herin knowing that your ladiship maye stand in stede sufficient in this mater wherein is only required iustice at the Marshalls hands'.[97] He is not asking her to further a suit already submitted to her husband, but rather states that she has the means to handle this suit herself, by seeking justice from the marshal. This example shows the significance of the role she occupied within her net-work: a woman with the social capital to intercede directly with the authorities on behalf of suitors.

Taken together then the network data provides a structural argument about Lady Lisle's influence and proximity to political power that provides a corrective to

---

[95] John Husee to Lady Lisle, 1 September 1537, SP 3/11 f.71.
[96] Lord Edmund Howard to Lady Lisle, 1535, SP 3/11 f.27.
[97] Gardiner to Lady Lisle, 20 June 1534, SP 3/14.

more dismissive evaluations of her role. Concerns such as education, land disputes, and hospitality may seem marginal to political concerns, but Lady Lisle's epistolary manoeuvres suggest a keen understanding of how such communications could maintain and extend the influence of her family with those at the epicentre of power. Given this it is striking Lady Lisle does not have her own entry in the *ODNB*. However, clearly it was recognised in her own time that she was engaging in social networks in a way that was rare for women: as well as the complaint about her 'intermeddling' in her husband's affairs discussed with Popley, Hussee also advised her to refrain from writing to Cromwell or Francis Bryan about the advancement of her daughter into the service of the queen, reporting that 'it is thought by my Lady Sussex and other your Ladyship's very friends that it is no meet suit for any man to move such matters, but for such ladies and women as be your friends.'[98] There were clear ideas about which matters were suitable for men and women to dabble in, and which networks were the correct and seemly ones for women to go through, which Lady Lisle challenged.

A final example from the list of women in Table 5.1c most frequently in positions of power is Julian (or Juliana) Penn. She occurs twice in position A, four times in position B, and three times in C. While her counts are smaller, she is a woman of note due to the fact that her position of power accrued from her own skills rather than those of an influential husband. As well as being highlighted through this ranking of feed-forward loops, she has the eleventh highest betweenness centrality ranking of all the women in our dataset; yet she has received relatively little scholarly attention. Her most prominent connection to the centres of power is via her sons Michael Hicks (secretary to Lord Burghley and later to his son Sir Robert Cecil), and Baptist Hicks (who sat in the House of Commons and was created Viscount Camden). She was married twice, first to Robert Hicks (an ironmonger and mercer, who died in 1558), and secondly Anthony Penn (who died in 1572). Her inheritance allowed her to establish herself as a moneylender, as well as continuing in the mercery business.[99] It is primarily through her financial activities that Penn is implicated in the network: Penn sends only three letters (to three different people), but receives sixteen from twelve different people. These letters trace a network of financial transactions that connect her to men and women at all levels of society, including some in positions of great influence.

The key relationship across every single feed-forward loop is that with Sir Robert Cecil. He wrote a letter on 3 October 1588 asking Penn to procure for him a silver bell, formerly belonging to Don Pedro, now in Lady Gore's possession, and instructing her to pay whatsoever she asks for it, and with the condition that 'it mowght not be knowen to her that I am to haue it for I wold not be beholding vnto her.'[100] We might assume that the connection between Cecil and Penn was initially made via her

---

[98] John Husee to Lady Lisle, 2 October 1537, SP 3/12 f.100.

[99] See Alan G. R. Smith, *Servant of the Cecils: The Life of Sir Michael Hicks, 1543–1612* (Rowman and Littlefield, 1977); and R. G. Lang, 'Social Origins and Aspirations of Jacobean London Merchants', *Economic History Review* 27:1 (1974), 28–47.

[100] Robert Cecil to Julian Penn, 3 October 1588, Lansdowne Vol/58 f.89r.

son Michael Hicks, who had forged a firm friendship with his master's son (although there is no letter between mother and son to enshrine this relationship as an edge). Importantly, we see the relationship between Penn and Cecil triangulating on several others seeking to borrow money from her, which suggests Cecil may have made the introduction, and that from Penn's perspective the relationship with Cecil would provide some kind of assurance that these third parties would repay her. Figures closing the triad include Cecil's nephew William (who writes requesting to borrow £50 and promising to pay 'more than ordinary interest'),[101] Sir Thomas Arundel, Sir John Haryngton, and Henry FitzGerald, Earl of Kildare. Such assurances were necessary: the reason that the Earl of Kildare appears in position B to her A, and C to her B is not because she was seeking a favour but rather chasing him for unpaid debts. In this letter dated 23 June 1591 she rebukes him for 'false sewrring [swearing]' and informs him she had 'complaned to the qwene who hath promes me that I shall take no wrong at mans hand'.[102] The suggestion here that Penn had access to the queen is an impressive one, and appears to have been successful: he replies that he means to stand by his word, but asks her to 'beare with me but till my mane retorne with mony owt of Ireland'.[103]

What is perhaps more interesting than the calculated rationale of her lending practices is the social capital Penn's lending practices bestowed upon her. The favour she had stored up by aiding the great and the good also allowed her to ask for help— both for others and for herself. Penn seems to have taken pity on a number of people brought into debt. In this period debtors were often detained in prisons, especially the Counters, until they could pay back their creditors—people like Penn.[104] However, once admitted to a Counter it was difficult for inmates to buy themselves out because they were required to pay for their own food, bedding, and clothing.[105] Despite her profession, Penn was clearly concerned about the impact of prison on people's lives, writing in a letter to one Hardwick that owed her money 'the sommer comes on apace, hott seasons are contagious especiallie in prisons, and such melancholy places', and offering him repose in her house instead.[106] Perhaps for this reason, Penn used her position with Cecil to seek help for one Mr Skynner, who required 'mitigacion of his fyne and enlargement owt of prison'.[107] Her favour may also have protected her when she gave shelter in her home to Charles Chester, who had been arrested on Cecil's orders on suspicion of being a Recusant.[108] Cecil was naturally troubled that this enemy of the state has been discovered in the home of the mother of his servant and

---

[101] Sir William Cecil to Julian Penn, 1599, Lansdowne Vol/103 f.268r.
[102] Julian Penn to the Earl of Kildare, 23 June 1591, Lansdowne Vol/68 f.207r. For another example of her chasing debts, see Thomas Churchyard to Penn, 1591, Lansdowne Vol/68 f.257r.
[103] Answer contained within the previous letter, see Lansdowne Vol/68 f.209r.
[104] Clifford Dobb, 'London's Prisons', *Shakespeare Survey* 17 (1964), 87–102 (p. 92).
[105] Sean McConville, *A History of English Prison Administration: Volume 1, 1750–1877* (Routledge and Kegan Paul, 1981), pp. 8–10 and 15–21.
[106] Penn to Mr Hardwick, Lansdowne Vol/108 f.33.   [107] See Cecil to Penn, Lansdowne Vol/107 f.106r.
[108] On his arrest and the discovery in his rooms of around twenty 'papistical' books, some written in Spanish, see Richard Young, Justice of the Peace, to Cecil, 19 June 1592, *Calendar of the Cecil Papers in Hatfield House: Volume 4, 1590–1594* (HMSO, 1892).

close colleague, and he wrote a series of letters upbraiding her, but this indiscretion appears to have had no lasting impact on her social standing, as her engagement with the family (e.g. her lending to William Cecil) continues after this event.

Taken together, the case studies above show us how the simple approach of sorting feed-forward loops by women's positionality can help us identify those women who were stepping out of the accustomed roles normally observed in female correspondence of the era, wielding power and granting petitions rather than issuing them, and receiving intelligence more usually associated with the male political sphere. Some of the women have received scholarly attention, but where they have their influence has often been diminished by assertions of lack of understanding or dismissal of their interests as domestic. However, our emphasis on structural positioning allows us to provide a different kind of evidence for their social standing, recentring them as figures of note.

Modelling Mediation

So far our attention has focused on the position of women within triads, which led us to consider single edges and categories of interactions we see across a given woman's triads, rather than the more traditional question that social scientists ask of feed-forward loops: how does the loop close? As such we've captured edges of petition, and edges of mediation, but have rarely been able to reconstruct the full dynamics of social credit and brokerage. While our method could direct us towards petitions by the hundred, the interactions further up the hierarchy are more often about political affairs. The main reason for this is that the full documentation of the fate of petitions is rarely contained in letter archives. Rather, as Daybell has noted, the fulfilment of requests are recorded elsewhere, for example in bishops' registers, Signet Office books, and Court of Wards records.[109] We wanted to discover, however, whether it was possible to automatically extract those rare cases for which the full petition process is marked by letters, revealing the identity of the mediator, and how the case is resolved. In this final section of the chapter we take a small detour, seeking to demonstrate how computational methods can be helpful not because there is a wealth of results to marshal and sort, but because the object of scrutiny is rare. Here computational methods become vital instruments for the close reader. Below we describe a way to extract the rare examples of full petition narratives in a triad—the needles in the haystack—providing the nubs of stories that can be reconstructed from these.

To search for petition narratives computationally we again consider all the 1,369 triads that contain at least one woman who is not one of the three monarchs Elizabeth I, Mary I, and Mary Queen of Scots. For all the feed-forward loops contained therein, we ask whether the first letter from A to B precedes a letter from B to C that mentions A, and in turn whether that letter from B to C precedes any correspondence

---

[109] See Daybell, *Women Letter-Writers*, p. 230.

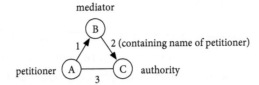

Feed-forward loop containing at least one woman

Figure 5.4 Illustration of the search criteria for petition narratives. The temporal sequence of the communications is indicated by 1, 2, and 3. Note that the link from A to C can go in either direction.

(in either direction) between A and C, signifying the closure of the triad (see Figure 5.4 for an illustration). We attempt to detect the mention of A in the letter from B to C by searching the calendar descriptions of the letters between B and C for the surname of A, which is taken to be the last word in the name label if the label does not contain a comma, and the last word before the first comma otherwise (as commas typically add the title of a person). This is not failsafe of course, but works often enough to generate a number of interesting cases to investigate further.

Amongst the eighty-nine cases the method presents as candidates, there are just a handful of examples that show us the entire petitioning process. Amongst the identified triads we also find a lot of diplomatic correspondence involving female monarchs and leaders, which is an interesting thing to model in its own right. It also captures a number of husband–wife triads, triangulating on third parties regarding various personal and business concerns (such as those involving Lord and Lady Lisle, Sabine and John Johnson, and Elizabeth and Laurence Wynyngton). While we ignore these examples here, these additional patterns in the data suggest other ways in which the method might also be used besides the modelling of petition and the mediation process, and ways that this work could be taken up by others.

One of the clearest demonstrations of the efficacy of the method for finding those needles in the haystack is James Parry's petition to Blanche Parry who was the longest-serving lady, and Chief Gentlewoman of Elizabeth I's privy chamber.[110] James Parry, imprisoned in the Fleet prison for debt, wrote to Blanche on 23 April 1587 asking her to sue Lord Burghley to relieve him.[111] It is unclear if he was a family member, but she clearly honoured this request: we see her writing to Burghley on 11 August to inform him that Thomas Games of Brecknockshire has offered his bond for the release of James Parry's debt and that Blanche will find another bondsman.[112] The triad is closed on the same day when James Parry also writes to Burghley, asking for two commissions (one to examine what has been taken by the sequestrators for the queen, the other to

[110] On the manner in which such ladies in waiting participated at the edge of the political arena, see Anna Whitelock, *Elizabeth's Bedfellows: An Intimate History of the Queen's Court* (Bloomsbury, 2013); Natalie Mears, *Queenship and Political Discourse in the Elizabethan Realms* (Cambridge University Press, 2005); and James Daybell (ed.), *Women and Politics in Early Modern England, 1450–1700* (Taylor and Francis Group, 2004).
[111] Lansdowne Vol/54 f.127r.   [112] SP 46/18 f.21r.

examine his suit with Shepham), and informing him that he has secured help from Blanche Parry and Thomas Games to pay his surety.[113]

Another example involves one of the Countess of Feria's ladies in waiting, Susan Tonge (known as Susan Clarencius, the widow of Thomas Tonge, Clarenceux King of Arms),[114] Chaloner (the diplomat, discussed above), and John Cuerton, an English merchant based in Spain, and regular correspondent of Chaloner's.[115] Cuerton sent Clarencius a letter on 12 October 1562 that seems to refer to a earlier petition on her part (which does not survive) for him to find service for her maid in Bilbao until her nephew comes out of England. His tone is short and he implies that she has rid herself of the maid because she does not wish to 'be at more charges with her' following a misunderstanding about a book (presumably of sensitive content) being placed in Clarencius's chest.[116] Cuerton clearly took the maid's side, explaining the book came not through the maid but a young man named Thomas, and reminding her that she is bound to set her maid free so that she might go back into her home country. Five further letters pass on the subject from Cuerton to Chaloner, the first two complaining that Clarencius does not look after the matter of her maid herself, specifically that she has made no provision for her raiment or other needs, and lamenting that the maid is not sent to England.[117] Later letters from Cuerton pass on news of the maid's plans to travel to London, and finally of her departure, one of which contains a statement of account, presumably for the costs incurred for the dispatch of the maid.[118] The loop is finally closed when Chaloner writes to Clarencius to inform her the maid had embarked for England six weeks previously, and reports receipt of a payment from her, presumably for the maid's costs.[119] While this is strictly a petition being granted, there are also other power dynamics at play: there is the clear expectation on Clarencius's part that Cuerton will do her bidding, seemingly due to his previous service to Chaloner, who was himself motivated to maintain a good relationship with the Countess of Feria and her ladies due to the value they offered as sources of news about the Catholic exile community and the court of Philip II (as discussed above).

The final full loop of petition we can reconstruct using this method concerns the petitions to Lord Burghley and Elizabeth, Countess of Lennox, by John Ingram c.1577 on behalf of the 'Queen's tenants' regarding the agistment of cattle north of the river Yore in Wensleydale (i.e. the proceeds of pasturage in the monarch's lands in England).[120] The dispute regards the true ownership of a parcel of land in Yorkshire: the tenant's assumption of being the queen's tenants is challenged by the countess, who replies to Ingram arguing that the lands are part of her jointure, following her

[113] SP 46/34 f.212r.

[114] David Loades, 'Tonge [née White], Susan [known as Susan Clarencius] (b. before 1510, d. in or after 1564)', ODNB, <https://doi.org/10.1093/ref:odnb/94978>.

[115] Sowerby, 'Elizabethan Diplomatic Networks', p. 310.

[116] Cuerton to Mrs Clarencius, 12 October 1562, SP 70/42 f.187.

[117] Cuerton to Chaloner, 29 October 1562, SP 70/43 f.172; and 9 November SP 70/44 f.109.

[118] Cuerton to Challoner, 7 January 1563, SP 70/48 f.136; 20 January 1563, SP 70/49 f.55; and 25 January 1563, SP 70/49 f.148.

[119] Challoner to Mrs Clarencius, 2 April 1563, SP 70/54 f.23.

[120] Petition to Burghley by John Ingram, SP 46/16 f.0073.

husband's death.[121] As discussed above, widows often needed to pursue legal recourse to protect their jointures. From two letters to Burghley in 1578, we see that the solution she sought for these land disputes was to devolve the earldom to her infant daughter, Arbella: she makes the case that the earldom had been granted to her husband and the 'heyres [i.e. heirs] of his body'.[122]

While there are only three full loops, the method also directs us to another small selection of triads where we have two sides of the petition loop, and a letter closing the loop on a separate matter. One example is the triad between Elizabeth and Francis Fowler and William Ashby. Francis Fowler was an English courtier who served a number of important figures, including the Earl of Leicester, and acted as adviser to James VI of Scotland and Archibald Douglas (the Scottish ambassador in London). Following Leicester's death Fowler retired to Scotland, leaving his wife behind in London. The exchange in question concerns the period following their estrangement, which was accompanied by concerns about her father's bond, regarding his house in the Spittle. The third party in the identified loop was the English ambassador to the Scottish Court, Ashby (via whom Thomas Fowler had been funnelling intelligence to Walsingham and Burghley since at least 1588). Ashby communicated with Elizabeth on 12 August 1589 expressing his happiness at having her husband with him, and his sorrow at her absence.[123] There is no surviving petition from Elizabeth to Ashby, but it is referred to in an earlier communication between Ashby and his nephew Robert Naunton, the month before, who informs his uncle that he had visited Elizabeth and her family, and that 'Mistress Mainie [Elizabeth's mother] toke your letters as kindlie as she had done your former silence unkindlie', and that her daughter (Elizabeth) is willing to go to Scotland, if her husband take order that it is with her parents' blessing and seemly convoy, and she asks Ashby's mediation.[124] The mediation appears to have happened because the same day that Asby sent his letter to Elizabeth, Thomas Fowler also writes to his wife (likely the letters were carried together), in which he says he is responding to her 'angry, threatening letter by Mr. Nanton [Robert Naunton]', apologises for his lack of communication, and responds to the issues of her father's bond, saying it has been sent.[125] Ashby's role, however, is only implied because the edge between the two men is marked by a letter of a later date, on a separate matter.

The rarity of these cases is, of course, due in part to the fact that the granting of formal petitions was documented in other archives, but also to the low representation of women's correspondence in this and other early modern archives. We need more methods for helping us to draw out the threads of women's lives, however few, so their histories can be reconstructed. This particular method in this section of course has broader applications and would render us larger returns if we removed the requirement of one node in our triad being a woman. It serves particular potential for

---

[121] Lady Lennox's answer to John Ingram's complaint, SP 46/16 f.0074.
[122] Lady Lennox to Burghley, 25 July 1578, Lansdowne Vol/27 f.9.
[123] William Ashby to Mrs Fowler, 12 August 1589, SP Scottish 2/598, f.36.
[124] Robert Naunton to William Ashby, 13 July 1589, SP Scottish, 2/598, f.9.
[125] SP Scottish 2/598, f.36.

thinking through the position of official mediators like diplomats and other foreign agents. But its interest here is the way it helps us detect rare features of the archive that would be almost impossible to uncover manually, or at least take many months to uncover. Computational methods can therefore help us with this process of amplifying women's history.

Conclusion

In their book *Data Feminism* D'Ignazio and Klein state that 'data feminism begins by analyzing how power operates in the world'.[126] If we are to be attentive to the role of women in the historic archive, we need to understand how they are positioned in relation to the centres of power. Explicitly, women were excluded from political office, and this is part of the reason that women's letters make up such a small percentage of the archive under examination in this book—less than 4% of correspondents. This statistical underrepresentation can present a pernicious problem in data-driven work: methods designed to look for statistical significance will repeatedly overlook already marginalised constituencies. However, we know that women were implicated in public and political life in manifold ways—to coin another of the tenets of D'Ignazio and Klein's practice, we recognise that the 'numbers don't speak for themselves'.[127] The challenge for us was how to capture the experiences of women when the data is sparse. The issue of scale was the reason we took a different kind of approach in this chapter, closer to the ground than the more 'distant' reading methods employed in previous chapters. By focusing on the network motif of the triad—the smallest unit, or building blocks, in a network beside the dyad—we proffered a method particularly attuned to close reading.

The utility of measuring women's position within feed-forward loops is that it provides heuristic for determining proximity to power. The examples in the previous pages show that identifying the triads in which women occupy position A provides a quick and largely accurate way to identify those moments in their lives when they are most disenfranchised and forced to petition. An important account of how power operates is provided when we turn to women's own accounts of their experiences of powerlessness and loss caused by bereavement, marriage breakdown, and other forms of deprivation—as well as attending to the narrative strategies they exploited to present themselves and their interests. At the other end of the scale the method is also effective in identifying the relationships within which women yielded power and influence—in position B or C—using letters to help others, manage their family's social position, or even in rare cases engage in international diplomacy. As such it allows us to pay close attention to the lives of these women, re-centring them in narratives that may have previously focused on their spouses or other male relatives.

---

[126] D'Ignazio and Klein, *Data Feminism*, p. 21.   [127] Ibid., p. 149.

More importantly, the method allows us to understand the relational nature of power, and that a woman's power was subject to multiple shifts as her circumstances changed throughout her lifetime.

By attuning ourselves to these shifts in power and fortune we do something to challenge the historical power dynamics of the archive. While we cannot do anything about the political marginality of women in the past, or what did not make it into the archive, by piecing together the threads of women's stories we amplify and elevate the position of these women within the dataset and the historical archive.

PART III
MOVEMENT

6

Information Flow

This chapter moves from metadata to data. In the previous chapters we mainly focused on correspondence metadata—the number of people to whom someone wrote, the number of people from whom they received letters, and their volume of correspondence—and showed how statistical measurements can allow us to examine their role in the network. Without looking at the contents of their letters, we were able to predict whether they might be diplomats or intelligencers, whether their letters were likely to have been intercepted, or whether they functioned as petitioners or mediators. These predictions could then be validated by targeted close reading of the individual letters by the identified figures of interest. This chapter, by contrast, begins with the letter contents, and the ways they can be 'read' en masse to yield insights about the movement of information.

For a large proportion of the letters in our database we have a data field that contains a description of the letter contents. This derives from the Calendars of State Papers, which contain a summary of the contents for each document. These summaries are a valuable source of information, even though there are some important inconsistencies of which we need to be mindful, as C. S. Knighton's overview of the history of the Calendars has shown. The first volume of the *Calendars of the State Papers Domestic*, edited by Robert Lemon and published in 1856, covered the reigns of Edward, Mary, and Elizabeth I up to the year 1580 in just 700 pages and was 'castigated for its brevity'.[1] Thankfully Edward and Mary's reigns were re-calendared in the 1990s, and followed the standard of Lemon's successor, Mary Anne Everett Green (née Wood), who sought to improve on Lemon's practice of 'indicating rather than describing' (in her forty years editing forty-one volumes). She determined that 'all the significant contents of a letter would be mentioned and key phrases might be printed verbatim; the summary of the rest would follow the structure of the original, trimmed of its superfluities'.[2] The State Papers Foreign also followed this benchmark up until July 1589, at which point (in 1950) the Calendar was discontinued, and its incumbent editor, R. B. Wernham, devised an abbreviated format, *The List and Analysis of State Papers Foreign* (1964–) which now extends to the end of 1596. In these volumes each document is identified, and the contents of all are woven into 'narratives for each politico-geographical component'.[3] But this means that for the letters in the SP Foreign dated 1589–96 the description field merely points to the relevant

---

[1] C. S. Knighton, 'The Calendars and their Editors, 1856–2006', *State Papers Online, 1509–1714* (Cengage Learning EMEA Ltd, 2007).
[2] Ibid.   [3] Ibid.

Tudor Networks of Power. Ruth Ahnert and Sebastian E. Ahnert, Oxford University Press. © Ruth Ahnert and Sebastian E. Ahnert 2023.
DOI: 10.1093/oso/9780198858973.003.0006

section in *List and Analysis*; and those from after 1596 are not calendared at all. Other local inconsistencies in the description fields are also introduced by value judgements of the editors: as James Daybell has noticed, women's letters suffer from some over-zealous contraction in the summaries.[4] More work needs to be done to characterise and quantify these biases.

Despite these inconsistencies and unfortunate absences, this data field provides an enormous amount of information about the contents of the letters in the State Papers. From one perspective it is a pity we do not have full transcriptions of all the letters in original spelling, as it would be a valuable dataset for examining Tudor language and orthography. However, the benefit of not having to deal with the complex spelling variations present in this period,[5] and the multiple languages in which foreign intelligence was transmitted (especially in the case of intercepted letters), is that we can more easily trace topics and news items as they were transmitted between correspondents and flowed across communities and national borders.

We began this process by extracting a ranked list of the key words for each calendar year using an algorithm that compares the frequency of a word in a document subset (here a year's worth) to the frequency in the total set of documents,[6] and ranked the words that changed most in usage over the time period as a whole.[7] The reason we did this is because the key words for a single year have limited utility: because the time period of a year is arbitrary we are often left with fairly common and uninteresting words, such as 'king', 'queen', and 'majesty' and associated pronouns among the top words (the relative usage of which fluctuated throughout the sixteenth century of course, due to the changing gender of the monarch).[8] Such a list is unlikely to lead us to the word 'armada', because it is relatively rare in the context of the entire century. If we look at Figure 6.1 we can see the usage of the word over time: the *x*-axis charts time by year, and the *y*-axis gives us the word in terms of its rank that year (on a logarithmic scale). While the word 'armada' seems to rank relatively highly in the opening years of Henry VIII's reign this is actually due to the lower numbers of surviving letters in those years; in reality in 1516 it was only used six times. By comparison, in 1588 we can see a small surge in usage, when it was used ninety-four times. This, of course, was the year of the Spanish Armada.

The change in usage, therefore, helps us to pinpoint newsworthy moments. We can produce similarly interesting graphs by thinking of words that are likely to generate graphs with sharp peaks and troughs. In the early stages of research for this chapter we would conjure words such as 'pope', which do indeed produce a revealing graph.

---

[4] James Daybell, *Women Letter-Writers in Tudor England* (Ashgate, 2006), p. 8.

[5] See, for example, Arja Nurmi, 'The English Language of the Early Modern Period', in *A New Companion to English Renaissance Literature and Culture*, ed. Michael Hattaway (Blackwell, 2010), pp. 15–26.

[6] To extract the keywords for a given year we used the *searcher.key_terms* function of the *whoosh* Python library on the document set of that year.

[7] Specifically we looked at the difference between the logarithms of the minimum and maximum annual ranks of the word over the time period of 1509–1603.

[8] On the need for filtering methods when working with word frequency, see Alistair Baron, Paul Rayson, and Dawn Archer, 'Word Frequency and Key Word Statistics in Historical Corpus Linguistics', *Anglistik: International Journal of English Studies* 20 (2009), 41–67.

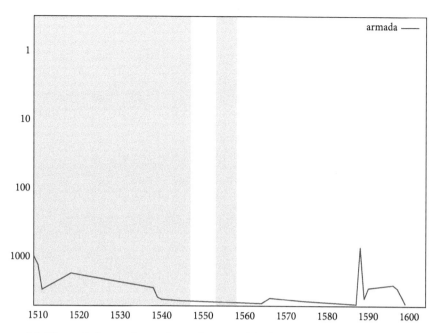

Figure 6.1 The rank (vertical axis, logarithmic scale) of the word 'armada' among the key words of each given year (horizontal axis) between 1509 and 1603. The reigns of the Tudor monarchs are shown in shades of grey.

The 'pope' graph (Figure 6.2) shows a clear drop in usage of the word following Henry VIII's break with Rome, passed by a series of acts between 1532 and 1534, a surge during the Catholic reign of Mary I, and another drop following the accession of Elizabeth I. While it is interesting to see the results of this graph, it is not hugely surprising. By relying on existing expertise and knowledge to generate graphs, it is likely that we will answer the questions we have formulated in the ways already anticipated. But how can we generate new questions, and find new areas of study, with this method?

We wanted to see if it was possible to find items of news through unsupervised methods: essentially, asking the computer to spot 'trending' topics for particular moments in Tudor correspondence. We discovered that extracting words with the greatest change in ranked usage over time, as outlined above, was an extremely effective method for discovering items of topical interest to the Tudor government. This automatically generated list of words acted as the starting point for the work in this chapter. In the following pages we use this list to discover words that share the same 'trend' over time; to use topic clusters to discover important events; and then to see how these surges in discourse manifest in the correspondence network (or, more simply put, who makes up the network of people discussing these events or topics). We create network visualisations of the communities using these words to discover how information travelled between people and over time; what particular network configurations can tell us about the management of information; and what general principles we can learn from examining the topographies of these networks.

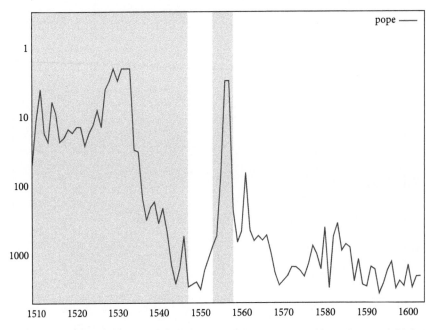

Figure 6.2 The rank (vertical axis, logarithmic scale) of the word 'pope' among the key words of each given year (horizontal axis) between 1509 and 1603. The reigns of the Tudor monarchs are shown in shades of grey.

As in previous chapters, the intention is to guide the reader through the development and utility of the method as much as it is about presenting the findings. The particular series of events we have chosen to engage with in the following pages are not the understudied or niche figures we have chosen to highlight in some of the previous chapters; rather, the first of the two extended case studies concerns one of the most overstudied episodes in history. However, our concern is less with the events themselves, and more with the networks within which these events were discussed: how information was transmitted, and what this reveals about the intelligence and communication networks that underpinned the Tudor government.

Words in Time

What can the change in a word's usage over time tell us? The first step to understanding its significance is to examine when the changes are taking place. To do this we can automatically generate plots like we did for the words 'armada' and 'pope' (in Figures 6.1 and 6.2).[9] What swiftly emerges when examining the graphs of the top-ranking most-changed words is that this method is very good at highlighting key events and topics of discourse from the sixteenth century. Sometimes the event is self-evident, as in the case of the Spanish Armada; in others it requires us to look at the letters to

---

[9] See <https://github.com/tudor-networks-of-power/code>.

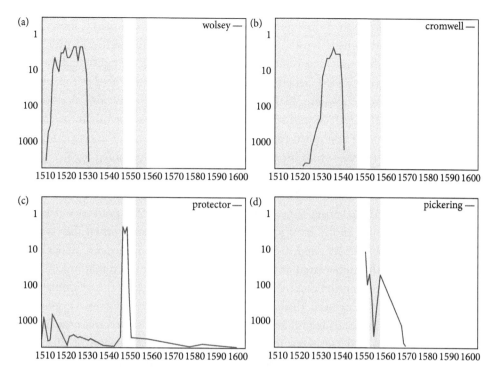

Figure 6.3 Personal histories: The ranks (vertical axis, logarithmic scale) of the words (a) 'wolsey', (b) 'cromwell', (c) 'protector', and (d) 'pickering' among the key words of each given year (horizontal axis) between 1509 and 1603. The reigns of the Tudor monarchs are shown in shades of grey.

understand why peaks occur at a certain moment. By digging into the letters to understand these profiles, we were able to identify three rough categories into which the graphs fall: the personal history, event-based history, and the narrative arc.

The personal history, as the name suggests, refers to those graphs that correspond to a particular person's life as it is reported in the archive of correspondence. In the case of the graphs of the names 'Cromwell' (9th in the list of words with largest changes) and 'Wolsey' (17th), shown in Figure 6.3, we can see that their curves are very similar, showing their rise to power, a period of administrative dominance, and a sharp demise. The reason that their period in power corresponds with their appearance at the top of the rankings for those years is self-evident: their personal archives make up a large percentage of the total number of letters in the State Periods during the period of their office (as discussed in Chapter 2). The only difference between the two graphs is that Wolsey's reign of power is slightly longer, and they occupy different slices of time; if we were to layer them over one another we could see how the demise of Wolsey coincides with Cromwell's rise. The 'protector' (7th ranked word) graph in Figure 6.3 is also easy to interpret: we have a sharp rise of the word coinciding with the beginning of Edward Seymour, the Duke of Somerset's Protectorate (1547–9).

Other cases are less obvious but sketch out in miniature the trajectory of key administrators, diplomatic agents, or subjects of Tudor surveillance. The 'Pickering' (ranked 169th) graph (see again Figure 6.3) is particularly interesting as it shows a fall and rise, as opposed to the rise and fall seen in the 'Wolsey', 'Cromwell', and 'protector' graphs. 'Pickering' here refers to William Pickering, who was the English ambassador in France from February 1551 (where we see him appear at a high level in the graph). As we have discussed elsewhere, Pickering was not part of the network as a correspondent between 31 July 1553 and 15 March 1558; during this period, however, and especially in 1553–4, he continued to be a topic of conversation.[10] The reason for this is that, after being released from his diplomatic post, Pickering joined Wyatt's rebellion (which arose from Mary I's determination to marry Philip II of Spain), before fleeing with Sir Peter Carew and other conspirators to the continent. From March 1554 to March 1555 Pickering is mentioned in a series of correspondence between royal agents in France and Mary's government, first in relation to their fear that he was in a position to intercept and decode Tudor intelligences (as former ambassador he had the key to the cipher used at this time), before they realised that he could be used to gather intelligence on continental conspirators in exchange for a pardon, after which he returned to England. Through intermittent later mentions we can infer his rehabilitation and ultimate appointment in 1558 as a royal agent to recruit mercenaries in the Netherlands and Germany for the French war. The accession of Elizabeth brought Pickering a last flash of notoriety (as we can see in the graph's second peak), when he was spoken about as a candidate for the queen's hand. Thereafter, apart from a place briefly on the Middlesex bench and a commission of lieutenancy for London at the time of the rebellion of 1569, Pickering received no further appointments, ending his days in semi-retirement and literary recreations—as demonstrated by the graph's long tail.[11]

The names of people, however, can also figure in the second category: of event-based history (see Figure 6.4). One such example is the 'Motte' (ranked 22nd in changes) graph in Figure 6.4, which points to the role of Valentin Pardieu de la Motte in key events within the Dutch Revolt occurring in 1578–9. The majority of the words found in our most-changed list fall into this category. Other names and titles include: 'Emperor', 'Bourbon', 'Regent', 'Sussex', 'Huntley', 'Desmond', 'Bothwell', 'Turlough', 'Tyrone', and 'O'Neill', amongst many others. The 'Bothwell' (46th) graph shows the distinction from the personal history graphs, which are normally spread over an extended period; rather, the sharp peaks correspond with discrete events, and indeed two different earls of Bothwell. The first peak in 1567 arises from discussion of James Hepburn, 4th Earl of Bothwell, who was one of those accused of having murdered Mary Queen of Scots's consort, Lord Darnley (the word 'murder' also peaks in this year). The latter pertains to Francis Stewart, 5th Earl of Bothwell, arrested in 1591 under charges of witchcraft. Other words that point to events of national interest

---

[10] Ruth Ahnert, 'Maps Versus Networks', in *News Networks in Early Modern Europe*, ed. Noah Moxham and Joad Raymond (Brill, 2016), pp. 130–58 (pp. 152–7).

[11] Pickering, Sir William (1516/17–75), of London and Byland and Oswaldkirk, Yorks. Published in *The History of Parliament: The House of Commons 1509–1558*, ed. S.T. Bindoff, 1982; available at <http://www.historyofparliamentonline.org/volume/1509-1558/member/pickering-sir-william-151617-75>.

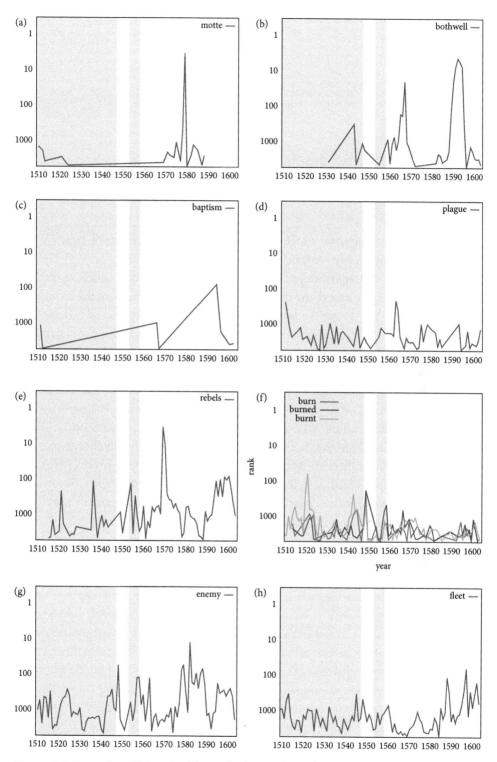

Figure 6.4 Event-based histories: The ranks (vertical axis, logarithmic scale) of the words (a) 'motte', (b) 'bothwell', (c) 'baptism', (d) 'plague', (e) 'rebels', (f) 'burnt'/'burn'/'burned', (g) 'enemy', (h) 'fleet', (i) 'wagon', and (j) 'labourers' among the key words of each given year (horizontal axis) between 1509 and 1603. The reigns of the Tudor monarchs are shown in shades of grey.

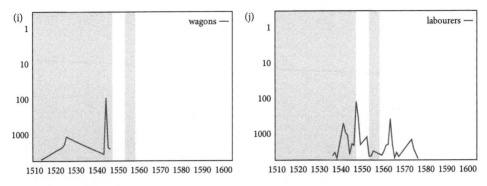

Figure 6.4 Continued

or concern include 'baptism', which has two peaks for the baptism of James VI of Scotland (1566) and Henry Frederick, Prince of Wales (1594).[12]

Other words that unequivocally point to events include 'plague', which unsurprisingly peaks in 1563, the date of the most devastating plague outbreak of the century in London (Figure 6.4). Among the graphs that correspond to event-based histories we also see a large category of geographical words (denoting places, nations, and national bodies), and those relating to military efforts. These cluster around key locations of interest, mostly within Scotland, Ireland, Spain and the Spanish Netherlands, France, and (to a lesser degree) the Ottoman Empire. Military language falls into two sub-categories: that which denotes discrete events, and more generic language that nevertheless points to key historic moments—although this distinction functions on a sliding scale. 'Rebels' (28th, Figure 6.4) is a general term that occurs regularly throughout the period 1509–1603, but there are notable peaks for the Pilgrimage of Grace (1536), the Rising of the North (1570), and Irish rebellion (throughout the 1590s). The words 'burnt', 'burned', and 'burn' are not obviously related to war, but the peak in 1544–5 in fact refers to the Burning of Edinburgh, the first major action of the war of the Rough Wooing. Other more generic words like 'enemy', 'war', 'truce', 'army', 'fleet', 'garrisons', 'adversaries', 'frontiers', and 'musters' produce graphs that are harder to read because there are so many peaks. The 'enemy' graph (Figure 6.4) shows that while the identity of the enemy changes with each respective military campaign, the concept of an enemy was always present. Even within these busy graphs, however, we see that momentous events rise to the surface, as in the case of 'fleet': while there are many small peaks throughout, the large ones in 1588 and 1597 demonstrate that the Spanish Armada of 1588 and Third Spanish Armada of 1597 loomed large in minds and missives of contemporaries. A number of other words have a surprising connection to military campaigns that are not immediately apparent, such as 'wagons' (the reason for its disappearance might be explained by the fact that a specific kind of wagon used

---

[12] On the celebrations surrounding the baptism of James VI at Stirling in 1566, see Michael Lynch, 'Queen Mary's Triumph: The Baptismal Celebrations at Stirling in December 1566', *Scottish Historical Review* 69 (1990), 1–21; on the celebrations surrounding the baptism of his son, see Michael Bath, '"Rare shewes and singular inventions": The Stirling Baptism of Prince Henry', *Journal of the Northern Renaissance* 4 (2012), <http://www.northernrenaissance.org/rare-shewes-and-singular-inventions-the-stirling-baptism-of-prince-henry/>.

by the English was not robust enough for the French roads),[13] and 'labourers' (which peaks in 1546 when labourers died at the Siege of Boulogne due to blockades stopping food entering, and in 1563 when a large number of labourers arrived in Le Havre shortly before the Siege 22 May–31 July 1563).

The third category of graph is the narrative arc (see Figure 6.5). Like the personal history, the narrative arc is characterised less by sharp peaks, and is instead suggestive of longer trends. One such example is the 'pope' graph discussed above; other examples include: 'holiness', 'Rome', 'Spain', 'imperial(ists)', 'religion', 'protestant(s)', 'congregation', 'christendom', 'heretics', 'bull(s)', 'Irish', 'catholic(s)', 'book(s)', 'conscience', 'theologians', 'Jesuit', 'divorce', 'nuncio', and 'papists'. The words 'Irish' and 'Spain' show the Tudor government's ongoing concern with these regions over the sixteenth century, whilst also helping pinpoint moments of focused anxiety or activity: once again there is a 1589 surge for Spain (the Spanish Armada); and the peak in the use of the word 'Irish' 1598 marks a key moment during the Nine Years War, the Battle of the Yellow Ford, during which up to 2,000 English troops were killed.

The dominance of religious words at the top of the ranked list of words falling into this category is unsurprising. The period of this study was marked by intense religious upheaval in England. The four separate monarchs (or five if you include the nine-day queen, Lady Jane Grey) imposed a range of religious positions on their subjects, enforcing orthodoxy with the threat of imprisonment and execution, which was all too often carried out. Not only were fifty-three evangelicals put to death for heresy in England and Scotland in the period 1527–46, Catholics also suffered incarceration and execution during Henry VIII's reign for failure to recognise their king as supreme head of the Church in England.[14] Famously, at least 282 perished under Mary I, gaining her the appellation 'bloody Mary'. Neither was Edward VI's Protestant reign without its religious casualties: a number of Protestant separatists were burnt for heresy, and certain high-profile Catholics languished in jail for much of the reign.[15] Like the 'pope' graph, the 'Rome' graph (Figure 6.5) captures the religious dominance of the pope during the first half of the sixteenth-century, the intense period of negotiation which preceded Henry's break with Rome, its subsequent decrease in prominence following the break, and the brief period of resurgence during Mary's reign. As the overlaying of the different graphs shows, 'holiness' and 'christendom' have similar plots; and with the decrease in Rome's influence in England we also see the disappearance of traditionally Catholic practices, like the issuing of papal bulls. Conversely, we see the virtual absence of the word 'protestant(s)' before c.1540 (the terms 'gospeller' or

---

[13] See Paul E. J. Hammer, *Elizabeth's Wars: War, Government and Society in Tudor England, 1544–1604* (Palgrave Macmillan, 2003), p. 26.

[14] See Brad Gregory, 'The Anathema of Compromise: Christian Martyrdom in Early Modern Europe', PhD thesis, Princeton University, 1996, p. 13; and Gregory, *Salvation at Stake: Christian Martyrdom in Early Modern Europe* (Harvard University Press, 1999), pp. 254–71.

[15] See Ruth Ahnert, *The Rise of Prison Literature in the Sixteenth Century* (Cambridge University Press, 2013), pp. 2–3.

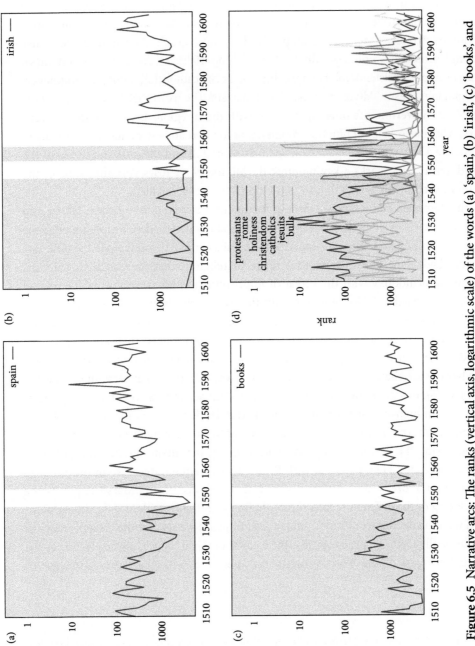

Figure 6.5 Narrative arcs: The ranks (vertical axis, logarithmic scale) of the words (a) 'spain', (b) 'irish', (c) 'books', and (d) 'protestants', 'rome', 'holiness', 'christendom', 'catholics', 'jesuits', and 'bulls' among the key words of each given year (horizontal axis) between 1509 and 1603. The reigns of the Tudor monarchs are shown in shades of grey.

'evangelical' were more common terms in the 1520s and 1530s),[16] and peaks during Edward's reign, and following Elizabeth's accession (although interestingly it decreases over her reign). The word 'catholic(s)' follows a similar trajectory to the word 'Rome' in the period up to Elizabeth's reign, but there is a surge of usage from the late 1570s, through the 1580s and 1590s, when the Tudor government was alert to the conspiracies of exiled English Catholics working in consort with Philip II of Spain; similarly, before the late 1570s the word 'Jesuits' was entirely absent, but also peaks in the 1580s and 1590s.

The narrative of the word 'books' is a little less obvious but a nice example of how a single word can provide a window onto an important issue.[17] We can see from Figure 6.5 that use of the word surges during the period 1526–39. This increase relates to the arrival of Lutheran tracts, English translations of the Bible, and other heretical and 'pestiferous books' (as they are termed in a letter to Wolsey from John Clerk, Bishop of Bath, and John Taylor) on English shores from the beginning of the 1520s, which was met with a programme of censorship and book burning.[18] In January 1521, Bishop Tunstall had written to Wolsey with the urgent recommendation that printers and booksellers be forbidden to import or translate Luther's works; but as the decade progressed the lists of proscribed books grew as a number of men were tasked with finding and reading these 'heretical' books. Scholarly discussions of this programme often foreground Thomas More's obsessive efforts, but these letters show the role of other lesser-known figures, such as John Hackett, who sent books from Antwerp and Mechelen to be burned.[19] From around 1530, however, the reference to books in letters subtly shifts. Alongside the continued anxiety to suppress heresy, we see an increase in correspondence seeking to find books supporting what is described euphemistically as the King's 'great matter': Henry's campaign to have the dispensation to marry his brother's widow Catherine of Aragon (granted in 1509) overturned so that he might be free to remarry. At the centre of these efforts is one Richard Croke, whose role is discussed at greater length below. What we see through the 1530s is a bookish battle between those 'writing in our favor',[20] and those writing books first against the king's great matter, and subsequently against his marriage to Anne Boleyn ('a Boke Agaynst this Iust Matrimonie').[21]

---

[16] See Alec Ryrie, *The Gospel and Henry VIII: Evangelicals in the Early English Reformation* (Cambridge University Press, 2003), pp. xv–xvi.

[17] 'Book' shows a similar pattern to 'books' between 1526 and 1539, but 'book' also has two sharp peaks in 1512 and 1551–2. Both these peaks are almost entirely due to Calendar descriptions of their archival history and material context: 'From a letter book' and 'John Johnson's letter book'.

[18] John Clerk, Bishop of Bath and Wells, and John Tayler to Wolsey, 1528, SP 1/48 f.93. On this topic, see James Simpson, *Burning to Read: English Fundamentalism and Its Reformation Opponents* (Harvard University Press, 2009).

[19] See, for example, Hackett's letters to Wolsey on 21 November 1526, Cotton Galba B/IX f.43; 24 November, SP 1/40 f.20; 1 December 1526, SP 1/40 f.42. There are forty-nine such letters to Wolsey, and further letters to Brian Tuke.

[20] Richard Croke to Girolamo Ghinucci, 25 January 1530, Cotton Vitellius B/XIII.

[21] George Browne to Cromwell, 6 July 1534, SP 1/85 f.35.

Topics and Their Transmission

The foregoing overview of these temporal word profiles shows that while individual graphs are unique, there are resemblances between graphs that can be revealing. For example, we can observe repeated surges on or around the same dates, such as the peak of the 'armada', 'fleet', and 'Spain' graphs in 1589. We also see narrative arcs that look very similar. Some map roughly the same trajectory over the whole century ('Rome', 'Pope', 'holiness', 'christendom'), while others track the same pattern for a few years before diverging ('catholic(s)' see Figure 6.5). This is not a coincidence; rather, the underlying reason is usually that they relate to the same event or series of events. What these shared profiles suggest is that we can detect word clusters or 'topics' that work together to signal the prevalence of a field of discourse at a specific moment in time. For example, the Italian wars of 1521–6 are marked by a surge in the usage of the words 'emperor', 'frontiers', 'Milan', 'league', and 'Imperial(ists)'; and The Nine Years War in Ireland by 'Irish', 'rebels', 'Tyrone', 'rebellion', 'revenge', and 'traitors'. Such clusters begin to emerge when we look through the profiles of the most changed words, as one notices the recurrence of certain dates and events. However, there are also ways of automating the process of identifying similar graphs.

The detection of topics in bodies of texts is a well-studied problem in natural language processing, and the aim of so-called 'topic models'. These models represent a family of algorithms that extract topics from texts, and have become a popular tool for the unsupervised analysis of text. As Shawn Graham, Scott Weingart, and Ian Milligan have written:

> Topic modeling programs do not know anything about the meaning of the words in a text. Instead, they assume that any piece of text is composed (by an author) by selecting words from possible baskets of words where each basket corresponds to a topic. If that is true, then it becomes possible to mathematically decompose a text into the probable baskets from whence the words first came. The tool goes through this process over and over again until it settles on the most likely distribution of words into baskets, which we call topics.[22]

The resulting baskets of words, or topics, therefore provide a latent representation of the corpus under examination, describing its contours in dominant and under-represented 'topics' of discourse. The method has been seized on in the digital humanities community, thanks to its accessibility via toolkits such as MALLET, although there has been a chorus of voices from within that community over the last decade urging caution in interpreting results where the underlying mechanisms are not fully grasped,[23] or where analysis of the outputs are not rooted in a deep engagement in the actual

[22] Shawn Graham, Scott Weingart, and Ian Milligan, 'Getting Started with Topic Modeling and MALLET', *The Programming Historian* 1 (2012), <https://doi.org/10.46430/phen0017>.
[23] Scott Weingart, 'The Myth of Text Analytics and Unobtrusive Measurement', <http://www.scottbot.net/HIAL/index.html@p=16713.html/>.

word counts that build them.[24] There are well-established statistical models to undertake this kind of analysis, the most common being latent Dirichlet allocation (LDA).

Our method is distinct from topic modelling as it takes advantage of the temporal dimension of our data by measuring the similarity of the changes in word usage over time, and then uses this similarity to define groups of words. More specifically we calculate the Pearson correlation between rank profiles of pairs of words. High values of the Pearson correlation (i.e. close to 1) correspond to profiles that display peaks and valleys at similar times.[25] This method is extremely successful at finding words that point to the same historical news events. For example, if we use this method to search for the 'closest' word to Walloons—a word that is only ranked in the top 5,000 overall during the period 1569–88, but has a sharp peak 1578–9—we discover that the following words have graphs with the closest shape (in ranked order):

'Selles', 'Beutrich', 'Motte', 'Douay', 'Malcontent', 'exercise', 'deputies', 'Maestricht', 'Montigny', 'Artois', 'Hainault', 'Noue', 'Ghent', 'Estates', 'monsieur', 'States', 'Spinola', 'inasmuch', 'Sommers', 'Lille', 'Casimir', 'Tomson', 'Bourbourg', 'colonels', 'negotiation'.

The Walloon people are an ethnic group native to modern-day Belgium; but during the sixteenth century they played an active role in the foundation of the Dutch state. What is striking about the list of words is that it is overwhelmingly composed of proper nouns pertaining to the Dutch Revolt, including key locations, administrative bodies, military leaders, and informants. The only exceptions are the words 'exercise', 'deputies', 'monsieur', 'inasmuch', 'colonels', and 'negotiation'; nevertheless the majority of these pertain to military activity, roles, and diplomatic activities that made up the history of the revolt ('monsieur' and 'inasmuch' are bits of common titles and filler words not excluded by the list of stop words). Moreover, even if we look at the long list that follows these top twenty-five results we see that the density of words pertaining to the Dutch Revolt continues quite far down the list, including words such as: 'Provinces', 'Orange', 'Antwerp', 'Pacification', 'Gravelines', 'Lalaing', 'Davison', 'union', and ' Zealand', amongst numerous others. We can also see the accuracy of these predictions by plotting the usage of these words over time onto the same graph, as seen in Figure 6.6.

What this figure makes clear is that when we discover a word with a seemingly interesting profile, we can immediately explore the field of discourse within which it most frequently appears. However, the aim of this chapter is not to discover topics, but rather to use that information to understand how such topics were transmitted through the network. Who were the key figures transmitting this information? What

---

[24] Ben Schmidt, 'Words Alone: Dismantling Topic Models in the Humanities', *Journal of Digital Humanities* 2 (2012), <http://journalofdigitalhumanities.org/2-1/words-alone-by-benjamin-m-schmidt/>.

[25] See <https://github.com/tudor-networks-of-power/code>. For related work, see Chenhao Tan, Dallas Card, and Noah A. Smith, 'Friendships, Rivalries, and Trysts: Characterizing Relations between Ideas in Texts', in *Proceedings of the 55th Annual Meeting of the Association for Computational Linguistics*, vol. 1: Long Papers (Association for Computational Linguistics, 2017), pp. 773–83.

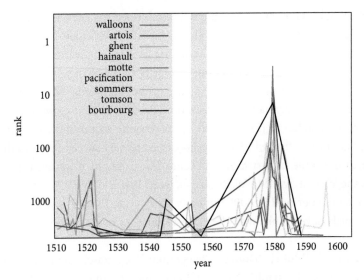

Figure 6.6 Words with similar time profiles to 'walloons', as measured using Pearson correlation of the time profiles. All show a peak around 1578–9.

was the topology of these networks? And can we learn any general principles about how information was disseminated in early modern Europe?

Using these generated word lists and topic clusters, we can create a network of the people who use specific words across the whole period or a given time window. We might call these 'topic networks'. To aid quick exploration of the epistolary networks that create these surges in the usage of specific words and topics we developed an algorithm to automatically generate these topic networks for any given word: this could be for the whole period of the archive or a custom period.[26] These network visualisations are colour-coded and numbered to indicate how the network evolves over time: the earliest edges appear in blue and the latest in red, and all the edges are numbered in the order in which the edge between two nodes first appeared, as well as providing the date of that first edge and the number of letters marking the edge in total. The following figures are accordingly rendered in colour where time is discussed, but in greyscale where the temporal dimension is not relevant.

These topic networks look very different depending on the kind of word and time window that is selected. With more generic words like 'papist', 'rebels', or 'books' it very much depends on the date range as to whether the graphical output is interpretable. As well as the network being huge, the changing usage over time and a potential lack of coterminous actors means that it is difficult to tell whether separation between communities is due to an interesting social phenomenon or a more banal reason. What we found most useful was to use the date-range of a given peak to determine the parameters of the visualisation. In those cases we found that with a few rare exceptions, the individuals involved in the topic network are almost all using the given word to

---

[26] This is done by searching the Calendar descriptions for a given set of keywords and extracting all correspondence that mentions at least one of the words. See <https://github.com/tudor-networks-of-power/code>.

refer to the same event, place, person, or concept. We can then meaningfully say that we have a visualisation of the network discussing that topic. In the following pages we will demonstrate how these topic networks can help us understand the correspondence networks underlying two different moments in Tudor foreign policy. The first is Henry VIII's undertaking to secure a divorce from Catherine of Aragon, a protracted negotiation that came euphemistically to be known as the 'king's great matter' and dominated the efforts of numerous statesmen, diplomats, lawyers, churchmen, and intellectuals over the best part of a decade—a series of events that has received extensive scholarly attention. The second is a chapter within the longer narrative of the Dutch Revolt (1566–1648), which occurred in the late 1570s.

These act as interesting comparison cases. They emerged organically through our initial explorations as the various words that refer to these events occur repeatedly in the top 3% of most-changed words. The king's great matter is a nice example to illustrate the method because the topic hardly needs introduction, so often has it been treated in scholarship, popular histories, and dramatisations. However, the approach allows us to see the surrounding debates and negotiations from another perspective: by emphasising the networks of people writing about this topic, it reveals how information was controlled and shared. By showing the networks pertaining to the king's great matter in comparison to those surrounding a conflict on foreign soil, and one in which the English became involved at a relatively late stage, we might expect to see quite a different network structure. While the Dutch Revolt graphs have their own family resemblance, they also share an important structural similarity with the 'divorce' graph. This helps us to see the different functions of correspondence within a government's foreign policy.

The King's Great Matter

The use of word clustering allows us to define a set of parameters through which to analyse the complex set of negotiations that constituted Henry VIII's 'great matter'. By beginning with the most obvious word that charts the events of these years— 'divorce'—we can define both a window of time and a field of discourse. The word 'divorce' peaks 1527–34, which makes sense given the timeline of events. By 1527 the king seemed to have come to 'the momentous conviction' that his marriage to Catherine of Aragon was against the law of God.[27] Although he had gained a papal dispensation following the death of his brother Arthur to marry his widow, Catherine, the continued failure of the marriage to yield an heir was reputedly interpreted by the king as a punishment from God for his act of adultery. In 1527 Catherine was 42 years of age, and Henry had already been pursuing Anne Boleyn for over a year. The contention that Pope Pius III did not have the authority to order a dispensation to marry

---

[27] G. W. Bernard, *The King's Reformation: Henry VIII and the Remaking of the English Church* (Yale University Press, 2005), p. 1.

Catherine was the argument that Henry took to Pope Clement VII in 1527 in the hope of having his marriage annulled. Diplomatic missions were sent to Rome in search of Clement's assent, and then later to seek permission to hold an ecclesiastical court hearing in England; other efforts were mobilised to consult leading theologians and philosophers who might support the English king's position. At the other end of this temporal window, in 1534, a series of acts and oaths marked the final break with Rome.

The words that have the most similar graphs to 'divorce' fall into four rough categories; a selection can be seen in Figure 6.7. The first are names and titles, and include 'Benet', 'Gregory', 'Ortiz', 'Foxe', 'Crumwell', 'Pope', 'Casale', 'Mai', 'nuncio', 'excusator' (the title given to Edward Carne), 'Karne' (Carne again), 'Ancona', 'Francis', and 'Salviati', amongst others. As discussed further below, these include the names of key actors within the diplomatic negotiations in Rome. The second category is the language of diplomacy and negotiation, including: 'speak', 'ask', 'refused', 'obtain(ed)', and 'treated'. The third pertains to the intellectual and legal consultation that supported Henry's undertaking: 'lawyers', 'learned', 'doctors', 'universities', 'read', 'counsel', 'books', 'learning', 'opinions', 'subscriptions', and 'theologians'. And the fourth main category includes words about legal process (especially regarding the legality of the papal dispensation): 'consistory' (i.e. a church council or court made up, in the Roman Church, of cardinals), 'dispensation', 'process', 'tried', 'judges', 'right'. The final word of interest to us in the ranked list of most similar words is 'conscience', which is used both by Henry VIII to justify his plea and by the pope to explain his inability to yield.

Each of these words provides a helpful window on the negotiations around Henry's great matter, but to focus on the structure and membership of the networks taking an

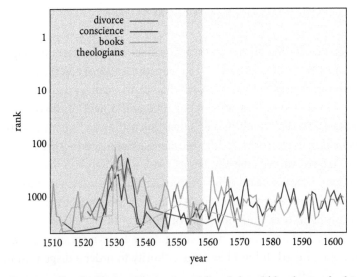

Figure 6.7 Time profiles for 'divorce', 'conscience', 'books', and 'theologians', which all peak between the mid-1520s and mid-1530s, around the time of Henry VIII's divorce from Catherine of Aragon.

interest in these processes we will limit ourselves to a sample of the topic networks for: 'divorce', 'conscience', 'books', and 'theologians' (see Figure 6.7), and we can see the networks of people who discussed these topics in their letters during the 'peak' period in Figures 6.8–6.11. Taken together, these topic networks chart the development of the great matter into an international debate, allowing us to understand how oppositional realms of debate intersect and who the mediating figures are between them. While there is a huge body of scholarship on this topic, this network perspective provides an abstraction of the debates that allows us to gain an overarching understanding of how information was managed in this complex and lengthy international negotiation, and to communicate visually how Henry's personal scruple functioned to divide Europe.

The topic network for 'divorce' in Figure 6.8 (peaks detected 1 July 1527–31 December 1534) comprises one large connected component, plus a smattering of free-floating dyads, triads, and one four-node component. Our concern here is with the large connected component, which clearly divides into two communities (in the top half and bottom half of the visualisation), held together only by a bridge, so that the main hubs on either side are separated by two degrees. This structure and its development over time can tell us a lot about the debate over the king's great matter, both in England and abroad, during these years.

The community in the top half of the figure focuses around Wolsey, who is the largest hub, and Henry, a smaller hub positioned just below him. From the blue colouring of the edges (indicating that they first occur early in the time window) we can see that initial communications were focused on Wolsey, which shows why Catherine put blame for the divorce at Wolsey's feet.[28] The way that Wolsey managed the discourse around the king's great matter in the earlier part of this period can be seen by looking at the letter he wrote to Henry VIII on 5 July 1527 (the second edge to form in the network), informing him of his meeting with John Fisher, Bishop of Rochester. He writes that on asking whether the bishop had had any communication with Catherine of Aragon, he said that a message had arrived from the queen 'by mowth' (suggesting covert means), stating that she desired his counsel. On asking Fisher if he had formed any conjecture what the matter could be, he answered that he knew nothing certain, but 'thinketh it was for a divorce to be had bitwene your highnes and the quene which to coniecte he was specially moved vpon a tale brought vnto him by his brother from London'. Wolsey then reports telling Fisher that the king had never intended to disclose this matter, but, seeing that Henry's good intentions had been misrepresented, he informs the bishop of the full matter, 'taking an othe of him to kepe it close and secrete'.[29]

The oath of secrecy tells us something about the small network in which epistolary discussion of the divorce initially took place (those connected by blue edges in Figure 6.8). Although Rochester hints at the way rumours had circulated beyond this small sphere, we gain a clear sense that Wolsey sought to contain discussion of the king's great matter. The limited number of people trusted with information in

---

[28] Bernard, *The King's Reformation*, p. 1.   [29] SP 1/42 f.155.

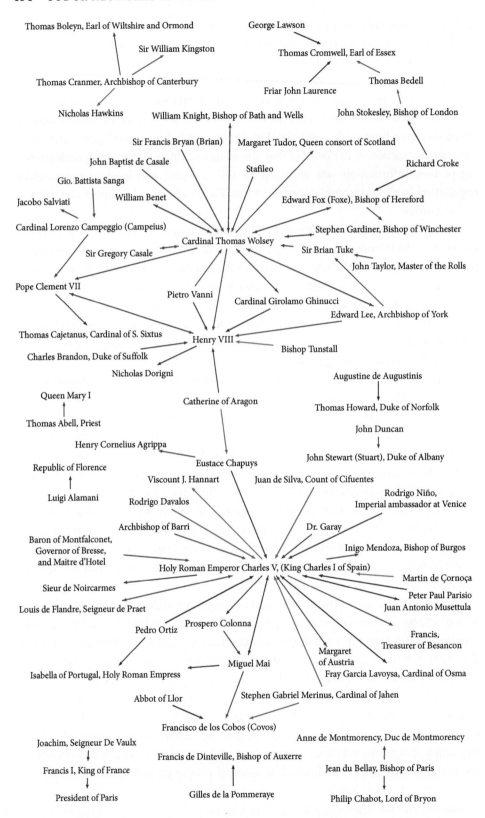

epistolary form around Wolsey includes only those formally assigned the responsibility of negotiating with the pope and his representatives in Rome, and the imperial ambassadors: Sir Gregory Casale (an anglicisation of Gregorio Casali, and 'Casale' in the list of names and titles above), England's resident ambassador to the Holy See, and the members of the three English embassies sent to treat with the pope between December 1527 and early 1529, Sir William Knight, Edward Fox ('Foxe' in the list of names and titles above), Stephen Gardiner, Sir Francis Bryan, and Pietro Vanni. Also included in Wolsey's confidence were Edward Lee, the Imperial ambassador to Charles V in Spain, and Girolamo Ghinucci, the Bishop of Worcester, who joined Lee in Valladolid 1526–9 as special ambassador, and also made numerous diplomatic trips to France.

The diplomats were trusted both with the job of negotiation on the king's behalf and to maintain a high level of secrecy. The desire for containment can be seen repeatedly in the correspondence between Wolsey and the imperial ambassadors Lee and Ghinucci. In a letter dated 1 August 1527 he opens by complimenting them on their circumspection, before going on to speak of the rumour that has sprung up in England that proceedings are being taken for a divorce between the king and queen: 'which is entirely without foundation, yet not altogether causeless; for there has been some discussion about the Papal dispensation, not with any view to a divorce, but to satisfy the French, who have raised the objection on proposing a marriage between the Princess and their Sovereign'.[30] He is clearly concerned that these rumours would reach the ears of Charles V, Catherine's nephew, and the letter concludes by stating that if the emperor mentions the subject they should make such a prudent reply as will overcome his prejudices. The concession here is that, if the rumours cannot be contained, at least the details of negotiations can be clarified ('entirely without foundation, yet not altogether causeless'). Importantly, this explains in part why the bridge to Charles V's section of the graph does not form until later, as can be seen by the redder hue of those bridging links in the network of Figure 6.8. He is also careful to draw the distinction between divorce and the dispensation sought to have the marriage declared invalid.[31] The distinction, however, did not seem to have bothered anyone else,

---

[30] Paraphrase of the Latin for SP 1/42 f.252 given in 'Henry VIII: August 1527, 1–10', in *Letters and Papers, Foreign and Domestic, Henry VIII, Volume 4, 1524–1530*, ed. J. S. Brewer (Longman, Green, Longman, & Roberts, 1875), pp. 1507–14. BHO, <http://www.british-history.ac.uk/letters-papers-hen8/vol4/pp1507-1514>.

[31] In fact Knight's initial mission in late 1527 was either to secure this declaration or to accept the other draft bull, permitting Henry to take on a second wife while remaining married to Catherine. See Catherine Fletcher, *The Divorce of Henry VIII: The Untold Story* (Vintage, 2014), pp. 9–13.

Figure 6.8 Topic network for 'divorce' in the time window from 1 July 1527 to 31 December 1534. The hub in the top half of the diagram with many blue connections is Thomas Wolsey (blue signifies that the first communication took place early in the time window, red that it took place late). The small hub just below him is Henry VIII, who connects to the other major hub in the bottom half of the diagram (the Emperor Charles V of Spain) via a bridge consisting of two nodes, Catherine of Aragon and Eustace Chapuys (the emperor's ambassador in England).

and Wolsey's imperial ambassadors and the members of the embassies to Rome used the word divorce as a shorthand, which is why the network of discussion around the divorce is so easy to draw.[32]

In Wolsey's correspondence with the diplomats sent to treat with the pope, by comparison, the concern was the persuasion of the pope as to the validity of Henry's arguments. In their lengthy account of their negotiations with the pope and his advisers dated 3 March 1528, Casale, Gardiner, and Fox detail the struggle they waged to secure the pope's support for the king's cause, and specifically permission to create an ecclesiastical court in England and a decretal commission to confirm in advance the sentence given by the legates.[33] Of their four-hour conference with the pope they described how he doubted whether the causes assigned for the divorce were sufficient, and desired 'Simonett' to consult his books. At the end of their conference the pope concluded that he had so much confidence in the king's conscience that he thought his cause was just; but because it must be tried before the world, and he did not have sufficient learning to discuss the matter, he must take the advice of counsel, because the emperor would employ the universities to respond to the issue.[34] This synopsis of this missive in the Calendar contains several of the keywords that peaked during the period of Henry's great matter: 'conscience', 'counsel', 'learning', 'universities'. Here we can see that the pope's concern to establish the intellectual basis for the king's arguments on the one hand, or the upholding of the marriage on the other, is also bound up with conflicting pressures he was receiving from Henry and the emperor via their respective ambassadors. This passage, then, also helps us to understand the larger international dynamics underpinning two key parts of the topic network: firstly, the papal arm of the network that extends to the left of Wolsey and Henry's hub; and secondly the bottom half of the network focused on the Imperial hub of Charles V.

The pope appears in the network situated between, and to the left of Wolsey and Henry VIII; and extending out from him are the nodes representing Campeggio, the legate whom he sent to England, and Cardinal Thomas Cajetan, who would ultimately write the decision rejecting Henry's appeal for divorce on the pope's behalf. However, while the pope here appears to be the bridging figure between the Tudor government (Henry and Wolsey) and Cardinal Campeggio, this representation is slightly misleading. The earlier edges—between Wolsey and the pope, and Campeggio and Pope Clement—in fact formed simultaneously when the two cardinals together wrote a report to Clement, following Campeggio's arrival in London on 8 October 1528. Campeggio, then, is the intermediary. But that joint letter (surviving in a draft in the hand of Vanni) gives a false impression of the unity of the two men. They inform Clement that having failed to persuade either Henry to yield to Catherine, or Catherine to Henry, they are now in the process of discussing the process by which they should try the case in the ecclesiastical court.[35] The fact that Campeggio's views differed from Wolsey became quickly apparent. In a letter from Wolsey to Casale on

[32] See ibid., p. xix.   [33] Ibid., p. 27.   [34] SP 1/47 f.144.
[35] Cotton Vitellius B/XI f.235.

1 November 1528, Wolsey complains that Campeggio has taken a course entirely different from his instructions, attempting to dissuade the king and queen from the divorce until he has made a report to the pope of what he has seen and heard here, and refusing to entrust Wolsey with the commission.[36] While the Tudor government and the pope's representative engaged in active debate and negotiation, their agendas and discourses ultimately diverged irreconcilably. Campeggio listened to evidence in the English ecclesiastical court for less than two months before Clement called the case back to Rome in July 1529. The failure to secure the annulment fell on Wolsey's shoulders: he was charged with praemunire in October 1529, and although he was subsequently pardoned in the first half of 1530, he was charged once more in November 1530, this time for treason, but died while awaiting trial. It is only at this late date that we see the edge between Henry and the pope form in the divorce network graph, when the king writes to complain of the outcome of the divorce proceedings and to upbraid the pope for being led by the 'ignoraunce of your counsaillors'.[37] What the letters marking those edges in the 'divorce' graph tell us, therefore, is that where we notice bridging structures between different powers, a great deal of pressure is exerted on those edges to reach consensus, and when that fails, the networks of communication bend and break.

The pressures placed on those bridges in the network are even apparent in the almost total separation between the Tudor government's sphere of discourse in the top half of the diagram in Figure 6.8 and the Imperial sphere on the bottom. The tenuous connection between them is maintained only by a bridge that consists of Eustace Chapuys, the emperor's ambassador in England, and Catherine of Aragon. In fact there is reason to argue that we should represent these two worlds as completely separate in their correspondence record regarding the divorce. The edge that forms between Catherine and Henry is not strictly marked by a letter, but instead the 'Records of the divorce of K. Hen. VIII. from Q. Catherine; remaining in the custody of the Lord Treasurer.'[38] If we remove this edge we see the two parts of the network separating completely, with Catherine relegated to the other side of the divide from her spouse. The visual structure of the topic network is therefore revealing: the opening of the fissure in the network's topology is symbolic of the political outcome of the proposed divorce.

Catherine's previous union with Henry's brother Arthur had been designed to cement political relations between the Holy Roman Empire and England, and the dispensation to allow her to marry Henry after his brother's death was motivated by the desire to maintain this powerful alliance. Charles V's displeasure at Henry's attempts to dissolve this marriage was not merely due to his allegiances to his aunt, Catherine, however; it also signalled his displeasure at Henry's infidelity to the Empire. On 27 January 1528 Henry and Francis I of France had jointly declared war on Charles V. England's alliances had shifted against the Holy Roman Empire. This is why no letters were passing between these two hemispheres; the main line of negotiation

---

[36] SP 1/50 f.219r–231.   [37] Cotton Vitellius B/XIII f.169.   [38] Lansdowne Vol/94 f.5.

between Henry's court and the Empire was through the Spanish ambassador Eustace Chapuys, who was requested by Catherine to represent her interests because of his legal background and knowledge of Latin. In fact the only reason we have the Spanish side of these discussion of the divorce is due to the two mechanisms that have introduced foreign data into the State Papers metadata: the editorial practice of John Sherren Brewer in the selection of material for the *Letters and Papers, Foreign and Domestic, of the Reign of Henry VIII*; and, to a lesser extent, the interception of foreign correspondence. As discussed in Chapter 4, Brewer, unlike the editors of the Calendars of later reigns, chose to include material from foreign archives.[39]

The Imperial sphere in the bottom half of the diagram, therefore, can be understood as a mirror image or inversion of the Tudor sphere above it: Charles pursued a diametrically opposed campaign to that of the Tudor court. In the same way he sought to influence the pope, but to reach the opposite conclusion: on 6 February 1529 he wrote to the Bishop of Burgos tasking him to labour on his behalf at Rome, specifically requesting that the cause may be determined in Consistory and not in England.[40] He also used his ambassadors Miguel Mai ('Mai' on the list of names and titles with similar temporal profiles, above), the Imperial ambassador to Rome, and Juan Antonio Muxetula (or Musettula, as in the figure), special envoy to Rome to persuade the pope regarding the validity of the earlier dispensation for Henry to marry Catherine issued by Pope Pius III (although we do not have evidence for those edges within the State Papers metadata). The original dispensation, according to Charles, was in his possession (see discussion in Chapter 5): in letters to Muxetula on 16 February he affirms that he cannot send the original safely because of its great significance, touching as it does not only the validity of the marriage, but also the authority of the Holy See.[41] Despite sending an authentic copy, however, a letter from Charles to Mai on 9 May 1529 discusses how the English ambassadors (presumably Bryan and Vanni) pressed the pope to declare it a forgery.[42] As part of his campaign to avert divorce Charles sought, through figures such as Cardinal Colonna, to cause the universities and other scientific institutions in the kingdom of Naples, as well as distinguished theologians and lawyers, to give their opinions in writing.[43] The intellectual and legal consultation undertaken by Spain once again can be seen as a mirror image of that undertaken by the English. This dimension of the king's great matter can be seen more explicitly through the category of similar words that includes: 'lawyers', 'learned', 'doctors', 'universities', 'read', 'counsel', 'books', 'learning', 'opinions', and 'subscriptions', etc.

We can begin to grasp the scholarly dimension of the great matter, and the different personnel that it involved, by looking at the topic networks for the words 'conscience' and 'books'. The 'conscience' topic network (peak detected 1 December 1527–31 December 1534) shown in Figure 6.9 exhibits some important structural similarities

---

[39] LP, vol 1, p. vii.   [40] BL, Add. MS 28,578, f.21. Modern copy from the Acad. de la Historia at Madrid.
[41] BL, Add. MS 28, 578, f.52. Modern copy from a draft from the archives of Simancas.
[42] BL, Add. MS 28,578, f.215. Modern copy.
[43] See the emperor's letter to Colonna dated 27 June: BL, Add. MS 28,580, f.201. Spanish draft, written by Alfonso de Valdes.

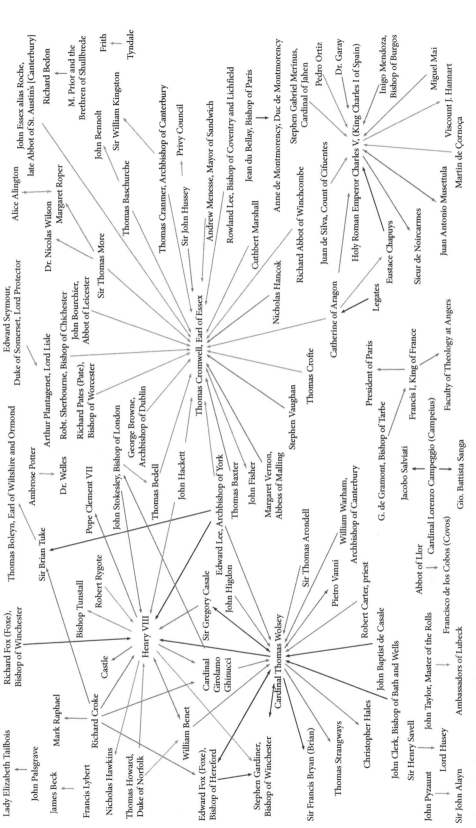

Figure 6.9 Topic network for 'conscience' in the time window from 1 December 1527 to 31 December 1534. The hubs of Henry and Wolsey are on the left-hand side, Cromwell is the central hub, connected to Emperor Charles V in the bottom right, via the bridging nodes of Catherine of Aragon and Eustace Chapuys.

to the 'divorce' network graph, and some revealing differences. The topic arises from the way Henry represented his motivations for seeking the dissolution of his marriage as due to his so-called scruple of conscience and the pope's conflicted position on this topic—a debate in which both sides sought to cite the Bible and theological tracts in support of their position. The topic also allows us to trace how the use of the word 'conscience' modulates and becomes tied up with the broader debates that developed out of the king's great matter, specifically the break with Rome and the difficult position in which this placed many English Catholics.

Compared to the 'divorce' network, Cromwell is much more dominant in this topic community. 'Conscience' is a word choice that emerged slightly later in the papal negotiations, and it was used particularly frequently by Cromwell (who used the word 'divorce' comparatively rarely). What is very similar to the 'divorce' topic network is the comparative placement of the three other hubs: Henry, Wolsey, and the emperor. Once again Charles V is connected into the main network only via the bridging figures of Catherine and Chapuys: an ideological divide corresponding with Henry's position on one side and Catherine's on the other. An important feature that distinguishes the 'conscience' network from the 'divorce' topic network, however, is the greater presence of lateral connections: people connecting not through but *around* the hubs, creating their own short paths. For example, there is a concentric ring of connections that form around Henry, which begins with Wolsey and loops through Edward Lee, Sir Brain Tuke (secretary to Wolsey and Henry), Richard Croke, and finally back to Wolsey via either Ghinucci, or Fox and Gardiner. All these men feature in the 'divorce' topic network, but with smaller numbers of connections. Amongst this list of men, Croke is perhaps the most interesting figure as he is the only one who is neither a diplomat (unlike Lee, Ghinucci, Fox, and Gardiner), nor the recipient of diplomatic bulletins (Wolsey or Tuke); he also has the highest degree apart from Wolsey. Croke's significance is due to his role in the intellectual wing of the king's great matter.

Croke was a Greek scholar who, between late 1529 and late 1530, was sent to Italy on a royal mission to find scholarly support for Henry VIII's divorce: specifically, the contention that the pope should not have made a dispensation permitting the king to marry Catherine. He sought to amass intellectual force behind these arguments through two kinds of scholarly witness: human and textual.[44] He collected, on the one hand, the subscriptions and writings of prominent philosophers, canonists, theologians, humanists, and rabbis; and on the other he scoured Venetian and Paduan libraries for patristic and other early Christian writings which would strengthen the king's cause. For example, in a 1529 letter to Gardiner he reports that he has collected writings or subscriptions from doctors Philip de Cremis, Hannibal, John Maria of Padua, de Barlaan, Donatus de Feltro, Mark of Sienna, Thomas prior of the Preachers, and various others who are either public preachers or professors.[45] Croke's centrality

---

[44] See Fletcher, *The Divorce of Henry VIII*, *passim*; Jonathan Woolfson, 'Croke, Richard (1489–1558)', *ODNB*, <https://doi.org/10.1093/ref:odnb/6734>; Gustavus Przychocki, 'Richard Croke's Search for Patristic MSS in Connexion with the Divorce of Catherine', *Journal of Theological Studies* 13 (1911–12), 285–95.

[45] Cotton Vitellius B/XIII f.56.

to this intellectual effort is even more apparent when we look at the topic networks for 'books' and 'theologians'.

The word 'books' is, as one might imagine, somewhat problematic because of its lack of specificity. As outlined above, references to books in the 1520s and 1530s were dominated by three main themes: the programme of book censorship and burning of heretical books; the consultation of libraries and universities in Europe to support the king's great matter; and the engagement with books in support of and against Henry's subsequent marriage to Anne Boleyn. The 'books' topic network for the two years 1529–30 shown in Figure 6.10, however, focuses largely on the second of these themes. Most importantly it helps us to see the significance of Croke, who forms a hub that is only slightly smaller than those of Wolsey, Cromwell, and Henry. His letters describe the process by which he sought access to libraries and gathered books for the king's cause, selections from which appeared in the government's propagandistic tracts of 1531, the *Gravissimae censurae academiarum* and its English translation, *The Determinations of the Moste Famous and Mooste Excellent Universities of Italy and Fraunce*, both printed by Thomas Berthelet. In a letter to Ghinucci from 1529 he discusses the pretences he used to obtain access, fearful that if the reason for his mission was known he would be denied: in this case he pretended to the Bishop of Chieti and Girolamo Aleandro, the Archbishop of Brindisi, that there were many princes who were desirous of founding a library, and he had been commissioned to search for books.[46]

We can further contextualise Croke's role by turning to the 'theologians' topic network in Figure 6.11, in which we can see a sparser version of the structure observed in the 'divorce' and 'conscience' graphs: two main communities, composed of English and Imperial actors respectively. The appearance of Charles V is unsurprising: the emperor, as we have already learned, had sought written statements against the divorce and in support of the original dispensation from distinguished theologians and lawyers and the universities and other scientific institutions in the kingdom of Naples. His letter to Colonna, which forms one edge in this network, includes the emperor's directive to acquire such statements. The other edges leading to Charles are constituted by reports from his ambassadors in Rome about the efforts of the English to amass scholarly and theological support for the divorce. Mai reports in a letter dated 10 August 1530 on his attempts to block the English efforts by securing a brief that no one should counsel, testify, or speak on the case of the king of England, except for conscience and truth, to which the English ambassadors complained that this was to forbid the faculty from giving an opinion, and, moreover, that as the terms of the brief required procedure according to canon law, it excluded the theologians.[47] Later letters give more specific details of the progress being made by the English and the names of those writing their opinions, including those made by Philip Decio and Rodrigo Niño against the queen.[48] Muxetula's letters express an even more explicit weariness:

---

[46] Cotton Vitellius B/XIII 30b.
[47] Mai to Charles V, 10 August 1530, BL, Add. MS 28581, f.24, modern copy from Simancas.
[48] Mai to Charles V, 10 January 1531, BL, Add. MS 28,582, f.286, modern copy from Simancas.

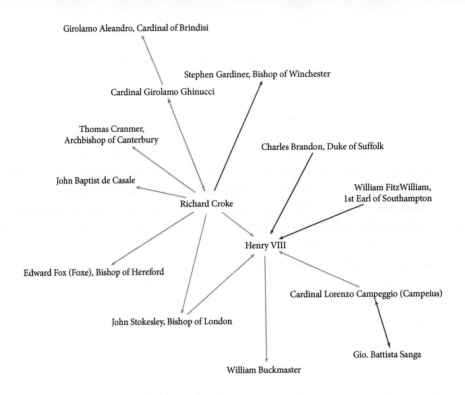

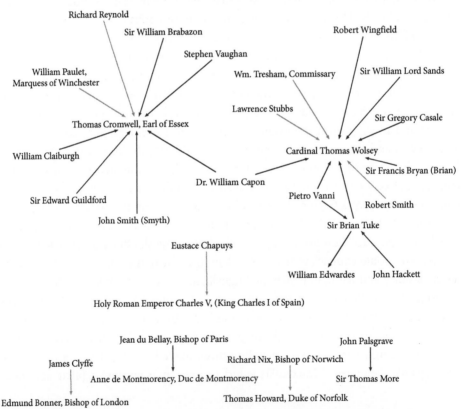

Figure 6.10 Topic network for 'books' in the time window from 1 January 1529 to 31 December 1530. The network consists of two main components, which are fully separated. The one in the top half of the diagram is focused on Henry VIII and Richard Croke, and the other one in the bottom half is focused on Wolsey and Cromwell.

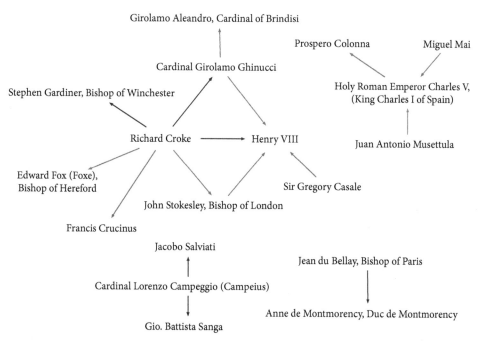

Figure 6.11 Topic network for 'theologians' in the time window from 1 January 1529 to 31 December 1531. The network consists of four small but separate components. The one in the top right is focused on Emperor Charles V. The component in the top left is focused on Richard Croke and Henry VIII. Two small components, with three and two nodes respectively, represent discussions of the English strategy regarding Henry's divorce among theologians.

he dismisses the supposed conscientious grounds of the divorce, and reports how he had amused the pope by suggesting a more accurate account would be that Henry had been crying because of the quarrel he had had with his mistress, and that the theologians had advised him to cry for the discharge of his conscience.[49] The free-floating dyad (the Bishop of Paris and Duc de Montmorency) and triad (Campeggio, Sanga, and Salviati) are also formed by letters discussing the English strategy, specifically the consultation of the theologians at the University of Paris.

The scholarly strategy of the English, then, was under much scrutiny. We can see why Croke sought to keep his role a secret upon his arrival in Italy. The reports talk about the efforts of the English ambassadors; however, what we can see is that, while there are an array of different diplomats in this network, it is Croke who is positioned at the centre of efforts to gather theological support. Croke in this context is a small hub. However, unlike bigger administrative hubs like Wolsey and Cromwell, where the dominant direction of information is into the hub, here we can see that all Croke's correspondence mentioning theologians is outgoing. This directionality shows us (along with the content of the missives) that he plays a managing role. He sent not

---

[49] Muxetula to Charles V, 23 January 1531, Add. MS 28,582, f.318, modern copy.

only reports on his progress but also requests for help in his mission: he sought to use the influence and contacts of his Italian associates and the resident ambassadors. The formation of nodes in both the 'books' and 'theologians' graphs suggest that Croke's most important partners in the mission were Ghinucci and John Stokesley, the Bishop of London. This is confirmed by the letters that mark these edges. Stokesley had been dispatched to Italy at the same time as Croke, accredited as an ambassador to the emperor. We see Croke reporting to his colleague on how, through Father Francis and his nephew, they looked set to gain the subscriptions of 100 theologians—in fact all the theologians and jurists of the Signory and Milan.[50] His correspondence with Ghinucci shows the role that the Italian played in helping him gain access to libraries and gather textual witnesses: writing on 14 January 1530, he thanks Aleandro for obtaining, on his behalf, permission to acquire books from St Mark's library, and reminds him that he needs the suffrages of theologians, such as Aleandro, whom he describes as both learned and good.[51] With the frequent and lengthy requests that Croke sent Ghinucci it seems that he strongly relied on his existing contacts and on intercession: he places a great deal of trust in Ghinucci during these first months, unlike the other Italian diplomats working for the English crown, Sir Gregory Casale (an anglicisation of Gregorio Casali) and his brother John Baptiste (or Giambattista), whom Croke accused of acting against Henry's interests (and who appears in the 'books' topic network).

However, Croke also let his mistrust spread to Ghinucci: in a letter dated 11 April 1530 he writes bluntly to the bishop that if he is not his sincere friend, he is not Croke's helper, but a spy upon the king's secrets.[52] This mistrust is significant because it tells us something about Croke's effectiveness in managing his network. These were not happy alliances. Although Croke used his English associates on the ground strategically upon his arrival, his behaviour acted to alienate them; eventually Ghinucci stopped replying to his letters. Historical opinion seems to agree that this was characteristic for Croke, who is described as lacking in social skills, quarrelsome, vitriolic, and 'anything but a diplomat'.[53] Whether this had a detrimental effect on the mission is hard to judge, for there were innumerable other dynamics at play. Croke's mission had been imagined originally as supplemental to diplomatic negotiations, but it so happened that Croke's presence in Italy coincided with a moment at which other processes stalled, other diplomatic agents fell silent, and allegiances were brought into question.[54] As a result, perhaps too much weight fell on a man who did not have the skills to manage his contacts to the best effect. In many ways he was very successful: Croke won over many individuals and institutions to the English cause. But this process required constant vigilance. This was a battle of two sides, as the four topic networks represented in Figures 6.8 to 6.11 so clearly show. One particular edge in the conscience

---

[50] Cotton Vitellius B/XIII f.55.   [51] Cotton Vitellius B/XIII 42b.   [52] Cotton Vitellius B/XIII f.71.

[53] Fletcher, *The Divorce of Henry VIII*, p. 124. Woolfson writes in his *ODNB* entry: 'For Thomas Baker he was "an ambitious, envious and discontented wretch" (Baker, 1.97); for J. T. Sheppard his character was "suspicious, touchy, conceited, zealous" (Sheppard, 23); for J. J. Scarisbrick he was "a whining, tiresome man, who seems to have been able to quarrel with anybody" (Scarisbrick, 256–7); for Diarmaid MacCulloch he was "a fussy and self-righteous Cambridge don who was more skilled at Greek than he was at human relationships" (MacCulloch, 51).'

[54] See Fletcher, *The Divorce of Henry VIII*, p. 128.

network diagram shows just how unstable the process of amassing support could be: the letter from Croke to Mark Raphael dated 14 October 1530 informs us that the 'Reverende pater' had previously written in support of Henry's cause. However, Croke had heard that, because he did not return Raphael's counsel in time, Raphael had then proceeded to write instead for the emperor, saying his former writing for Henry was merely an exercise. Croke asserts that it is plain that he has written against his conscience, and warns him to return to his former position, and to excuse himself by saying that he had written for the emperor unwillingly.[55] This example shows the tenuousness of the English position: even their seeming allies could default.

Taken together, the four topic networks reveal something of the complexity of Henry's diplomatic negotiations, touching as they did on the authority of Rome and the dynamics of Imperial power. The network diagrams fall into two groups: those for 'divorce' and 'conscience' give a more comprehensive insight into patterns of communication and alliances, whereas the network graphs for 'theologians' and 'books' elucidate a specific strategy for the consolidation of authority. As a result, we see Croke emerging from the peripheries of the first two network graphs to occupy a central position within that particular set of activities. What the topic network for 'theologians' shares with 'divorce' and 'conscience', however, is that it demonstrates the irreconcilability of Henry's desires with the imperial agenda. Taken together, these network diagrams act as a warning: the fissures opening up in each of them foreshadow the rift that would end ultimately with the break with Rome. The break was achieved finally in 1534 following a series of acts passed in the preceding two years.

More generally, by retelling what is perhaps a well-worn episode for history from a different perspective we can understand something about the value of the method we have developed both for providing macroscopic insights and for identifying individuals who occupied important roles in the transmission of information, but may have been marginalised in historical accounts.[56] As such the narrative above demonstrates the benefit of such a method for orienting research, or structuring teaching of a given topic, when there exists a mass of documentation: it traces a path through those records, and shows how the parts relate to one another. However, the benefits of the overview perspective become even stronger when we begin to apply such a method to multiple historical episodes in ways that allow us to begin to take an even more distant view of the archive and recognise abstract network structures across them, such as the separated spheres of influence observed in Figures 6.8–6.11. For this is not a feature that is peculiar to the king's great matter.

---

[55] Cotton Vitellius B/XIII f.123.
[56] Croke, for example, receives a single-sentence mention in G. W. Bernard's tome *The King's Reformation*.

The Netherlands 1578–9

The fissures we observed in the 'divorce', 'conscience', and 'theologians' network graphs are an important feature that can be observed in numerous other topic networks. This tendency is especially noticeable in the case of words and topic clusters concerning international relations, diplomatic negotiations, or war. In some topic networks we see a complete separation of these two spheres. In such cases it is apparent that the two worlds are constituted by separate intelligence activities. In general, the largest connected component is a product of the network of intelligencers reporting to the Tudor government, whereas the next largest component is made up of the actors whose aims and agendas are opposed to those of the Tudor government. These come into our data through two means. In the Henrician period, a role is played by Brewer's editorial policy of inclusion in his *Letters and Papers*, as discussed above; but beyond this it can be attributed to the kinds of interception and surveillance discussed in Chapter 4. One such example can be seen in the correspondence emerging from a period within the Dutch Revolt during the years 1578 and 1579, as highlighted in relation to the Walloon topic cluster above.[57]

The Dutch Revolt is the name given to the decades-long struggles of the northern, largely Protestant, provinces of the Low Countries against the Roman Catholic rule of Spain. Tensions began when Charles V abdicated in 1555 and the seventeen provinces were handed over to his son Philip II, who absorbed them into the wider Spanish empire; but the first key eruptions are often cited as the *Beeldenstorm*, the wave of attacks on Catholic art and iconography that began in the summer of 1566. The southern provinces initially joined in the revolt but later submitted to Spain, and, by the end of the war in 1648, large areas of the Southern Netherlands had been lost to France, which had allied itself with the Dutch Republic against Spain.[58] When thinking about such a long, drawn-out process it is hard to consider particular periods of time in isolation without focusing on single battles or treaties. Even important events, such as the Pacification of Ghent in 1576, only take meaning by understanding them within the context of what happened before and after. In many ways this captures the very challenge at the heart of writing history: we must necessarily extract, simplify, and exclude, setting (sometimes) arbitrary start and end points. The use of word frequency as a guide, however, allows us to think about topics from new perspectives, by separating out strands of narratives, and defining discrete time periods that might not occur to us otherwise. Above we discussed the word frequency profiles that were most similar to 'Walloons', which peaked in the two-year period 1578–9. These grouped

---

[57] For an overview of the English role in the Dutch Revolt during Elizabeth's reign, see Wallace T. MacCaffrey, *Elizabeth I: War and Politics, 1588–1603* (Princeton University Press, 1994), chapters 13 and 14; Susan Frye, *Elizabeth I: The Competition for Representation* (Oxford University Press, 1996), pp. 78–85; Charles Wilson, *Queen Elizabeth and the Revolt of the Netherlands* (Macmillan, 1970); Peter Iver Kaufman, 'Queen Elizabeth's Leadership Abroad: The Netherlands in the 1570s', in *Leadership and Elizabethan Culture*, ed. Peter Iver Kaufman (Springer, 2013), chapter 5.

[58] See James D. Tracy, *The Founding of the Dutch Republic: War, Finance, and Politics in Holland, 1572–1588* (Oxford University Press, 2008).

profiles can help us to understand the way that the events in the Netherlands were reported to the Tudor government in these years, and how international relations were observed and managed.

The reason for the surge in references to 'Ghent', 'Artois', 'Hainault' [i.e. Hainaut], 'Mechlin' [i.e. Mechelen], 'Pacification', 'Walloons', 'States', 'Motte', and 'Casimir' during this two-year window becomes apparent when we examine the history of this period, and the events leading up to them. Following the eruption of revolt in 1566 Philip II sent Fernando Álvarez de Toledo, Duke of Alba, to impose military rule and act as governor-general. During the decade that followed, Elizabeth I watched carefully without getting involved, despite an embassy from the rebel States of Holland and Zeeland in January 1576 offering to make her their sovereign. As John Guy and Susan Doran have argued, in these years her aims were to reconcile the rebellious provinces to Philip's obedience, to persuade him to restore their ancient liberties, and to keep the Netherlands free from an occupying foreign army.[59] Her attitude changed, however, following the Sack of Antwerp in November 1576 by mutinying Spanish troops, when 8,000 people in Antwerp lost their lives. This shocking event stiffened many against the Spanish Habsburg monarchy. The States-General signed the Pacification of Ghent, unifying the rebellious provinces with the loyal provinces with the goal of removing all Spanish soldiers from the Netherlands and stopping the persecution of heretics; Elizabeth supported the Pacification and offered the States military aid provided they preserved their obedience to the King of Spain.[60] The increased English engagement supported by a new embassy to the Netherlands explains why we see a peak in references to events in the Netherlands from 1577 onwards.

In keeping with the terms of the Pacification, the Spanish troops were removed, but in the summer of 1577 Don John of Austria (the new governor-general) began a new campaign against the Dutch rebels, and in early 1578 he roundly defeated the rebel armies at Gembloux. Elizabeth saw the need for intervention, but, anxious about the ramifications of explicitly siding against Spain, she arranged and paid for John Casimir, Count Palatine of Simmern (and brother to the Elector Palatine), to lead a mercenary army into the Netherlands. However, in Ghent Casimir committed acts of violence and oppression that exacerbated religious disputes. In response, the largely Catholic provinces of Walloon Flanders, Hainaut, and Artois refused to contribute to the general war effort.[61] Instead, they turned to Alessandro Farnese, the Duke of Parma and new governor-general for protection. Hainaut reported that unless the Pacification of Ghent was ratified a second time, the Walloons would continue to believe that the king's only reason for accepting it had been for him to 'cover up some sinister design'.[62] When Farnese suggested to Valentin Pardieu de la Motte (the governor of Gravelines that had previously sold out to the previous governor-general) that the Pacification

---

[59] John Guy, *Elizabeth: The Forgotten Years* (Viking, 2016), p. 32; Elizabeth Doran, *Elizabeth I and Foreign Policy, 1558–1603* (Routledge, 2000), pp. 11, 35.

[60] Doran, *Elizabeth I and Foreign Policy*, p. 36.

[61] Mack P. Holt, *The Duke of Anjou and the Politique Struggle During the Wars of Religion*, p. 113.

[62] Monica Stensland, *Habsburg Communication in the Dutch Revolt* (Amsterdam University Press, 2012), p. 89.

be made less demanding, La Motte's reply was that the Pacification would have to be accepted in its entirety without amendments. The negotiation between Farnese and the southern Walloon provinces resulted in them signing the Union of Arras (6 January 1579): in return for restoration of law and order the States of the Walloon provinces agreed to maintain their loyalty to Philip II and not tolerate Calvinism. Other provinces and towns, such as Mechelen followed suit, reconciling with Philip on the same terms. In opposition, however, was the Union at Utrecht, signed on 23 January by several northern Protestant provinces including Holland and Zeeland. As Mack P. Holt has observed, the leaders of these two unions were 'unaware in 1579 that they had taken the first step toward a permanent division of the Netherlands'.[63]

Despite the brevity of this outline of events, we can see the reason for the peaks in the usage of these specific words 'Ghent', 'Artois', 'Hainault' [i.e. Hainaut], 'Mechlin' [i.e. Mechelen], 'Pacification', 'Walloons', 'States', 'Motte', and 'Casimir'. Our concern, however, is less with the words themselves, than the way they help us identify the different communities using them, and what this in turn reveals about the government's management of information. For this reason we compare the topic networks of seven of the aforementioned words within the cluster in Figure 6.12a–g).

By comparing them, we can begin to see that it is highly likely they are generated by the same intelligencing activities. The 'Artois' (Figure 6.12a) and 'Hainault' (Figure 6.12c) network diagrams look almost identical, like mirror images of each other, with two clear communities separated noticably by time (blue edges early, red late), and bridged by very few figures. The topic networks for 'Mechlin' (Figure 6.12d), 'Motte' (Figure 6.12e), and 'pacification' (Figure 6.12f) differ from those two, as the two main communities in these networks are *fully* separated; the components in the top half of the 'Motte' and 'pacification' networks share some similar structural features with the community that appears in the left hemisphere of the 'Hainault' and the right hemisphere of the 'Artois' network graphs. Of the seven networks, 'Walloons' is the least complex, focusing around one main hub with a few free-floating dyads and triads. By contrast, 'Ghent' is the most complex, but it is in essence a more populated version of the bridged structures seen in the 'Artois' and 'Hainault' topic networks.

What unites all of these networks is that the membership of the two main 'communities'—whether bridged or unbridged—remains strikingly consistent. The first and larger community in both of these diagrams is what we might dub the Tudor diplomatic network. The second main community, usually only slightly smaller than the first, represents the key individuals, governing bodies, and provinces warring and negotiating over the shape of the Netherlands in these years, including the States-General (often at its centre), the Estates of Artois, and Deputies of Hainaut. The Tudor diplomatic network focuses around small intelligence hubs including Francis Walsingham (Principal Secretary with Thomas Wilson), William Cecil Lord Burghley (Lord High Treasurer), and Elizabeth I. In all the topic networks, with the exception of 'Pacification', the most connected figure is William Davison. Davison was in the

---

[63] Holt, *Duke of Anjou*, p. 114.

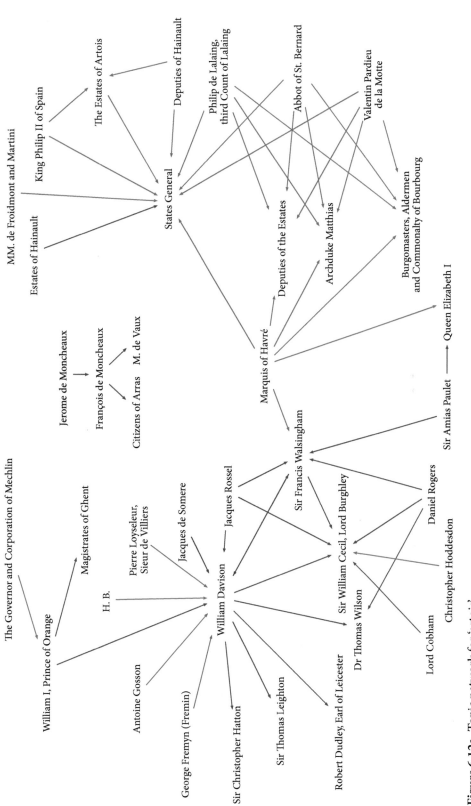

Figure 6.12a Topic network for 'artois'.

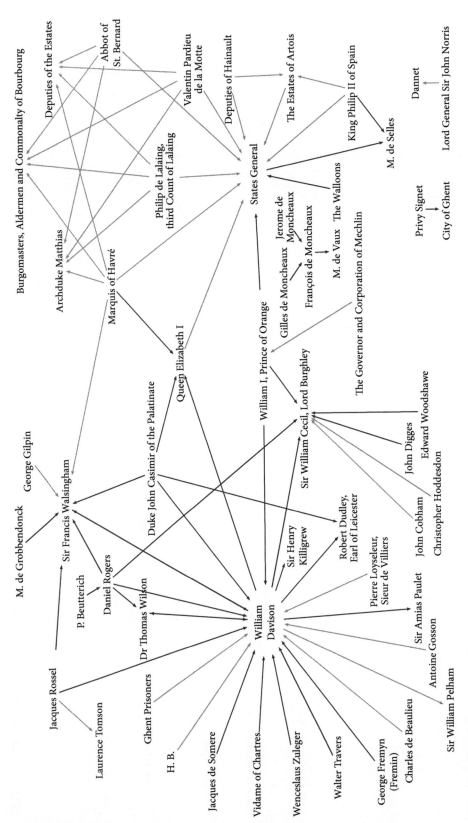

Figure 6.12b Topic network for 'ghent'.

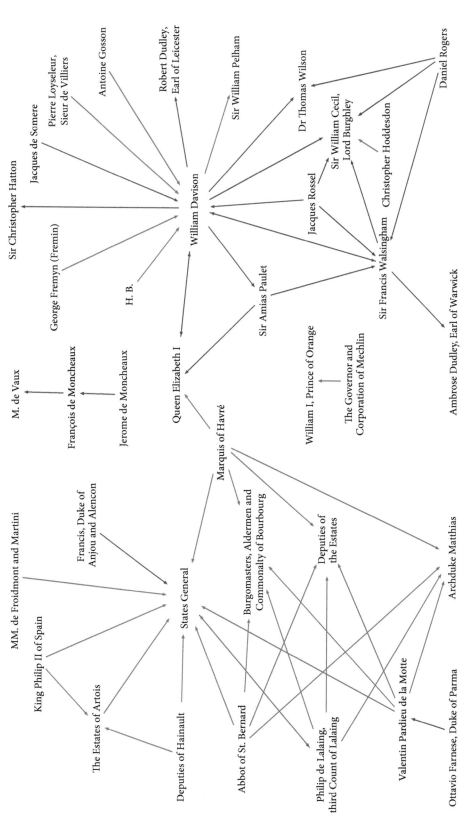

Figure 6.12c Topic network for 'hainault'.

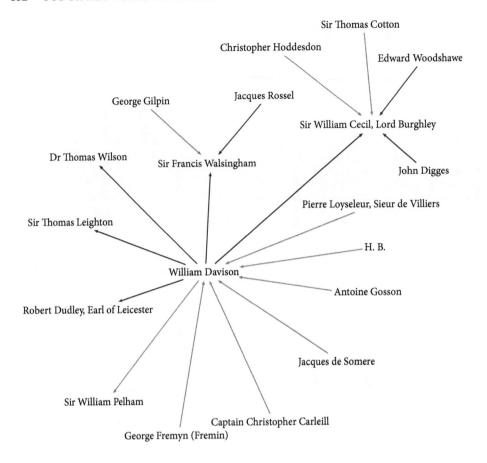

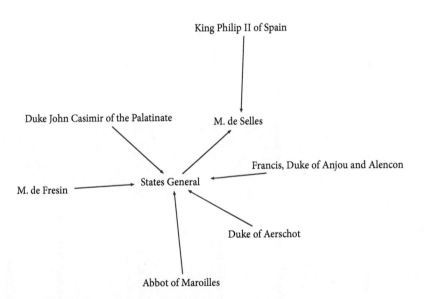

Figure 6.12d Topic network for 'mechlin'.

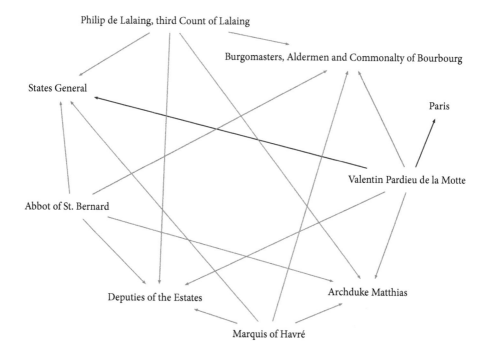

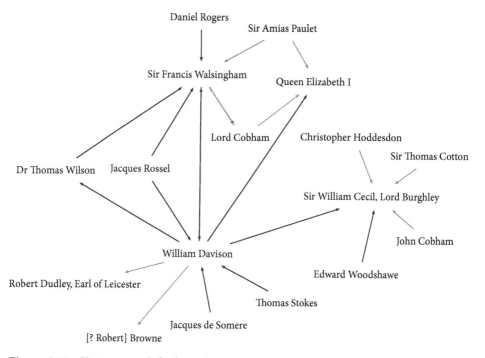

Figure 6.12e Topic network for 'motte'.

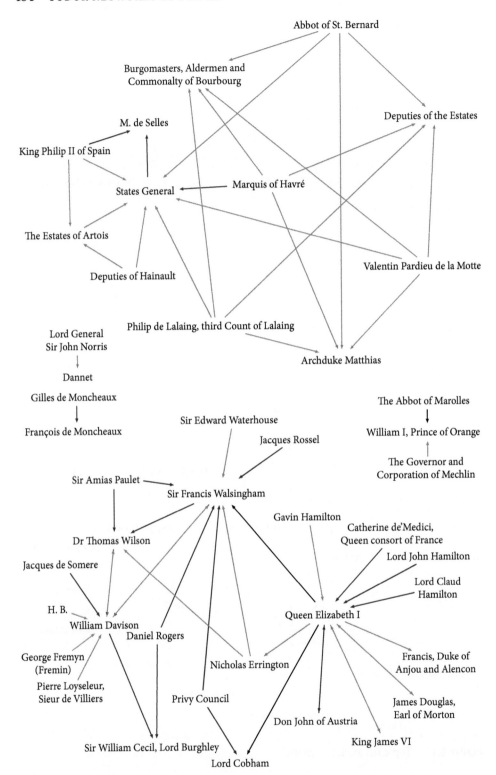

Figure 6.12f Topic network for 'pacification'.

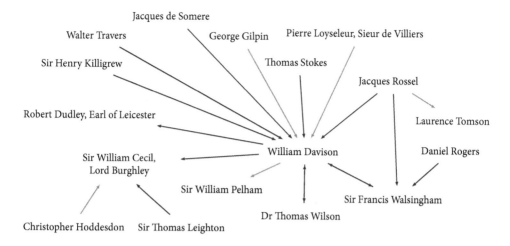

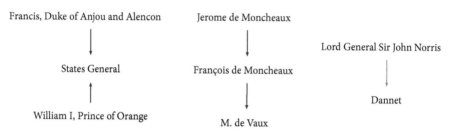

Figure 6.12g Topic network for 'walloons'.

Netherlands as the resident agent from August 1577 to May 1579, and sent regular intelligence reports to the secretaries Walsingham and Wilson, to Burghley, and to Robert Dudley, the Earl of Leicester, who was a strong proponent of English intervention in the Netherlands. Davison himself consistently argued that the Netherlands was the key to English security to the extent that he faced accusations that he had not defended Elizabeth's decisions over military aid. In a letter from Davison to Secretaries Walsingham and Smith he writes: 'I vnderstoode at my retvrne by Gand [i.e. Ghent] that the D. Casimire findinge himself grevid with my negociac[i]on had written to her Majestie in complaint of me as of a man that had therin exceedid his limittes.'[64] Despite these misgivings, the topic networks show how, as we would expect from a resident ambassador, Davison was positioned at a crucial intersection within the flow of intelligence, not only sending, but receiving intelligence.

Davison received letters both from key foreign leaders (such as Casimir and the Duke of Orange, discussed further below), and from other Tudor agents, which include both ambassadors and the heterogeneous kinds of 'intelligencer' discussed in Chapter 4. There was some change in the make-up between these correspondents after he was recalled in May 1579, which helps us understand the way that geographical

---

[64] 3 December 1578, SP 83/10 f.57r.

location affected the kinds of networks used for information management. Those he received letters from only during his embassy (1577–9) include Daniel Rogers (2 letters), Wenceslaus Zuleger (2), Jacques Rossel (1), Walter Travers (1), Thomas Stokes (1), Jean de Ferrières, Vidame de Chartres (1), and a group of Ghent prisoners (1). While some of his correspondents on embassy sought Davison's help—such as the Vidame de Chartres (who had previously been a recipient of English shelter and financial aid) and the prisoners from Ghent—the remainder were figures able to furnish Davison with valuable information. Rogers was a diplomat who served on missions to the Low Countries in the 1570s, meeting regularly with William of Orange and John Casimir, Count Palatine, to carry out Elizabeth I's policies towards the Low Countries.[65] Zuleger was a member of the Palatine Church council who provided an important point of access to Casimir and information on his actions in Ghent at the end of 1578.[66] Rossel had served the States as quarter-master and muster-master, and (seemingly in order to gain a commission from Her Majesty) sent frequent and highly sensitive material to Walsingham totalling sixty-three letters and numerous inter-cepted missives, as will be discussed further below. Travers was an English Puritan exile and chaplain to the English Merchant Adventurers at Antwerp, writing to Davison a letter with news of the religious atmosphere there.[67] And Stokes (already mentioned in Chapters 2 and 4) was a merchant-intelligencer used extensively by Walsingham, to whom Stokes sent at least 111 letters, providing not only detailed news reports on events in the Netherlands, but also acting as a conduit for others' intelligences: in a letter to Davison dated 31 December 1578 he says that he has forwarded two large packets of letters from Rogers to England.[68]

Davison's reliance on his correspondence networks became more acute after his return to England. In this period we see the emergence of new informants and con-tacts within his network (who may have provided oral intelligence prior to his depart-ure), as well as the continued use of a few trusted intelligencers. Appearing across Figures 6.12a–g those individuals that people who wrote to him only after he was recalled (and up until 1580) include: Pierre Loyseleur, Sieur de Villiers (15 letters), Anthoine Gosson (4 letters), George Gilpin (1), Charles de Beaulieu (1), one 'H. B.' (1), and Christopher Carleill (1). Two further figures corresponded throughout this whole period: Georges Fremyn (19), and Jaques de Somere (9). Three of these figures have histories that are fairly well documented and appear in the *ODNB* or in continental dictionaries of national biography. The first is Gilpin, secretary for the Merchant Adventurers in Antwerp and one of the queen's most trusted agents in her negotiations with the states of the Low Countries.[69] The second, Carleill, was an English soldier who had fought on behalf of Dutch Protestant allies in 1573 and 1578–81, during which

[65] Mark Loudon, 'Rogers, Daniel (c.1538–1591)', *ODNB*, <https://doi.org/10.1093/ref:odnb/23969>.

[66] *The Reformers of England and Germany in the Sixteenth Century: Their Intercourse and Correspondence*, ed. H. Schmettau and B. H. Cowper (Hatchard & Company, 1859), p. 146. See Zuleger to Davison on 5 December and 17 December 1578: SP 83/10 f.60r and SP 83/10 f.85r.

[67] 12 November 1578, SP 83/10 f.26.   [68] SP 83/10 f.108.

[69] Gary M. Bell, 'Gilpin, George (d. 1602)', *ODNB*, <https://doi.org/10.1093/ref:odnb/10758>.

time he sent military intelligence back to Walsingham and other key government figures.[70] The third is de Somere, who was an administrator and diplomat (and poet) from Ghent.[71] Unlike the former figures, who regularly communicated with Walsingham, de Somere only communicates with Davison, to whom he delivered news from Ghent following the violence, reporting that Artois was on the point of being reconciled to the King of Spain, and the attempts to bring in Lille, Tournay, Douay, and Orchies; he also offered an additional point of access to the Prince of Orange.[72] Interestingly—and perhaps indicating his status in the Netherlands—de Somere did not expect news only to pass in one direction. In the letter dated 16 August 1579 he adds a postscript saying that he had just heard that the Duke of Alençon had arrived in England, and remarks, 'Vous etes sur le [place] auoir nouvelles intéressantes' (you are in the place to have interesting news) of him, implying that news of the duke's negotiations for marriage to Elizabeth might be sent by return post to de Somere.[73]

The other figures to correspond with Davison after he left the Netherlands are much harder to trace: they are a heterogeneous group of intelligencers, and where we find any trace of them in scholarship they are referred to in passing only, in terms of the intelligence they were able to furnish; biographical details are sketchy. The one to correspond most frequently with Davison was Villiers, who had become a close associate of Walsingham's in the 1570s before, in 1577, joining the Prince of Orange as chaplain and adviser.[74] He provided detailed accounts of shifting loyalties and factions between districts, as war broke out such as news of war between the districts of Tournay and Cambray on one side, and Artois and Hainaut on the other.[75] Charles de Beaulieu (again solely Davison's correspondent) was appointed by the Duke of Orange in 1575 and the provisional government of Zealand to provide passports for goods imported,[76] but his skills also seem to have stretched to cryptography as in a letter dated 2 October 1579 he writes to Davison telling him that he has been employed by Villiers to decipher the dispatches from Bernardino de Mendoza to the Duke of Parma, whereby they got at the truth of their enemies' secrets.[77] Fremyn (already briefly mentioned in Chapter 4) has been described by Roger Kuin as a French captain in the service of States, later governor of Saftingen, who was a regular correspondent and intelligencer for Walsingham and provided Davison with detailed military reports from his camps at Thiméon and Ligny, and later from Antwerp and Ghent.[78] H.B. (unidentified) wrote once to Davison on 26 July 1579 regarding a peace conference in Cologne, but all we know of him is the observation of Calendars editors that the writer (apparently a Fleming) wrote Davison's drafts of two letters dated 1 and 13

---

[70] D. J. B. Trim, 'Carleill, Christopher (1551?–1593)', *ODNB*, <https://doi.org/10.1093/ref:odnb/4668>.
[71] Available at: <http://www.academieroyale.be/academie/documents/FichierPDFBiographieNationaleTome2046.pdf#page=394>.
[72] De Somere to Davison, 7 December 1578, SP 83/10 f.82r; and 16 December 1578, SP 83/10 f.82r–83r.
[73] SP 83/12 f.56.
[74] *The Correspondence of Sir Philip Sidney*, ed. Roger Kuin, vol. 1 (Oxford University Press, 2012), p. lxi.
[75] Villers to Davison, 17 October 1579, SP 83/12 f.93.
[76] Andrew Spicer, *The French-Speaking Reformed Community and Their Church in Southampton, 1567–c.1620*, Southampton Record Series, 39 (Sutton, 1997), pp. 136–7.
[77] SP 83/12 f.87.   [78] *The Correspondence of Sir Philip Sidney*, ed. Kuin, vol. 1, pp. xlii–xliii.

April 1579, so we might infer that the writer had served Davison in some secretarial capacity.[79] Gosson, Seigneur de Wavrin, again writes solely to Davison, whom he seems to hold as a friend as well as an associate, passing him not only reports on the movement of key leaders and developments in the peace process, but all lamenting the absence of his associate whose guidance he desires on the issue of marriage.[80]

By exploring, even very superficially, the make-up of Davison's region of the network in the seven topic networks we can see that an ambassador was only as successful as the network he built. Part of his success and status derives from having correspondents to which nobody else in the Tudor government had access (thereby bridging structural holes), like de Somere, Gosson, and the anonymous H.B. However the effective management of information seems to have been arranged so that Davison and Walsingham held certain intelligencers in common: for the most valuable agents it made sense to make sure that information was passing along multiple routes back to the Tudor government in case of interception or delays. Of these associates held in common, perhaps the most important in this period of Dutch history was Jacques Rossel. This is demonstrated clearly in the Hainault, Motte, and Walloons graphs (Figures 6.12b, 6.12e, and 6.12g), where he triangulates between Davison and Walsingham. Rossel seems to have been a Burgundian adventurer, before he entered the service of the States as commissary and muster-master.[81] He corresponded first with Burghley (and seemingly only once) on 23 March 1578 before becoming a regular correspondent of Walsingham's, sending him at least sixty-three missives, as well as one surviving letter addressed to Elizabeth I. Arthur Butler has inferred from the correspondence between Rossel and Walsingham that the pair sought actively to sidestep Davison, of 'whose astuteness in obtaining information the Secretary perhaps had not a very high opinion'. At the same time, however, he remarks that Rossel's information about the Prince of Orange and those in his closest confidence should be taken with caution: 'Besides being an inveterate scandal-monger, he seldom fails in his references to that group and its chief to adopt a rather spiteful tone'.[82]

Nevertheless it is undeniable that Rossel was able to deliver vital intelligence to the Tudor government. Through access to intercepted correspondence, he sent Walsingham information from within enemy circles, from news of the death of Philip II's son Ferdinand in 1578, to the burning of villages near Bouchain and Valenciennes by the Malcontents (a group of military companies captained by French-speaking nobles who refused to obey the States-General until their wages had been paid).[83] More importantly for our view of the topic at the heart of these network diagrams, Rossel also sent intercepted letters and documents to Walsingham. In a letter dated

---

[79] SP 83/12 f.40.

[80] On his marriage see Gosson to Davison, 30 April 1580, SP 83/13 f.23.

[81] I can find no evidence for assertion that he was an unfrocked monk in Baron Kervyn de Lettenhove's *Les Huguenots et les Gueux: Étude historique sur vingt-cinq années du XVIe siècle (1560–1585)* (Beyaert-Storie, 1884), p. 48.

[82] 'Preface', in *Calendar of State Papers Foreign: Elizabeth, Volume 13, 1578–1579*, ed. Arthur John Butler (HMSO, 1903), pp. v–lx. BHO, <http://www.british-history.ac.uk/cal-state-papers/foreign/vol13/v-lx> (accessed 16 August 2017).

[83] See Rossel to Walsingham, 9 November 1578, SP 83/10 f.19; and 6 August 1580, SP 83/13 f.44.

13 December 1578, he states that he had sent a copy of the latest treaty made by the Estates with the Duke of Anjou, which clearly demonstrates the aims of the French, and the various intelligences they had received from de la Motte and of the brothers de Lalaing and Montigny.[84] And in a letter dated 15 March 1579 he confirms that he had sent Walsingham 'les lettres et protestes, des seniors Visconte de Gant, de Captaine de Capre, Conte de Lallain, Montigny, la Mothe, et auetres et la responce de messieurs des Estats Generaulx aux Estats dartois'.[85] It is unclear whether these documents were freely handed over to Rossel by the representatives within the States-General, or whether he gained them by covert means, as with the interceptions, but as he observes, from this package of communication Walsingham can judge the intentions of those various actors.

The presence of correspondence bundles like this within the State Papers shows clearly the means by which we are able to reconstruct the second main cluster apparent across Figures 6.12a–g. The packet to which Rossel refers in the latter missive is almost certainly the three letters and documents bundled together and sent on 20 February 1579 (based on the date and the identity of the figures discussed therein). They contain: a letter from Philip de Lalaing, the 3rd Count of Lalaing, to the States-General that informing them that the Duke of Guise is amassing a large force in France; a copy of the protest signed by Robert de Melun, Viscount of Ghent, Oudart Bournonville, Baron of Capres, and Emmanuel de Lalaing, Baron de Montigny asserting that they stand by the Pacification of Ghent and the general union; and an account of what Montigny promised Guillaume de Homes, Lord of Hèze.[86] The people named in these documents were at the centre of a battle being waged by Farnese (then governor-general) on behalf of Philip II over the loyalty of the 'Malcontents', the Catholic nobles of the south: Montigny was the first to be won over to the Spanish fold, followed by his brother Lalaing, the Viscount of Ghent, Charles Philippe de Croÿ, Marquis d'Havré, Hèze, and Capres.[87] Around this time there seems to have been a special effort to intercept letters pertaining to this issue of alliance as we have several further bundles of correspondence between foreign bodies on this matter. One of the biggest bundles contains seven separate letters dating from February 1579: (1) d'Havré to the Archduke Matthias (the figure that the rebel provinces wanted as their governor-general) seems to date from before his defection to the Spanish side because it mentions the pernicious devices of de Selles, Philip II's ambassador; (2) Lalaing to the Deputies of the Estates at Antwerp is a request to be made to the Governor of Bouchain; (3) the Abbot of St Bernard and d'Havré to the States-General on the discontent of the Viscount of Ghent and Capres, and the risk of Artois and Hainaut separating from the States; (4) Philip II to the Burgomasters, Aldermen, and Commonalty of Bourbourg offers them his support for the maintenance of the Catholic faith in return for their allegiance; (5) and (6) two further letters from de la Motte on behalf of Philip making the same offer.[88]

[84] SP 83/10 f.76.   [85] SP 83/11 f.201.   [86] SP 83/11 f.134.
[87] Wilson, *Queen Elizabeth and the Revolt of the Netherlands*, p. 73.   [88] SP 83/11 f.148r–151r.

What is important about these two packages of letters is that they form the backbone of the second main 'community' in five of the seven network visualisations for the keywords—the two exceptions being 'Mechlin' and 'Walloons'.[89] Therefore, in Figures 6.12a–c and e–f we see the same individuals, governing bodies, and provinces featured as senders and recipients of these intercepted letters: Archduke Mattias, Philip II, de la Motte, Lalaing, d'Havré the States-General, representatives of Bourbourg, Artois, Hainaut. For the 'Motte' and 'Pacification' graphs (Figures 6.12e and f) this cluster of actors forms a disconnected island. These communities of correspondence form islands precisely because of their seizure. But in the three topic networks discussing 'Artois', 'Ghent', and 'Hainault' (Figures 6.12a–c) we see that there are bridges between the main Tudor diplomatic network and the body of seized correspondence focused on the key actors in the Dutch Revolt. These bridges help to highlight two key diplomatic relationships. The 'Hainault' and 'Artois' network graphs are the easiest to interpret: we can see that the key bridging figure here is d'Havré, who corresponds both with Elizabeth I and Walsingham. In the Ghent topic network, in addition to the d'Havré bridge, we can also see that the Prince of Orange bridges an important structural hole. Orange's letters date from before d'Havré's, but they also help to paint a picture of the latter's role in Anglo-Dutch relations. D'Havré's value derived, in part, from the fact that in the earlier part of the 1570s he had served as a commander and messenger to Philip II; however, when the king would not make him governor of Antwerp Castle, he defected and joined the services of the States-General, and was subsequently entrusted with the post of Ambassador in England.

What their positions in these network graphs make clear is that both d'Havré and Orange acted as crucial brokers on this international stage. Despite comparable structural positions in terms of the communities (and structural holes) that they bridged, these two men represented very different interests. Orange's letters written from Ghent in January 1578 describe the tense relationship between d'Havré's position and his own. In the first, he writes to Davison that he is concerned because he has heard from some friends that d'Havré and Adolf van Meetkercke, when reporting their negotiation to the States, declared that Elizabeth had counselled them to maintain the Roman religion in which they were born and bred.[90] This referred to the English queen's promise to help the States with money and troops if they promised to observe the terms of the pacification and maintain the old religion.[91] This forced Orange, as the leader of the rebel Protestant states, into a position where he needed to seek guidance on how to speak with d'Havré without giving offence to Elizabeth: he recognised their need for financial aid, but her position on religion was necessarily damaging to his

---

[89]   Mechlin features another, separate bundle, dated 29/30 September 1578, and we see other items of interception across both these graphs.
[90]   4 January 1578, SP 83/5 f.3r.
[91]   Wallace T. MacCaffrey, *Queen Elizabeth and the Making of Policy, 1572–1588* (Princeton University Press, 2014), p. 228.

agenda. As he expressed in further letters to Davison and Burghley, he feared that he may lose his credit as a negotiating force and as a leader of the Protestant cause.[92]

To conclude this case study, we can see that the abstract approach of tracing topic networks allows us to identify not only communities of discourse concerning the Dutch Revolt, but identifying precisely the means by which they were bridged, via acts of diplomatic brokerage and espionage. In this case we have identified two intermediary figures with different religious affiliations and political agendas. D'Havré, in a letter to Elizabeth dated 24 May 1579, updates her on the peace conference at Cologne (called by Emperor Rudolf II to attempt reconciliation between the Catholic delegates, Orange, and the Calvinists), which he predicted would ultimately fail because of treaties entered into by Hainaut and Artois (i.e. The Union of Arras). He had been sent on a mission to Artois with Meetkercke, but it was during this very mission that d'Havré defected back to the camp of Philip II. This was not necessarily inevitable, despite the issue of religion: Charles Wilson has argued that if Orange had had the financial resources of Farnese, and better backing from England, d'Havré and the other Catholic nobles might have been persuaded differently.[93] Orange and d'Havré functioned as two separate bridges, two routes by which the English sought to influence and negotiate with the States; but the differences between them tell us in miniature the story of the Netherlands in the year 1578–9. These diplomatic routes might have led to the desired aim of reconciliation, but ultimately we see them splitting along confessional lines, in a country that was irreparably divided. Once again, as in the case of Henry's 'great matter', we are faced with a history of separation.

Modularity

What unites the two case studies—on the king's great matter and the short episode within the Dutch Revolt—is the way in which topic networks help us to detect different epistolary communities and to understand their relationship to one another. In particular, the structural insights that this method offers enable us to identify subcommunities within the topic networks that correspond to the diplomatic network on the one hand and to foreign parties captured through editorial work or interception on the other. While our analysis of the communities was derived from reading and interpreting the graphs one by one, these separate communities within a graph can also be detected algorithmically by measuring the 'modularity' of a graph. High modularity means that one can partition a network into sub-regions that are densely connected, but the connections between those separate regions are much sparser or even nonexistent. By this definition the topic network for 'divorce' would have a relatively high modularity because the network divides into two main communities that are

---

[92] See Orange to Davison, 5 January 1578, SP 83/5 f.7r; and Orange to Burghley, 14 January 1578, SP 83/5 f.17r.
[93] Wilson, *Queen Elizabeth and the Revolt of the Netherlands*, p. 74.

connected only by one bridge. 'Pacification' would also have high modularity because the two main communities are entirely separated.

The fact that this kind of feature can be measured means that the observations gleaned from our two case studies can be generalised in order to discover other topics that feature high modularity. We were interested to see whether other graphs with high modularity scores would also point to issues of foreign policy and help us to detect other acts of interception. As observed above, acts of interception may create disconnected islands or communities that are connected by bridges, but in both cases they are clearly discernible as a separate cluster from the main intelligence networks. To search systematically for this kind of feature we developed a method that consists of four key steps that unify several of the methods outlined above. The first step was to return to the words with the most changed use over time, to identify topics that were newsworthy in a bounded period of time. Secondly, whereas in our analysis above the peaks of discourse were undertaken by manually identifying the period of the peak, we then undertook a step for automatic 'peak-extraction' which, as the name suggests, identifies where the peak period lies. From that information, we then automatically generated a network graph of the topic for that period, and finally measured that graph for its modularity and ranked all the results from highest to lowest modularity.[94]

One indication of the success of the method is the fact that amongst the ranked list of topic networks with the highest modularity are several of the topics that we have already encountered. In the top 3% most-modular networks we get several that pertain to Henry VIII's great matter: 'universities' (1530–1), 'influence' (1529–32), 'witnesses' (1531–3), 'marry' (1525–34), 'recovered (1529–30), and 'Wiltshire' (1530–3). We have encountered the significance of the word 'universities' before. Wiltshire refers to Thomas Boleyn, ambassador to the pope at Bologna, and ambassador to Charles V in 1532. Many of the letters using the word 'witnesses' in the synopsis are Spanish (meaning this is a translated word), most referring to the special *remissoriae* that would be granted by the Roman tribunal to enable the statements of witnesses for Catherine's side to be collected for presentation at the trial.

'Marry' in fact is more disparate in its inclusion because of the longer time frame (nine years): in the latter part of the period it contains many references to Henry's marriages to Catherine and Anne, but we also have references to Charles V's marriage to Isabella of Portugal and the engagement of Eleanor of Austria to Francis I, both in 1526, amongst others. The 'marry' graph therefore points us towards a facet of the method that should be considered in analysis of the results. The method of automatic peak extraction can mean that sometimes the peak is very long, because the usage is very high over an extended period of time (i.e. when the word remains consistently in the top 5,000 ranked words throughout this period). The longer the period, the more likely there will be modulations in the topics to which the word refers. The word 'marry' thus refers to the nuptials of multiple couples. In a similar way, as discussed

---

[94] See <https://github.com/tudor-networks-of-power/code>. The modularity is based on communities assigned by the Louvain algorithm.

above, the word 'books' was a trending topic in different communities over the 1520s and 1530s, from those seeking to burn 'pestiferous' heretical books, to those gathering theological support for Henry's great matter, to those writing against Henry's marriage of Anne Boleyn. But in other cases the method of peak extraction will extract single years, where a sharp peak pushes a word over that baseline. In these cases we have much sparser data, which also leads to higher modularity: the less data we have, the more likely we are to get free-floating islands of nodes in the network graphs. For the most part, cases that fall in between these extremes tend to yield the most interesting and helpful data, pointing us to genuinely discrete events and the communities of discourse behind them. But the extremes should be kept in mind when interpreting the graphs.

The process of ranking topic networks by their modularity allows us to confirm that the highest modularity is often observed for words relating to foreign policy, rather than domestic issues. It also allows us to observe important shared features across these topic networks. As in the case studies previously discussed, the graphs with highest modularity often feature an organisational structure in which the largest cluster is made up of members identifiable with the Tudor diplomatic community, and the next biggest represents a community that are the target of the government's intelligence gathering; these are either separate or connected by very few edges. Moreover, within the larger Tudor diplomatic community we see a recurring pattern: there will usually be two or three larger hubs, often including the monarch and/or secretary of state alongside another important statesman; and between them we find several figures who are poised as connectors. In each case these figures are revealed to occupy a position of diplomatic significance. For example, in the 'german' (1545–6) network graph (Figure 6.13a) these are Christopher Mont and Walter Buckler, the two men who were dispatched to Germany by Henry VIII to create an alliance between England, the German princes, and the King of Denmark.[95] In the 'Constantinople' (1539–42) network graph (Figure 6.13b) the figure is Edmund Harvel, a merchant turned agent in Venice who provided Cromwell with extensive reports on Mediterranean and Turkish matters.[96] In the 'Marseilles' (1533–4) network graph (Figure 6.13c) the individual is Pietro Vanni, who in his capacity as collector of papal taxes travelled in 1533 to Rome, Avignon, and Marseilles.[97] In the 'Naples' (1535–6) graph (Figure 6.13d) it is Richard Morison, an exile in Italy who sent Cromwell intelligence for a stipend.[98] The 'Romans' (1531–5) topic network (Figure 6.13e) refers to the title 'King of the Romans' used by German kings prior to their election as Holy Roman Emperor: here the figures are Gregory Casale (also known as Gregorio Casali) and Mont, who were Henry VIII's ambassadors in Rome and Germany respectively. The 'Antwerp' (1539–40) topic network (Figure 6.13f) is a little more complex, as the number of hubs mean that there are more bridging figures, including Stephen Vaughan,

[95] Luke MacMahon, 'Mont, Christopher (1496/7–1572)', *ODNB*, <https://doi.org/10.1093/ref:odnb/18994>.
[96] Jonathan Woolfson, 'Harvel, Edmund (d. in or before 1550)', *ODNB*, <https://doi.org/10.1093/ref:odnb/39717>.
[97] L. E. Hunt, 'Vannes, Peter (c.1488–1563)', *ODNB*, <https://doi.org/10.1093/ref:odnb/28097>.
[98] Jonathan Woolfson, 'Morison, Sir Richard (c.1510–1556)', *ODNB*, <https://doi.org/10.1093/ref:odnb/19274>.

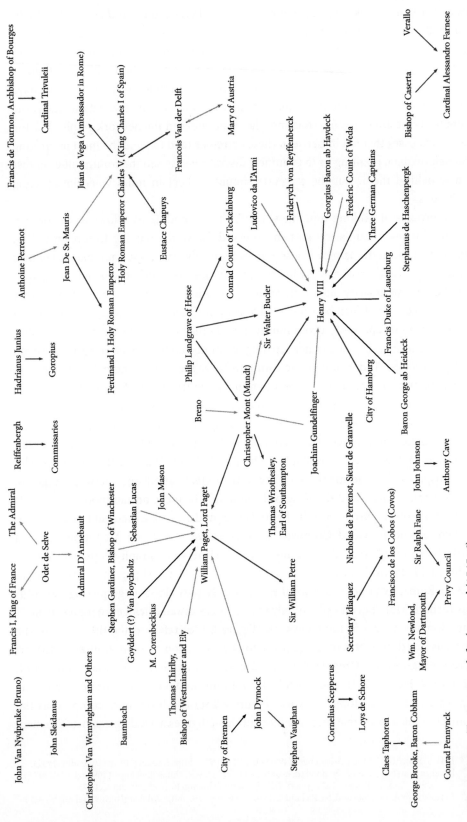

Figure 6.13a Topic network for 'german' (1545–6).

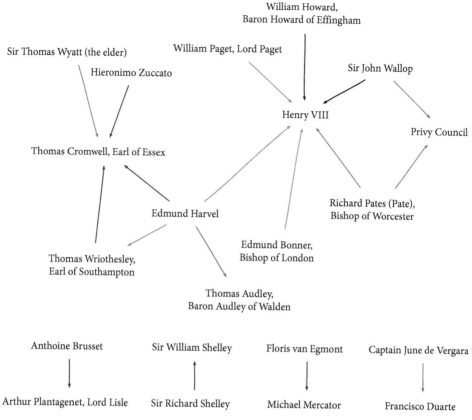

Figure 6.13b Topic network for 'constantinople' (1539–42).

Richard Pates, Nicholas Wotton, and Thomas Wyatt the elder; Mont also makes an appearance. These men served ambassadorial roles in a number of different locations at that time: Stephen Vaughan in the Low Countries, Pates and Wyatt at the court of Charles V, Wotton in Cleves, and Mont in Germany.

The second largest community in each graph is usually focused around the foreign powers' intelligence structures. In fact, in all six graphs the person at the centre of that foreign intelligence network component is Charles V—as it was in the graphs discussed with regards to Henry's 'great matter'. The evidence for these foreign intelligences enter our dataset through two key means, as discussed previously in Chapter 4 and above: editorial labour (specifically Brewer's editorial policy of inclusion in his *Letters and Papers*, as discussed above) and interception. The majority derive from the Spanish archives of Simancas and some other European archives, consulted by Brewer and his associates. But in addition, some other letters are from English archives, such as the British Library's MS Cotton Vespasian C/II (from the library of Sir Robert Cotton), which is a collection of correspondence, both originals and transcripts, concerning England and Spain (April 1522–October 1524). Cotton's own political career makes it more likely that these papers ended up in English hands through interception.

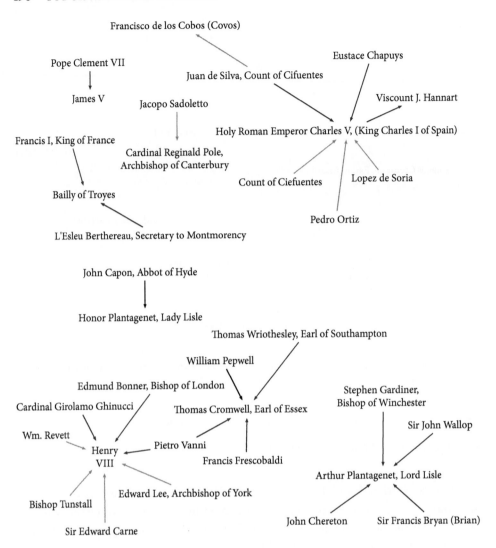

Figure 6.13c Topic network for 'marseilles' (1533–4).

This brings us to another observation. The six examples above are representative in that the vast majority of the topic networks with the highest modularity derive from Henry's reign, suggesting that the editorial effect has a larger impact than acts of interception. However, if we limit ourselves to topic networks dating from after Henry's reign, we see interception looming much larger. For example, the topic network for 'edict' (1576–7) (Figure 6.14a) refers mainly to the Edict of Beaulieu (1576) passed by Henry III of France, which gave Huguenots the right of public worship for their religion, and ended the Fifth war of Religion, although at the tail end of the period there are also some references to the Perpetual Edict of 1577, which provided for the removal of Spanish forces from the Netherlands. Notably John Casimir, Count Palatine of Simmern, was implicated across both events. Once again the largest component, occupying the left side of the figure, represents the diplomatic routes that information on these events took. The smaller component, focused around Henry III in the top right, is clearly the result of interception. With the exception of the correspondence with Casimir, these edges

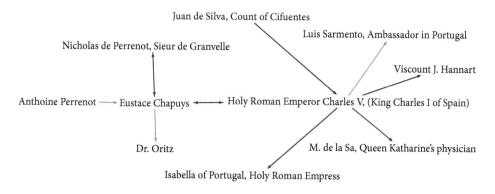

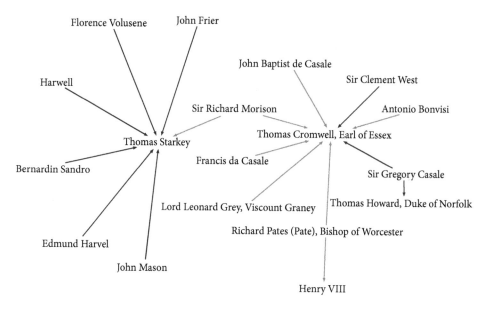

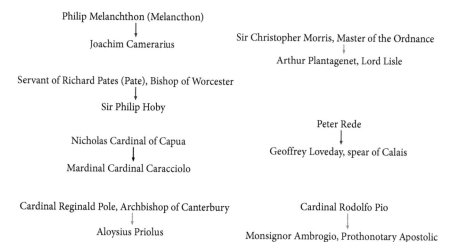

Figure 6.13d Topic network for 'naples' (1535–6).

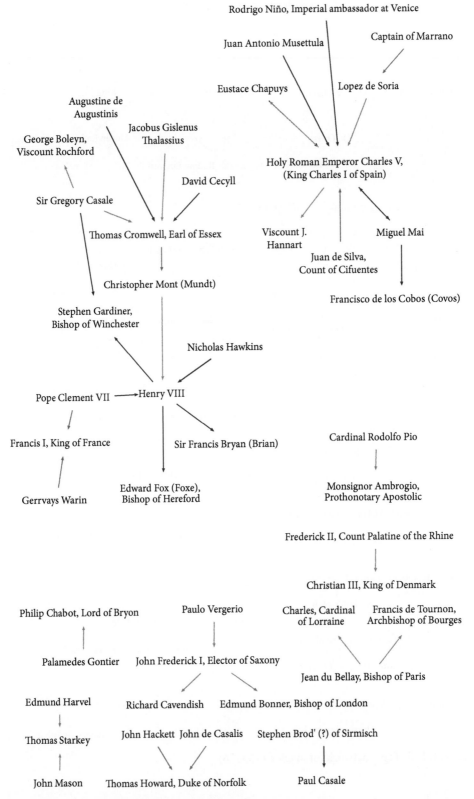

Figure 6.13e Topic network for 'romans' (1531–5).

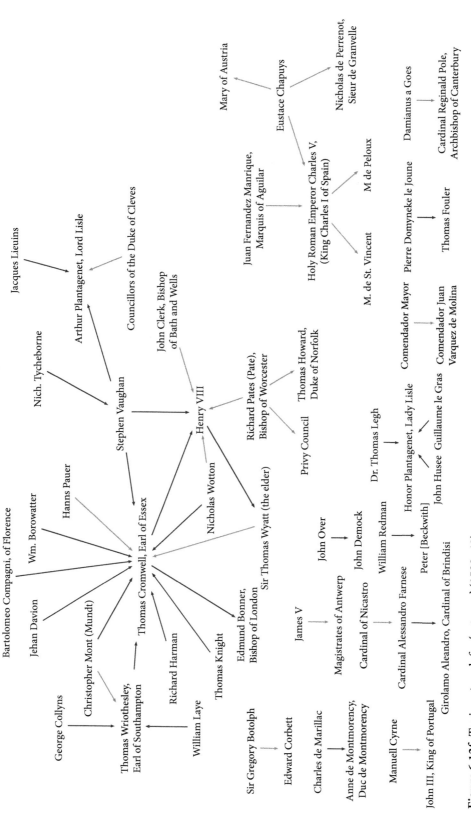

Figure 6.13f Topic network for 'antwerp' (1539–40).

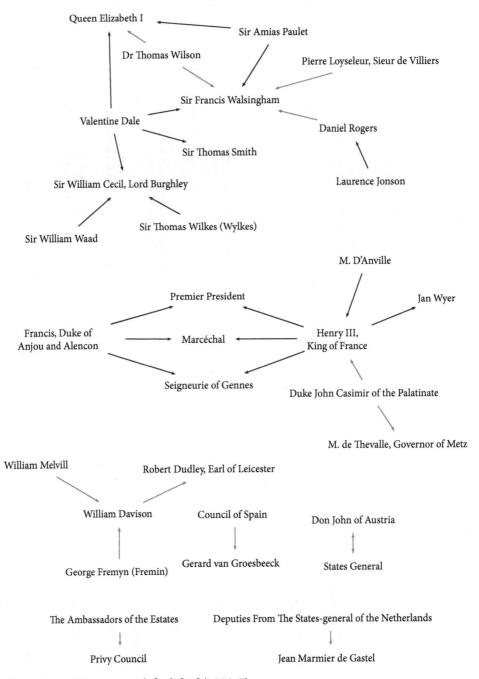

Figure 6.14a Topic network for 'edict' (1576–7).

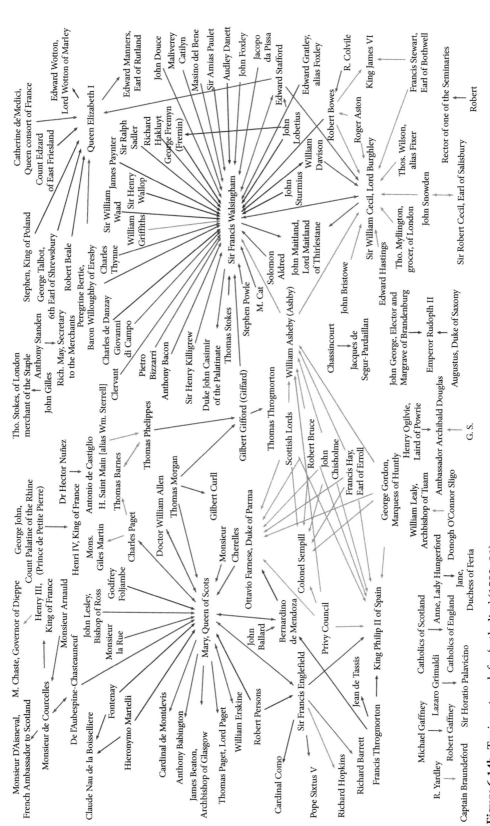

Figure 6.14b Topic network for 'catholics' (1583–91).

surrounding Henry are from a single packet of letters, marked as a 'Copy'.[99] Casimir's letters to Henry are copies 'sent by Daniel Rogers and endorsed by him'.[100]

Another more obvious example is the discourse around 'catholics' (1583–91), shown in Figure 6.14b. This is of course a diffuse topic that collects together a broad range of foreign threats focused on the Elizabethan state, including several conspiracies intent on deposing Elizabeth and replacing her on the throne with Mary Queen of Scots (which led to the surveillance of Mary discussed in Chapter 4). The right-hand side of the network comprises the government hubs of Elizabeth I, Burghley, and Walsingham. On the left, by comparison, we see the objects of interception. The largest hubs are Mary—who we know was the subject of systemic interception implicating her and many of her correspondents—Philip II, and Ottavio Farnese, Duke of Parma. Arrayed around them are a network of English Catholic exiles such as Francis Englefield, as well as known conspirators Thomas and Charles Paget, the religious leaders and architects of various plots, Robert Persons and William Allen, and Anthony Babington (after whom the Babington plot was named). We also find French diplomats, secretaries, and agents such as Nicholas Leclerc, Sieur de Courcelles, Albert Fontenay, and Hieronymo Martelli (the alias of the French Jesuit and conspirator Henry Samier, who spent months in disguise as Mary's physician). It is unsurprising, therefore, that we should observe that Gilbert Gifford is one of the bridges between these two spheres, given his identity as the double agent who secured the evidence that finally condemned Mary.

What this method is able to provide—for the period following Henry VIII's reign at least—is a concise visual summary of the twofold intelligence strategy employed by the Tudor government as outlined in Chapters 3 and 4: the parallel use of diplomatic missives and of forwarded correspondences, including letters intercepted through international surveillance and espionage. By comparing many of these graphs, we can see the structural continuity of diplomats across graphs and identify the roster of individuals who fulfilled this specific role. As such it is a method that at once allows us to identify general patterns, and also to single out specific people, events, and regions that might be worthy of further attention. For example, as we browse across the highest modularity topic networks we observe Mont appearing in several (as well as across an extended period of time), showing his crucial infrastructural role in Anglo-Germanic relations from entering royal service in the late 1520s until his death in 1572 (with only a brief period out of favour during Mary I's reign). However, the only full article to focus on Mont's career, by Esther Hildebrandt, accounts for the extended service and success of this 'second-rank diplomat' via his surprisingly cosmopolitan profile, as a German-born Englishman, who attended a French church in Strasbourg, who was 'on good terms with theologians, ex-patriates, and diplomats'.[101] We can imagine a way of using these network graphs in the aggregate to identify other

---

[99] Letters from the French king and the Duke of Anjou, SP 70/146 f.97.
[100] See Duke Casimir to the French king, 1 October 1577, SP 81/1 f.66, and 2 October 1577, SP 81/1 f.68.
[101] Esther Hildebrandt, 'Christopher Mont, Anglo-German Diplomat', *Sixteenth Century Journal* 15:3 (1984), 281–92 (p. 292).

careers like his that are worthy of attention, and to help us understand the common features of successful diplomatic careers.

Conclusion

This chapter has offered a set of research steps that can be used alone or in combination by researchers using our Tudor letters dataset—or indeed many other datasets containing text fields. We have described how users can chart the change in a word's usage over time, and how we can rank words by the magnitude of this change in order to identify potential newsworthy items. We showed how words with similar temporal profiles very often share these patterns because they refer to the same topic, and that by clustering words with the most similar temporal profiles we can uncover the vocabulary that surrounds certain historical episodes.

Taken alone, these steps have clear value for scholars working with textual datasets, especially those newer to digital approaches. Of course, the computational analysis of text is a vibrant field that is moving apace thanks to new AI-assisted technologies. However, in many cases, the most cutting-edge method is not necessary to allow humanities scholars to explore their data and to ask and answer the questions that are pertinent to them. In this case we have offered simple, transparent methods as the first step in sifting our data to select topics of interest. It is worth stressing here again the point we have made at various moments throughout the book, that we have sought to foreground approaches that let the data speak for itself, telling us which avenues might be fruitful for further analysis, rather than going into the data with preconceived hypotheses in which we are particularly interested. Of course there is a process by which we use our human judgement to sort the wheat from the chaff of our preliminary results, which is akin to the step of 'winnowing' described by Jo Guldi in her article 'Critical Search'.[102] What we are looking for in this sifting process is a combination of statistical significance and historical interest.

The two extended case studies we selected in this chapter are in many ways representative of the kinds of preliminary results that we receive from quantitative analysis, which are often dominated by events well documented in both the contemporary record and modern historiography—episodes such as Henry VIII's 'great matter'. They are well studied for a reason, but the predominance of such material in preliminary results will often elicit criticism that digital methods tell us things we already know. However, as we have argued elsewhere, it is important that such results are returned because it proves the value and utility of the methods, and gives us faith when less-studied topics and events are brought to the fore alongside these. Moreover, a computational analysis of well-known events can also yield different kinds of insight that are not possible through analogue research processes. Therefore, unlike our practice in

---

[102] Jo Guldi, 'Critical Search: A Procedure for Guided Reading in Large-Scale Textual Corpora', *Journal of Cultural Analytics* 3:1 (2018), <https://doi.org/10.22148/16.030>.

most of the previous chapters, where we have sought to explore those less studied figures and events, in this case we returned to two well-worn episodes to show how our
methods reveal broader patterns in our data.

In our case these broader insights are yielded by taking the outcomes of the linguistic analysis and examining them through the lens of the network. Our approach of
mapping the topic networks for some of our most-changed words allows us to better
understand the topology of the communities involved in the dissemination of particular
news items and topics of discourse. This process invites an interrogation of the temporal
resolution of a topic's dispersal, the key people and processes by which information
was transmitted and captured within the dataset. For the topic networks involved in
Henry VIII's great matter and the period 1578–9 within the Dutch Revolt, we discovered
that these graphs were typified by fissures which saw the networks forming two main
communities in each. In all cases the first represented the state's perspective on events,
and the second a foreign set of viewpoints on those same affairs. These are present in
our data as a result of two mechanisms: the first is the contemporary interception of
foreign intelligence; and the latter is editorial policy of the Victorian editors of the
Letters and Papers, who decided to include in their catalogues descriptions of papers
from foreign archives pertinent to English state affairs.

We would suggest that while the individual steps in the research process that we
outline have utility on their own, some of the most interesting avenues for research
announce themselves when we combine approaches. In our final section we suggested
a research process that combined all the previous steps and, as a final step, automatically
measured and compared the modularity of graphs. In so doing we found that topic
networks with the highest modularity allowed us to home in on key foreign affairs
for the Tudor government. Moreover, the method offered a rough impression of
the span of the government's international interests, the reach of its intelligence
networks over the period 1509–1603, and key recurring actors in the transferral of
information—the weak ties that we discussed at the beginning of Chapter 3, such as
Mont. However, to fully understand the reach of the Tudor government's foreign
intelligence networks, we need to consider another dimension of our dataset that we
have largely ignored heretofore: the geolocation of the letters. In the seventh and final
chapter of the book, therefore we turn to a set of methods for analysing communications networks within their geographical context.

7

Itineraries

The networks of these moving, intersecting writings compose a manifold story that has neither author nor spectator, shaped out of fragments of trajectories and alterations of spaces.

Michel de Certeau, *The Practice of Everyday Life.*[1]

Communication networks are often imagined and presented on a geographical map. In Chapter 1 we presented our interactive visualisation, in which an individual's correspondence can be explored through a cartographic projection. However, in the intervening chapters we have focused on the construction and measurement of our epistolary networks in *mathematical* space. Where we have visualised these networks, the position of the individual in such renderings—up, down, left, or right—does not map to any kind of longitude or latitude. As Scott Weingart puts it, 'there is no x or y axis, and spatial distance from one node to another is not inherently meaningful.'[2] Our attention has focused rather on network-based definitions of distance and proximity, such as the length of the shortest path that connects two nodes in a network. These short paths underpin network measurements such as betweenness centrality, which have helped us to identify people that are located in structurally significant positions within our correspondence network.

But structural significance is not divorced from geographical location. Often a person's role as an information broker is determined by their location. We might recall that when Pietro Bizzarri (discussed in Chapter 4) travelled to the continent to oversee the printing of his literary works, his period in Venice helped him supply a gap in diplomatic coverage (the English had no resident ambassador in Venice at that time), and capitalise on being in this strategic entrepôt for the trade of regional and international news. As Filippo De Vivo writes: 'Locked between opposite blocks—Bourbons and Hapsburgs, Catholics and Protestants, Christians and Turks—Venice became an arena for espionage not wholly unlike central European capitals during the Cold War.'[3] The significance of specific locations at particular moments in history explains why various projects on correspondence have used maps to represent the

---

[1] Michel de Certeau, *The Practice of Everyday Life*, tr. Stephen Rendall (University of California Press, 1984), p. 93.

[2] Shawn Graham, Ian Milligan, and Scott Weingart, *Exploring Big Historical Data: The Historian's Macroscope* (Imperial College Press, 2015), p. 250.

[3] Filippo De Vivo, *Information and Communication in Venice: Rethinking Early Modern Politics* (Oxford University Press, 2007), p. 74.

Tudor Networks of Power. Ruth Ahnert and Sebastian E. Ahnert, Oxford University Press. © Ruth Ahnert and Sebastian E. Ahnert 2023. DOI: 10.1093/oso/9780198858973.003.0007

passage of information, including *Mapping the Republic of Letters*, and Cameron Blevin's work on the US Post Offices in the nineteenth-century West.[4]

The increasing use of Geographic Information Systems (GIS), sometimes called the 'spatial turn', in history and literary studies in some ways mirrors the proliferation of network visualisation and quantitative network analysis in the humanities.[5] Specialists in the discipline of Archaeology have been employing GIS since the early 1980s, whereas in disciplines such as History, equivalent fields of digital research have only 'emerged' over the past two decades.[6] One project that has successfully merged network analysis and GIS is the highly cited *Science* article, 'A Network Framework of Cultural History', and its associated *Nature* video which reconstructs aggregate intellectual mobility over two millennia through the birth and death locations of more than 150,000 notable individuals.[7] The resulting network of locations provides a macroscopic perspective of cultural history, which retraces cultural narratives of Europe and North America using large-scale visualisation and quantitative tools to derive historical trends beyond the scope of specific events or narrow time intervals. The video developed from this research shows how these cumulative migrations play out over time, revealing the emergence of particular towns and cities as cultural centres at specific historical moments.

Correspondence gives us another way of thinking about large-scale spatial trends from a network perspective. Letters all have a point of origin, although authors do not always record this. Of the 132,474 letters in our dataset 62.1% list their place of sending. If we return to Figure 1.6 in Chapter 1, we can see an excerpt of our data in which the geo-coordinates of these origins are plotted on a blank canvas. This simple visualisation is striking in the way it provides a pointillist impression of England and continental Europe, with England densely filled, continental Europe more sparsely described but still discernible, and detail reducing markedly in Spain, Portugal, and Eastern Europe. It shows immediately the extent and the limits of the Tudor worldview via the spread and coverage of its intelligence networks, as well as the way that voyage and discovery was expanding its peripheries. Written from its farthest reaches (and beyond the visual scope of Figure 1.6), we have letters sent from the seat of the

---

[4] *Mapping the Republic of Letters*, <http://republicofletters.stanford.edu/>, and *Geographies of the Post*, <http://cameronblevins.org/gotp/>.

[5] On the 'spatial turn' see Jo Guldi's introduction <http://spatial.scholarslab.org/spatial-turn/>. For fuller discussions, see David J. Bodenhamer, John Corrigan, and Trevor M. Harris, eds., *The Spatial Humanities: GIS and the Future of Humanities Scholarship* (Indiana University Press, 2010); Anne Kelly Knowles and Amy Hiller, eds., *Placing History: How Maps, Spatial Data, and GIS are Changing Historical Scholarship* (ESRI Press, 2008); and Ian N. Gregory, *A Place in History: A Guide to Using GIS in Historical Research* (Oxbow, 2003).

[6] Patricia Murrieta-Flores, Christopher Donaldson, and Ian Gregory, 'GIS and Literary History: Advancing Digital Humanities Research through the Spatial Analysis of Historical Travel Writing and Topographical Literature', *Digital Humanities Quarterly* 11 (2007). Archaeology was also one of the earliest adopters of network analysis in the humanities. For a good introduction to the field, see Tom Brughmans, Anna Collar, and Fiona Coward, eds., *The Connected Past: Challenges to Network Studies in Archaeology and History* (Oxford University Press, 2016).

[7] Maximilian Schich, Chaoming Song, Yong-Yeol Ahn, Alexander Mirsky, Mauro Martino, Albert-László Barabási, Dirk Helbing, 'A Network Framework of Cultural History', *Science* 345:6196 (2014), 558–62. DOI: 10.1126/science.1240064. For the *Nature* video, see <https://www.nature.com/news/humanity-s-cultural-history-captured-in-5-minute-film-1.15650>.

Spanish colonial government of the Philippines in Manila (a letter from the city to Philip II of Spain by the 'city'),[8] from the Inopay Valley in Peru (an ethnographic account of the inhabitants of this area sent by Brother Nicolas Mastrillo to Juan Sebastian),[9] and from Cochin in India (Lourenço Rodrigues's account of his outward voyage sent to Rodrigo Alvares Mascarenha).[10]

The way in which our accumulated data draw a partial map of Europe is reminiscent of Michel de Certeau's concept of 'Walking the City' in his book *The Practice of Everyday Life*. The quote that opens this chapter describes the way that de Certeau imagines walkers moving through the city blindly 'writing' it as they walk, shaping out of the 'fragments of their trajectories' a 'manifold story that has neither author nor spectator'. Given the developments in network visualisation and quantitative analysis since de Certeau's book was written, it is perhaps tempting to suggest that we now have the technology to tell this manifold story in its totality, to see it all at once and become the spectator. Indeed, in recent years location data from mobile phones has been used to map and study the movement of hundreds of thousands of individuals.[11] However, de Certeau pre-empts these technologies and suggests their limitations, writing that 'operations of walking can be [...] transformed into points that draw a totalling and reversible line on a map. They allow us to grasp only a relic set in the nowhen of a surface of projection.' His issue with these 'imaginary totalizations' is loss of information: 'The trace left behind is substituted for the practice. [...] It causes a way of being in the world to be forgotten.'[12]

De Certeau's meditations are useful for thinking about how to work with geographic data, and they guide the manoeuvres we employ in this chapter. While Figure 1.6 has its value for showing us the richness of the geographical data that we have at our disposal, by collapsing the temporal dimension into one surface it represents a moment that never was: all-people, in all-places, all-at-once. This chapter shows how we can move from this 'imaginary totalization' towards a method that allows us to extract those 'fragments of trajectories'. By time-ordering our correspondents' outgoing correspondence (where place-of-writing is given), we can reconstruct their movements and compare the itineraries of different individuals and categories of writer. As such we can look for exceptional journeys—gleaning fragmentary glimpses of journeys to the edge of the Tudor purview, into sites of conflict, dispute, and

---

[8] The city to Philip II, 1565, SP 94/4 f.162.

[9] Brother Nicolas Mastrillo wrote to Juan Sebastian on 26 October/5 November 1595, SP 94/5 f.56. Mastrillo, with Father Joan Font, was one of two Spanish Jesuit priests who were exploring the jungle east of Jauja and Andamarca. For a fuller account of this expedition, see Stefano Varese, *Salt of the Mountain: Campa Ashaninka History and Resistance in the Peruvian Jungle* (University of Oklahoma Press, 2004), pp. 43–52.

[10] The city of Manila to Philip II, 1565, SP 94/4 f.162; Brother Nicolas Mastrillo to Juan Sebastian, 26 October/5 November 1595, SP 94/5 f.56; and Lourenço Rodrigues to Rodrigo Alvares Mascarenha, 'the copie of a Portugal letter translated into English the 8 October 1602', SP 89/3 f.16. The fact that the correspondence from these most distant locations is in Spanish and Portuguese, and sent to Spanish and Portuguese recipients, suggests how interception was a key mechanism for extending the geographical purview of the Tudor government. Rodrigues's letter, for example, was found in the ship *St Valentine* which was taken at Cezimbra in June 1602 during an attack led by the English naval officer Richard Leveson.

[11] Marta C. Gonzalez, Cesar A. Hidalgo, and Albert-Laszlo Barabasi, 'Understanding Individual Human Mobility Patterns', *Nature* 453 (2008), 779.

[12] De Certeau, *Practice of Everyday Life*, pp. 93, 97.

opposition—or find sites of intersection. Intersections, as one might expect, are dominated by people who were in London, and to a lesser extent places like Paris or Dublin. These are much less likely to reveal personal interactions than finding two people in a small Welsh village on the same day. But, as we show, statistical modelling can suggest the likelihood of two people being in the same place by chance. Amongst the most unlikely—and thus potentially 'significant'— intersections we find a high number of people brought together by wars and sieges, as well as a significant number resulting from the visitations undertaken during Henry VIII's dissolution of the monasteries. We observe therefore that this strategy takes us to locations at specific moments in their history, when authors are witnessing them at a moment of 'alteration', or perhaps revealing themselves to be actors bringing about those moments of change.

One of the most important things that this kind of approach offers to the study of history is the way that it allows us to grasp 'manifold stories'. We can reconstruct networks on the ground that might not be apparent from the epistolary metadata, showing particularly how diplomats or other agents might have harnessed the intersecting intelligences available at a specific location and built a local network of informants. We can also deduce where the government sought to ensure its access to intelligence through multiple routes to ensure they were not without information if letters were lost or intercepted, as well as to ensure the trustworthiness of their informants. The method therefore captures the manner in which the Tudor government sought to corroborate its sources, in a manner that also allows the historian working with this archive to corroborate theirs.

'Fragments of Trajectories'

As a genre, the letter is one that draws attention both to the temporal and spatial dimensions of its composition: it was, and remains, common practice that letter writers record both the time and place of writing. These dual dimensions suggest why the temporally collapsed cartographic representation found in Figure 1.6 is inadequate for the complexity of epistolary data. In recent years a number of researchers have moved towards a temporal approach to historical and literary geographies.[13] Patricia Murrieta-Flores, Christopher Donaldson, and Ian Gregory have worked on methods for reconstructing itineraries of historical writers. Their source material was the travelogues of three canonical, eighteenth-century British travellers: the poet Thomas Gray (1716–71), the naturalist Thomas Pennant (1726–98), and the agriculturist Arthur Young (1741–1820). Like our letter data, the entries in these travelogues provide a series of geolocations that are fixed in time and space; but these researchers

---

[13] For an interdisciplinary collection of approaches, see Sybille Lammes, Chris Perkins, Alex Gekker, Sam Hind, Clancy Wilmott and Daniel Evans, eds., *Time for Mapping: Cartographic Temporalities* (Manchester University Press, 2018).

seek to recreate the route travelled by these three men using GIS software to 'simulate the natural corridors, determining the most efficient route for travelling over the terrain taking into account the relief of the Lake District's topography'.[14] Contrary to many mapping projects, therefore, this work emphasises what de Certeau calls 'a way of being in the world', the process of moving through the landscape.

In a similar way it is possible to generate itineraries for each of the writers in the State Papers archive that corresponded from more than one location. Here, as ever, there is a tension between the scale of the dataset and the granularity of the itineraries that we are able to reconstruct. The approach used by Murrieta-Flores et al. provides highly granular detail, and therefore fairly accurate estimates of the miles travelled by the respective individuals on each day of their journey. This approach also allows us to infer the things that the writers of these travelogues may have seen but are perhaps not mentioned. There is much to recommend this approach to a study of early modern correspondence: it would have significant value for the study of early courier routes and the development of a European postal network—an area of scholarship that continues to flourish, and has been aided in recent years by developments in digital methods. However, the approach taken by these researchers is only possible because they are working with three travellers. By contrast, we have 3,026 people who wrote from more than one location. In this context we have to allow for a more coarse-grained approach to the data, reconstructing approximate itineraries by, effectively, joining the dots created by their time-ordered correspondences.

The construction of itineraries of this kind is achieved simply by ordering an individual's correspondence in time and extracting the place IDs associated with these letters, in that order.[15] Linking these sequences of points with straight lines 'as the crow flies' does not, of course, provide real itineraries; these are merely 'fragments of trajectories', in the words of de Certeau. If we had time to read all the letters and cross-refer with external sources we could build up a much more detailed picture. But what we must necessarily sacrifice in terms of granularity, we make up for in computational power. We have already made these itineraries available to explore through the interactive visualisation we published in collaboration with Kim Albrecht, and some of the figures featured in this chapter use this online tool.[16] Moving beyond the visual, we can also, with just a few lines of code, calculate an estimate of their miles travelled. Among the 3,026 itineraries the longest total distance travelled by any single individual is 31,420 miles; the largest number of journey legs is 1,051; and the largest number of distinct places visited is 109. There are 371 itineraries with 10 or more separate locations, and 572 that are longer than 1,000 miles.

---

[14] Patricia Murrieta-Flores, Christopher Donaldson, and Ian Gregory, 'GIS and Literary History: Advancing Digital Humanities Research through the Spatial Analysis of Historical Travel Writing and Topographical Literature', *Digital Humanities Quarterly* 11:1 (2017), <http://www.digitalhumanities.org/dhq/vol/11/1/000283/000283.html>.

[15] Place IDs are the unique identifiers assigned to each place in the data-cleaning process. Where there is a range of uncertainty in the dates we use the beginning of the date range.

[16] Kim Albrecht, Sebastian E. Ahnert, and Ruth Ahnert, *Tudor Networks* interactive visualisation <http://tudornetworks.net/>.

Table 7.1 Ranked list of correspondents with the largest mileage travelled, according to letters bearing a place of writing

Rank	Name	Distance (miles)
1	Charles V, Holy Roman Emperor	31,420
2	Elizabeth I	18,329
3	Francis I, King of France	17,261
4	Lord General, Sir John Norris	15,280
5	Sir Thomas Smith	14,641
6	Thomas Randolph	14,201
7	John Clerk, Bishop of Bath and Wells	13,227
8	William FitzWilliam, 1st Earl of Southampton	12,787
9	Robert Wingfield	12,280
10	William Cecil, Lord Burghley	12,253

The most basic problem when presented with all this data is how to identify trajectories that are particularly notable. One answer is to rank these itineraries by their total mileage. The ten people who travelled the furthest according to their epistolary trail are listed in Table 7.1. Digging down into these results we find that there are two main factors contributing to the 'most travelled' statistics. The first, and most obvious, is travel to far-flung places. The second factor is the quantity of letters. The reason for the latter is illustrated neatly by Burghley's appearance in this list. Burghley did not frequently travel abroad, but the massive quantity of his correspondence (he sent 592 letters with identified locations), means that even though the distances he travelled were only small, the miles quickly add up. Monarchs of course exemplify both attributes: they wrote much and travelled often. Early modern monarchy was peripatetic in nature: kings and queens progressed around their realms. James Daybell discusses the extraordinary posts required for the movement of the monarch to not interfere with governmental decision-making.[17] The size of the realm governed had an effect on the amount of travel: the vast nature of the Holy Roman Empire meant that Charles V travelled more than 30,000 miles across the 549 letters with identified locations in this archive, as demonstrated in Figure 7.1. The figure provides a good sense of the extent of the empire under his rule, and suggests that Edward Armstrong may have been right to call him the 'travelling director of the Hapsburg syndicate'.[18]

Norris, Smith, and Randolph (at ranks 4–6 in Table 7.1) represent the dominance of diplomatic and military leaders not only in the top ten, but throughout the top fifty by this measure. For diplomats and military leaders alike, it is precisely their travel to foreign locations that is the occasion of their writing (as discussed in Chapter 3). They

[17] James Daybell, *The Material Letter in Early Modern England: Manuscript Letters and the Culture and Practices of Letter-Writing, 1512–1635* (Palgrave Macmillan, 2012), p. 121.
[18] Edward Armstrong, *The Emperor Charles V*, vol. 1 (Macmillan, 1902), p. 157.

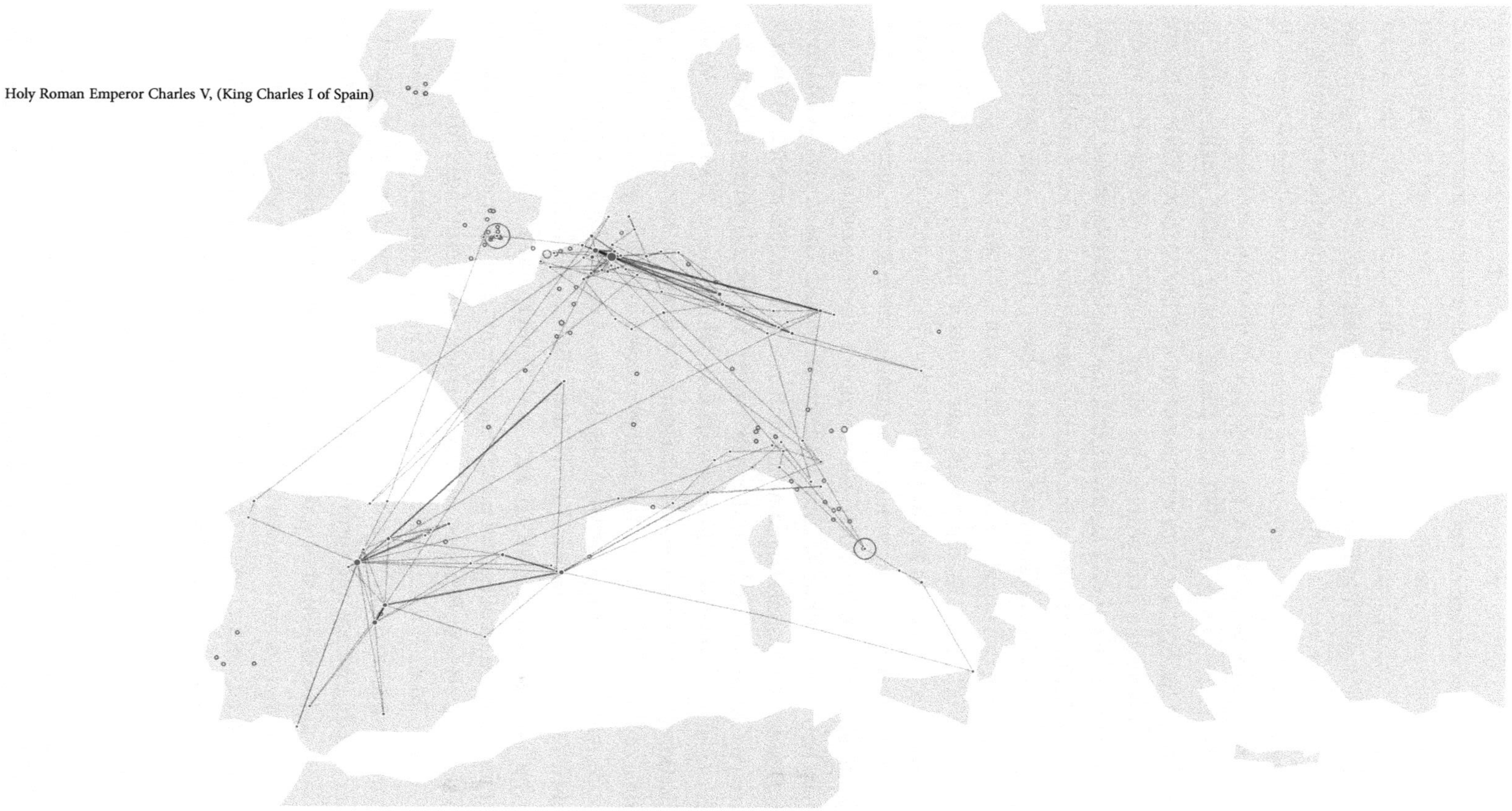

Holy Roman Emperor Charles V, (King Charles I of Spain)

Figure 7.1 Geographical view of Charles V's correspondence in the Tudor Networks visualisation (<http://tudornetworks.net>). Red dots mark locations from which he sent letters, and the lines between them show the temporal sequence, thus creating an approximate itinerary. Image credit: Kim Albrecht.

have been dispatched for the purposes of the realm's foreign interests, to maintain diplomatic relations or engage in military campaigns, and regular correspondence is central to their effective service. Smith (whose itinerary is visualised in Figure 1.4) appears high in this ranking because he was both Principal Secretary (and therefore a frequent correspondent when in England) and an ambassador who served in France 1562–6 and 1572.[19] Norris was a renowned military leader who, as the visualisation in Figure 7.2 shows, travelled extensively, serving in Ireland, France, and the Netherlands during the years of 1573–87, as well as participating in the unsuccessful plan to attack Portugal with Sir Francis Drake in 1589, and commanding a small English army in Brittany preventing the Spanish from winning control of the province 1591–4, before returning to Ireland for the final years of his career. Randolph also travelled across numerous countries: as Figure 7.3 clearly charts, the English ambassador spent most of his professional life in Scotland at the courts of Mary Queen of Scots and her son James VI, but in 1568–9 he was sent on a special embassy to Russia, visiting the court of Ivan IV, and serving on special embassies to France in 1573 and 1576.[20]

The dominance of monarchs, diplomats, and agents at the top of the ranking of most travelled correspondents is also helpful for identifying anomalous travellers who fall outside the more obvious categories. Interestingly, the first two anomalies are, in fact, more in line with the popular conception of the expanding world of the Renaissance, both in geographic and intellectual terms. The more well-known example is Desiderius Erasmus (ranking at number 47). A sizeable portion of his collected correspondence is folded into the State Papers. Of the 291 letters he sent, 240 have an identified place entered in the metadata field, which covers 7,186 miles. While the visualisation of his itinerary shown at Figure 7.4 does not have the long-range links of some of the diplomats, the darker lines connecting the larger red dots show that he made multiple journeys between the key locations of London, Cambridge, Antwerp, Brussels, Louvain, and Basel. In the years 1514–21 he was chiefly in Brabant, moving frequently between Louvain, Bruges, and Antwerp due to his involvement in the project for a trilingual college at Louvain, his appointment as an imperial councillor, which kept him close to Brussels, and his oversight of the printing of his works in Basel.[21] Erasmus himself comments on these frequent journeys in a letter to Christopher Urswick from St Omer, dated 5 June 1517, writing how his 'genius of a horse' had carried him back and forth from St Omer to Basel twice, and that he had visited so many universities that he was now as wise as Homer's Ulysses.[22]

The second example is the itinerary of Captain Henry Duffield, who might loosely be described as an adventurer, and gains scant mention in scholarship. A visualisation of his itinerary looks very uninteresting because it is a single line marking a return

---

[19] Gary Bell, *A Handlist of British Diplomatic Representatives: 1509–1688* (Cambridge University Press, 1995), entries F81, F100, F103–4, F106–11, F115–16, F121–2, LC43.

[20] Bell, *Handlist*, F126, F131, R2, SC28, SC33–5, SC46, SC48–9, SC56, SC62, SC71.

[21] James McConica, 'Erasmus, Desiderius (c.1467–1536)', *ODNB*, <https://doi.org/10.1093/ref:odnb/39358>.

[22] P. S. Allen, ed., *Opus Epistolarum Des. Erasmi Roterodami*, vol. 2: *1514–1517* (Oxford University Press, 1910), Item 416. *'Eqvi tui genius mihi fuit magnopere felix; nam bis iam Basileam...Sapit iam non minus quam Homericus Vlysses, si-quidem mores hominum multorum vidit et vrbes; tot adiit vniuersitates.'*

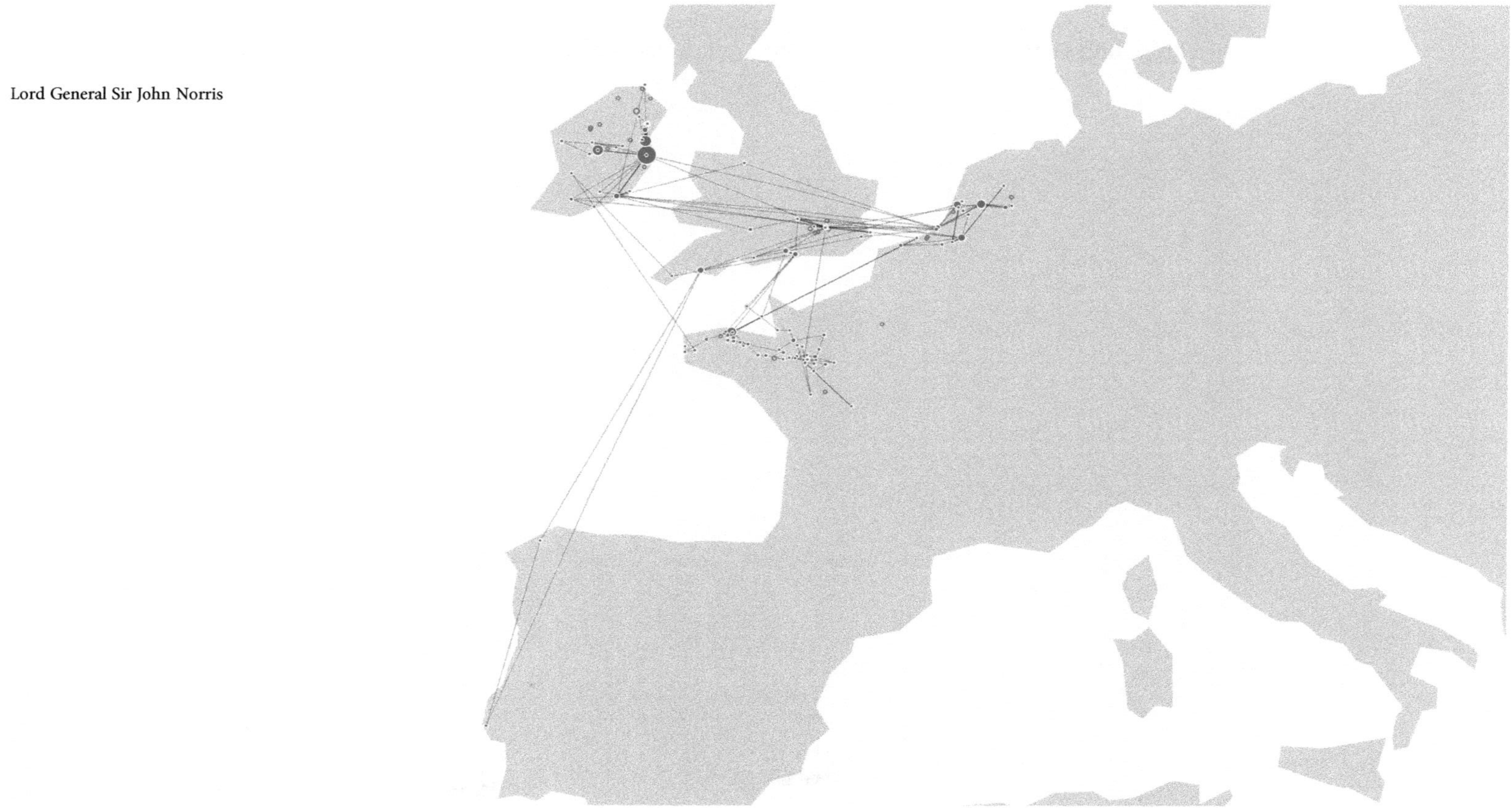

Lord General Sir John Norris

Figure 7.2 Geographical view of the correspondence of Lord General Sir John Norris in the Tudor Networks visualisation (<http://tudornetworks. net>). Red dots mark locations from which he sent letters, and the lines between them show the temporal sequence, thus creating an approximate itinerary. Image credit: Kim Albrecht.

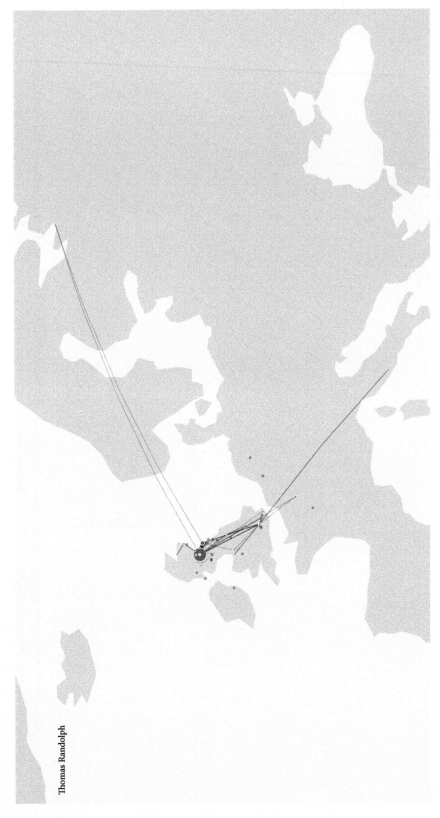

Thomas Randolph

Figure 7.3 Geographical view of Thomas Randolph's correspondence in the Tudor Networks visualisation (<http://tudornetworks.net>).

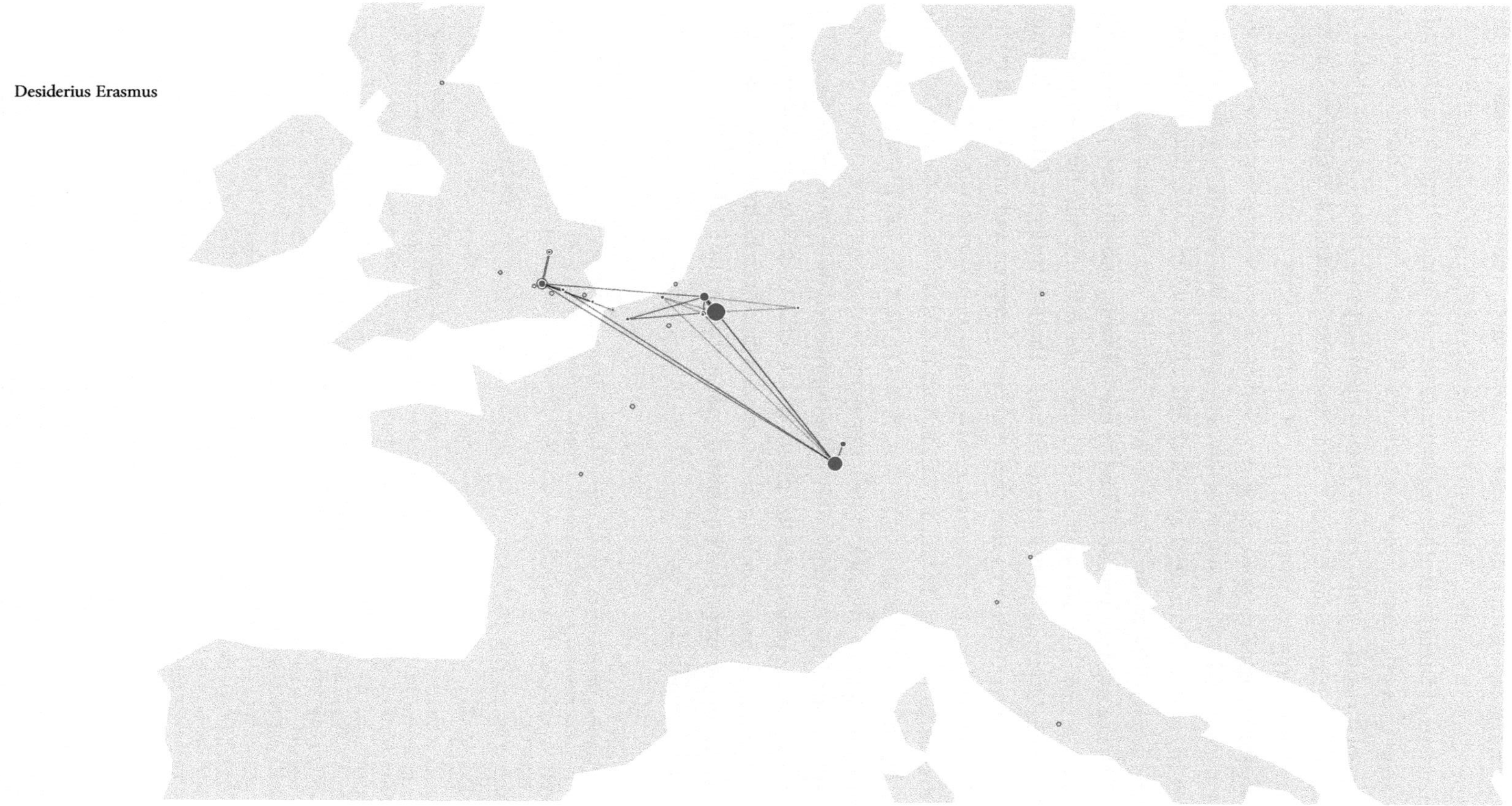

Desiderius Erasmus

Figure 7.4 Geographical view of Desiderius Erasmus's correspondence in the Tudor Networks visualisation (<http://tudornetworks.net>). Image credit: Kim Albrecht.

journey of 9,329 miles from the Tower of London to Havana, and back to the Marshalsea prison in London. Trying to join the dots of that sparse itinerary by looking for mentions of Duffield in other correspondence, we gain a glimpse of a life made up of fascinating but dangerous journeys. He was likely the Captain Duffield listed as commander of the ship *Crane*, one of a fleet of eight ships sent into the West Indies in 1591 to intercept a rich Spanish fleet.[23] The reason for Duffield's 1594 imprisonment in the Tower seems to place him in the pay of Philip II, King of Spain: according to a letter from Paul Crushe to Lord Burghley, Duffield was commissioned to burn the navy at Chatham.[24] Duffield subsequently appears on the fleet list of the ill-fated expedition of royal and private ships which left Plymouth in 1595, under the command of Sir Francis Drake and John Hawkins, with the aim of capturing the city of Panama.[25] Drake and Hawkins both died in the following months, and in April 1596 we have a letter from Havana addressed to the Lord Admiral and the Earl of Essex written by Duffield (along with Richard Gifford, Thomas Brugges, Edward Boorde, and Thomas Bewser), reporting that they had been captured and imprisoned by the Spanish fleet, and asking for deliverance.[26] Deliverance, however, was not forthcoming: just over three years later Duffield writes from the Marshalsea prison, in which he describes his three years' imprisonment in Spain (where he was presumably transported after his capture), the lack of help to pay his ransom, and the means by which he eventually secured his freedom, only to be imprisoned once more in England. The reason for his arrest appears to be the means of his return into England, and the confession of the Spanish man Don Juan de Gusman, with whom he travelled, which suggested that this opportunist had developed connections with English Catholic exiles in the service of Philip II.[27]

[23] Richard Polwhele, *The History of Cornwall, Civil, Military, Religious, Architectural, Agricultural, Commercial, Biographical, and Miscellaneous*, vol. 4 (T. Flindell for Castell & Davies, 1816), p. 76.

[24] SP 12/241 f.171. See also Benjamin Beard's letter to Sir John Puckering, dated 11 May 1594 from the Fleet prison, SP 12/248 f.226.

[25] For the fleet list, see Kenneth R. Andrews, ed., *The Last Voyage of Drake and Hawkins* (Hakluyt Society, 1972), p. 25.

[26] SP 12/257 f.2.

[27] The details of his return from Spain to England can again be pieced together from fragments. He writes, 'If I went about to deceive the Spaniards and brought away a young man with me [de Gusman], it was done to procure my liberty' (Henry Duffield to Sir Robert Cecil, 24 April 1599, in *Calendar of the Cecil Papers in Hatfield House: Volume 9, 1599*, ed. R. A. Roberts (HMSO, 1902), pp. 126–50. BHO, <http://www.british-history.ac.uk/cal-cecil-papers/vol9/pp126-150>.) A sighting of Duffield, Thomas Brugges, and de Gusman in Bayonne seeking passage into England is reported in a letter from Humphrey Parkes to the Earl of Essex dated 22 November 1598. A fuller narrative of how they finally made passage is laid out in two documents penned by Richard Tomson: a letter to Cecil dated 17 May 1599, and Tomson's translation of the account given de Gusman, who had been entrusted to Tomson's custody (*Cecil Papers*, pp. 167–89, <http://www.british-history.ac.uk/cal-cecil-papers/vol9/pp167-189>). Gusman's account describes the series of promises and deceptions by which Duffield persuaded the Spaniard to bring him and Brugges into England: first to deal with the Bishop of Lugo and Don Diego Brochero, general of the galleys and army of Spain to have Duffield deliver into his custody, and then to consent to give them liberty, on the promise that they would take him to England 'where there was noe Inquisition, and [I] might lyve according to my conscience frelye, and did assure me that I should be verye welcome to Her Majestie [...] and her Council for soe good a service' (SP 12/270 f.132.). On this promise he secretly hired a barque with six mariners, and came to France, where they found passage in a ship of Plymouth, with merchandise for Bristol. However, in a further colourful twist, the ship was sent off course and, after three weeks, landed in Ireland, where they were arrested and imprisoned. Following dealings with the Earl of Desmond they were given a passport and servant to guide them to Limerick, where they embarked on one of the six or seven barques full of soldiers, who were to march the next morning and take the ship out of the power of Tekew Mahona.

Table 7.2 List of the top twenty-six people ranked by miles per letter

Rank	Person	Miles	Number of letters	Miles per letter
1	Henry Duffield	9,329	4	2,332
2	Edward Collins	2,109	2	1,054
3	Baptista Servigi	1,625	2	812
4	Thomas Bannister	3,938	6	656
5	Humphrey Locke	1,902	3	634
6	Nicholas Oseley	1,722	3	574
7	Alexander White	1,114	2	557
8	Robert Crichton, 8th Lord Crichton of Sanquhar	1,663	3	554
9	Ahmad al-Mansur, Sultan of the Saadi dynasty	2,143	4	536
10	John de Cardenas	1,537	3	512
11	Thomas Alabaster	2,039	4	509
12	Jan Łaski (John a Lasco)	984	2	492
13	Thomas Cely	956	2	478
14	John Chereton	1,420	3	473
15	Patrick Lumbarde	940	2	470
16	The Cardinal of Burgos, Francisco Mendoza de Bobadilla	935	2	467
17	Pedro de Mendoza	924	2	462
18	Hieronymo Martelli	1,376	3	459
19	Gerard Veltwyk	911	2	455
20	Henry Richards	1,800	4	450
21	Roger How	899	2	450
22	Robert Persons	2,213	5	430
23	Marchionne Langus, Nuncio in England	1,749	4	437
24	Brian M'Geoghegan	2,158	5	431
25	George Everett	1,290	3	430
26	Sir Thomas Cotton	3,351	8	419

The anomalous case of Duffield, amongst foreign leaders and diplomats in the list of most travelled, suggests a certain kind of itinerary that is useful to search for more systematically. How can we find similarly intriguing fragments of trajectories that take us to the edge of the Tudor purview? What is distinctive about Duffield's journey is the number of miles he covers over a sequence of very few letters. What this suggests is that one way of finding other 'movable' figures is to look for others with a similarly high mileage per letter (i.e. the mileage totals used to generate the list above, divided by the number of letters sent that include place data), and create a list of authors ranked by those total number of miles. By this measure Duffield appears as the

Eventually they came with a gentleman of Limerick to Waterford, and thence to Bristol. Other references to him in the archive, and in the State Papers following in James I's reign, suggests he may be worth further analysis if we want to understand the kinds of motivations that caused English men to align with the Spanish. See Francis Edwards, *Plots and Plotters in the Reign of Elizabeth I* (Four Courts Press, 2002), pp. 242–7.

highest scorer, followed by a host of other interesting figures who can be found in Table 7.2.

In contrast to Table 7.1, which was organised simply by distance and is almost entirely diplomatic in nature, the individuals found in Table 7.2 are much more heterogeneous. As well as those on embassy or in the service of diplomats we find a sultan, a nuncio, captains, merchants, religious leaders, and Catholic conspirators. Like Duffield, the figures with the highest miles per letter share the fact that they have few data points. Across this list, the figure with the most letters with identifiable locations is Sir Thomas Cotton (7); most of the others only send between 2 and 4. The result is that we have a much more fragmentary picture of their movements. However, the lack of data points combined with a large mileage per letter implies that at least one location in their itinerary must take them far from their point of origin. As such the resulting list is made up of people with fascinating journeys.

If our aim from such a search is to discover snapshots of far-flung locations, we can look to John de Cardenas, sent on embassy to Morocco and who wrote in 1589 to Walsingham from 'The Playe' (the harbour at Agadir),[28] or Cotton, a merchant trading with Constantinople who wrote in 1568 from Zante, in Greece. In the reverse case we have those who travelled from distant locations to England, such as the Polish reformer Jan Łaski who, shortly after becoming pastor of a Protestant church at Emden in 1542, came to England, where from 1550 he superintended the Strangers' Church of London until the accession of Mary I.[29] The mileage per letter also draws attention to the international movements of Sultan Ahmad al-Mansur who (with his brother Abd al-Malik) was forced to flee his elder brother Abdallah al-Ghalib and live in exile in the Regency of Algiers and Constantinople for seventeen years, before returning to Morocco in 1576 to depose his uncle.[30] Perhaps one of the most fascinating itineraries on this list is that of Thomas Bannister, whose letters chart a trajectory from London to St Nicholas (the northern port on the White Sea used by merchants travelling into Russia), the Narva river at the Russian border, Vologda, Kashan (in modern-day Iran), and Shemakhi (Azerbaijan). He and Geoffrey Duckett, employees of the Muscovy Company, began this journey as servants to Thomas Randolph on his 1568 embassy to Russia (mentioned above), with the commission of advising him on the affairs of the company, and developing trade with Persia.[31] On 3 July 1569 Bannister and Duckett embarked on a mission into Persia, beginning at Yaroslavl with some twelve English sailors and forty Russians. Following their departure the next surviving letter we have from Bannister is one written from Kashan, Iran, in April 1570, which tells of a dramatic voyage in which their ship was attacked by almost 300 Nogai Tartars, which resulted in eleven of their number being killed and a further twenty-five wounded, including Bannister. Thereafter, reaching Astrakhan on 20 August,

---

[28] See Thomas Stuart Willan, *Studies in Elizabethan Foreign Trade* (Manchester University Press, 1959), p. 124, n. 1.

[29] Dirk W. Rodgers, 'À Lasco [Laski], John (1499–1560)', *ODNB*, <https://doi.org/10.1093/ref:odnb/16081>.

[30] See Mercedes Garcia-Arenal, *Ahmad Al-Mansur: The Beginnings of Modern Morocco* (One World, 2009).

[31] C. F. Beckingham, 'Banister, Thomas (d. 1571)', *ODNB*, <https://doi.org/10.1093/ref:odnb/47037>.

the town was attacked by an army of Ottomans, Crimean Tartars, Nogais, and Cherkes, estimated at over 120,000, which drove Bannister and his associates to discharge their goods and sink their barque and become men of war for the defence of the town.[32] From Kashan Bannister visited Tehran ('where never any English travelled before'),[33] spent five or six months at Ardabil, visited Shah Tahmasp in Qazvin, and travelled to Tabriz, Tiflis, and finally Shemakhi, where he wrote his final letter that survives in this archive, laying out his foregoing journey. From Shemakhi he organised the transportation of goods intended for England, including 200 camels,[34] before going to Arrash to buy raw silk, where he died in July 1571, probably of malaria.

But as well as highlighting individuals who travelled long distances, the list also helps us to focus on significant locations. In Table 7.2 we have a list of only twenty-six people. Given the exhaustive array of locations to which they could have travelled, it is striking that there are several locations that occur in more than one of these twenty-six itineraries. This suggests either that such locations are of particular strategic importance, or that a significant event happened there. One example is the Bay of Cádiz, which was the home of the Spanish Navy and became an important entrepôt for exploration and trade in the sixteenth century because of its proximity to the western Mediterranean and North Africa. Those writing from this region include John Chereton, Lord Lisle's agent (who set off on a voyage with Italian merchants to the Mediterranean in 1533, taking in Cádiz, Leghorn, Pisa, and Candia),[35] and Thomas Cely (a former soldier as part of Elizabeth's 'garde extraordynare', writing in 1579). Cely had been sent to the Bay by the Spanish Inquisition as a galley slave, but used his strategic location to provide intelligence to the queen and Burghley on Spanish preparations for war despite being 'sworn by the Inquizision of spayne nether yet to speke nether to wryte nothynge tochyn the secretes of the ynquizision'.[36]

A second example is Terceira, the site of the Conquest of the Azores. The conquest occurred on 2 August 1583, in the Portuguese archipelago of the Azores, between forces loyal to the claimant Dom António (often referred to in letters by his supporters as King of Portugal), supported by the French and English troops, and the Spanish and Portuguese forces loyal to Philip II of Spain. England's support of Dom António made strategic sense not only because of the ongoing antagonism with Spain throughout the Elizabethan period, but also because Terceira was in a key location in the Atlantic for English pirates to get food, water, and firewood on their voyages during the period of raids on the Caribbean. For this reason the English sent forces, including those under the command of Captain Henry Richards who wrote from Terceira to Walsingham on 22 June 1582. His letter describes the arrival of his ship at Terceira, alongside that captained by one Sachfield and several ships commanded by Monsieur

---

[32] Thomas Bannister to Cecil, 16 April 1570, SP 70/111 f.76.   [33] Ibid.

[34] Bannister to Cecil, May 1571, SP 70/118 f.8.

[35] Alwyn A. Ruddock, *Italian Merchants and Shipping in Southampton: 1270–1600* (Southampton: University College, 1951), p. 248.

[36] Thomas Cely to Elizabeth I, 12 December 1579, SP 94/1 f.28. See also Cely to Burghley, 12 December 1579, SP 15/26 f.88.

L'Andereau, which required them to pass through the fleet of Spanish ships, in the process of which the French captain was slain.[37] David Quinn states that this act brought Captain Richards great prestige, and soon after his arrival he was at work with his men and the Terceirans constructing defences.[38] The other journey through Terceira is that of Baptista Servigi (to whom we can find no references in the scholarship on this conquest), who writes to Walsingham from Angra on Terceira on 6 March 1583, pledging his service to Elizabeth and expressing his pleasure she has vowed to assist Dom António.[39] From Paris later that year he writes a lengthy letter in Italian to Captain Tomaso Sasetti that provides a detailed account of the conquest from the perspective of 'one who knows the truth not only concerning the proud enemy who gained the unexpected victory, but also as to the defenders, both French and of other nations', attributing Terceira's loss to ill-fortune, the malgovernance of the Viceroy, and the proud and unskilled Portuguese.[40]

These two examples point to another way in which the data can help us to navigate the archive in new ways. They illustrate how different itineraries overlap and interweave, constituting what de Certeau might call 'moving, intersecting writings'. Those points of intersection direct our attention both towards the individuals on these trajectories and the significance of their meeting points.

'Moving, Intersecting Writings'

We might argue that the significance of a place is constituted precisely by its identity as a site of intersection. Tim Ingold has argued that:

> Places [...] are like knots, and the threads from which they are tied are lines of wayfaring. A house, for example, is a place where the lines of its residents are tightly knotted together. But these lines are no more contained within the house than are threads contained within a knot. Rather, they trail beyond it, only to become caught up with other lines in other places, as are threads in other knots.[41]

Ingold's formulation gives us a different perspective on how we might utilise letter data to understand the significance of specific places within these Tudor communication networks. Rather than pulling out single threads because of certain exceptional

---

[37] Henry Richards to Walsingham, 22 June 1582, SP 89/1 f.233.

[38] David B. Quinn, *England and the Azores, 1581–1582: Three Letters* (Coimbra, 1979), p. 207.

[39] Batista Servigi to Walsingham, 6 March 1583, SP 89/2 f.21.

[40] Paraphrase of the Italian from the Calendar; Batista Servigi to Captain Tomaso Sassetti, 29 November/ 9 December 1583, SP 89/2 f.21. We have not been able to find any scholarly engagement with this account of the conquest. The recipient might be the same as the author of the account of the Saint Bartholomew's Day Massacre, see *The Massacre of Saint Bartholomew: Reappraisals and Documents*, ed. Alfred Soman (Martinus Nijhoff, 1974), 99–152. Sasetti is also listed as a decipherer in Robert Hutchinson, *Elizabeth's Spymaster* (Orion, 2011), pp. 85, 289, 309.

[41] Tim Ingold, 'Against Space: Place, Movement, Knowledge', in *Boundless Worlds: An Anthropological Approach to Movement*, ed. Peter Wynn Kirby (Berghahn Books, 2009), pp. 29–43 (p. 33).

properties, such as their length or the distance between the points on their itinerary, Ingold suggests that we should look for the knots along these 'lines of wayfaring'.

We can do this by comparing the itineraries of individuals and identifying points in time and space at which they may have shared a location. For example, if person A writes from location X on 3 January and 5 March 1584, and from nowhere else in between, and if person B writes from X on 20 February 1584, we can infer that they are likely to have overlapped at location X at least on 20 February. The fact that we only use single days of writing from one origin or uninterrupted series of such days, as outlined in the example above, means that we almost certainly underestimate the duration that individuals spend in a particular location, which makes our list of estimated overlaps highly conservative. However, even with these restrictive terms we find 100,630 total intersections, of which 2,538 are flagged as significant.[42]

This shows quite clearly that our data is full of knots. But how can this help us? Theoretically it can aid us in discovering whether people met, or whether a particular location was significant at a specific moment because of the cast of people meeting there. More generally it can be used as a tool for enriching our narratives of particular historical events. As the example of Servigi's journey to Terceira and his subsequent account of the conquest shows, intersecting itineraries provide a powerful tool for identifying alternative perspectives on the events that occurred in those locations, thereby corroborating or undermining existing narratives.

The latter use is perhaps the easiest to implement as one can begin with the people and places in which one is interested to generate a list of other people at that location during the period of interest. The benefit of targeted queries is that the volume of correspondence identified for close reading is more tractable. By contrast, finding ways of sifting the *whole* dataset to uncover notable knots is more challenging because of the distorting effect of hubs. In previous chapters (especially Chapter 2) we have used this word to refer to individuals with many epistolary connections. In this case, however, the issue is geographical hubs: cities and influential ports that have a disproportionate amount of traffic passing through them. In Figure 7.5 we can see a graph plotting the distribution of the number of letters sent for all the places of writing in our database on logarithmic axes. The x-axis charts the number of letters, and the y-axis the number of places with that number of letters. The roughly diagonal distribution indicates a power-law distribution, which is similar to the degree distribution of the people in this network discussed in Chapter 2. It shows us that while thousands of places in our dataset have only one letter sent from them (represented by the point in the top-left position in the graph), just a handful of places have thousands of letters written from them (the points in the bottom right-hand corner of the graph). The biggest hub of course is London: 6,419 of the 82,479 letters with a known place of writing are assigned 'London'; but the actual number of letters originating in the capital is even greater, as a further 1,335 letters give 'Westminster' as their origin, 1,227

---

[42] We use a conservative multiple hypothesis correction method (Bonferroni) and a 5% significance cutoff. For full documented code to reproduce these results, see <https://github.com/tudor-networks-of-power/code>.

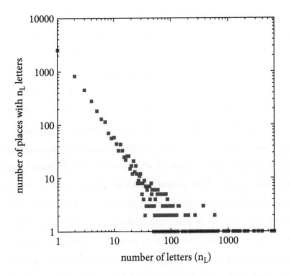

Figure 7.5 Distribution of the number of letters sent from all the places of writing in our database, on logarithmic axes. Note that the points fall on a diagonal (to a good approximation), indicating a power-law distribution.

letters give 'Greenwich', and more letters are associated with further London locations. A total of 12,222 letters originate inside a ten-mile radius around the City of London.[43]

Due to the disproportionate representation of the English capital in our data, we sought to exclude the 'London' place label from our investigations of intersections. Nevertheless, other place-hubs create a distorting effect. For example, if we look at a ranked list of people with the most intersections outside London, eight out of the top ten were leading political figures in Ireland, with most of their overlaps in Dublin.[44] It is not that hubs like Dublin are not interesting as locations. The problem is that merely knowing that two people were in Dublin at a specific time does not necessarily tell us that they knew or spoke to one another. It is, however, possible to unpick these knots on particular lines of wayfaring to determine whether there was in fact a documented contact between a given individual and those with whom he or she intersected geographically, or whether their interaction is otherwise significant.

[43] The difference between this set of letters and the subset of 6,417 that are explicitly labelled 'London' highlights the resolution problem one encounters when dealing with place data, which relates to the more general problem of encoding uncertainty in historical datasets. In the case of place data geo-coordinates can help to address this problem, as in our example above. But the ambiguity of location labels, which is due to the fact that any precise location is typically signified by a hierarchy of area identifiers (England, London, Westminster, Westminster Abbey) complicates the quantitative analysis of historical place data.

[44] The top ten are Geoffrey Fenton (323 intersections excluding London), Adam Loftus (310), Sir Richard Wingfield (272), Christopher Peyton, Auditor of Ireland (251), Sir Henry Wallop (242), Patrick Bermyngham (235), George Bourchier (235), Robert Dillon (221), George Gilpin (218), and Masino del Bene (218). The exceptions are Gilpin (a diplomat in the Netherlands during the Dutch Revolt) and de Bene, a former soldier apparently in the service of Catherine de Medici, who wrote a number of intelligence reports to Walsingham, Burghley, and Sassetti. References to del Bene (sometimes Delbene) with regard to his connection to the Tudor government are scarce. See, for example, the passing reference to him in E. John B. Allen, *Post and Courier Service in the Diplomacy of Early Modern Europe* (Nijhoff, 1972), p. 110; and John Bossy, *Giordano Bruno and the Embassy Affair* (Yale University Press, 2002), p. 93.

There are two ways in which we can go about doing this, but the best route depends on the nature of the research question. The first is an assisted manual means of verifying potential interactions, from the perspective of the individual correspondent. Such an approach is useful if one's interest is in a particular historical figure or community. We generated a very simple HTML interface, for which we provide the code in our GitHub repository,[45] that allowed us to explore the intersections of each individual in our dataset who fulfils the criteria of having intersecting itineraries. It allows us to select an individual and see a full list of all the people with whom they intersected; the dates of that intersection; whether that intersection was either preceded or followed by correspondence; and (as discussed further below) in cases where they do not correspond, read the Calendar descriptions of letters that contain likely *mentions*. This mode of exploration has some obvious uses. It can tell us whether the pattern or content of their communication changed following a potential meeting. If, for example, two people only correspond following an intersection we might infer that their co-location at a particular moment was significant—perhaps the occasion of their first meeting, or that a personal relationship (marked only by conversation) shifts to a remote relationship that necessitates further correspondence.

Within this granular approach our interest was focused on the cases where there was an intersection but no correspondence between the individuals. Here, we determined, was an opportunity to expand our understanding of the movement of information in the Tudor period beyond the network of correspondence. This addresses one particular shortfall that presents itself when working with letters as the sole source of data, as Scott Weingart has observed:

> By only looking on one axis (letters), we get an inflated sense of the importance of spatial distance in early modern intellectual networks. Best friends never wrote to each other; they lived in the same city and drank in the same pubs; they could just meet on a sunny afternoon if they had anything important to say. Distant letters were important, but our networks obscure the equally important local scholarly communities.[46]

The intersections of itineraries reveal *potential* local networks, but these connections need to be validated. In order to determine whether an intersection resulted in an actual meeting, one can automatically search all the letters for likely mentions, using the lists of alternative name labels associated with every person in the correspondence data (which are a by-product of the disambiguation and deduplication process described in Chapter 1). By searching letter abstracts for these labels one can identify potential mentions of the corresponding individuals in the body of the letter, with the limitation of only using name labels, or name parts, if they are not elsewhere

---

[45] See <https://github.com/tudor-networks-of-power/code>.

[46] Scott Weingart, 'Networks Demystified 8: When Networks are Inappropriate', <http://www.scottbot.net/HIAL/index.html@p=39600.html>.

attributed to another person (e.g. the label 'Mr Eden' cannot be used as it maps to a Thomas Eden in one manuscript and a Richard Eden in another). This method detects four different ways in which a mention-connection can occur for two individuals X and Y who overlap in a specific location: X mentions Y (to a third person Z), X is mentioned to Y (by Z), Y mentions X (to Z), Y is mentioned to X (by Z). Because this approach combines the spatio-temporal overlaps with textual analysis of the letter synopsis (thereby combining two different parts of the letter metadata), it provides an effective way to automatically generate a list of the overlaps that were most likely to result in actual meetings, even though they were never marked by letter exchange. From our explorations of this data we would suggest that a research area to which this tool might fruitfully contribute is a systematic study of diplomats' and agents' local networks of informants, how these varied, and how this contributed to different levels of success on embassy.

Perusing the interface shows the massive volume of potential interactions generated by our methods. But unless one has a set of individuals in whom one is interested, it is difficult to know where to begin. A second approach, therefore, for engaging with the intersection data employs statistical modelling to determine the significance of an intersection within the dataset as a whole. As we have already discussed above, itineraries will often overlap in centres, such as London, Paris, or Dublin, which is unlikely to be interesting unless there is other evidence, such as mentions, connecting the two individuals in question. However, if the location is a remote one, through which not many people in our dataset passed, the fact that two people appear in it at the same time may be much more significant. We can search for such cases systematically by calculating the probability that two particular individuals overlapped by chance given the durations they spent in a particular place, and assessing the significance of this overlap given the lengths of time other people spent in the same place and the number of people who spent time there across our entire dataset.[47] In other words, the rare appearance of a location in the dataset as a whole makes it likely that the two people were in the location at the same time for the same reason.

'Alterations of Spaces'

But why does it matter to be able to detect these statistically rare intersections? When we examine the people at the top of the ranking for their significance of intersection, it directs us to places that appear rarely in our dataset, but more significantly it directs us to moments of historical significance in those locations. If we look at the top fifty individuals according to their most significant overlaps we see that they are often at the site of a specific event; and the most common category of event in this list is war and siege. The method therefore provides an automated way not merely of identifying

---

[47] In addition one needs to filter out co-authorships of letters, which are otherwise a dominant signal in this analysis. See <https://github.com/tudor-networks-of-power/code>.

genuine knots in itineraries, but also of identifying historical crossroads. Moreover, we find that the authors of the letters are often more than mere witnesses of these events; frequently they are also figures who had a material impact on those events, fighting in battles or participating in diplomatic negotiations. This observation returns us to de Certeau's quotation: 'The networks of these moving, intersecting writings compose a manifold story that has neither author nor spectator, shaped out of fragments of trajectories and alterations of spaces.' Here we can see clearly how the intersecting writings of these correspondents are indeed creating 'alterations of spaces'. After these intersections occur, these places are no longer the same.

The locations of war and siege most obviously fill this function of alteration. Reading down the list of people ranked by their most 'significant' intersections we encounter examples like that of Fernando d'Ávalos, 5th marquis of Pescara, and Charles III, Duke of Bourbon (two of the forty-five people in joint first place by this measure), who intersect at the Camp before Marseilles during the 1524 Siege of Marseilles. This is unsurprising given that these men together led the army of the Holy Roman Empire. However, it shows the power of automatic detection, and shows links that would not have been marked by letters passing between them because they were travelling together. The value of finding such pairs of correspondents is that it will offer us accounts of the events that may offer corroboration, or different perspectives. Comparable examples, from other locations of violence and destruction, include: James Douglas, Earl of Morton, and John Erskine, Earl of Mar (also joint first by this measure) intersect in the Camp before Edinburgh at the end of 1571 during the Lang Siege (1571–3), when the castle was held by supporters of Queen Mary, against the rule of new regent the Earl of Lennox, who after being shot was succeeded by Erskine;[48] Geoffrey Fenton and Captain William Piers the younger (joint 87th place) intersect at the Camp at Smerwick during the Siege of Smerwick in 1580, during the Second Desmond Rebellion in Ireland; and Sir John Ogle and Sir Robert Drury (joint 179th place)[49] intersect at Grave during the Siege of Grave, which took place between 18 July and 20 September 1602 as part of the Eighty Years War and the Anglo-Spanish War. The alterations of space that resulted from these events were dramatic. D'Ávalos ruthlessly looted the surrounding countryside after the Siege of Marseilles. The Lang Siege left Edinburgh castle and the town in ruins, and its inhabitants short of both food and fuel.

An overlapping category of significant intersections are those in named houses and castles. In these cases we see that these often coincide with further battles and sieges, as in the case of Cardinal Lorenzo Campeggio and Cardinal Benedetto Accolti (joint 179th), who found themselves together with others such as Pope Clement VII and Gregory Casale in Castel Sant'Angelo before and after the Sack of Rome in May 1527.[50]

---

[48] Harry Potter, *Edinburgh under Siege 1571–1573* (The History Press, 2003).

[49] We retain the number of people in our rankings. Thus joint first is followed by joint 28th, followed by joint 30th, joint 34th, etc.

[50] William E. Wilkie, *The Cardinal Protectors of England: Rome and the Tudors Before the Reformation* (Cambridge University Press, 1974), p. 178.

Similarly, Sir Henry Unton, the ambassador to France, overlaps with Edmund Yorke, master of the ordnance and musters of army in Normandy (joint 30th) at Fontaine-le-Bourg in April 1592, a seigniorial manor house in Normandy that was repeatedly besieged and served as a home in 1592 to King Henri IV during the military campaign against the troops of Alessandro Farnese, Duke of Parma. Later in 1597 Henri IV stayed for a couple of days at the Château de Picquigny before sieging Amiens; and there in Picquigny we see Captain Arthur Chichester (later Baron Chichester), William Lille, and Sir John Aldrich intersecting in May of that year.

Country houses and castles also function as the site of important meetings, either because of their strategic location, or other practical considerations. One notable example is the intersection in July 1528 of Sir Thomas Heneage (the elder) and Dr John Bell (joint 297th) at Tyttenhanger House. Tyttenhanger House was the country seat of the Abbot of St Albans—a title Wolsey had been bestowed in 1522—and it was so large that in 1528 Henry VIII and his retinue removed there to avoid the deadly sweating sickness that was sweeping London. Heneage and Bell were both part of Henry's inner circle in this period. Heneage was a member of the privy chamber.[51] Bell had made himself useful in promoting the king's divorce from Catherine, for which he worked tirelessly, although the two letters he wrote from Tyttenhanger demonstrate that he was employed by Henry more broadly in church matters, directing Wolsey regarding the king's wishes concerning the bestowal of church offices.[52] What is perhaps notable about this example is that although the location may have changed, the court continues to function unaltered, so accustomed were early modern courts to functioning peripatetically.[53] We might see Henry's adoption of the space as a harbinger of the events of 1539 when the house entered crown hands in the dissolution of the monasteries.

The programme of reformation imposed by the crown during Thomas Cromwell's period in office, culminating in the legal process known as the dissolution of the monasteries (1536–41), is a recurrent feature of these freighted sites of intersection throughout the top 200 people. Ranked joint first is the intersection of Adam Becansaw and John Vaughan in Gresford in October 1535, as part of the monastic visitations; Gresford is otherwise written from on only two other occasions. The first visitations began following the 1535 act that sought to redirect the first fruits paid to Rome by episcopal sees to the crown, which was followed by the appointment of commissioners to visit each ecclesiastical institution and report on their financial situation. A second commission followed in the autumn of that year to evaluate adherence to

---

[51] Michael Riordan, 'Heneage, Sir Thomas (b. before 1482, d. 1553)', *ODNB*, <https://doi.org/10.1093/ref:odnb/12920>.

[52] Susan Wabuda, 'Bell, John (d. 1556)', *ODNB*, <https://doi.org/10.1093/ref:odnb/2010>. See his letters to Wolsey, dated 7 July 1528, SP 1/49 f.84, and 10 July 1528, SP 1/49 f.95.

[53] The itinerary of the court over the Tudor period would be a fascinating small project in its own right, and is now rendered more tractable thanks to the availability of *The Elizabethan Court Day by Day* by Marion E. Colthorpe, which is licensed under an Attribution-ShareAlike 4.0 International licence. See <https://folgerpedia.folger.edu/The_Elizabethan_Court_Day_by_Day>.

'new procedures for discipline'.[54] Eighty-six questions were to be put to the inhabitants of these monasteries, many of which were concerned about the monks' and nuns' sincerity to their vocation, including their chastity. That concern with sexual behaviour can be seen in the letters of Becansaw and Vaughan, and the changes that their visits wrought.[55] Vaughan's letters paint a picture of Gresford reformed, informing Cromwell that:

> according to your instruccions [...] we haue put to execucion suche enormities and sinful lyuinge as we haue found here both to the pleasure of God [...] and to the comforte of all good people, for syns our comynge many a score of them that kepte concubines openly in ther houses beinge sengle men and sengle women hauinge betwixte them many children be now married. The priests with ther concubines be now reformed and haue left the concubines, and every man that was founde by deteccion gilty, we punished openly in the face of the country. The people not only the good but also the badd, thankinge God highely that euer suche power shuld come emongst them to call them from ther sinfull lyuinge.[56]

The alteration of space described here is a moral one. However, in his letter to Cromwell Becansaw expresses his anxiety that one of the other commissioners, Ellis Price, was coming with a new commission, which he feared 'shalbe slaunderouse vnto the said visitation in so moche he ridethe about the country with his concubyne openly'.[57] This site thus remained one of dispute as the crown sought to extend its agenda of reform.

Other examples associated with the appointed commissioners tasked with visiting religious houses include: Thomas Legh and John ap Rice, who intersected in Walden Abbey on 16 October 1535 (ranked joint 51st for significance) and travelled together visiting numerous other religious houses at Worcester, Lacock Abbey, Bruton Abbey, Wilton, Wherwell, Witney, Reading, Haliwell, and Royston. Robert Southwell and Edward Carne intersected at Malmesbury (ranked joint first) and both wrote from this location on 16 December 1539, the day after Malmesbury Abbey was surrendered to them as the king's commissioners. Richard Watkins coincided with Rowland Lee in Burton-upon-Trent on 27 June 1533 (ranked 179th), where the two were sent to speed the election of one of the abbots to the rank of Abbot of Westminster (the highest office known to have been attained by any monk of Burton), an event which has been described as foreshadowing the ultimate dissolution of the monastery.[58]

[54] See G. W. Bernard, *The King's Reformation: Henry VIII and the Remaking of the English Church* (Yale University Press, 2005), p. 245.

[55] See Glanmor Williams, *Renewal and Reformation: Wales c.1415–1642* (Clarendon, 1987), pp. 282–3.

[56] Vaughan to Cromwell, 14 October 1535, SP 1/98 f.5.

[57] Becansaw to Cromwell, 14 October 1535, SP 1/98 f.4. On Price, see Peter R. Roberts, 'Price [Prys], Ellis [*called* y Doctor Coch] (c. 1505–1594)', *ODNB*, <https://doi.org/10.1093/ref:odnb/22748>.

[58] *A History of the County of Stafford*, vol. 3 (Victoria County History, London, 1970), pp. 199–213, available at: <https://www.british-history.ac.uk/vch/staffs/vol3/pp199-213> (accessed 20 December 2018). For the letters, see Watkins to Cromwell, 27 June 1533, SP 1/77 f.90, and Lee to Cromwell, 25 June, SP 1/77 f.80.

And Richard Pollard and John Russell, Earl of Bedford, intersected in Wells (ranked joint 418th, but still in the top 10% of most significant intersections) on 16 November 1539. Pollard, by then General Surveyor of the Court of Augmentations, assisted Cromwell in administering the surrender of religious houses by visiting the premises and making a detailed valuation of the house's assets and income. In this role in September 1539 Pollard was among the commissioners sent to Glastonbury Abbey, which the abbot Richard Whiting had refused to surrender. After finding money and plate walled up in secure vaults, Whiting was arrested and sent to the Tower of London, where he was questioned by Cromwell and then subsequently sent back to Glastonbury with Pollard, reaching Wells on 14 November, where he was tried and convicted of robbing Glastonbury church. The next day he was transported to Glastonbury, drawn through the town upon a hurdle, and executed on Torre Hill, as detailed in both Pollard's and Russell's letters. Russell adds the detail that the abbot was beheaded and quartered, with one quarter left standing at Wells, another each at Bath, Ilchester, and Bridgwater, and his head upon the abbey gate at Glaston. Russell was probably present in his capacity as Lord President of the Council of the West, and seems to have been involved in the trial as he sends Cromwell the details of the inquest that passed on the abbot. It is also worth mentioning that Russell, like Legh and various other commissioners, directly benefited from the dissolution of the monasteries in the south-west, having earlier that year been granted about 30,000 acres, drawn primarily from the former monastery of Tavistock in Devon and valued at £648 12s. per annum.

As with the example of sieges, the intersections relating to the dissolution of the monasteries are not passive: figures like Legh, Southwell, Pollard, and Russell are not drawn to these locations because something is happening, but rather they are key actors in those events, the very forces bringing about 'reform', the seizure of church assets, and the beneficiaries of those distributions of land and wealth. Once again these events occasion alterations of spaces, as has been discussed in the scholarship of James Simpson, Jennifer Summit, and Margaret Aston, amongst others, who describe how in the sixteenth century England 'acquired a whole suite of ruins. [...] And the architectural fossils which remained as testimonies to the royal guillotining of the monastic past fostered a growing nostalgia for what had been swept off in this break.'[59] From this perspective we can see the men intersecting at the locations as agents of destruction, and their respective itineraries leaving behind ruins in their wake.

Other examples near the top of our rankings for significance direct us to travellers who made forays into new territories for the purposes of trade and conquest, of the kind we encountered in the first sections of this chapter. One example is the intersection of Sir Francis Drake, Sir John Norris, and Anthony Asheley at Cascais on 2 June

---

[59] Margaret Aston, 'English Ruins and English History: The Dissolution and the Sense of the Past', *Journal of the Warburg and Courtauld Institutes* 36 (1973), 231–55 (pp. 231–2). See also James Simpson, *The Oxford English Literary History, Volume 2, 1350–1547: Reform and Cultural Revolution* (Oxford University Press, 2002), chapter 1; Jennifer Summit, 'Leland's Itinerary and the Remains of the Medieval Past', in *Reading the Medieval in Early Modern England*, ed. Gordon McMullan and David Matthews (Cambridge University Press, 2007), pp. 159–76.

1589 (Asheley and Drake are ranked joint 167th). What is significant about this inter-section was that it was essentially bungled. Following the defeat of the Armada, Drake and Norris were commissioned to seek out and destroy the remaining ships, to sup-port the rebels in Lisbon against King Philip II (then King of Spain and Portugal), and take the Azores if possible. Drake was to command a fleet, and Norris was to lead his army overland to Lisbon, where Drake and the fleet were to reinforce him. However, upon arrival at Lisbon on 23 May, the English troops found the fortress was too strong and the army too weak. Meanwhile Drake brought the fleet up to the mouth of the Tagus River to Cascais but made no attempt to reach Lisbon.[60] Puzzled by his delay, Norris eventually abandoned Lisbon, leaving behind many of his sick and wounded troops, and by the time he made connection with Drake and his fleet in Cascais, he had lost a third of his forces. From here we get three accounts. Asheley complains that this is the result of the lack of timely supplies from England, and the lack of explicit demonstration in favour of King António from the Portuguese.[61] Drake and Norris write together, interestingly, providing a unified narrative, rather than laying blame with the other, and citing the same causes as Asheley.[62] Three days later Norris and Drake wrote to the Council that, having no hope of supplies from England, they resolved to sail for St Michael's and the rest of the Azores.[63]

Many of the moments of intersection listed above are relatively well known within the scholarship of their relative historical fields and geographical territories. For example, the dissolution of the monasteries has a vast library of scholarship docu-menting it. Similarly the explorations and adventuring of the Elizabethan period has received plentiful attention. However, what this chapter shows is the power of auto-mation: by determining a set of rules to identify significant locations at particular moments, these events emerge from the mass of data. This of course has the effect of what Lara Putnam has noticed of enabling both knowledge and ignorance: 'Digital search offers release from place-based research practices that have been central to our discipline's epistemology and ethics alike.'[64] However, this is crucial for an under-standing of the process that brought the State Papers archive into being, and the resulting reconstruction of the purview of the Tudor government, specifically of the Secretary of State, and of the way he accumulated knowledge across borders. This is a move away from a process of specialisation that has carved up the archive to answer place-specific research questions.

Taking a networked overview however necessarily relies on the deep scholarship of these specific knowledge domains and geographies. The fact our algorithms can iden-tify moments and places of interest that have been the subject of deep scholarship allows us to validate the method and to identify new avenues. As we have noted

---

[60] D. J. B. Trim, 'Norris [Norreys], Sir John (c.1547×50–1597)', *ODNB*, <https://doi.org/10.1093/ref:odnb/20276>.

[61] Asheley to Walsingham, 2 June 1589, SP 12/224 f.117.

[62] Norris and Drake to the Council, 2 June 1589, SP 12/224 f.114.

[63] Norris and Drake to the Council, 5 June 1589, SP 12/224 f.129.

[64] Lara Putnam, 'The Transnational and the Text-Searchable: Digitized Sources and the Shadows They Cast', *American Historical Review* 121 (2016), 377–402 (p. 379).

elsewhere, '[i]t is extremely important that the method confirms what we already know. That means it works, and that we can put some trust in it when it draws attention to things we might not have observed before.'[65] One such case is the journey of Seth Cocks, and his intersections with Nicholas Perkins. Cocks is almost impossible to trace outside the Calendars, yet his intersection with Perkins in Cracow is ranked in the top 10% of most significant intersections. The case has some important lessons for the ways that the Tudor government managed information gathering at the edges of its geographical reach, and how it constructed a 'manifold story' from different epistolary perspectives, to shore up its information networks and verify the veracity of its intelligences.

A 'Manifold Story': Perkins and Cocks

Seth Cocks and Christopher Perkins intersected in Cracow in April 1595, and both wrote letters from Prague within eight days of each other in July 1593. The reason for Perkins's presence on both occasions was formal diplomatic business. The intersection allows us to assemble the correspondence of the two men to tell a 'manifold' account of English interests in these locations, and also to shed light on the careers of both men.

Perkins's life prior to his diplomatic service, as outlined in Chapter 2, was far from standard for an ambassador. He left England for the continent in 1565, presumably for religious reasons, as he subsequently entered the Society of Jesus in Rome in 1566, was ordained at Augsburg in 1575, and in 1580 was put forward by Robert Persons and William Allen for the Jesuit mission to England. How he came to serve as an agent for the Tudor government is hard to determine; so too are his religious affiliations, and doubts regarding the steadfastness of his loyalty to the crown continued throughout his career. However, by October 1589 he was already communicating intelligence to Walsingham and in or before December 1591 he was granted an annuity of 100 marks, after being 'sent on her Majesty's necessary affairs to Poland, Prussia and other parts of the East Country' the previous year.[66] Thereafter Perkins was used on a number of foreign missions, even though in March 1596 the pope offered 'near £2,000 for his life' because, Perkins claimed, he had 'boldly resisted the insolent proceedings' of the clergy and the pope's legate against the dignity of Her Majesty.[67]

By comparison, almost nothing is known about Seth Cocks. Cocks wrote seven letters to Robert Cecil in the years 1593–8. He is mentioned, as far as we have been able to discover, in only three locations: the *List and Analysis of State Papers*, which gives

[65] Ruth Ahnert and Sebastian E. Ahnert, 'Protestant Letter Networks in the Reign of Mary I: A Quantitative Approach', *English Literary History* 82 (2015), 1–33.

[66] See Thomas M. McCoog, 'Perkins [Parkins], Sir Christopher (1542/3–1622)', *ODNB*, <https://doi.org/10.1093/ref:odnb/21968>, and *History of Parliament*, <https://www.historyofparliamentonline.org/volume/1558-1603/member/parkins-(perkins)-christopher-1545-1622>.

[67] Perkins to Robert Cecil, 9 May 1598, SP 12/267 f.13r.

no history of Cocks, just the details of the events on which he reported; a one-sentence reference to him in Jonathan Wolfson's book, *Padua and the Tudors*, describing him as an intelligencer and supplying the information that he matriculated at Magdalen College, Oxford, in 1579; and a history of the Cocks family that mentions one Seth as the son of Thomas and Elizabeth Cocks (whose dates fit the matriculation dates), notes the lack of information about Seth except for an inscription on his brother's memorial that suggests he was killed fighting in the Irish wars in 1599.[68] The combined roles of intelligencer and soldier are a familiar combination, as we have discovered by examining the variety of figures who gathered intelligence in the Tudor period. These activities create an interesting itinerary, placing him in Prague in July 1593, in Padua by the end of November, where he stays until March 1594, before leaving for Leipzig, returning to Padua in June, and to Cracow in April 1595. The mechanism by which he became an intelligencer working for Cecil, and the official reason for his presence both in Italy and Eastern Europe, however, is not apparent from his letters.

What we do know, by reading their letters, is that the intersection of Perkins and Cocks in Prague and Cracow was not an accident. They were reporting on the same incidents, and, more importantly, Cocks provided accounts of Perkins's diplomatic negotiations and mentions having passed intelligence to him (although Perkins does not mention Cocks). Given the two intersections and common interest, we might assume that the two had therefore travelled together, as in the case of Randolph, Bannister, and Duckett going into Russia (discussed above). The obvious suggestion might be that Cocks is a servant of Perkins. However, from the contents of the letters we see that although their co-location may have been coordinated by the Tudor government, the men do not travel together, and Cocks provides a different perspective on events that suggests he had his own agenda. His letter from Prague dated July 1593 talks about events 'after Mr Perkins arryual heare', which suggests that Cocks was already in situ on this date, and a subsequent letter written from Padua in late November or early December 1593 discusses events in Prague following Perkins's departure.[69] Moreover, Cocks's critique of Perkins's negotiations strongly suggests his independence.

Perkins had travelled to Prague to meet with the Holy Roman Emperor Rudolf II concerning the ongoing land war between the Habsburg Monarchy and the Ottoman Empire in the years 1593–1606, known as the Long Turkish War (or Thirteen Years War). In his meetings with the emperor Perkins defended Elizabeth against accusations of defending the Turks, and he offered the services of the queen's ambassador in Constantinople, Edward Barton, as a mediator in the dispute between the Turks and the Empire. In return Elizabeth hoped that the emperor would advise the pope and

---

[68] *List and Analysis*, vols. 5 and 6, *passim*; Jonathan Woolfson, *Padua and the Tudors: English Students in Italy, 1485–1603* (Clarke, 1998), p. 133; and J. V. Somers Cocks, *A History of the Cocks Family* (1967, rev. 1999), p. 42, <http://homepages.xnet.co.nz/~sremos/history.pdf>. The Cocks family history does not mention his Oxford affiliation, or any of his travels in Poland, Prussia, or Italy.

[69] SP 80/1 f.154r, and SP 85/1 f.163.

the Spanish king to pursue a peaceful resolution in their war with England, France, and Holland.[70] Perkins provides a positive account of his negotiations, writing that the emperor 'would be inclined to iust condicions of Peace'.[71] Cocks, however, provides additional context which paints a more complex picture:

> Thobtayning of his [the emperor's] great victories being presently after Mr Perkins arryual heare, hath beane I think a greate occasion that his entertainment hath beane much the colder, and her Majesties gratious offer not so gladly axepted as otherwise they wold haue beane. But trewly Mr Perkins omytted no meanes [...] to draw them to accept.[72]

Cocks is referring to the impact of the recent Habsburg victory at the Battle of Sisak. He implies this success had given the emperor and Croatian forces greater confidence, perhaps making them feel less in need of Elizabeth's help, and resulting in a 'colder' reception for Perkins.

Cocks also provides an account of Perkins's embassy to Poland in 1595. According to Perkins's letter to Burghley dated 15 March 1595, on arriving in Cracow he found that the pope's legate and the clergy had spread 'diuers odious rumours [...] of her Majesties intention'. Their specific accusation was that Perkins had been sent 'to hinder the confederation against the Turk', for which ambassadors from the emperor, the electors and princes of Germany (except the Palatine of the Rhine), Transylvania, Wallachia, and Moldovia were pressing. Perkins gives a long account of how he dispelled these rumours, presenting himself as a valuable and effective diplomat.[73] Cocks's account of these events provides a different picture, however. His letter to Robert Cecil suggests that Perkins's diplomatic visit was far from successful, due in large part to his demeanour, which acted as a barrier to negotiations. He writes that: 'ix days before thend of the parlement arryued heare D. Perkins, a man lyttle gratefull to this king and court, as appered by the skornfull audience, and cold visage he receaued.'[74]

It is, of course, good policy to seek multiple sources of intelligence on foreign affairs. Here we see the combination of formal diplomatic embassy with informal intelligence networks being employed as a means of validating Perkins's accounts. Cocks provides a corrective to the optimistic accounts provided by Perkins that sought to provide a positive evaluation of his missions, suggesting that on both occasions he received a chilly reception. As such, Cocks's letters also form a missing link in

---

[70] Thomas M. McCoog, *The Society of Jesus in Ireland, Scotland, and England, 1589–1597: Building the Faith of Saint Peter upon the King of Spain's Monarchy* (Routledge, 2016), p. 147.

[71] Perkins to Barton, 18 July 1593, SP 81/7 f.140r.

[72] Cocks to Sir Robert Cecil, 26 July 1593, SP 80/1 f.154.

[73] SP 88/1 f.217. This letter also contains a lovely account of his journey, reporting having arrived in Cracow 'ten days before thend of the Parlamente hauing sustained by the way all the labours and incommodities that the wynter season, in the extreme could, and barren cuntries might yeald, hunger, could, dyfficultie of the waies, for the horrable quantitie of ise and snowe, and in summa, the desire I had of expedition as the matter required, afforded me verie little ease'.

[74] Cocks to Cecil, 8 April 1595, SP 88/1 f.221.

the existing accounts of Perkins's career. In the 1590s Perkins periodically begged for preferment 'to some living without cure', so that he could continue to serve the queen.[75] However, such preferment was not offered (although his situation improved at the end of the decade when he was appointed master of requests extraordinary in 1598 and Latin secretary on 21 August 1601). With no more income than the annual stipend of 100 marks promised in December 1591, 'Perkins suspected that the government discriminated against him, despite his years of service and loyalty, because of his foreign education and his former Catholicism.'[76] Cocks's letters, however, suggest an additional factor may have been the ineffectiveness of Perkins's missions, and perhaps we can even trace back the lack of promotion directly to Cocks's negative reports. Cocks's evaluation is borne out by other parts of Perkins's mission to Poland in 1594–5. For example, in July 1594 Perkins had been in Elbing (which was the Chartered English Eastland Company's entrepôt for Baltic trade at this time), where part of his mission was to negotiate the Company's trade relations. In a letter to Burghley dated 1 July 1594 Perkins assured him that the King of Poland would do nothing which might lead to the deterioration in Anglo-Polish relations. However, while Perkins asserted that Poland had no interest in exporting grain to Spain against the wishes of the Queen of England, Polish grain was nevertheless transported to Spain in Danzig ships.[77]

The 'intersecting writings' thus directs us to correspondence that provides an additional perspective on Perkins's diplomatic career, which may also suggest that Cocks played a role in Perkins's arrested advancement. But it is not merely the diplomatic realm to which these intersections direct us; they also draw attention to Prague and Cracow as locations of esoteric activity that captivated the Tudor government—suggesting the twofold interest of the English government in these locations. In the 1580s John Dee, the English mathematician, astronomer, astrologer, occult philosopher, and adviser to Queen Elizabeth I, had sought the patronage of both Emperor Rudolf II in Prague, and King Stefan of Poland in Cracow. Travelling with him was Edward Kelley, an occultist and alchemist. Although our letter data does not automatically reveal intersections with Kelley (because we have no letters in our dataset from him after 1591), the contents of Perkins's letters written from Prague in 1593 and Cracow in 1595 show a triad forming between Kelley, Cocks, and Perkins. Perkins had in fact previously met Kelley and Dee in Prague in 1589, and in June 1589 Kelley accused him of being a papal emissary complicit in a plot to assassinate Elizabeth I. Interestingly, as Thomas McCoog has observed, on returning to England Perkins expressed his belief that Kelley was attempting a similar plot against the English throne, following 'the counsel of his friends and ghostly fathers the Jesuits', producing evidence for them by means of a letter from Sigismund III.[78] Although Perkins was temporarily held in the custody of John Young, Bishop of Rochester,

---

[75] Salisbury MSS, 4.583, quoted in McCoog, 'Perkins [Parkins]'.   [76] McCoog, 'Perkins [Parkins]'.
[77] Henryk Zins, *England and the Baltic in the Elizabethan Era*, tr. C. Stevens (Manchester University Press, 1972), p. 263.
[78] McCoog, 'Perkins [Parkins]'.

Elizabeth and Burghley do not seem to have taken either accusation very seriously: Perkins was quickly exonerated, and both Elizabeth and Burghley repeatedly sought Kelley's expertise, as we see from Burghley's letter to him in May 1591, entreating him to return home and soliciting from him a remedy to ease his gout.[79]

Cocks's intersection acts as a line of reconnection between Perkins and Kelley in 1593 and 1595, as well as once more providing an alternative view. In 1591 the emperor imprisoned Kelley on a charge of killing an official named Jiri Hunkler in a duel, and perhaps also, as has been suggested, to ensure that he did not leave with his supposed alchemical secrets.[80] In his 1593 letter from Prague, in which he reports on Perkins's embassy, Cocks also provides a report on Kelley. In fact, the detail he provides on Kelley covers many more lines of the letter than his intelligence on Perkins, which indicates the level of the government's interest in the alchemist. He reports how he has 'thoroughly sifted owt the means he vied to manytayne his pompe':

> I find by those that [are] weall thoroughly acquaynted with many of his shyfts that the philosophers stone hath beane nothing els then the quintisence of 6 thousand ducats of the baron of Rosenbergs together with an extraction of certayne iewells which by the credyt he had by the L: Rosenburgh [...] owt of the which being pawned to the Iews he dystylled to the valew 16 m ducats whereof he melted many and sent the wadges to bee sold to the goldsmith, which gaue such as an opynion of his skyll that yt was thought there wold not be any led enough in the country for thoperacion of his powder, and this he lymed for a while in his glory tyll breaking twice with themperor for performance of the grand profe he promysed, and his creditors which weare many and exclayming for their doubtes, he resolued to run away by night, but was brought back againe and hath remained ever since yn pryson, where he hath had tyme enough to haue vsed the vertew of the philosophers stone for the procurment of his lyberty; but I can heare of no effectes but tryfles which may be wrought by many deceits.[81]

The alternative view provided by Cocks is the sure-sighted corrective to the deceits wrought and promises made by Kelley, which seem to have intrigued and beguiled not only the emperor but also Elizabeth and Burghley at home in England. He outlines the series of investments that Kelley had sought to finance his alchemy, the numerous creditors to whom he owed money, the mounting number of doubters when he twice failed to perform his transformation of lead into gold, and finally the implication of guilt when Kelley sought to escape his debts. Despite this report, however, interest in Kelley's activities both in England and the Baltic continued. In Cocks's 1595 letter from Cracow he writes: 'I am now within these 2 dayes to depart hence

[79] Lansdowne Vol/103 f.208r.

[80] Michael Wilding, 'A Biography of Edward Kelly, the English Alchemist and Associate of Dr. John Dee', in *Mystical Metal of Gold: Essays on Alchemy and Renaissance Culture*, ed. Stanton J. Lindon (AMS Press, 2007), pp. 35–90.

[81] Cocks to Cecil, 26 July 1595, SP 80/1 f.154.

and mean to passe by Prage, by cause I wyll see Sir Edward Kelley who they say enioy-eth his former fauour with themperor.'[82]

What we know about Cocks may be fragmentary, but his intersection with Perkins provides an important demonstration of the way that information from remote loca-tions was obtained by the Tudor government in this period. The concerns that the state had in eastern Europe, and the picture it derived from the intelligence coming out of this region, were multifarious, layered, and intersecting. The diplomatic con-cerns were bound up with the religious context of ongoing war, trade relations, as well as the access to information about esoteric activity. The densely intersecting topics of information in Cocks's writing, however, are directly inverse to the number of inter-secting itineraries that we can derive from the State Papers archive in the geographical region in which he travelled. An overview of our data shows the scarcity of epistolary coverage in Eastern Europe during this period, meaning that those charged with sup-plying information from such locations were clearly required to serve multiple func-tions. The value, therefore, of Cocks's intelligence was high. However, as with so many of the intelligencers discussed in this book, that value does not appear to have equated to preferment: despite his service and offer in a letter of 1598 to serve Cecil on his return to England, this is the last time he appears as a correspondent in the State Papers, suggesting he did not progress to a more formal engagement before his death in Ireland the following year. It is why Cocks and so many like him have failed to emerge in histories of the period heretofore.

Conclusion

This chapter has traced its own methodological itinerary, and it has led us to what data scientists might describe as an 'edge case': that is, a situation that occurs only at an extreme operating parameter. As one of the most statistically unlikely intersec-tions, the meeting point of Cocks's and Perkins's itineraries in Prague and Cracow show us how this kind of modelling helps to identify meaningful 'knots' in wayfaring, where we are able to observe multiple textual accounts of specific historical events. It is also an edge case in that it brings to the fore more marginal—and in the case of Cocks, virtually unknown—figures represented in the archive. The fact that a given person has been understudied is not, however, justification itself for studying them. We might argue that they are marginal for good reason. Our contention here, as with the lives of other intelligencers and agents that we have pieced together from frag-ments in other chapters, is that it is precisely these 'fragmentary trajectories' that we must assemble if we are to understand how networks of these moving, intersecting writings compose a manifold story of Tudor foreign policy.

This edge case is emblematic of the way in which intelligence was assembled by the Tudor government. The methods outlined in this chapter show us that diplomatic postings were only the tip of the iceberg in terms of how local intelligence was

---

[82] SP 88/1 f.221.

sourced. We know *where* the Tudor government had the most intelligence coverage, which is so evocatively illustrated by Figure 1.6, which projects onto a blank canvas the coordinates of the writing place of letters for which we have geographical information. Diplomatic postings make up a small percentage of this coverage; information from these other locations is supplied by the broad 'plat' of intelligencers outlined in Chapter 4, as well as intelligence derived from intercepted correspondence, as discussed in Chapters 4 and 6. Moreover, Figure 7.5—which plots the distribution of the number of letters written from a given place on a logarithmic scale—shows that numerous places were marked by moderate or high numbers of letters, meaning that the Tudor government often would have had multiple contacts in these locations who could supply corroborating evidence or alternative accounts on events. In other cases administrative tasks and missions were built with what we might think of as an information insurance policy in place: by dispatching teams—whether that be pairs of commissioners sent out as part of the visitation of the monasteries, or the entourage sent into Russia including Randolph, Bannister, and Duckett—they had greater assurance that information would reach the government, if lines of communications were compromised. Perhaps more importantly, it provided a means of corroborating accounts.

While this was a sensible information strategy on the part of the government, the maintenance of multiple lines of information undoubtedly caused tensions and competition for favour. We can already infer that Cocks's reports contributed to Perkins's failure to secure preferment 'to some living without cure', and elsewhere we see anxieties that the use of parallel intelligence reports ran the risk of undermining an individual's status. An example highlighted by our method can be found in a letter from Henry Stanley, Earl of Derby, to Secretary Walsingham. It was sent from the Bourbourg conference in 1588, a key peace negotiation within the Dutch Revolt. The mission was led by Derby, and he was joined by Comptroller Sir James Croft, William Brooke, Lord Cobham, Amyas Paulet, and Valentine Dale. Our method shows that Derby and Dale both overlap with a Flemish merchant called Andreas de Loo (perhaps better known as a collector of Holbein's works),[83] who was commissioned as an agent to treat informally with Alessandro Farnese, Duke of Parma, on behalf of Elizabeth. However, Derby clearly felt uneasy about this parallel means of negotiation, writing to Walsingham:

> Sir, I wolde haue written oftener to yowe either by myselfe or by my man but that Mr Comptroller and Andreas de Loo maketh secrete despacches into Englande withowte making me preuie or my Lord Cobham or anye of the other Comyssioners for the which if yowe wolde giue theyme some chekke or aduice in yowre nexte letters it wolde be vsed no more.[84]

---

[83] Lesley Lewis, *The Thomas More Family: Group Portraits After Holbein* (Gracewing, 1998), p. 4.
[84] Derby to Walsingham, 3 July 1588, Bourbourg, SP 77/4 f.204.

The reference to 'secrete despacches' suggests Derby's discomfort that he and his fellow commissioners did not know the contents of de Loo's letters, and were not given the opportunity to verify their contents. Such mistrust must have been endemic within the complex network of informants established by the principal secretaries.

While our attention has turned here to what the method allows us to say about the Tudor government's strategy around the spatial management of intelligence, the potential of these linked approaches is more general. The search for alternative or verifying accounts is not just the business of governments, but of scholars too. We believe that this chapter, perhaps more than any of those preceding it, has many books' worth of possibilities contained within it. Its methods are both an intuitive and powerful means for engaging with digitised archives. They bear the most in common with the Victorian project to calendar the State Papers (discussed in Chapter 1). The Calendars arranged the papers not only chronologically, but also by subject and region, allowing researchers to more easily discover related clusters of documents. This method achieves this more powerfully, speedily, and at scale, making explicit connections that are latent or hidden within a mass of documentation or obscured by the contextless search mechanisms of the online interface, which is now often the default mode of engagement. We hope that others will take up these methods to find those journeys that intersect with the individuals, the communities, the places, and the events that they study as a means of shoring up their research process, corroborating and problematizing the narratives they have constructed.

Afterword

A 'conclusion' is not fitting for a book such as this, in which the primary aim is to open up new entry points into a historical letter archive by rendering it as network data. Our intention in the foregoing chapters was to scope just some of the potential avenues that future researchers could take by developing experiments that focused on different dimensions of the data, from the basic metadata to the descriptions of the letter contents, and from its gendered dimension to its geographical facets. We sought to show how these approaches allow researchers to analyse the archive at different scales, using different theoretical frameworks, and how one might design customised methodologies within those frames. As such, each chapter resulted in a very different pathway through the network. These multifarious threads do not cohere into one unified thesis about the State Papers archive, but such a task is perhaps impossible for an archive of such richness and variability. Indeed, we have sought to quantitatively describe, and trace dimensions of that archive, which was created by the monarch's Principal Secretary; which captures domestic correspondence, intercepted missives, and entire family archives that were seized by the crown; and one that has also undergone losses both random and targeted, from the neglect of the descendants of individual secretaries to acts of intentional destruction.

Instead of trying to formulate a conclusion, we offer in this afterword a reflection on where such work might go next. We believe that this dataset, now made available for all to use, has the potential to generate numerous new projects—and indeed the data is in the process of being incorporated into several other pieces of research.[1] However, if the community is to fully benefit from the new insights and approaches offered through each of our experiments, it is important that others take up this work and develop it in new directions. This is why we have made the data and the code for each chapter available for others, following the values of the open research community. The aim of open research is to ensure that our results are reproducible and verifiable, but—perhaps more importantly—that others can take both the data and code and further develop our collective understanding of the State Papers archive, its making, the histories that can be told with it, and how these missives might relate to cognate collections. However,

---

[1] Work published/in-press: Kim Albrecht, Sebastian E. Ahnert, and Ruth Ahnert, *Tudor Networks*: Interactive web visualisation (2020), available at: <http://tudornetworks.net/>; Rachel Midura, Sebastian E. Ahnert, and Ruth Ahnert, 'Shadow Networks: Intercept Letters in the British State Papers, 1580–1603', in *Network Analysis and the Early Modern Archive*, ed. Ruth Ahnert, Philip Beeley, Esther van Raamsdonk, and Yann Ryan, as a special issue of *Huntington Library Quarterly* (forthcoming). In-progress projects reusing the data: 'Networking Archives: Assembling and Analysing a Meta-archive of Correspondence, 1509–1714' (AH/R014817/1), PI Howard Hotson; 'In Our Name: Pragmatics, Materiality and Ideologies of Power and Nation in the Correspondence of James V and Henry VIII, 1513–1542' (SRG2021\210819), PI Mel Evans.

Tudor Networks of Power. Ruth Ahnert and Sebastian E. Ahnert, Oxford University Press. © Ruth Ahnert and Sebastian E. Ahnert 2023.
DOI: 10.1093/oso/9780198858973.003.0008

these opportunities open in different directions for those approaching this material from a data-driven perspective and those working within the historiographical context of Tudor government and early modern epistolary exchange.

For those approaching this book with interests more squarely in Tudor political history, or in the history of early modern communication practices, the openings for future research tend to focus on individual biographies and collective histories. While we have taken the time to tell at greater length the stories of certain individuals—such as Pietro Bizzarri, Edward Courtenay, the Earl of Devon, or Seth Cocks—there are many cases in the preceding pages where our quantitative evaluations suggest individuals who might merit article- or even book-length studies or re-evaluations. One such example, highlighted in Chapter 2, is the Principal Secretary Sir William Paget who, unlike many secretaries, is shown to be statistically important within the archive as a whole, but to whom just one book-length study has been devoted, compared to the plethora of studies in which figures such as Thomas Cromwell, Francis Walsingham, and William Cecil, Lord Burghley, have been the subject. We would contend that a comparative study is overdue. Similarly, at the end of Chapter 7 we touch briefly on the persistent structural importance of the diplomat Christopher Mont in news and intelligence transmission—a figure that has (as far as we can tell) received detailed attention only in the form of one article-length study. Mont in particular may benefit from our call, repeated at several junctures throughout the book, to reconsider the history of diplomacy and intelligence trading through meso-level analysis, or collective biographies, in order to understand community-level commonalities. Chapters 3 and 4 suggest several approaches that buttress current lines of scholarly enquiry into early modern diplomacy, providing additional structural evidence for the professionalisation and the changing face of diplomatic personnel over the sixteenth century. Our similarity method helps to provide a more fulsome reckoning of the heterogeneous group of 'intelligence producers' identified by William H. Sherman, which include: scholars, secretaries/clerks, merchants, lawyers/antiquaries, architects/surveyors, military men, ecclesiastical leaders, and foreign intelligence. These are figures whose stories have almost been totally elided. Where their names are mentioned at all in scholarship, the focus is on the events they reported rather than on the men themselves and their intelligence roles. However, while individually these men may not be deemed worthy of their own histories we would contend that, when considered as a group, they are. A call to write a collective history of this extra-diplomatic category, if answered, would allow us to extend the existing scholarship on early modern diplomacy.

Further key insights regarding the mechanisms of foreign intelligence gathering were explored in Chapters 4 and 6. Surveillance is a topic that has not been understudied, thanks to the fascination of the more prominent Tudor conspiracies against Elizabeth I, and there is a growing interest in the operational realities of such practices as letter interception, thanks to the work of figures such as Nadine Akkerman.[2]

---

[2] See Nadine Akkerman, 'The Postmistress, the Diplomat, and a Black Chamber?: Alexandrine of Taxis, Sir Balthazar Gerbier and the Power of Postal Control', in *Diplomacy and Early Modern Culture: Early Modern Literature in History*, ed. Robyn Adams and Rosanna Cox (Palgrave Macmillan, 2011), pp. 172–88.

Chapter 4 provides general methods that can be adopted for a broader understanding of the impact of interception on the shape of the State Papers archive, as well as the everyday realities of Tudor intelligencing—which we have also called for elsewhere.[3] Our methods can be further developed and fine-tuned to understand the methods by which interception was implemented, its personnel, and nature of the materials collected through this process, from the most incendiary conspiratorial plots to the banal and workaday reports. Such work is important to understand the continuities and differences of practice not only between different English secretaries, but also—if we compare different nations' State Papers—between different national contexts. Chapter 6 demonstrates how we can use modularity scores to identify disconnected islands in networks of news dissemination, which often represent examples of letter interception and the archiving of letter bundles.

Returning to meso-scale analysis and the idea of collective biographies, we are hopeful that our chapter on the women that appear in the State Papers will be useful to researchers working in several areas. Our simple heuristic for finding women in petitioning roles will supplement legal studies of early modern women, particularly with regards to the legal and social processes available to widows, estranged wives, and the wives of imprisoned men. The structural argument provided also helps to add support to those scholars who have begun to argue for the influence of different categories of women (such as ladies-in-waiting) or individual women who have previously been dismissed as naive holders of power (such as Honor Plantagenet, Viscountess Lisle, or Jane, Duchess of Feria). In this case, we hope people will be encouraged to use our existing tables of results, made available through our supplementary materials, as well as to adapt the method to other collections.

The usability of our methods for historians not trained in digital methods is a key issue, and one of the reasons that we developed the interactive visualisation *Tudor Networks* alongside our more quantitatively advanced methods for the book.[4] We are hopeful that the materials sitting behind Chapters 6 and 7 might be especially useful as a starting point for other scholars' historical research. The words that change most in usage over the course of the century can open many avenues depending on one's particular research interests. We might look, for example, to work such as the TIDE Project's *Keywords of Identity, Race, and Human Mobility in Early Modern England*, which provides definitions for keywords associated with early modern conceptions of race and identity.[5] We can provide supplementary material for such approaches to conceptual and social history; or a more aggregate approach can aid the now active field of study around early modern news, to explore concrete questions around the transmission of news, with particular attention to speed and geography of dissemination. Chapter 7 also provides various sets of results for those interested in early modern mobility, with tables of the most-travelled people, as well as ways of identifying

---

[3] Midura, Ahnert, and Ahnert, 'Shadow Networks'.   [4] See Albrecht et al., <http://tudornetworks.net/>.
[5] See Nandini Das, João Vicente Melo, Haig Smith, and Lauren Working, *Keywords of Identity, Race, and Human Mobility in Early Modern England* (Amsterdam University Press, 2021), from the ERC-funded project, Travel, Transculturality, and Identity in England, c.1550–1700, <http://www.tideproject.uk/> PI Nandini Das.

those with intersecting itineraries. While the probabilistic ranking of those most stat-istically significant intersections is one of the more sophisticated ways that the mater-ial can be used (particularly for the identification of local intelligence networks for diplomacy and espionage), there is a lot to recommend a more simple and elegant use of the intersections method as a way of identifying people in a certain location on the date of an important event. Such a method allows historians more rapidly to discover other accounts of events, which could either verify or bring into question the veracity of those with which they have been working.

But we also hope that the audience and impact of this book will take us beyond historians of Tudor politics, diplomacy, news, and epistolary culture. We believe that the experiments in each chapter also provide methodological openings for those interested more broadly in data-driven approaches to cultural heritage data. The data-set can be an important testing ground for taking our methods forward; but equally these methods can be applied to other collections data. Other letter collections are the obvious place to start, and excellent efforts are being made by various projects to digi-tise letters, so the opportunities are manifold. Importantly, the potential of the methods we have scoped in the foregoing chapters also scale with the size of the col-lections under question. Follow-on research, which we have conducted with the team behind *Early Modern Letters Online* (EMLO) as part of the Networking Archives pro-ject, has sought to create a 'meta-archive' of almost 450,000 early modern letters by merging the dataset at the heart of this book with the newly curated letters from the Stuart State Papers (1603–1714), and nearly 150 further catalogues brought together in EMLO (a collection broadly shaped by the brief to reassemble the missives of the Republic of Letters). The aims of this follow-on project are both specific and general. Specifically, we are interested to understand how combining these overlapping data-sets provides the basis for experimental case studies that will help us to understand the intersections between the international republic of letters, and the communica-tions networks in the service of the English state. This works at the level of the individual—for example, understanding how the oeuvre of one figure (such as John Milton)[6] relates to the broader economy of information exchange around them—as well as at the level of whole communities and nations.[7]

The more general challenge presented by work like this is how we can understand the impact of the contours of these new digital corpora on the analytical outcomes we can derive and, in turn, the histories we can write. For, while layering up multiple cor-respondences and collections will give us a lot of data, it cannot capture the true world of early modern communication. To what extent is this a problem for the research we can undertake? One of the key criticisms levied at digital humanities research

---

[6] Esther van Raamsdonk and Ruth Ahnert, 'John Milton's Network & The Republic of Letters', in *Digital Approaches to John Milton*, ed. Richard Cunningham and Harvey Quaman, as a special issue of *Renaissance and Reformation/Renaissance et Réforme* 44:3 (2022), 81–110.

[7] The outcomes of this work are reported in Ruth Ahnert, Sebastian E. Ahnert, Philip Beeley, Howard Hoston, Miranda Lewis, Esther van Raamsdonk, and Yann Ryan, *Correspondence Networks in Early Modern Europe: Experiments in Digital History* (work in progress).

concerns the biases of the corpora with which we are working. These biases are multi-layered: they are shaped firstly by collection practices of the originators of the archive, such as the secretaries of state in our case; secondly by what survives the vicissitudes of time; thirdly by the collection policies of libraries and archives, who have been the judges of what is worth collecting; and finally by the coverage of digitisation, which has been driven by piecemeal institutional and national 'policies' (if they can even be called that) and the patchwork coverage of projects. These have created collections that are often without design, as well as being structurally biased, marginalising the voices of women, of racial minorities, and of those otherwise outside the structures of power. In the early days of cultural analytics research scholars worked with the assumption that the scale of the data that they were suddenly able to access would, to some extent, ameliorate the aforementioned biases. However, increasingly, scholarship is engaging with the vital work of examining the extent of such bias in qualitative and quantitative terms. It is of vital importance, because it not only affects large-scale data-driven work, but also small-scale analogue histories (although in these cases source criticism is an easier task to manage).

Our work in Chapter 2 is a contribution to the toolbox of methods needed to undertake this work, and we strongly advocate that all projects working with collections data at scale should undertake such foundational work before they begin on more specific research questions to understand the 'shape' of their archive.[8] Others are taking this work forwards in exciting directions. One route that has proved fruitful for Kaspar Beelen and his collaborators on the Living with Machines project is a method they have termed the 'environmental scan', which constructs a contextual dataset against which to measure digitised corpora to understand their dimensions. In their case, in order to establish how representative was their dataset of ~40 million pages of newspapers of the Victorian press as a whole, they digitised a series of press directories, which provide not only a list of titles, but also additional information about them, including: frequency of publication, price, self-declared political leaning, area of circulation, whose interests they promoted, and the name of the publisher. This provides the authors with vital contextual data at scale to understand the outcomes of their analysis, allowing them to see how, for instance, an overrepresentation of liberal newspapers, or uneven geographical coverage might bias their findings.[9] However, such contextual data is not always possible to identify or create. In this case we can use the inverse logic, as in the piece of work undertaken by Sebastian in collaboration with Yann C. Ryan. To understand how missing epistolary data might be affecting the outcomes of network analysis, they conducted experiments designed to simulate the impact of the kinds of loss often seen in historical correspondence data, including

[8] See also Yann Ryan, Sebastian E. Ahnert, and Ruth Ahnert, 'Networking Archives: Quantitative History and the Contingent Archive', *Proceedings of the Workshop on Computational Humanities Research* (CHR 2020), <http://ceur-ws.org/Vol-2723/>.

[9] See Kaspar Beelen, Jon Lawrence, Daniel C. S. Wilson, David Beavan, 'Victorian Perspectives on Digital Newspapers: Addressing Bias and Representativeness in Digital Heritage Collections', *Digital Scholarship in the Humanities* (2022), <https://doi.org/10.1093/llc/fqac037>.

random document loss, missing years, and errors in the disambiguation and deduplication process. The results show that most network centrality measures maintain robustness until a very large proportion of the data (typically 60% or more) is removed. They conclude with the optimistic news that researchers working with similar historical correspondence datasets might be able to consider network analysis results to be robust in most cases, rather than work on the assumption that missing data would lead to very different findings or results.[10]

Two areas that we are particularly keen to see advanced are the methods and insights of Chapters 6 and 7, which intersect with two very active areas of research: textual analysis and geospatial analysis. The methods presented here are relatively modest compared with cutting-edge data-driven research in these areas. However, the techniques are fitting for the kinds of questions with which humanities scholars might approach collections like this. There are important ways that our work could be taken forward: as well as using the geographical origin of a letter, we can further explore the movement of information and the geographical reach of an individual's intelligence networks by extracting the place names contained within descriptions of letter contents. We are seeing progress in this area in work undertaken by Juri Opitz, and also as part of the Networking Archives project (in a chapter led by Yann C. Ryan).[11] The latter utilises Named Entity Recognition (NER) to 'read' letters for place names contained therein in order to reconstruct the geographical reach of the intelligence network surrounding Undersecretary of State Joseph Williamson—a figure who dominates the Stuart State Papers. This work has the potential to support emerging research into postal routes, undertaken (for different periods) by figures such as Cameron Blevins and Rachel Midura.[12]

The letter descriptions are perhaps one of the areas of this dataset ripest for further methodological interventions and the enrichment of our data. Chapter 7 uses our disambiguated and deduplicated person name lists to search the descriptions of the letter contents for people who mentioned one another before or after intersecting in a given location. However, the more general ability to extract mentions of people from letter contents has the potential to massively enrich this dataset and extend our understanding of the early modern social network. Of course merely using the pre-existing list of senders and recipients severely limits the number of people we can identify. However, using NER as in the work on geographical networks offers huge potential—although it would also require a large effort of curation due to the issues of disambiguation and deduplication we have outlined at length in Chapter 1. This would be another project

---

[10] Yann C. Ryan and Sebastian E. Ahnert, 'The Measure of the Archive: The Robustness of Network Analysis in Early Modern Correspondence', *Journal of Cultural Analytics* 7:57 (2021), <https://doi.org/10.22148/001c.25943>.
[11] See Juri Opitz, 'Automatic Creation of a Large-Scale Tempo-Spatial and Semantic Medieval European Information System', *Proceedings of the Workshop on Computational Humanities Research (CHR 2020)*, <http://ceur-ws.org/Vol-2723/>.
[12] See Cameron Blevins, *Paper Trails: The US Post and the Making of the American West* (Oxford University Press, 2021); Rachel Midura, 'Itinerating Europe: Early Modern Spatial Networks in Printed Itineraries, 1545–1700', *Journal of Social History* 54 (2021), 1023–63.

in its own right, but the outcome could be extremely valuable for scholars of early modern history.

As we have outlined, person and place names (alongside the names of organisations and Calendar dates) offer themselves as the connective tissue that allows us to link, aggregate, and analyse material across multiple archives and collections—not just letters but across the breadth of material collected and catalogued by heritage institutions. The biggest challenge facing research is the siloing of collections data, which is scattered across multiple institutions with their own data standards. National funding councils are finally beginning to tackle this issue. In the UK, the Culture is Digital white paper issued by the Department for Digital, Culture, Media and Sport in 2018 asserted that 'the UK's future will be built at the nexus of our [. . .] cultural creativity and our technical brilliance', and contended that libraries and archives need a 'strategic and coordinated approach to enable more connections and curated content to be available across multiple digitised collections'.[13] However, until recently the UK has lacked investment both in the human and technical infrastructures needed to realise that vision. Inroads are currently being made through the vision projects such as *Towards a National Collection*, which, as the name suggests, is supporting research that breaks down the barriers that exist between the UK's outstanding cultural heritage collections, with the aim of opening them up to new research opportunities and encouraging the public to explore them in new ways.[14] At the moment progress towards this larger vision is being explored through a series of smaller projects under that project's banner, seeking between them to develop tooling, frameworks, and sample collections that will move cultural heritage institutions closer to realising this vision.

These contributions intersect with the more abstract and technical debates around the need to develop common data standards and practices to support the interoperability of datasets both within cultural heritage and research institutions. Such interventions vary from those focused specifically on one kind of document (and engaging with a more historical readership), such as Howard Hotson and Thomas Wallnig's important set of recommendations from the COST-Action Reassembling the Republic of Letters, published in their edited collection *Reassembling the Republic of Letters in the Digital Age: Standards, Systems, Scholarship*,[15] to broader recommendations for shared ontologies and research infrastructures.[16] While such concerns may seem like they are distant from the core concerns of this book, we would contend that the contributions we have made in the previous pages, and in the data, tools, and methods that underpin the book, move us in important ways towards the reality of linked

---

[13] <https://www.gov.uk/government/publications/culture-is-digital>.

[14] Towards a National Collection (AH/V000802/1), PI Rebecca Mary Bailey, see <https://www.nationalcollection.org.uk/>.

[15] Howard Hotson and Thomas Wallnig, eds., *Reassembling the Republic of Letters in the Digital Age: Standards, Systems, Scholarship* (University of Göttingen Press, 2019).

[16] See, for instance, Alison Langmead, Jessica M. Otis, Christopher N. Warren, Scott B. Weingart, and Lisa D. Zilinksi, 'Towards Interoperable Network Ontologies for the Digital Humanities', *International Journal of Humanities and Arts Computing* 10 (2016), 22–35; and Arianna Ciula, Julianne Nyhan, and Claudine Moulin, 'ESF Science Policy Briefing on Research Infrastructures in the Digital Humanities: Landscapes, Ecosystems and Cultures', *Lexicon Philosophicum* 1 (2013), 277–87.

collections, through the development both of tools for the cleaning and linking of collections data and of methods that can help researchers make sense of such data at scale. This feels fitting for a collection like the State Papers, which began, in its own way, as a national project. We are therefore keen for this cleaned and linked data to come full circle, and be integrated as a key component of a future national collection.

Bibliography

Primary Sources

The primary material focuses on the data underlying Parts I–IV of *State Papers Online, 1509–1714* (Thomson Learning EMEA Ltd, 2007). As detailed further in Chapter 1, the letters were extracted from the underlying XML data from this resource (kindly provided by Gale Cengage on hard-drives), and curated for the specific purpose of this project. It has been released as a standalone dataset:

Ruth Ahnert, Sebastian E. Ahnert, Jose Cree, and Lotte Fikkers, '*Tudor Networks of Power -* Correspondence Network Dataset', <https://doi.org/10.17863/CAM.99562>.

Individual documents from within this dataset are referenced in the footnotes using their original shelfmark for the purposes of reproducibility.

Other Primary Sources and Catalogues

Beale, Robert, 'Treatise of the Office of a Counsellor and Principal Secretarie', printed in Conyers Read, *Mr Secretary Walsingham and the Policy of Queen Elizabeth*, 3 vols. (Clarendon Press, 1925), vol. 1, pp. 423–43.

Bowes, Robert, *The Correspondence of Robert Bowes, of Aske, Esquire, the Ambassador of Queen Elizabeth in the Court of Scotland*, ed. Revd J. Stevenson (J. B. Nichols and Son, 1842).

Brewer, J. S., et al., eds., *Letters and Papers, Foreign and Domestic, of the Reign of Henry VIII: Preserved in the Public Record Office, the British Museum, and Elsewhere in England*, 21 vols., vols. 1–4 arr. and catalogued by J. S. Brewer; vols. 5–13 arr. and catalogued by J. Gairdner; vols. 14–21 arr. and catalogued by J. Gairdner and R. H. Brodie (Longman, Green, Longman, & Roberts, 1862–1910).

Danyell, Jane, 'Misfortunes of Jane Danyell', The National Archives, HAD D/F/TYS 71/9.

Danyell, John, 'Danyells Dysasters', The National Archives, HAD D/F/TYS 71/9.

Erasmus, Desiderius, *The Correspondence of Erasmus: Letters 1122 to 1251, 1520 to 1521*, tr. R. A. B. Mynors and annotated by Peter G. Bietenholz (University of Toronto Press, 1988).

Erasmus, Desiderius, *Opus Epistolarum Des. Erasmi Roterodami*, vol. 2: *1514–1517*, ed. P. S. Allen (Oxford University Press, 1910).

Hackett, Richard, *The Letters of Sir John Hackett, 1526–1534*, ed. Elizabeth Frances Rogers (Morgantown, West Virginia University Library, 1971).

Pole, Reginald, *Epistolae Reginaldi Poli S. R. E. Cardinalis et aliorum ad ipsum*, ed. A. M. Quirini, 5 vols. (Bavarian State Library, 1744–57).

Pole, Reginald, *The Correspondence of Reginald Pole, Volume 1, A Calendar, 1518–1546: Beginnings to Legate of Viterbo*, ed. Thomas F. Mayer (Routledge, 2002).

Roberts, Richard Arthur, et al., eds., *Calendar of the Manuscripts of the Most Honourable the Marquess of Salisbury: preserved at Hatfield House, Hertfordshire*, 24 vols., vols. 1–13 issued as Gt. Brit. Parliament. Papers by command; vols. 11–12 edited by R. A. Roberts; vols. 13–14 by E. Salisbury; vols. 15–20 by M. S. Giuseppi; and vols. 21–4 by G. D. Owen. (HMSO, 1883–1976).

Schmettau, H., and B. H. Cowper, eds., *The Reformers of England and Germany in the Sixteenth Century: Their Intercourse and Correspondence* (Hatchard & Company, 1859).

Wernham, Richard Bruce, ed., *List and Analysis of State Papers, Foreign Series: Elizabeth I*, 6 vols. (HMSO, 1964–89).

Secondary Sources

Adams, Robyn, 'A Most Secret Service: William Herle and the Circulation of News', in *Diplomacy and Early Modern Culture*, ed. Adams and Cox, pp. 63–81.

Adams, Robyn, and Rosanna Cox, eds., *Diplomacy and Early Modern Culture: Early Modern Literature in History* (Palgrave Macmillan, 2011).

Ahnert, Ruth, 'Maps Versus Networks', in *News Networks in Early Modern Europe*, ed. Noah Moxham and Joad Raymond (Brill, 2016), pp. 130–58.

Ahnert, Ruth, *The Rise of Prison Literature in the Sixteenth Century* (Cambridge University Press, 2013).

Ahnert, Ruth, and Sebastian E. Ahnert, 'Metadata, Surveillance, and the Tudor State', *History Workshop Journal* 87 (2019), 27–51.

Ahnert, Ruth, and Sebastian E. Ahnert, 'Protestant Letter Networks in the Reign of Mary I: A Quantitative Approach', *English Literary History* 82 (2015).

Ahnert, Ruth, Sebastian E. Ahnert, Catherine N. Coleman, and Scott B. Weingart, *The Network Turn: Changing Perspectives in the Humanities* (Cambridge University Press, 2020),

Akkerman, Nadine, *Invisible Agents: Women and Espionage in Seventeenth-Century Britain* (Oxford University Press, 2018).

Akkerman, Nadine, 'The Postmistress, the Diplomat, and a Black Chamber? Alexandrine of Taxis, Sir Balthazar Gerbier and the Power of Postal Control', in *Diplomacy and Early Modern Culture*, ed. Adams and Cox.

Albert, Reka, and Albert-László Barabási, 'Statistical Mechanics of Complex Networks', *Rev. Mod. Phys.* 74 (2002), 47–97.

Albrecht, Kim, Sebastian E. Ahnert, and Ruth Ahnert, *Tudor Networks*: Interactive web visualization (2020), available at: <http://tudornetworks.net>.

Alford, Stephen, 'Politicians and Statesmen II: William Cecil, Lord Burghley (1520–98)', *State Papers Online, 1509–1714* (Thomson Learning EMEA Ltd, 2007). Available at: <https://www.gale.com/intl/essays>.

Alford, Stephen, 'Some Elizabethan Spies in the Office of Sir Francis Walsingham', in *Diplomacy and Early Modern Culture*, ed. Adams and Cox, pp. 46–62.

Alford, Stephen, 'State Papers of Edward VI, Mary I and Elizabeth I', *State Papers Online, 1509–1714* (Thomson Learning EMEA Ltd, 2007). Available at: <https://www.gale.com/intl/essays>.

Alford, Stephen, *The Watchers: A Secret History of the Reign of Elizabeth I* (Penguin, 2012).

Allen, E. John B., *Post and Courier Service in the Diplomacy of Early Modern Europe* (Nijhoff, 1972).

Andrews, Kenneth R., ed., *The Last Voyage of Drake and Hawkins* (Hakluyt Society, 1972).

Armstrong, Edward, *The Emperor Charles V*, vol. 1 (Macmillan, 1902).

Aston, Margaret, 'English Ruins and English History: The Dissolution and the Sense of the Past', *Journal of the Warburg and Courtauld Institutes* 36 (1973), 231–55.

Badeloch, Noldus, Marika Keblusek, and Hans Cools, eds., *Your Humble Servant: Agents in Early Modern Europe* (Uitgeverij Verloren, 2006).

Bannister, Scott-Smith, *Names and Naming Patterns in England 1538–1700* (Oxford University Press, 1997).

Barabási, Albert-László, *Linked: The New Science of Networks* (Perseus, 2002).

Barabási, Albert-László, and Reka Albert, 'Emergence of Scaling in Random Networks', *Science* 286 (1999), 509–12.

Barker, Nicolas, 'The Perils of Publishing in the Sixteenth Century: Pietro Bizari and William Parry, Two Elizabethan Misfits', in *England and the Continental Renaissance: Essays in Honour of J. B. Trapp*, ed. Edward Chaney and Peter Mack (Boydell and Brewer, 1990), pp. 125–42.

Baron, Alistair, Paul Rayson, and Dawn Archer, 'Word Frequency and Key Word Statistics in Historical Corpus Linguistics', *Anglistik: International Journal of English Studies* 20 (2009), 41–67.

Barry, Judith Hudson, 'Norris, Sir Thomas (1556–1599)', *ODNB*, <https://doi.org/10.1093/ref:odnb/20285>.

Bath, Michael, '"Rare shewes and singular inventions": The Stirling Baptism of Prince Henry', *Journal of the Northern Renaissance* 4 (2012), <http://www.northernrenaissance.org/rare-shewes-and-singular-inventions-the-stirling-baptism-of-prince-henry/>.

Bartlett, Kenneth R., 'Bizzarri, Pietro (b. 1525, d. in or after 1586)', *ODNB*. Available at: <https://doi.org/10.1093/ref:odnb/2487>.

Bartlett, Kenneth R., '"The misfortune that is wished for him": The Exile and Death of Edward Courtenay, Earl of Devon', *Canadian Journal of History* 14 (1979), 1–28.

Beckingham, C. F., 'Banister, Thomas (d. 1571)', *ODNB*, <https://doi.org/10.1093/ref:odnb/47037>.

Beelen, Kaspar, Jon Lawrence, Daniel C. S. Wilson, and David Beavan, 'Victorian Perspectives on Digital Newspapers: Addressing Bias and Representativeness in Digital Heritage Collections', *Digital Scholarship in the Humanities* (2022), <https://doi.org/10.1093/llc/fqac037>.

Beer, Barrett L., and Sybil M. Jack, eds., *The Letters of William, Lord Paget of Beaudesert, 1547–63*, Camden Fourth Series, vol. 13 (Camden Society, 1974).

Behrens, Betty, 'The Office of the English Resident Ambassador: Its Evolution as Illustrated by the Career of Sir Thomas Spinelly, 1509–22', *Transactions of the Royal Historical Society* 16 (1933), 161–95.

Bell, Gary M., *A Handlist of British Diplomatic Representatives* (Royal Historical Society, 1990).

Bell, Gary M., 'Gilpin, George (d. 1602)', *ODNB*, <https://doi.org/10.1093/ref:odnb/10758>.

Bernard, G. W., *The King's Reformation: Henry VIII and the Remaking of the English Church* (Yale University Press, 2005).

Bevan, Amanda, 'State Papers of Henry VIII: The Archives and Documents', *State Papers Online, 1509–1714* (Cengage Learning EMEA Ltd., 2007). Available at: <https://www.gale.com/intl/essays>.

Bindoff, S. T., ed., *The History of Parliament: The House of Commons 1509–1558*, 3 vols. (Published for the History of Parliament Trust by Secker & Warburg, 1982).

Biow, Douglas, *Doctors, Ambassadors, Secretaries Humanism and Professions in Renaissance Italy* (University of Chicago Press, 2002).

Blanchard, Ian, 'Vaughan, Stephen (b. in or before 1502, d. 1549)', *ODNB*, <https://doi.org/10.1093/ref:odnb/28146>.

Blevins, Cameron, *Paper Trails: The US Post and the Making of the American West* (Oxford University Press, 2021).

Bode, Katherine, *A World of Fiction: Digital Collections and the Future of Literary History* (University of Michigan Press, 2018).

Bodenhamer, David J., John Corrigan, and Trevor M. Harris, eds., *The Spatial Humanities: GIS and the Future of Humanities Scholarship* (Indiana University Press, 2010).

Borgatti, Stephen P., 'Centrality and Network Flow', *Social Networks* 27 (2005), 55–71.

Bossy, John, *Giordano Bruno and the Embassy Affair* (Yale University Press, 1991).

Bowden, Caroline M. K., 'Cecil [née Cooke], Mildred, Lady Burghley (1526–1589)', *ODNB*, <https://doi.org/10.1093/ref:odnb/46675>.

Bowden, Caroline M. K., 'The Library of Mildred Cooke Cecil, Lady Burghley', *The Library: Transactions of the Bibliographical Society* 6 (2005), 3–29.

Bowden, Caroline M. K., 'Women as Intermediaries: An Example of the Use of Literacy in the Late Sixteenth and Early Seventeenth Centuries', *History of Education* 22 (1993), 215–23.

Brownlees, Nicholas, '"Newes also came by Letters": Functions and Features of Epistolary News in English News Publications of the Seventeenth Century', in *News Networks in Early Modern Europe*, ed. Joad Raymond and Noah Moxham (Brill, 2016), pp. 394–419.

Brughmans, Tom, Anna Collar, and Fiona Coward, eds., *The Connected Past: Challenges to Network Studies in Archaeology and History* (Oxford University Press, 2016).

Burge, Caitlin, 'Letters, Networks of Power, and the Fall of Thomas Cromwell, 1523–1547' (unpublished doctoral thesis, 2022). Available from: <https://qmro.qmul.ac.uk>.

Burt, Ronald S., *Structural Holes: The Social Structure of Competition* (Harvard University Press, 1992).

Burton, Antoinette M., ed., *Archive Stories: Facts, Fictions, and the Writing of History* (Duke University Press, 2005).

Bush, M. L., 'The Lisle–Seymour Land Disputes: A Study of Power and Influence in the 1530s', *The Historical Journal* 9 (1966), 255–74.

Carley, James P., 'Blount, William, Fourth Baron Mountjoy (*c.*1478–1534)', *ODNB*. Available at: <https://doi.org/10.1093/ref:odnb/2702>.

Carrafiello, Michael L., 'English Catholicism and the Jesuit Mission of 1580–1581', *The Historical Journal* 37 (1994), 761–74.

Centola, Damon, and Michael Macy, 'Complex Contagions and the Weakness of Long Ties', *American Journal of Sociology* 113 (2007), 702–34.

Certeau, Michel de, *The Practice of Everyday Life*, tr. Stephen Rendall (University of California Press, 1984).

Chibi, Andrew A., 'Sampson, Richard (d. 1554)', *ODNB*, <https://doi.org/10.1093/ref:odnb/24594>.

Ciula, Arianna Julianne Nyhan, and Claudine Moulin, 'ESF Science Policy Briefing on Research Infrastructures in the Digital Humanities: Landscapes, Ecosystems and Cultures', *Lexicon Philosophicum* 1 (2013), 277–87.

Clough, Cecil H., 'Gigli, Silvestro (1463–1521)', *ODNB*, <https://doi.org/10.1093/ref:odnb/10671>.

Cocks, J. V. Somers, *A History of the Cocks Family* (J. Somers Cocks, 1967, rev. 1999).

Cohen, Deborah, and Peter Mandler, 'The History Manifesto: A Critique', *American Historical Review* 120:2 (2015), 530–42.

Coleman, Catherine N., 'Seeking the Eye of History: The Design of Digital Tools for Enlightenment Studies', in *Digitizing Enlightenment: Digital Humanities and the Transformation of Eighteenth-Century Studies*, ed. Simon Burrows and Glenn Roe (Liverpool University Press, 2020).

Collett, Barry, 'Giustinian, Sebastian (1460–1543)', *ODNB*, <https://doi.org/10.1093/ref:odnb/70789>.

Colthorpe, Marion E., *The Elizabethan Court Day by Day*, available at: <https://folgerpedia.folger.edu/The_Elizabethan_Court_Day_by_Day>.

Craigwood, Joanna, 'Sidney, Gentili, and the Poetics of Embassy', in *Diplomacy and Early Modern Culture*, ed. Adams and Cox, pp. 82–100.

Crankshaw, David J., 'The Tudor Privy Council, c.1540–1603', *State Papers Online, 1509–1714* (Thomson Learning EMEA Ltd, 2007). Available at: <https://www.gale.com/intl/essays>.

Crummé, Hannah Leah, 'Jane Dormer's Recipe for Politics: A Refuge Household in Spain for Mary Tudor's Ladies-in-Waiting', in *The Politics of Female Households: Ladies-in-Waiting Across Early Modern Europe*, ed. Nadine Akkerman and Birgit Houben (Brill, 2013), pp. 51–71.

Curtis, Cathy, 'Pace, Richard (1483?–1536)', *ODNB*, <https://doi.org/10.1093/ref:odnb/21065>.

Das, Nandini, João Vicente Melo, Haig Smith, and Lauren Working, *Keywords of Identity, Race, and Human Mobility in Early Modern England* (Amsterdam University Press, 2021).

Dawson, Jane E. A., 'William Cecil and the British Dimension of Elizabethan Foreign Policy', *History* 74 (1989), 196–216.

Daybell, James, *The Material Letter in Early Modern England: Manuscript Letters and the Culture and Practices of Letter-Writing, 1512–1635* (Palgrave Macmillan, 2012).

Daybell, James, *Women Letter-Writers in Tudor England* (Oxford University Press, 2006).

D'Ignazio, Catherine, and Lauren F. Klein, *Data Feminism* (The MIT Press, 2020).

Dobb, Clifford, 'London's Prisons', *Shakespeare Survey* 17 (1964), 87–102.

Doran, Susan, *Elizabeth I and Foreign Policy, 1558–1603* (Routledge, 2002).

Edwards, Francis, *Plots and Plotters in the Reign of Elizabeth I* (Four Courts Press, 2002).

Ellis, Steven, 'Centre and Periphery in the Tudor State', in *A Companion to Tudor Britain*, ed. Robert Tittler and Norman Jones (Blackwell, 2004), pp. 133–50.

Ellis, Steven, *Tudor Frontiers and Noble Power: The Making of the British State* (Clarendon, 1995).

Everett, Martin G., and Thomas W. Valente, 'Bridging, Brokerage and Betweenness', *Soc. Networks* 44 (2016), 202–8.

Eyers, Tom, 'The Perils of the "Digital Humanities": New Positivisms and the Fate of Literary Theory', *Postmodern Culture: Journal of Interdisciplinary Thought on Contemporary Cultures* 23:2 (2013).

Finnegan, David, 'Fitzgerald, Gerald [Garret, Gearóid], Eleventh Earl of Kildare (1525–1585)', *ODNB*, <https://doi.org/10.1093/ref:odnb/9557>.

Firpo, Massimo, *Pietro Bizzarri, esule italiano del cinquecento* (Giappichelli, 1971).

Fletcher, Catherine, *Diplomacy in Renaissance Rome: The Rise of the Resident Ambassador* (Cambridge University Press, 2015).

Fletcher, Catherine, *The Divorce of Henry VIII: The Untold Story* (Vintage, 2014).

Flynn, Dennis, *John Donne and the Ancient Catholic Nobility* (Indiana University Press, 1995).

Freeman, Linton C., 'Set of Measures of Centrality Based on Betweenness', *Sociometry* 40 (1977), 35–41.

Frigo, Daniela, *Politics and Diplomacy in Early Modern Italy: The Structure of Diplomatic Practice, 1450–1800* (Cambridge University Press, 2002).

Fritze, Ronald H., 'Yonge, John (1466/7–1516)', *ODNB*, <https://doi.org/10.1093/ref:odnb/30227>.

Frye, Susan, *Elizabeth I: The Competition for Representation* (Oxford University Press, 1996).

Gammon, Samuel Rhea, *Statesman and Schemer: William, First Lord Paget, Tudor Minister* (David & Charles, 1973).

Garcia-Arenal, Mercedes, *Ahmad Al-Mansur: The Beginnings of Modern Morocco* (One World, 2009).

Gladwell, Malcolm, *The Tipping Point: How Little Things Can Make a Big Difference* (Little, Brown, 2000).

Goldring, Elizabeth, Jayne Elisabeth Archer, and Elizabeth Clarke, eds., John Nichols, *The Progresses and Public Processions of Queen Elizabeth: Volume III: 1579 to 1595* (Oxford University Press, 2013).

Gonzalez, Marta C., Cesar A. Hidalgo, and Albert-Laszlo Barabasi, 'Understanding Individual Human Mobility Patterns', *Nature* 453 (2008), 779.

Gorden, Andrew, 'Recovering Agency in the Epistolary Traffic of Frances, Countess of Essex and Jane Daniell', in *Women and Epistolary Agency in Early Modern Culture, 1450–1690*, ed. James Daybell and Andrew Gordon (Routledge, 2016), pp. 182–206.

Gordon, Andrew, and James Daybell, 'Living Letter: Re-reading Correspondence and Women's Letters', in *Women and Epistolary Agency, 1450–1690*, ed. James Daybell and Andrew Gordon (Routledge, 2016), pp. 1–20.

Gould, Roger V., and Roberto M. Fernandez, 'A Formal Approach to Brokerage in Transaction Networks', *Sociological Methodology* 19 (1989), 89–126.

Graham, Shawn, Ian Milligan, and Scott Weingart, *Exploring Big Historical Data: The Historian's Macroscope* (Imperial College Press, 2015).

Graham, Shawn, Scott Weingart, and Ian Milligan, 'Getting Started with Topic Modeling and MALLET', *The Programming Historian* 1 (2012). Available at: <https://doi.org/10.46430/phen0017>.

Granovetter, Mark S., 'The Strength of Weak Ties', *American Journal of Sociology* 78 (1973), 1360–80.

Gregory, Brad, *Salvation at Stake: Christian Martyrdom in Early Modern Europe* (Harvard University Press, 1999).

Gregory, Brad, 'The Anathema of Compromise: Christian Martyrdom in Early Modern Europe' (unpublished PhD thesis, Princeton University, 1996).

Gregory, Ian N., *A Place in History: A Guide to Using GIS in Historical Research* (Oxbow, 2003).

Greteman, Blaine, *Networking Print in Shakespeare's England: Influence, Agency, and Revolutionary Change* (Stanford University Press, 2021).

Grummitt, David, 'Plantagenet, Arthur, Viscount Lisle (b. before 1472, d. 1542)', *ODNB*, <https://doi.org/10.1093/ref:odnb/22355>.

Guldi, Jo, 'Critical Search: A Procedure for Guided Reading in Large-Scale Textual Corpora', *Journal of Cultural Analytics* 3:1 (2018), <https://doi.org/10.22148/16.030>.

Guldi, Jo, 'What is the Spatial Turn?', <https://spatial.scholarslab.org/spatial-turn/>.

Guldi, Jo, and David Armitage, *The History Manifesto* (Cambridge University Press, 2014).

Gunn, S. J., 'Brandon, Charles, First Duke of Suffolk (c.1484–1545)', *ODNB*. Available at: <https://doi.org/10.1093/ref:odnb/3260>.

Gunn, Steven, *Early Tudor Government, 1485–1558* (Palgrave, 1995).

Guy, John, *Elizabeth: The Forgotten Years* (Viking, 2016).

Hackel, Heidi Brayman, *Reading Material in Early Modern England: Print, Gender, and Literacy* (Cambridge University Press, 2005).

Hammer, Paul E. J., *Elizabeth's Wars: War, Government and Society in Tudor England, 1544–1604* (Palgrave Macmillan, 2003).

Hammer, Paul E. J., *The Polarisation of Elizabethan Politics: The Political Career of Robert Devereux, 2nd Earl of Essex, 1585–1597* (Cambridge University Press, 1999).

Hampton, Timothy, *Fictions of Embassy: Literature and Diplomacy in Early Modern Europe* (Cornell University Press, 2009).

Hanawalt, Barbara A., 'Lady Honour Lisle's Network of Influence', in *Women and Power in the Middle Ages*, ed. Mary Erler and Maryanne Kowaleski (University of Georgia Press, 1988), pp. 188–214.

Haynes, Alan, *Walsingham: Elizabethan Spymaster & Statesman* (The History Press, 2007).

Hildebrandt, Esther, 'Christopher Mont, Anglo-German Diplomat', *Sixteenth Century Journal* 15:3 (1984), 281–92.

Hoak, Dale, 'Re-habilitating the Duke of Northumberland: Politics and Political Control, 1549–53', in *The Mid-Tudor Polity, c.1540–1560*, ed. Jennifer Loach and Robert Tittler (MacMillan, 1980), pp. 29–51.

Holland, Paul W., and Samuel Leinhardt, 'A Method for Detecting Structure in Sociometric Data', *American Journal of Sociology* 76 (1970), 492–513.

Holland, Paul W., and Samuel Leinhardt, 'The Statistical Analysis of Local Structure in Social Networks', *NBER Working Papers 0044*, National Bureau of Economic Research (1974).

Holt, Mack P., *The Duke of Anjou and the Politique Struggle During the Wars of Religion* (Cambridge University Press, 1986).

Hotson, Howard, and Thomas Wallnig, eds., *Reassembling the Republic of Letters in the Digital Age: Standards, Systems, Scholarship* (University of Göttingen Press, 2019).

Hoyle, R. W., 'Darcy, Thomas, Baron Darcy of Darcy (b. in or before 1467, d. 1537)', *ODNB*, <https://doi.org/10.1093/ref:odnb/7148>.

Hughes, Charles, 'Nicholas Faunt's Discourse Touching the Office of Principal Secretary of Estate, & c.1592', *English Historical Review* 20 (1905), 499–508.

Hughes, Jonathan, 'Somerset, Charles, First Earl of Worcester (c.1460–1526)', *ODNB*, <https://doi.org/10.1093/ref:odnb/26004>.

Hunt, L. E., 'Vannes, Peter (c.1488–1563)', *ODNB*, <https://doi.org/10.1093/ref:odnb/28097>.

Hutchinson, Robert, *Elizabeth's Spymaster* (Orion, 2011).

Hyvönen, Eero, Ruth Ahnert, Sebastian E. Ahnert, Jouni Tuominen, Eetu Mäkelä, Miranda Lewis, and Gertjan Filarski, 'Reconciling Metadata: Semi-Automated Tools', in *Reassembling the Republic of Letters in the Digital Age: Standards, Systems, Scholarship*, ed. Howard Hotson and Thomas Wallnig (Göttingen University Press, 2019), pp. 223–36.

Infelise, Mario, 'From Merchants' Letters to Handwritten Political *avvisi*: Notes on the Origins of Public Information', in *Correspondence and Cultural Exchange in Europe*, ed. Francisco Bethencourt and Florike Egmond (Cambridge University Press, 2007), pp. 41–2.

Ingold, Tim, 'Against Space: Place, Movement, Knowledge', in *Boundless Worlds: An Anthropological Approach to Movement*, ed. Peter Wynn Kirby (Berghahn Books, 2009).

Jacks, Philip, and William Caferro, *The Spinelli of Florence: Fortunes of a Renaissance Merchant Family* (Penn State University Press, 2001).

Jardine, Lisa, *Temptation in the Archives: Essays in Golden Age Dutch Culture* (UCL Press, 2015).

Jardine, Lisa, and William Sherman, 'Pragmatic Readers: Knowledge Transactions and Scholarly Services in Late Elizabethan England', in *Religion, Culture and Society in Early Modern Britain: Essays in Honour of Patrick Collinson*, ed. Anthony Fletcher and Peter Roberts (Cambridge University Press, 1994), pp. 102–24.

Jenkins, J. G., ed., *A History of the County of Stafford*, vol. 3 (Victoria County History, 1970).

Johnson, Margot, 'Ruthall, Thomas (d. 1523)', *ODNB*, <https://doi.org/10.1093/ref:odnb/24359>.

Jones, Norman, *Governing by Virtue: Lord Burghley and the Management of Elizabethan England* (Oxford University Press, 2015).

Kaufman, Peter Iver, 'Queen Elizabeth's Leadership Abroad: The Netherlands in the 1570s', in *Leadership and Elizabethan Culture*, ed. Peter Iver Kaufman (Springer, 2013), chapter 5.

Keblusek, Marika, and Badeloch Vera Noldus, eds., *Double Agents: Cultural and Political Brokerage in Early Modern Europe* (Brill Publishers, 2011).

Ketelaar, Eric, 'Tacit Narratives: The Meanings of Archives', *Archival Science* 1:2 (2001), 131–41.

Kinney, Arthur F., and Jane Lawson, *Titled Elizabethans: A Directory of Elizabethan Court, State, and Church Officers, 1558–1603* (Palgrave Macmillan, 2014).

Knecht, R. J., *The French Civil Wars, 1562–1598* (Longman, 2000).

Knighton, C. S., 'The Calendars and their Editors, 1856–2006', *State Papers Online, 1509–1714* (Thomson Learning EMEA Ltd, 2007). Available at: <https://www.gale.com/intl/essays>.

Knighton, C. S., 'The Principal Secretaries in the Reign of Edward VI: Reflections on Their Office and Archive', in *Law and Government Under the Tudors: Essays Presented to Sir Geoffrey Elton Regius Professor of Modern History in the University of Cambridge on the Occasion of His Retirement*, ed. Claire Cross, David Loades, and J. J. Scarisbrick (Cambridge University Press, 1988), pp. 163–76.

Knowles, Anne Kelly, and Amy Hiller, eds., *Placing History: How Maps, Spatial Data, and GIS are Changing Historical Scholarship* (ESRI Press, 2008).

Koenigsberger, H. G., *Monarchies, States Generals and Parliaments: The Netherlands in the Fifteenth and Sixteenth Centuries* (Cambridge University Press, 2001).

Konnert, Mark W., *Local Politics in the French Wars of Religion: The Towns of Champagne, the Duc de Guise, and the Catholic League, 1560–95* (Taylor and Francis, 2017).

Kuin, Roger, ed., *The Correspondence of Sir Philip Sidney*, vol. 1 (Oxford University Press, 2012).

Lamal, Nina, 'Communicating Conflict: Early Modern Soldiers as Information-Gatherers', *Journal of Medieval and Early Modern Studies* 50 (2020), 13–31.

Lammes, Sybille, Chris Perkins, Alex Gekker, Sam Hind, Clancy Wilmott, and Daniel Evans, eds., *Time for Mapping: Cartographic Temporalities* (Manchester University Press, 2018).

Lang, R. G., 'Social Origins and Aspirations of Jacobean London Merchants', *Economic History Review* 27:1 (1974), 28–47.

Langmead, Alison, Jessica M. Otis, Christopher N. Warren, Scott B. Weingart, and Lisa D. Zilinksi, 'Towards Interoperable Network Ontologies for the Digital Humanities', *International Journal of Humanities and Arts Computing* 10 (2016), 22–35.

Latour, Bruno, 'Anti-Zoom', <http://www.bruno-latour.fr/sites/default/files/P-170-ELIASSON-GBpdf.pdf>.

Latour, Bruno, Pablo Jensen, Tommaso Venturini, Sébastian Grauwin and Dominique Boullier, '"The whole is always smaller than its parts": A Digital Test of Gabriel Tardes' Monads', *British Journal of Sociology* 63 (2012), 590–615.

Leadham, I. S., *Selden Society: Select Cases before the King's Council in the Star Chamber*, vol. 2 (B. Quaritch, 1903–11).

Leimon, M., and G. Parker, 'Treason and Plot in Elizabethan Diplomacy: The "Fame of Sir Edward Stafford" Reconsidered', *The English Historical Review* 111:.444 (1996), 1134–58.

Lewis, Lesley, *The Thomas More Family: Group Portraits after Holbein* (Gracewing, 1998).

Lewis, Miranda Arno Bosse, Howard Hotson, Thomas Wallnig, and Dirk van Miert, 'Time', in *Reassembling the Republic of Letters in the Digital Age: Standards, Systems, Scholarship*, ed. Howard Hotson and Thomas Wallnig (University of Göttingen Press, 2019), pp. 97–118.

Lincoln, Matthew, 'Confabulation in the Humanities', available at: <https://matthewlincoln.net/2015/03/21/confabulation-in-the-humanities.html>.

Loades, David, 'Tonge [née White], Susan [known as Susan Clarencius] (b. before 1510, d. in or after 1564)', *ODNB*, <https://doi.org/10.1093/ref:odnb/94978>.

Loomie, Albert J., *The Spanish Elizabethans: The English Exiles at the Court of Philip II* (Burns and Oates, 1965).

Loudon, Mark, 'Rogers, Daniel (*c.*1538–1591)', *ODNB*, <https://doi.org/10.1093/ref:odnb/23969>.

Loughlin, Mark, 'Maitland, William, of Lethington (1525×30–1573)', *ODNB*, <https://doi.org/10.1093/ref:odnb/17838>.

Lugioyo, Brian, *Martin Bucer's Doctrine of Justification: Reformation Theology and Early Modern Irenicism* (Oxford University Press, 2010).

Lynch, Michael, 'Queen Mary's Triumph: The Baptismal Celebrations at Stirling in December 1566', *Scottish Historical Review* 69 (1990), 1–21.

McCabe, Richard Anthony, *'Ungainefull Arte': Poetry, Patronage, and Print in the Early Modern Era* (Oxford University Press, 2016).

MacCaffrey, Wallace T., *Elizabeth I: War and Politics, 1588–1603* (Princeton University Press, 1994).

MacCaffrey, Wallace T., *Queen Elizabeth and the Making of Policy, 1572–1588* (Princeton University Press, 2014).

McClure, Ellen M., *Sunspots and the Sun King: Sovereignty and Mediation in Seventeenth-Century France* (Chicago University Press, 2006).

McConica, James, 'Erasmus, Desiderius (*c.*1467–1536)', *ODNB*, <https://doi.org/10.1093/ref:odnb/39358>.

McConville, Sean, *A History of English Prison Administration: Volume 1, 1750–1877* (Routledge and Kegan Paul, 1981).

McCoog, Thomas M., 'Perkins , Sir Christopher (1542/3–1622)', *ODNB*, <https://doi.org/10.1093/ref:odnb/21968>.

McCoog, Thomas M., *The Society of Jesus in Ireland, Scotland, and England, 1589–1597: Building the Faith of Saint Peter upon the King of Spain's Monarchy* (Routledge, 2016).

McDonough, Katherine, 'Putting the Eighteenth Century on the Map: A Proposal for Early Modern French Geospatial Data Development', in *Digitizing Enlightenment*, ed. Glenn Roe and Simon Burrows, (Oxford Studies in the Enlightenment/Liverpool University Press, 2019).

McEntegart, Rory, *Henry VIII, the League of Schmalkalden, and the English Reformation* (Boydell and Brewer, 2002).

McGladdery, C. A., 'Bowes, Robert (d. 1597), *ODNB*, <https://doi.org/10.1093/ref:odnb/3059>.

MacMahon, Luke, 'Mont, Christopher (1496/7–1572), *ODNB*, <https://doi.org/10.1093/ref:odnb/18994>.

Magnusson, Lynne, 'A Rhetoric of Requests: Genre and Linguistic Scripts in Elizabethan Women's Suitors' Letters', in *Women and Politics in Early Modern England, 1450–1700*, ed. James Daybell (Taylor and Francis Group, 2004), pp. 51–66.

Mancell, Peter C., *Hakluyt's Promise: An Elizabethan's Obsession for an English America* (Princeton University Press, 2010).

Mattingly, Garrett, *Renaissance Diplomacy* (Houghton Mifflin, 1955).

Mears, Natalie, *Queenship and Political Discourse in the Elizabethan Realms* (Cambridge University Press, 2005).

Mears, Natalie, Ludovic Moncla, and Matje van de Camp, 'Named Entity Recognition Goes to Old Regime France: Geographic Text Analysis for Early Modern French Corpora', *International Journal of Geographical Information Science, Special Section: Spatial Computing and Digital Humanities* 33 (2019), 2498–522.

Midura, Rachel, 'Itinerating Europe: Early Modern Spatial Networks in Printed Itineraries, 1545–1700', *Journal of Social History* 54 (2021), 1023–63.

Midura, Rachel, Sebastian E. Ahnert, and Ruth Ahnert, 'Shadow Networks: Intercept Letters in the British State Papers, 1580–1603', in *Network Analysis and the Early Modern Archive*, ed. Ruth Ahnert, Philip Beeley, Esther van Raamsdonk, and Yann Ryan as a special issue of *Huntington Library Quarterly* (forthcoming, June 2023).

Miller, Clarence H., 'Chaloner, Sir Thomas, the Elder (1521–1565)', *ODNB*, <https://doi.org/10.1093/ref:odnb/5040>.

Milligan, Ian, *The Transformation of Historical Research in the Digital Age* (Cambridge University Press, 2022).

Morgan, Hiram, 'The Fall of Sir John Perrot', in *The Reign of Elizabeth I: Court and Culture in the Last Decade*, ed. John Guy (Cambridge University Press, 1995), pp. 109–25.

Murrieta-Flores, Patricia, Christopher Donaldson, and Ian Gregory, 'GIS and Literary History: Advancing Digital Humanities Research through the Spatial Analysis of Historical Travel Writing and Topographical Literature', *Digital Humanities Quarterly* 11 (2007).

Newcombe, D. G., 'Tunstal, Cuthbert (1474–1559)', *ODNB*, <https://doi.org/10.1093/ref:odnb/27817>.

Newman, Mark E. J., *Networks: An Introduction* (Oxford University Press, 2010).

Nurmi, Arja, 'The English Language of the Early Modern Period', in *A New Companion to English Renaissance Literature and Culture*, ed. Michael Hattaway (Blackwell, 2010), pp. 15–26.

Opitz, Juri, 'Automatic Creation of a Large-Scale Tempo-Spatial and Semantic Medieval European Information System', *Proceedings of the Workshop on Computational Humanities Research* (CHR 2020), <http://ceur-ws.org/Vol-2723/>.

Ormrod, W. Mark, *Women and Parliament in Later Medieval England* (Palgrave Macmillan, 2020).

Overell, Anne M., 'A Nicodemite in England and Italy: Edward Courtenay, 1548–56', in *John Foxe at Home and Abroad,* ed. David Loades (Ashgate, 2004), pp. 117–35.

Overell, Anne M., *Italian Reform and English Reformations, c.1535–c.1585* (Routledge, 2008).

Parmiter, Geoffrey de C., *The King's Great Matter: A Study of Anglo-papal Relations 1527–1534* (Barnes & Noble, 1967).

Pawlicka-Deger, Urszula, and Christopher Thomson, *Digital Humanities and Laboratories: Perspectives on Knowledge, Infrastructure and Culture* (Routledge, forthcoming in 2023).

Peeples, Matthew, 'Network Science and Statistical Techniques for Dealing with Uncertainties in Archaeological Datasets', <http://www.mattpeeples.net/netstats.html>.

Pettegree, Andrew, *The Invention of News: How the World Came to Know About Itself* (Yale University Press, 2014).

Pieper, Renate, 'Trading with Art and Curiosities in Southern Germany before the Thirty Years' War', in *Markets for Art, 1400–1800,* ed. Clara Eugenia Núñez (Universidad de Sevilla, 1998), pp. 87–101.

Polwhele, Richard, *The History of Cornwall, Civil, Military, Religious, Architectural, Agricultural, Commercial, Biographical, and Miscellaneous,* vol. 4 (T. Flindell for Castell & Davies, 1816).

Potter, David, 'Mid-Tudor Foreign Policy and Diplomacy, 1547–63', in *Tudor England and Its Neighbours,* ed. Glenn Richardson and Susan Doran (Macmillan, 2005), pp. 106–38.

Potter, Harry, *Edinburgh under Siege 1571–1573* (Stroud, 2003).

Prescott, Andrew, 'What Price Gale Cengage?', blog post available at: <https://medium.com/digital-riffs/what-price-gale-cengage-668d358ce5cd>.

Przychocki, Gustavus, 'Richard Croke's Search for Patristic MSS in Connexion with the Divorce of Catherine', *Journal of Theological Studies* 13 (1911–12), 285–95.

Putnam, Lara, 'The Transnational and the Text-Searchable: Digitized Sources and the Shadows They Cast', *American Historical Review* 121 (2016), 377–402.

Quinn, David B., *England and the Azores, 1581–1582: Three Letters* (Imprensa de Coimbra, 1979).

Raamsdonk, Esther van, and Ruth Ahnert, 'John Milton's Network & The Republic of Letters', in *Digital Approaches to John Milton,* ed. Richard Cunningham and Harvey Quaman, as a special issue of *Renaissance and Reformation/Renaissance et Réforme* 44:3 (2022), 81–110.

Rapoport, Anatol, 'Spread of Information through a Population with Socio-structural Bias: I. Assumption of Transitivity', *Bulletin of Mathematical Biophysics* 15 (1953), 523–33.

Rawson, Katie, and Trevor Muñoz, 'Against Cleaning', in *Debates in the Digital Humanities 2019,* ed. Matthew K. Gold and Lauren F. Klein (University of Minnesota Press, 2019), chapter 23.

Richardson, W. C., *Stephen Vaughan, Financial Agent of Henry VIII: A Study of Financial Relations with the Low Countries* (Louisiana State University Press, 1953).

Riordan, Michael, 'Heneage, Sir Thomas (b. before 1482, d. 1553)', *ODNB,* <https://doi.org/10.1093/ref:odnb/12920>.

Robertson, Karen, 'Negotiating Favour: The Letters of Lady Ralegh', in *Women and Politics in Early Modern England, 1450–1700,* ed. James Daybell (Taylor and Francis Group, 2004), pp. 99–113.

Rodgers, Dirk W., 'À Lasco [Laski], John (1499–1560)', *ODNB,* <https://doi.org/10.1093/ref:odnb/16081>.

Rodriguez-Salgado, M. J., 'Suárez de Figueroa [née Dormer], Jane, Duchess of Feria in the Spanish Nobility (1538–1612)', *ODNB,* <https://doi.org/10.1093/ref:odnb/7836\>.

Rossiter, William, and Jason Powell, eds., *Authority and Diplomacy from Dante to Shakespeare* (Ashgate, 2013).

Rowse, A. L., 'Edward Courtenay, Last Earl of Devon of the Elder Line', in *Court and Country: Studies in Tudor Social History* (University of Georgia Press, 1987), pp. 61–101.

Ruddock, Alwyn A., *Italian Merchants and Shipping in Southampton: 1270–1600* (University College, Southampton, 1951).

Ryan, Yann C., '"More Difficult from Dublin than from Dieppe": Ireland and Britain in a European Network of Communication', *Media History* 24 (2018), 458–76.

Ryan, Yann C., and Sebastian E. Ahnert, 'The Measure of the Archive: The Robustness of Network Analysis in Early Modern Correspondence', *Journal of Cultural Analytics* 6:1 (2021), <https://doi.org/10.22148/001c.25943>.

Ryan, Yann C., Sebastian E. Ahnert, and Ruth Ahnert, 'Networking Archives: Quantitative History and the Contingent Archive', *Proceedings of the Workshop on Computational Humanities Research* (CHR 2020), <http://ceur-ws.org/Vol-2723/>.

Ryrie, Alec, *The Gospel and Henry VIII: Evangelicals in the Early English Reformation* (Cambridge University Press, 2003).

Schich, Maximilian, Chaoming Song, Yong-Yeol Ahn, Alexander Mirsky, Mauro Martino, Albert-László Barabási, Dirk Helbing, 'A Network Framework of Cultural History', *Science* 345:6196 (2014), 558–62.

Schmidt, Ben, 'Words Alone: Dismantling Topic Models in the Humanities', *Journal of Digital Humanities* 2 (2012), <http://journalofdigitalhumanities.org/2-1/words-alone-by-benjamin-m-schmidt/>.

Schneider, Gary, *The Culture of Epistolarity: Vernacular Letters and Letter Writing in Early Modern England, 1500–1700* (University of Delaware Press, 2005).

Schobesberger, Nikolaus, Paul Arblaster, Mario Infelise, André Belo, Noah Moxham, Carmen Espejo, and Joad Raymond, 'European Postal Networks', in *News Networks in Early Modern Europe*, ed. Joad Raymond and Noah Moxham (Brill, 2016), pp. 19–63.

Schofield, John, *Philip Melanchthon and the English Reformation* (Ashgate, 2006).

Schreurs, Eugene, 'Petrus Alamire: Music Calligrapher, Musician, Composer, Spy', in *The Treasury of Petrus Alamire: Music and Art in Flemish Court Manuscripts 1500–1535*, ed. Herbert Kellman (Ghent Ludion, distributed by the University of Chicago Press, 1999), pp. 15–27.

Scott-Warren, Jason, *Sir John Harington and the Book as Gift* (Oxford University Press, 2001).

Shen-Orr, Shai S., Ron Milo, Shmoolik Mangan, and Uri Alon, 'Network Motifs in the Transcriptional Regulation Network of Escherichia Coli', *Nature Genetics* 31:1 (2002), 64–8.

Sherman, William H., 'Research Intelligence in Early Modern England', *Studies in Intelligence* 37:5 (1994), 95–104.

Simpson, James, *Burning to Read: English Fundamentalism and Its Reformation Opponents* (Harvard University Press, 2009).

Simpson, James, *The Oxford English Literary History, Volume 2, 1350–1547: Reform and Cultural Revolution* (Oxford University Press, 2002).

Smith, G. R., *Servant of the Cecils: The Life of Sir Michael Hicks, 1543–1612* (Rowman and Littlefield, 1977).

Smithies, James, 'Digital Humanities, Postfoundationalism, Postindustrial Culture', *Digital Humanities Quarterly* 8:1 (2014), <http://www.digitalhumanities.org/dhq/vol/8/1/000172/000172.html>.

Snow, C. P., *The Two Cultures*, with an introduction by Stefan Collini (Cambridge University Press, 1998).

Soman, Alfred, *The Massacre of Saint Bartholomew: Reappraisals and Documents* (Martinus Nijhoff, 1974).

Sowerby, Tracey A., 'Elizabethan Diplomatic Networks and the Spread of News', in *News Networks in Early Modern Europe*, ed. Joad Raymond and Noah Moaxham (Brill, 2016), pp. 305–27.

Spicer, Andrew, *The French-Speaking Reformed Community and their Church in Southampton, 1567–c.1620*, Southampton Records Series 39 (Sutton, 1997).

Stensland, Monica, *Habsburg Communication in the Dutch Revolt* (Amsterdam University Press, 2012).

Stewart, Alan, 'Familiar Letters and State Papers: The Afterlives of Early Modern Correspondence', in *Cultures of Correspondence in Early Modern Britain*, ed. James Daybell and Andrew Gordon (University of Pennsylvania Press, 2016).

Stewart, Alan, 'Francis Bacon's Bi-literal Cipher and the Materiality of Early Modern Diplomatic Writing', in *Diplomacy and Early Modern Culture*, ed. Adams and Cox, pp. 120–34.

Subrahmanyam, Sanjay, 'Introduction', to *Merchant Networks in the Early Modern World*, ed. Sanjay Subrahmanyam (Variorum, 1996).

Summit, Jennifer, 'Leland's Itinerary and the Remains of the Medieval Past', in *Reading the Medieval in Early Modern England*, ed. Gordon McMullan and David Matthews (Cambridge University Press, 2007).

Tosh, Will, *Male Friendship and Testimonies of Love in Shakespeare's England* (Palgrave Macmillan, 2016).

Tracy, James D., *The Founding of the Dutch Republic: War, Finance, and Politics in Holland, 1572–1588* (Oxford University Press, 2008).

Travers, Jeffrey, and Stanley Milgram, 'An Experimental Study of the Small World Problem', *Sociometry* 32 (1969), 425–43.

Trim, D. J. B., 'Carleill, Christopher (1551?–1593)', *ODNB*, <https://doi.org/10.1093/ref:odnb/4668n>.

Trim, D. J. B., 'Norris [Norreys], Sir John (*c*.1547×50–1597)', *ODNB*, <https://doi.org/10.1093/ref:odnb/20276>.

Trouillot, Michel-Rolph, and Hazel V. Carby, *Silencing the Past: Power and the Production of History* (Beacon Press, 2015).

Underwood, Ted, 'The Stanford Literary Lab's Narrative' (2017), <http://www.publicbooks.org/the-stanford-literary-labs-narrative/>.

Valente, Thomas W., and Kayo Fujimoto, 'Bridging: Locating Critical Connectors in a Network', *Soc. Networks* 32:3 (2010), 212–20.

Varese, Stefano, *Salt of the Mountain: Campa Ashaninka History and Resistance in the Peruvian Jungle* (University of Oklahoma Press, 2004).

Vivo, Filippo de, *Information and Communication in Venice: Rethinking Early Modern Politics* (Oxford University Press, 2007).

Wabuda, Susan, 'Bell, John (d. 1556)', *ODNB*, <https://doi.org/10.1093/ref:odnb/2010>.

Waddell, Brodie, ed., *Petitions in the State Papers, 1600–1699, British History Online*, <http://www.british-history.ac.uk/petitions/state-papers>.

Warren, Christopher N. Daniel Shore, Jessica Otis, Lawrence Wang, Mike Finegold, and Cosma Shalizi, 'Six Degrees of Francis Bacon: A Statistical Method for Reconstructing Large Historical Social Networks', *Digital Humanities Quarterly* 10:3 (2016), <http://digitalhumanities.org/dhq/vol/10/3/000244/000244.html>.

Watts, Duncan, and Steven Strogatz, 'Collective Dynamics of "Small-World" Networks', *Nature* 393 (1998), 440–2.

Weingart, Scott, 'The Myth of Text Analytics and Unobtrusive Measurement', <http://www.scottbot.net/HIAL/index.html@p=16713.html>.

Weingart, Scott, 'Networks Demystified 8: When Networks are Inappropriate', <http://www.scottbot.net/HIAL/index.html@p=39600.html>.

Wernham, R. B., *After the Armada: Elizabethan England and the Struggle for Western Europe, 1588–1595* (Clarendon Press, 1984).

Wershler, Darren, Lori Emerson, and Jussi Parikka, *The Lab Book: Situated Practices in Media Studies* (University of Minnesota Press, 2022).

Whitelaw, Mitchell, 'Generous Interfaces for Digital Cultural Collections', *Digital Humanities Quarterly* 9:1 (2015), |<http://www.digitalhumanities.org/dhq/vol/9/1/000205/000205.html/>.

Whitelock, Anna, *Elizabeth's Bedfellows: An Intimate History of the Queen's Court* (Bloomsbury, 2013).

Wilding, Michael, 'A Biography of Edward Kelly, the English Alchemist and Associate of Dr. John Dee', in *Mystical Metal of Gold: Essays on Alchemy and Renaissance Culture*, ed. Stanton J. Lindon (AMS Press, 2007).

Wilkie, William E., *The Cardinal Protectors of England: Rome and the Tudors before the Reformation* (Cambridge University Press, 1974).

Willan, Thomas Stuart, *Studies in Elizabethan Foreign Trade* (Manchester University Press, 1959).

Williams, Glanmor, *Renewal and Reformation: Wales c.1415–1642* (Clarendon, 1987).

Williamson, Elizabeth R., *Elizabethan Diplomacy and Epistolary Culture* (Routledge, 2021).

Williamson, Elizabeth R., ' "Fishing after News" and the Ars Apodemica: The Intelligencing Role of the Educational Traveller in the Late Sixteenth Century', in *News Networks in Early Modern Europe*, ed. Noah Moxham and Joad Raymond (Brill, 2016), pp. 542–62.

Wilson, Charles, *Queen Elizabeth and the Revolt of the Netherlands* (Macmillan, 1970).

Woolfson, Jonathan, 'Croke, Richard (1489–1558)', *ODNB*, <https://doi.org/10.1093/ref:odnb/6734\>.

Woolfson, Jonathan, 'Harvel, Edmund (d. in or before 1550)', *ODNB*, <https://doi.org/10.1093/ref:odnb/39717>.

Woolfson, Jonathan, *Padua and the Tudors: English Students in Italy, 1485–1603* (Clarke, 1998).

Woolfson, Jonathan, 'Morison, Sir Richard (c.1510–1556)', *ODNB*, <https://doi.org/10.1093/ref:odnb/19274>.

Yale, Elizabeth, 'The History of Archives: The State of the Discipline', *Book History* 18:1 (2015), 332–59.

Zins, Henryk, *England and the Baltic in the Elizabethan Era*, tr. C. Stevens (Manchester University Press, 1972).

Index

In the case of monarchs, foreign princes and princesses, emperors, and popes, we have adopted the convention of including them in the index under first names (e.g. Mary I, Queen of England); otherwise, we have indexed under individual family names, rather than titles (e.g. Blount, William, 4th Baron Mountjoy). In the case of women, we have used the surname she was using for the main period of writing discussed in this book, with maiden and other former names given in parentheses. Due to the subject matter of the chapter in which most women are discussed (on petitioning and mediation), most appear under by their married names, and we provide cross-references within the index for those women also known by their maiden names (e.g. those who have ODNB entries or similar). The one exception we have made is for the wives of Henry VIII, where we have followed the convention of using their maiden names.

For the benefit of digital users, indexed terms that span two pages (e.g., 52–53) may, on occasion, appear on only one of those pages.